To Kelly
Best wishes
and lots of lo
Happy Chris
Chri

NINA & VIC

First published in 2004 by

WOODFIELD PUBLISHING
Bognor Regis, West Sussex, England
www.woodfieldpublishing.com

ISBN 1-903953-69-3

Nina & Vic

A World War II Love Story

The wartime letters of
Nina Chessall and **Vic Vinnell**

Edited by
Janine Harrington

Woodfield

2003

*60th Anniversary of the formation of
RAF 100 Group, November 1943*

2004

*60th Anniversary of D-Day and the ill-fated
final flight of Mosquito DK292*

*'… one day, dear Nina, I shall write a book
about the most beautiful love story that ever was.
The story of Nina and Vic'*

Vic Vinnell, 1944

They shall not grow old, as we that are left grow old:

Age shall not weary them, nor the years condemn.

At the going down of the sun and in the morning

We shall remember them.

Nina, my mum, was a Visionary.

She believed in the magic of dreams. The Power of Prayer.

She was a woman who lived by faith.

Brought up in a family of Quakers, from the start, her life was one of absolute honesty, absolute purity, absolute truth, absolute integrity, absolute Love.

She was a very moral woman, which was often hard, especially when we as her children were young and rebellious, testing the limits of that love.

But she never let go. She was always there for us.

And for me, her first born, she was special.

Together we spent many happy hours, sharing our dreams, our hopes and our love.

Contents

Introduction

This is the story of a young girl whose life unfolds like a tapestry of rich colours through the pages you are about to read. It is the life of an ordinary girl living in extraordinary times, against the backdrop of the Second World War. Her name was Nina. She was my mother, who in latter years became my soul-mate, through our mutual sharing of experiences. And this is her story – a true story – told in her own words from memories, diaries and the hundreds of letters that she and Vic, her wartime sweetheart, shared.

This is also Vic's story – a navigator in the RAF 100 Group, who together with Jack Fisher, the pilot with whom he flew, disappeared on the night of 26/27 November 1944.

Nina and Vic shared a love that will never die and I am proud to be their voice, because I believe their story should be told and shared. It is a love story which holds so many lessons for us all, especially today. I feel privileged to have been a part of Nina's life as her daughter, her first-born, and to have shared the writing of this book with her. In seeing it published I am fulfilling a promise first made in the summer of 1944 by Vic to Nina, and later by myself to my mum, who passed away in the summer of 1996.

It has become my personal tribute to her as well as a memorial to the short lives of Vic and Jack, whose final resting place is still unknown.

Love is Eternal, Rest in Peace

Janine Harrington, 2004

Dedication

Mum, thank you for sharing your story and entrusting me to be your Voice.
Through these pages, the true spirit of Love lives on.
* * * * *

Jo, as my own First-Born, this book is written for you and your generation.
Vic was just one who gave his life that you might live free today.
You are now of the age that Vic was when his life was taken from him.
As a young person today you are the Hope of the World.
It is with you, therefore, that the future of this country rests.
* * * * *

Audrey, I hope that you feel this constitutes, in part at least,
a fitting memorial to your brother Jack Fisher, pilot of the Mosquito
in which he and Vic lost their lives. Thank you for sharing personal
memories for inclusion in this book.
* * * * *

My thanks also goes to all those in the **RAF 100 Group Association** many of
whom wrote to Mum in the months before she died, and who have since
made me feel welcome and so much a part of the Association today. Thank
you also for the shared personal memories, documents and letters of the day.
* * * * *

Ian, thank you for all your support, your strength, your love.
Your own experience of Service Life together with the continuing research
you have undertaken has proved invaluable. In helping to complete this
book you have put something of yourself within its pages.
* * * * *

Nina Chessall 1944.

NINA CHESSALL

NINA CHESSALL was born in Cheshire on 9th April 1918. Her father, also a man with a rocklike faith, passed away when she was just six years old, leaving her as the eldest, to take responsibility, especially in later years, for her two younger brothers and her mother who was poor in health.

Nina and her Dad were close. His death affected her deeply. And for a year or more after, she was taken out of school to spend time at home, away from the pressure of study, where she might more easily be comforted and supported and come to terms with her grief as a small child. This time became the first of her 'Desert Experiences', where she sought out God as a solace and strength. Her Mum would play on the family organ, singing out the words: 'Nearer my God, to Thee, nearer to Thee', while Nina read the Bible through several times over, thirsting after the kind of strength and love that might see her through.

God was a living part of the family. Prayer times were important. Grace was said before meals. Sundays were given over to worship. And while her mother never married again, she became a local Speaker, sharing her own experiences of Faith.

In 1939/40, Nina's two brothers went away to war. Their home was bombed, and, living in rented accommodation, her mother's health deteriorated. Nina became her carer, until, in February 1943, she joined the WAAF, and was posted away from home to RAF Wheaton Aston, Little Onn, Staffordshire, where, on 3rd December that same year; she met Vic.

Vic Vinnell 1944.

VIC VINNELL

Henry VICTOR Alexander VINNELL was a Flight Lieutenant in the Royal Air Force Volunteer Reserves. Vic, as he became known, was born on 21st September 1922. His Education Record shows that he reached the standard of Senior Oxford School Certificate, and on leaving school, had qualified with R.S.A French 1, R.S.A English 1, and London Chamber of Commerce Handwriting. He was interested and actively involved in cricket, tennis and squash, and he counted amongst his hobbies: photography and radio. Civil employment prior to joining the RAF was as an assistant salesman in a wholesale grocers.

Vic volunteered for service in the RAF in December 1940 and was awarded his Flying Badge in March 1942. He went on to join 418 (R.C.A.F) Squadron on Night Intruding missions in July 1942, and had completed 13 sorties before leaving for No. 1 Radio School, Cranwell, for remustering from NAV/B to NAV.B/W in May 1943. He qualified as NAV.B/W in September of that same year, and in October, was posted to RAF Wheaton Aston pending a further posting.

It was at the RAF base at Wheaton Aston in the December of that same year, that he met and fell in love with Nina, who was also stationed there.

In 1944, Vic was moved to RAF Foulsham, 192 Squadron, in Norfolk, where he had been specially chosen to become part of the 100 Group, a Special Operations Unit aimed at seeking out and jamming enemy radar and radio signals, flying over the bombers which masked their approach until they were clear.

Through letters they shared over this year and the daily diaries Nina kept, it is possible to follow their love story, their dream marriage and a family based on a firm foundation of faith and unconditional love against the backdrop of the Second World War.

Sadly, The Dream was not to be. They became engaged. The wedding day was set, the wedding dress and rings bought. But then ... Vic failed to return from a mission. On the night of 26/27 November 1944, so near the end of the war, he went missing on a flight to Munich with Jack Fisher, and the wreckage of their Mosquito has never been found.

He was just twenty-two years old.

Jack Fisher 1944

JACK FISHER

Jack Glen Millan Fisher was a Pilot Officer with the Royal Canadian Air Force. Born August 30th 1923 on a farm homestead in Canada, Jack was the oldest of seven children and special being the only boy. His father served in World War One in France and Belgium. His youngest sister Audrey recalls:

'Jack was a good son, the apple of his mum's eye; with a bit of an adventurous streak, like trying to ride a bull as soon as our parents were gone, or attempting to ride the unbroken stallions. And of course, with six younger sisters he was a big tease!'

Jack was always scribbling little rhymes and verses in his school notebook and liked to read Determined to finish High School, he took several jobs to qualify. His first job after Graduation was with the Prairie Farm Rehabilitation Act, a Government Agency to improve farming methods and ways. He joined the RCAF as soon as he could in 1940 in Regina, Saskatchewan; the same day as his father rejoined the Army. Jack loved every minute of his air force training in Ontario -

'I remember Jack coming home on leave when I was about ten years old and he would come to school with me in his pilot's uniform, holding my hand'.

Jack joined 192 Squadron, 100 Group, in August 1944, based at RAF Foulsham. Vic was Jack's navigator, and they were the only crew on board the mosquito DK292 when it went missing on the night of 26/27 November 1944.

Jack was just 21 years old.

Nina's faith was tested to its limits over the ensuing five years following Vic and Jack's sudden and drastic disappearance. And yet, from within, came a very special kind of strength. Out of that suffering, came the realisation that Vic would always be a part of her life. No-one could take away the love they had shared.

Exactly one year later, on 27th November 1945, she won first prize for an article written for 'Mother and Child' magazine entitled *'This, My Dream Home ... by the WAAF whose man went to war'*, which went on to be published with a photograph of herself in uniform on 5th December 1945 by the *Daily Express*. It shared with readers the kind of marriage and family for which she and Vic had planned and dreamed when the world might once more be at peace.

Readers were touched, and responded by writing to her, especially those who had themselves lost to the war someone they loved. One man also serving in the RAF who heard about her through a friend, wrote his own letter to her. They corresponded for a while and then met anonymously on a railway platform. They fell in love. And later still, they married, and went on to have three daughters, the eldest of whom they named Janine (combining their names John and Nina). Me.

It was in later years, that Mum and I came to share a very special relationship, and together, we joined the 100 Group RAF Association in an attempt to discover more about Vic and what happened to him, the pilot and their plane. Through ensuing years, Mum had kept in contact with the family of the Canadian pilot Jack Fisher, who had been flying the mosquito with Vic as navigator. And as we gathered information, it became like a thousand piece jigsaw trying to assimilate the fragments of maps, documents and materials that came our way.

Nina Chessall passed away on 22nd July 1996 from cancer, still not knowing what had become of her beloved Vic.

For her today, I believe there are no more secrets. But my own search continues. And, in turn, I gave Mum my promise to carry forward Vic's promise to her that one day their story would be shared.

Beginnings

These words, written by Nina about her father, were found after her death in 1996. They provide an understanding about her beginnings and the person who was to have the greatest influence over the life that was to come:

'This is a collection of personal reminiscences about my childhood background, and in particular about my father, whom I adored, and who had a very strong influence during my formative years.

I was born in Cheshire – Cheshire Cat with a grin from ear to ear in a village called Heswall, just across the river from North Wales. My parents kept the only newsagents shop. My earliest memory is of standing on a high stool behind the counter collecting pennies with one hand, and giving out newspapers with the other.

'Pennies first, please!' I used to say.

Oh, it was a wonderful time! Reading all the comics: such as *Tiger Tim's Weekly* and many more. At the age of two I used to sit outside the shop on sunny days, surprising everyone by giving a fair imitation of being able to read – '*Tiger Tim said to the bear: 'Let's go and play with the other animals. So they did.*'

My father was also the village barber. I must have been a precocious child. All the men waiting in the salon were my ready-made audience. I used to ask awkward questions like, 'Do you say your prayers?' and if there was no response I would say 'Would you like to hear me say mine?'

And I would!

> '*Gentle Jesus, meek and mild,*
> *Look upon this little child.*
> *Pity my simplicity,*
> *Suffer me to come to Thee.*'

My father used an open cut throat razor in those days, no safety razors then. I remember a text that used to hang on the wall just in line with the customer's eye when he tilted back his head for a shave. In front of him would be father, and just above his head they would see:

'Prepare to meet thy God'.

My parents used to work very hard and very long hours. My father's day must have started about 5am, because he had to meet the first train arriving at 6am station three miles away,and push the heavy load of papers up the hill on his bicycle. And yet, in spite of the long hours and hard work from early morning to late at night, six days a week, we were all of us at Church on Sunday mornings – myself and two younger brothers (one in a pram left in the church porch), mother and father and our housekeeper.

I was baptised in a Methodist Church, so we all attended there in the mornings. In the evenings, we attended the Presbyterian church because it was nearer. My father was really a Quaker, so he believed in attending all the Christian denominations and belonging to none. He was a Lay Preacher, and my mother too was much in demand as a speaker or pianist or soloist. You name it, she could do it!

Sunday afternoons, my parents led a Gospel meeting: PSA – 'Pleasant Sunday Afternoons'. I understand this was how they met. Father had been a visiting speaker, mother was the soloist. During the week, my father led a boys Bible Class for the Brethren at the Gospel Hall.

When I was four and had acquired a baby brother, we retired from business due to health reasons and bought a biggish house on a hill with some land, and an old cottage adjoining where my father went in for poultry farming with some 300 hens.

These were wonderful, golden days for me. I followed my father everywhere. I helped him to feed the hens, to collect their eggs, and watch the chicks hatch out – my first lesson in learning how life begins. I also grew vegetables and fruit. I specially loved the fresh green peas and raspberries.

One day, I was caught crouching behind a lone of peas with my mouth full, sampling the goods:

'Thou God seest me.'

I have never since been entirely free of the feeling that God is a silent watcher of all my actions.

Father taught me to read from a book called: 'Reading Without Tears'.

'*A is a man with his legs astride,*

B is a house with two windows wide.'

Sometimes, I would sit at my bedroom window and look across the river to the houses on the other side. When the sun was shining, there was one house I specially loved. I used to call it 'The House with the Golden Windows'. It was tucked halfway up the hillside and I used to dream about the wonderful people who might live there, and how wonderful it would be if we could live there too.

Some years later, we went to North Wales for our Sunday School Outing. And I saw the house for myself. It was dark and peeling and ivy-covered with ordinary glass windows and a cross old couple living there. No golden windows. No good little children for me to play with. But I happened to look back across the river to where our own house should be. There it was, at the top of the hill. And I couldn't believe it – our house had golden windows instead! But I had to leave its warmth and shelter first before I really found this out.

My father took me to school on my first day. He was able to see me in the playground because our garden backed on to the school. And so it was that he saw me pushed to the ground by one of the bigger girls. He was over the wall in a trice, picking me up from the middle of the puddle in which I had fell, my knees bleeding and muddy.

It's a strange thing that I cannot remember his face – and yet I remember the protection of his arms, the gentleness of his hands, the reassurance of his voice. Just like a Shepherd must feel to a little lost lamb. And it was the meaning of the hymn he taught me to say as my prayer each night as he knelt at my bedside with me. It is also one of the prayers I taught my own children to sing together at bedtime:

> *'Jesus, tender Shepherd, hear me,*
> *Bless Thy little lamb tonight.*
> *Through the darkness be Thou near me,*
> *Keep me safe till morning light ...'*

Years later, when my husband and I were settling into our first Pastorate in a small village in Wiltshire, there was a message from an old lady nearby, nearly 90 years old, to visit her. She specially wanted a visit from the new minister's wife because it was a church that had not had a minister for ten years. I went along with the three children. She sat propped up among the pillows, her white hair flowing to her shoulders, her thin hands clasped on the counterpane. She told us she used to belong to a choir in her young days. So I asked her if she would like the children to sing their bedtime prayer. And there, in that small room, I was taken back to times when my father and I had shared the same words of that prayer with so much meaning for me as I remembered the way we had been. About this time, the Salvation Army wanted to start weeknight meetings in the village where we lived. There was no accommodation for them available. So my father offered them one of our large rooms, complete with organ and piano which my mother played for them. We sang lots of hearty choruses: 'In my Heart there rings a melody', 'Count your blessings one by one', 'Build on the Rock', 'Blessed Assurance, Jesus is mine'. The whole house was filled with children and the sound of their music, until the meeting got so big that they had to transfer to larger premises. And sadly, the two Army Officers who had been staying with us had to leave too. But not before, to my parents great joy, I had insisted on walking out to the penitent form and offered my life to God.

I was just seven years old.

Soon after this, my father died, probably believing that he had done very little to serve the Master he loved. Just an ordinary obscure little shopkeeper, leaving behind very little more than a widow and three young children. Yet here am I, forty years or so later, talking to my own children about him. Sharing the experience of a man, my father, who had such a profound influence over my life'.

1939 – 'War is declared'

PERSONAL DETAILS – NINA CHESSALL

Name:	Nina Chessall
Age:	20 years old
Address:	23 Ilford Avenue
	Wallasey
	Cheshire
Background:	I live with my mother and two brothers: Joe and Fred, both younger than I. Nunkie, my mother's brother, also lives with us. My father died when I was six years old. I also have a boyfriend, Bill. He lives at Saughall Hotel some ten miles distance away, where his father is Manager. I work at Post Office Telephones, India Buildings, Liverpool where I am a shorthand typist.
Interests:	I am secretary to the Presbyterian Church Guild. I enjoy tennis, hockey, walking and reading.
Birthday:	9th April 1918
Weight:	8 stone, 8lbs
Height:	5' 3"
Size in shoes:	5
Size in hats:	61/2
Size in gloves:	61/2

APRIL

9 Sunday I'M 21 TODAY! Nunk gave me a beautiful wristlet watch and Mum woke me first with Dressing Table Set. Dear Mum! Manicure set from boys. Bill called with Dressing Table Set (!?) and daffodils.

   Memo: This weekend is the loveliest time of my whole life, and my life has held many peaks of happiness. Everybody has been so sweet and kind; it almost makes me weep with the joy of it all. I can see beauty everywhere, and I'm glad, so glad to be alive and part of this glory called Life.

27 Thursday CONSCRIPTION HAS COME! for all men between 20-21. And the burning question is – Is it War?

28 Friday Met Bill at 6pm and chose large and handsome suitcase and very dainty powder compact in exchange for his duplicated dressing table set given on my birthday. Had tea at Reece's café and home about 9pm. Hadn't seen Bill for a whole week!

31 Thursday MORE men called up and Correspondence Course started between Hitler and Chamberlain. Bill and I discussed events in front room. Mum in bed and doctor not at all pleased with her progress. Mum fidgeting about and in mood all evening. I just about stuck it out till Bill went at 10.15. When she came to Bill's visits happening too often and that I had to do my own washing on Saturday afternoons and never go out, I couldn't stand it any more. I wept till it hurt in kitchen at 11.30 and crept back to bed half an hour later.

SEPTEMBER

3 Sunday WAR DECLARED. It sounds very strange. Go for a walk into fields and country. Seems absolutely unbelievable that there could be a war, with the sun and the birds.

---

4 Monday WAR DECLARED BY BRITAIN AND FRANCE The Fleet moves into position. Great Britain declared war on Germany at 11 o'clock yesterday morning. Six hours later, at 5pm, France declared war.

Broadcasting last evening from his study at Buckingham Palace, the King said – "In this grave hour, perhaps the most fateful in our history, I send to every household of my people, both at home and overseas, this message, spoken with the same depth of feeling for each one of you as if I were able to cross your threshold and speak to you myself. For the second time in the lives of most of us we are at war …

The task will be hard. There may be dark days ahead and war can no longer be confined to the battlefield. But we can only do the right as we see the right and reverently commit our cause to God.

May He bless and keep us all."

WAR CABINET OF NINE. Churchill is now First Lord.'

'LONDON HEARS ITS FIRST RAID WARNING.'

'PETROL WILL BE RATIONED.'

Bill has been to join the RAF. Told to come again early. Meet Bill in Park at 6pm. How I love Bill. He's so understanding and sympathetic. Home at 8.30. House all dark due to ARP curtains and 'blued' windows.

5. Tuesday <u>RAF RAIN LEAFLETS OVER GERMANY</u> Royal Air Force planes flying by night carried out extensive reconnaissance over Northern and Western Germany. They were not engaged by enemy aircraft. More than 6,000,000 copies of a note to the German people were dropped over a wide area.

Bill is accepted for RAF, and has medical exam on Thursday. Meet with Bill at 6pm and go to Liverpool to Jewellers for 'Love Tokens'. I'll always remember how silly and self-conscious I felt choosing my bracelet and Bill's signet. Tea and biscuits at Reece's. So happy, happy!

7 Thursday Bill passes Medical Test A1 and has to report to RAF tomorrow morning. Meet him at Birkenhead Park and put on each other's presents. I'll wear this always and kiss it Goodnight. Talk of our hopes and fears till 7.30, then home.

8 Friday Meet Joan at Park Station while waiting to see Bill off. Talk for the shortest 20 minutes I ever remember and kiss him Goodbye, still smiling, but with a heavy heart. Show everyone my bracelet; I'm proud of it. Come home at usual time and darn stockings and go to bed at 9.30 – to sleep, perchance to dream.

9 Saturday Letter from Bill to say I'm in his thoughts and he loves me always. Last day at Birkenhead office. Do shopping and sit in park with Mum. Tea. More darning, and bed. A dreary day, and I can see nothing but a long succession of dreary days ahead till my Lover comes back again.

10 Sunday Help Mum with ideas for ARP blackouts. Listen to service on wireless. Mum says can't be in love – sleep too well!

11 Monday On Leave. Make black curtains and hang them with Fred's help. Also make Gas Mask covers for Mum.

20 Wednesday Write to Bill enclosing enlargement of the photo he took at Mold last Bank Holiday. Brother Joe is worried about becoming 18 – military age.

21 Thursday Read book called 'Rebecca' by Daphne du Maurier. I shouldn't like to be a second wife for anybody. (Nina, you are learning sense!)

23 Saturday: <u>RUSSIA GETS TWO-THIRDS OF POLAND</u>
New Frontier passes through Warsaw

GASBAGS FOR CARS HERE SOON

Black-out time: tonight is 6.57, tomorrow 6.54

28 Thursday Hurray! At last a letter! I think I enjoy this one better than any other he has written, I suppose because of the waiting. Read 'The Citadel' by A.J.Cronin. Have seen film with Bill.

OCTOBER

---

6 Friday   HITLER: COLONIES AND WORLD CONFERENCE

'Peace' terms are his last offer: he wants to make new Polish State. 'If the allies do not agree with my demands it will be my last offer. On the West we await the enemy.' Hitler made these declarations in his much-trumpeted 'Peace Plan' speech to the Reichstag this afternoon.

The chief points of his plan are:

> the return of colonies – 'the most important German political demand'. This demand is not an ultimatum and should not be carried out by force.' The colonial claim is justified by the necessity of a new distribution of the world's raw materials.

> The creation of a just and enduring German frontier.

> The various races throughout German sovereign territory and throughout South-Eastern Europe to be put in order.

>The building up of a Polish State whose security will be guaranteed by Germany and Russia, and the Government of which will allow no intrigues against either of those countries.

After Hitler had outlined these proposals, he said: 'Should Mr Churchill refuse this, then this, my declaration, will be the last. Mr Churchill may be convinced that Great Britain will be victorious. I do not doubt that Germany will be victorious. May God help so that my thoughts are understood and so that not only Germany, but all the nations of Europe may enjoy peace.

---

7 Saturday Get dressed for Bill's arrival after dinner. Decide to have apple fritters for tea, so out to buy cream cakes to have with them. Bill arrives WITH UNIFORM about 5pm. He looks a most wonderful person, but just a bit strange and the cap takes a bit of getting used to. Ready to leave about 7,30 and walk along Prom to Seacombe, stopping by a seat just long enough for Bill to break his watch. That first kiss for a week! 8.30 boat across (how lovely to sail into the future alone together) and a last caress and he is gone. But thank heavens it's Saturday and I will see him again tomorrow.

8 Sunday He brings me a big box of chocolates, the darling, and I try to whisper words of love to him before that cursed bus bears him away from me (for three months, this time).

---

15 Sunday <u>HITLER'S PROBLEM – WHAT CAN HE DO NEXT?</u>
Hitler is all in a bother over the contemptuous turning down of his peace offer. Messages from Berlin yesterday describe him as 'pale with anger'.

---

17 Tuesday <u>FIRST BOMBS ON BRITAIN – 4 NAZI PLANES DOWN</u>
German bombs fell on Britain yesterday for the first time since war began. In a clear Autumn sky Nazi bombing aeroplanes, believed to number fifteen, swooped over the Pentland Hills, dived down on the Firth of Forth and aimed bombs at the famous Forth Bridge and at Rosyth Great Naval Base. Ten bombs were dropped. All fell in the River Forth. It was later officially announced: 'There were no civilian casualties. No property was damaged.' The raiders were driven off by gunfire and by British fighting planes.'

Letter! He gets ten days Leave at Xmas!!

18 Wednesday Joe's birthday – house shoes from me, military brushes from Mum. Write Bill a long letter consisting of five pages and send him snaps. None of them have turned out well.

---

23 Monday <u>BRITAIN WINS FIRST WEEK OF AIR WAR</u>
14 Nazi bombers shot down in 6 days. Every enemy air raid on the British coast has been driven off with heavy loss to the Germans. Another Nazi bomber – the fourteenth in six days – was shot down yesterday in the sea off the east coast of Scotland.

NOVEMBER

2 Thursday <u>RATIONING</u> When butter and bacon are rationed, ham will be rationed too. The rations announced last night will probably begin on December 16. They will be a quarter of a pound each of butter and bacon for every individual a week. That means a pound of bacon and a pound of butter for a family of four. There will also be three kinds of ration books – a general one for men, women and children over six years old; a child's book for children under six, and a travellers book for people who do not permanently live at home.

8 Wednesday Letter from Bill together with lovely Wishbone brooch.

9 Thursday <u>HITLER ESCAPES EXPLOSION IN A BEER CELLAR</u> 6 dead, 60 hurt: reported attempt with time-bomb. Twenty-seven minutes after Hitler ended a hysterical speech in the Buergerbrau Beer cellar at Munich last night – a speech in which he cried that he was ready for a five-years' war with Britain – the building was shaken by an explosion which killed six members of the 'Old Guard' of the Nazi party, and injured sixty other people.

17 Friday Experience first air raid today. One plane driven off! Marvellous! I think I feel more sorry for the poor lonely plane.

DECEMBER

4 Monday Terrible shock when I hear of Marion's death. Start letter to Bill asking him not to volunteer for Air Crew, probably no use.

29 Friday <u>SUGAR & MEAT WILL BE RATIONED</u> Morrison announces his new food plans, and tells housewives potatoes and raisins are good substitutes. By the end of February you will be rationed for sugar, meat, bacon and ham, and butter. Your rations each week will be:

Sugar	¾ pound
Meat	about 2lb
Bacon and ham	¼ lb
Butter	¼ lb

Mr W. S. Morrison, Minister of Food, announced yesterday that sugar and meat would be rationed – because 'rationing makes possible a greater dedication of our shipping services to the prosecution of the war'.

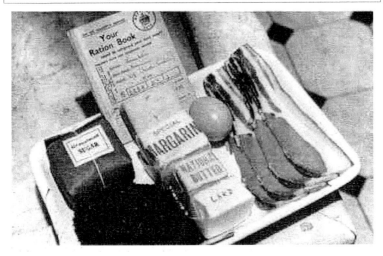

31 Sunday A Happy New Year to us all! But I wonder what 1940 has in store for us – probably a lot of disappointments and maybe sorrow and pain. I don't expect it to be easy. And although 1939 has not been such a very lucky year for anyone, I would not have it any different. I have made mistakes, lots of them, but it has also brought me the greatest joy I have ever known.

1939 has given me the greatest joy and the greatest pain. It's funny how those two go hand in hand: -

- I was 21 and crossed the line from girlhood to womanhood,
- I fell in love and tasted for the first time the 'bitter-sweet' Adventure of Love,
- Then came War and now we, Bill and I, are forever saying 'Goodbye'. But please God, my biggest wish is that I NEVER say Goodbye to him for the last time – no, never!

1940

'Every man – and woman – will prepare himself to do his duty,
whatever that might be, with special pride and care …'
Winston Churchill

JANUARY

11 Thursday BILL'S BIRTHDAY. First rehearsal of play tonight with Church Guild, or rather, just the first reading over. I rather fancy Enid, sweet country girl, but chosen instead for Aunt Agatha. I only sounded like that because I've no letter from my love.

February

1 Thursday Post letter and parcel to Bill. Mother is very much worse – I think she has got flu. Rehearsal of play at Church with Duncan, trudging there and back through the snow.

3 Saturday Bill arrives at 12.30 this morning. A lovely surprise! But Nunk has to come downstairs to let him in – I didn't hear him. He looks cold and starved and fed up, but after a bath and rest, he calls for me at 7pm and we go to The Capitol. Rotten picture, but it doesn't matter very much because I am with Bill. Home at 11.15, but Mum and Nunk still up. Nunk falls over in 'black-out' and hurts his ribs.

4 Sunday Mum in bed all day. A very disappointing day! I planned to leave tea all ready and then meet Bill this afternoon and stay at his house for tea. But Mother said No! So I had to see the family fed until Bill calls at 7.30. I light a fire in the parlour and we just make the best of it.

MARCH

13 Wednesday <u>REDS 'CEASE FIRE' AT NOON TODAY</u> Moscow announced early this morning that the war in Finland, which began with the Soviet Army's invasion 104 days ago, will end at midday today. Although Helsinki so far has not confirmed it, Moscow claims that a peace treaty has been signed with Finland. Under it, Stalin gets almost everything he demanded when he went to war.'

22 Friday Mum lets me down and goes out with Nunk, so I have to stay home and darn stockings.

23 Saturday Dancing at Tower Ballroon with Bill.

24 Sunday Out with Mum, and just because I go to Bill's for tea, a terrible fuss, and Mum in tears. It is not fair.

25 Monday More fuss. Chester with Bill. Lovely day.

27 Wednesday Lunch with Bill and Jim at Cooper's before they go back.

APRIL

9 Tuesday My birthday – and 21 no more! Lovely time and unexpected presents. People were very kind. Rehearsal for play.

OSLO FALLS TO GERMANS: SEA, AIR BATTLES RAGING Germany today occupied a protesting Denmark without resistance, invaded Norway in a lightning offensive on the southern and western coasts and challenged the combined Allied naval and aerial forces in the North Sea. A naval battle was reported raging off the Norwegian coast. British and French Governments announced their intention to rush 'full aid' to Norway.

23 Tuesday 'Doctor's Orders' play by Guild. Great Success!!

25 Thursday BRITAIN SENT 1,500 RAW TROOPS WITHOUT ARTILLERY OR PLANES TO NORWAY – AND SLAUGHTER.'

28 Sunday WHAT WAR IS COSTING US The money must and can be found. Introducing a Budget of mammoth proportions, Sir John Simon, Chancellor of the Exchequer, told the world that to win victory money must and can be found. Two thousand six hundred and sixty-seven million pounds is the present estimate of the cost of the war.

The principal Budget proposals announced by the Chancellor, in addition to the new Purchases Tax, may be summarised as follows:

Beer –Increase equivalent to a penny a pint;

Spirits –whisky, gin, and brandy will be increased by 1s 9d a bottle, making whisky 16s a bottle, gin 15s a bottle;

Tobacco – increase equivalent to 3d an ounce. Cigarettes which have been 10 for 7d will in future cost 8 1/2d;

Matches – Penny boxes of matches will in future cost 1 1/2d. Duty on Lighters will increase from 1s to 2s 6d.

Post – Letter post will be 2 1/2d per 2oz packet instead of 1 1/2d and Postcards will be 2d instead of 1d, but correspondence to the Forces overseas will be at the old rates.

Telephone – There will be 15 per cent increase on all telephone charges.

CALL FOR WOMEN Another 250,000 drop in workless total. Britain's industrial army is mobilising at a faster pace every week, and the Government will shortly appeal to women workers to play a bigger part in the industrial war effort. In some areas, particularly the Midlands, the limit of the available man power has almost been reached. That is why the Government is to ask more women to come forward for factory work.'

MAY

10 Friday: NAZIS INVADE HOLLAND, BELGIUM, LUXEMBURG: MANY AIRPORTS BOMBED.

'YOU MUST CARRY YOUR GAS MASK: ARP should be on alert. The carrying of gas masks by the public is once more necessary. They should acquaint themselves with the position of shelters and first aid post in their neighbourhoods. Householders are recommended to overhaul their domestic preparations against air attack.'

---

14 Tuesday '2,000 TANKS IN BIG BATTLE Between 1,500 and 2,00 tanks are engaged in a great battle between French and German motorised forces north-west of the Belgian fortress of Liege. The Germans are making their main attack in this sector, and their advance is being held.

CHURCHILL'S ORDER OF THE DAY 'What is our policy? I say it is to wage war – war by sea, land and air; war with all our might and with all the strength that God can give us ... what is our aim? It is victory, victory at all costs, victory in spite of all terrors; victory, however long and hard the road may be.' (Mr Churchill's speech in the House of Commons)

JUNE

5 Wednesday <u>DUNKIRK AT LAST ABANDONED, THE WITHDRAWAL COMPLETE</u>

NEVER SURRENDER 'We shall defend our island whatever the cost may be. We shall fight on the beaches, we shall fight on the landing grounds, in the fields, in the streets, in the hills. We shall never surrender.'

Mr Churchill.

11 Tuesday <u>ITALY TAKES THE PLUNGE</u> Italy is today at war with France and Britain, after eight hours' notice of her decision. At 4pm yesterday, Count Ciano informed the Allied Ambassadors in Rome that Italy would enter the war on the side of Germany at midnight.

17 Monday <u>A WAY TO END HOSTILITIES</u> 'I must tell you that today the fighting must cease. During the night I have been in touch with the enemy to see whether they can agree with me an old soldier, a means of putting an end to the hostilities.' Marshal Petain, the new French Premier, made this announcement to the French nation at 12.30pm today. He said: 'Frenchmen! At the call of the President of the Republic, I have assumed the Government of France, I am sure of the faith of our soldiers, who have been fighting with admirable heroism against an enemy superior in numbers and in arms'.

FRANCE ASKS PEACE France asked Adolf Hitler for 'peace with honour' today, but Great Britain fought on alone. Hitler was reported by Nazi sources as likely to accept nothing but complete capitulation. He arranged to meet with Premier Mussolini to discuss the French proposal broadcast by Premier Marshal Henri Phillipe Petain as German armies thundered southward through the beaten and exhausted ranks of Poilus.

Leaders of the British Government took the position that the fight must go on and that France probably would join other refugee governments to carry on outside French soil, especially with the French naval forces that are so vital to Britain. But that may depend on the meeting between Hitler and Mussolini.

18 Tuesday 'EVERY MAN TO ARMS! France's decision to 'cease the fight' led yesterday to a great rush in London of men and women eager to serve. The new RAF recruiting inquiry bureau was thronged.

19. Wednesday LEADERSHIP, GIVE US LEADERSHIP 'The battle of France is over. I expect that the battle of Britain is about to begin.' Thus, Mr Churchill in the House of Commons yesterday, and now there can be no illusions in anybody's mind about the ordeal before us. 'Hitler', he said, 'knows he will have to break us in this island or lose the war.'

LET ALL CHILDREN GO TO SAFETY About 340,000 children remain in Greater London. Arrangements should be made at once to remove all children from crowded cities – if necessary to Canada, which has offered to shelter thousands. 'We shall fight better if we know that the children are safe.'

20 Thursday MASSED BOMBING BEGINS Hitler last night launched his greatest air attack of the war on Britain. Swarms of raiders swooped on the east coast of Scotland, on Yorkshire and on its coast; on Co. Durham, down to Lincolnshire and as far south as towns on the south-east coast.

22 Saturday Overtime till 6pm. Fed-up! And still more fed-up!! Boys out, Mum out, and all the tea things to wash.

23 Sunday FRENCH SIGN ARMISTICE: British Government's grief and amazement. Churchill appeals to Frenchmen: 'Fight on'.

Looks like rain all day, but it doesn't. Walk after tea with Mum round Upton and Arrowe Park across the fields. But still fed-up! Why can't I go out on my own instead of always with Mum?

> **24 Monday GERMAN'S TERMS – COMPLETE CAPITULATION OF FRANCE** She must hand over stocks, material, and territory for war on Britain; fleet to be called to home ports and disarmed.

No letter from Bill, and I did expect one. Lengthen mauve frock, darn and wash stockings. Buy gas mask-cum-handbag for Mum's birthday.

25 Tuesday First air-raid at 2am. Seem to do nothing all evening except play the piano.

27 Thursday Letter from Hilda that Bill's brother is missing.

29 Saturday Go straight from office to Upton and buy strawberries for tea at Marjorie's. Meet two Frenchmen, talk to them a bit and buy them strawberries. Go a walk after tea with Marjorie and meet two other French soldiers, one being Paul Strass, a schoolteacher. We get on famously and he is very entertaining. Promise to see him again next Saturday. Home very late, just before midnight.

30 Sunday Marvellous day! Go for a walk with Mum and Nunk to Woodchurch and lo and behold! Paul Strass again! Speak to him and promise to see him tomorrow night. Very excited! Home for tea and to learn some French.

JULY

1 Monday Marjorie's birthday, so sort her a card. Buy her a handbag from Bon Marche sale. Go to Arrowe Park to keep appointment, but Paul is not there, although I wait half an hour. Walk to Upton Station and home rather sadly. Letter from Bill.

2 Tuesday Hear that French soldiers have left Arrowe Park, so that is the reason Paul was missing.

> **20 Saturday YIELD OR DIE, HITLER ROARS AT BRITAIN** Speaking before the German Reichstag, Hitler yesterday offered England 'peace of destruction'. 'I feel myself obliged to make one more appeal to reason to England,' he said, 'not as a victor but for the triumph of common sense.' He made it clear that a rejection of this appeal would result in a 'final' attack on England.

23 Tuesday Hilda tells me that Bill in Saughall camp last night and is sailing this morning. Go to landing stage and see 'Reina del Pacifico' being loaded, but cannot see Bill. Go again at night and stay to tea in town with Hilda, and lo! Bill! Wave and throw kisses until it is too dark to see him. Air-raid.

24 Wednesday Bill now in mid-river, but although I go over on Seacombe boat, cannot see him. The boat sails this afternoon, whither I know not where. Tidy up writing desk at home and sort Bill's letters into datal order.

25 Thursday Jim rings up from Rank's re: Bill's address. Barrage balloons now along landing stage.

AUGUST

8 Thursday Another air-raid. Been happening all week. This time a bomb dropped in Benton killing a girl.

9 Friday A most awful Air-Raid! I have never been so frightened before. Bombs dropped in Gorsey Lane and St Paul's Road (only 200 yards away from Ilford Avenue where we live).

---

13 Tuesday <u>**BIGGEST AIR RAIDS OF ALL**</u> The Battle of Britain is on: Hitler throws in more and more bombers. Portsmouth heavily bombed. All day long there were terrific battles over the Channel and along the coast. And last night the Air Ministry announced we had shot down thirty-nine more Germans and had lost nine RAF fighters. After dark, the raiders returned – over the south-east, the south-west, north-east and Wales.

---

31 Saturday Go round the shops for a bit and have dinner at Reece's. Have a cup of tea with Mum at 4pm and then to bed. But a horrible screaming bomb wakes me up at 8.30 and we are under the stairs till 3.30am. It is more worrying because Joe is out on the bike and Nunk has gone for a walk. Town Hall is hit twice and many houses demolished near there. Custom's House, Liverpool, also hit. Gregson injured and PO man killed.

SEPTEMBER

5 Thursday Three Air-Raids during day. Move beds about. Mum now sleeps under stairs and I sleep in front room, while Nunk crawls under kitchen table. Joe and Fred patronise the Public Shelters. Raids from 10pm to dawn.

7 Saturday Postcard from Bill (3). Two raids during morning. Meet Hilda and stay in town to shop. We have lunch at Lyons in Church Street and home at 4.30. Enjoy a lovely bath, and so to bed. Feel terribly tired. Three Air-Raids during night, but comparitively quiet and enjoy a night's sleep. London is getting it all. They have had the biggest and heaviest raid of the war. 400 people killed, and 1300 – 1400 seriously injured.

8 Sunday NATIONAL DAY OF PRAYER. Three Air-Raids today, but only one plane playing hide-and-seek in the clouds.

12 Thursday PALACE BOMB Buckingham Palace has been bombed. A time bomb dropped into the terrace on the North Wing just outside the King's sitting room. The King and Queen, who have used the Palace regularly throughout the raids, were away for the night.

TERRIFIC LONDON BARRAGE MEETS GREATEST RAID London Blitz night No 5 was a sensation. It began at 8.34 after three daylight raids. Goering intended it to be a Super-Blitz night. He sent over bigger-than-ever formations of bombers, and sent fighters to protect them. And what a surprise they had: All around them broke the biggest anti-aircraft barrage London has ever seen. From every part of London A.A guns flashed and roared. Only a few raiders got through to drop bombs on Inner London. Most had to drop their bombs haphazard on the outskirts. And all the time the intense gunfire drowned the noise of the bombs. The indescriminate bombing of London now stands revealed by the Premiere as part of the invasion plan.

Hitler's plans for invading Britain are nearing completion. Mr Churchill last night said the invasion may be launched at any time. Next week must be regarded as 'very important'. Germany, he said, is massing barges and ships in ports from Hamburg down to the Bay of Biscay. Preparations have also been made to carry a force from Norway. While the Army stands confident and ready for the assault, the Navy and RAF are shelling and bombing every one of Hitler's invasion ports. Barges and harbours are being continuously and heavily bombed.

Mr Churchill (in a broadcast last night) gave warning that invasion may be attempted soon and made this call to the nation:

'Every man – and woman – will therefore prepare himself to do his duty, whatever it may be, with special pride and care ...With devout but sure confidence I say that God defends the right.'

22 Sunday 5 little Raids. Rearranged beds again. Mum and Nunk now go under table and I sleep on couch under the stairs. Joe and Fred go to Shelter. Write to Bill on couch.

OCTOBER

Tuesday Birkenhead Argyle Street got it again.

1 Friday Lovely day. Buy gorgeous pair of shoes, crepe soles, from Hinde's and a feather and two sprays of flowers. Really enjoy myself trying them on. Coat and 2 dresses back from cleaner's so sewed buttons on coat and feather on hat.

2 Saturday Wear my new bronze hat and dress for first time and the girls at office seem to like it. Afterwards, have lunch with Nora at Lyon's and a good cry when we see 'Nurse Edith Cavell' at Prince of Wales Theatre. Home at 4.30. Mend and listen to wireless.

NOVEMBER

1 Friday Bombs fell in Victoria Road, New Brighton

3 Sunday Get bathed and then a walk with Mum from Leaseford to Hoylake along the Prom. See barbed wire entanglements and new defence methods. Wash hair and cut up lunches.

4 Monday Letter from Bill (No. 9) and the code works! He is at Port Suez. Short Air-Raid and a few warnings during night – they make quite a change!

6. Wednesday The Queen comes to Wallasey. I wish I could have seen her. Nunk said she looked beautiful. Think out plans for Xmas presents.

19. Tuesday Little boys pick up shrapnel on beach. Air raid sirens all through night.

20. Wednesday Start next letter to Bill. Receive perfume from Cairo – very strong, and pay 5d. Customs. Do more embroidery. Hilda says her mother had a letter from the War Office to say that Bill's brother, Jim, must be presumed dead, and pilot's wife came to see them on Sunday.

DECEMBER

21 Saturday Mr Alston waiting at office to subscribe to a wreath. Have lunch at Maison Lyon's and then stay overtime till 4.30. Meet Hilda and go to her home with Xmas presents. Then call on Marjorie and there 5 minutes when siren goes. Dash to Bermuda Road, but no buses running, and then the guns start! That walk back to Chatterton's I shall never forget. Sit in their Shelter till 2am and eventually sleep at Marjorie's 4am till 9.30.

22 Sunday Come home at 11.30. So glad to find Mum and everyone whole. Mrs Potter calls and Uncle Johnston. He is helping to clear debris at the top of the road. Sirens start at usual time, 6.40, but not quite so bad, go upstairs at 6.15am – hardly worth it.

23 Monday Unexploded bomb opposite.

25 Wednesday <u>CHRISTMAS DAY</u> Aunt Lucy has been bombed and gone to Sandbach with Aunt Amy. Have dinner and then finish making 2 presents. One of the bombs explodes in the park.

---

31 Tuesday HITLER PLANNED MONDAY SWOOP Hitler meant to start the second Great Fire of London as the prelude to an invasion. This was the belief held in well-informed quarters in London yesterday. The Nazis planned to set big fires burning all over London before midnight. Relays of bombers laden with H.E would then have carried out the most destructive raid of the war. The New Year invasion was to have followed.

1941

JANUARY

1 Wednesday <u>New Year's Day</u> Thick frost and very cold. Letter No. 18 and Xmas card from Bill together with three photographs. Write out reply in rough till sirens go at 9.15pm. Planes pass over at regular intervals but there are no guns. Go with Nunk as far as the steps of the Public Shelter and it is bitterly cold. I think Nunk is scared of fire bombs. Few bombs drop at 6am.

3 Friday Get afternoon off and see film 'Pride and Prejudice' with Greer Garson and Laurence Olivier – two of my favourites. Home at 6.10. Finish off letter No 12 to Bill. Water-pipes in bathroom frozen. Sleep in bed socks, hood, and gloves to keep out the cold.

12 Sunday Fred stays in all day to learn guitar. Shelter at 8pm.

26 Sunday Joe has bought a ukelele, practises with Fred all day.

27 Monday Joe and Fred still twanging and strumming – fill my ears with cotton wool and calmly continue sewing.

28 Tuesday Tonight there is peace and quiet for a change – just Mum and I and the wireless. (Joe at night school, and Nunk on fire-watching duties).

29 Wednesday Post letter No. 15 to Bill. It is announced that the 18-19s, and 40s are the next in turn to register for Military Service That means Joe! Oh, it's a shame, he looks so very young. We all have a good talk about it after tea.

'Night is the only time I live,
Wherein I find delight,
For then I dream my lover's near
To make a day of night.
But when I wake from those sweet dreams,
And find that he's away,
My night again begins its course
With every break of day.'
   W.H. Davies (Tramp poet)

FEBRUARY

1 Saturday Joe goes to Renshaw Hall, Liverpool, to volunteer for the Air Force. He has his medical a week on Monday.

2 Sunday Joe and Fred go to a meeting of the local Fire-Watchers in a room behind the Wine Shop at 9.15pm. The notice sounded like an ultimatum from the under-world and I expected to read 'Burn this as soon as you have read it'. They return at 11.15. A very strange idea!

5 Wednesday Announcement in Echo that Bill's brother must be presumed dead. He has been missing eight months now.

7 Friday Volunteer for fire-fighting at the office, but I sincerely hope I won't be called upon. Write letter to Bill No. 16.

10 Friday Joe goes for his Medical today and he rings me up afterwards. He has passed A1 except for his eyesight and has to report on Wednesday morning for service as Air Mechanic. That's about the best thing he could be because he wants to get out of an office. Tells us all about it at night. Nunk on fire-watching duty all night and stays in room behind the wine shop.

12 Wednesday Kiss Joe au revoir. Post Letter No. 16 to Bill. It seems funny at home without Joe, and Mum is a bit upset.

13 Thursday Joe back home on deferred service and will probably report again for service in a month's time.

21 Friday Mabel Jones gets her promotion today. I am a bit hurt because she is five below me on the Seniority List. Goodness knows why! If I asked for an explanation I wouldn't get any satisfaction, so what's the use? Chin up, Nina. You're not the Career Girl you used to think you were.

22 Saturday Streatie very concerned about the Promotion and goes down to see Reg Thomas who is going to take the matter up with the Region. Meet Marjorie and go for a walk round Greasby and Thurstaston. Tea at the Cottage Loaf. Sleep with Marjorie.

27 Thursday Have an interview with Mr Robbins re: this promotion business and it seems that nothing can be done about it now, but he assures me that the question has been taken up by Mr Barclay and it won't happen again.

MARCH

1 Saturday Another blow to my pride – Jean Robertson has been promoted in front of me. I can't understand it, but one thing's certain, I am not going to take this lying down. Mr Robbins' assurances evidently carry no weight.

2 Sunday Draft out letter to Chief Clerk protesting about the recent promotions.

3 Monday Write out protest on official paper and take it down to him by hand. Draft out next letter to Bill.

5 Wednesday The anticipated, but dreaded interview with the Chief Clerk. His answer is that it is only quite recently that I have shown outstanding ability and that if I work hard for the next six months I might then be considered. The whole thing is so unfair because it is so untrue. That is not the truth, and if I tell the truth, I shall only be put down as tactless – a vicious circle! And this injustice is for what we are fighting. I am furious with Clements and his cronies and the whole rotten system. I'd take another job tomorrow.

7 Friday Letter for Joe to join up on the 20th and to report at Cardington (wherever that is!) – South Wales.

11 Tuesday Write Letter No. 19 to Bill
Sirens at 8.45pm. Learn that Mac has been reported 'missing believed killed'. It is a fortnight since I last saw him.

12 Wednesday Marie back from Leave and I am surprised to discover that she hasn't heard about Mac. She is very upset about it, it's such a shock. We talk about him in the retiring room and that helps.

Sirens at 8.30 and from that moment until 3.30 the next morning there is no respite. The raid is concentrated on Wallasey and Birkenhead and the atmosphere in the Underground Shelter is intense. The noise of bursting shells is nothing; we are almost glad to hear them, but the land-mines which glide down so silently and which create so much havoc are dreadfully near. The bombs whistle over our heads and they land in front of us and six times the lights are blown out. Incendiaries are everywhere, and there are eight roaring furnaces.

I am cold and stiff and ready waiting to swallow the brown earth above my head. I wouldn't mind if all the houses were hit, so long as the Shelters were safe. There are 300 people in ours, and I cling to the man next to me for courage.

At 4am it is over and the fires and sirens and dirt is everywhere. Erskine Road is still blazing. Fred and I breathe a prayer of thankfulness. There is no gas, no water, no electricity, so we sit in the kitchen and wait for morning.

13 Thursday No office today. Tidy up the house and Fred boards up windows and with a couple of suitcases each, we wend our way to Heswall. Joe and Fred sleep at Slater's and I sleep with Mum at Thelwell's. Glad to forget everything in merciful oblivion. But frosty reception from Mum's old friends (good Methodists both) who greet us with unsmiling faces and the words 'We don't mind being thrutched upon – 'thrutched' apparently being an amalgam of thrust/'foisted'. We are very dirty, dishevelled, unwashed, tired, hungry.

14 Friday People at office were very anxious about my not turning up yesterday. Home at lunch-time to see if Mum knows of a house for Marie, but this is all forgotten when I see what used to be 23 Ilford Avenue, our home. A bomb was dropped next door in last night's raid, only 15 yards from the Shelter and the house is a shambles. Take as much with me in my case and go back to office. Hilda offers to store our furniture at their house, and Mr Corkhill (PO Inspector) takes a couple of big cases to Saughall in his car.

15 Saturday Promotion question seems very unimportant now, but give my moral support to the deputation to the Chief Clerk. There is another promotion today.

Go to Wallasy and help Mum to stack the furniture and food in one of the downstairs rooms, board up the windows again and nail up the door. A furniture conveyance is practically unobtainable, but Uncle Johnston says he can come on Monday evening. This may be too late as there is an unexploded bomb behind our house as a result of last night's raid again. Can't do anything else but leave it. Pay 30s for a taxi to Heswall. Mrs Thelwell not very kind. She will not allow us to leave two suitcases at her wretched place.

17. Monday Go to Wallasey at night to help Mum load the furniture on Uncle Johnson's lorry. Can only take half of it, and the two boys go to Saughall to unload. They have to walk all the way back to Heswall, all the buses are full up. All very tired. Mum has found us a house in Oban Drive, off Milner Road. Could have kissed her all over.

18 Tuesday Mr and Mrs Thelwell are very nasty (about 'evacuees' and 'hotels'). A very narrow-minded pair, making not very subtle jokes at our expense. Anyway, it is the last day, thank goodness.

Home with Hilda to await the rest of our furniture. Wait till 8pm. Transpires that Uncle Johnson is required to work overtime very night this week on demolition work, so will have to wait till Monday for the furniture. Dark night and a long time finding the house in Oban Drive, but I like it very much. Go to sleep surrounded by suitcases, boxes and clothes, but who cares now? We've got a roof over our heads and a decent bed and I've still got Bill.

20 Thursday Get up early to accompany Joe to Lime St. Station to see him off safely. How I hate stations! I seem to be losing everyone – Bill, Mac, Joe and the house!

APRIL

7 **Monday** <u>NAZIS INVADE YUGO-SLAVIA, GREECE</u> British in action. Greeks destroy 10 German tanks. The German Army invaded Yugo-Slavia and Greece at 5.30am yesterday. Later, the British Government announced that Imperial troops had landed in Greece. The British statement said: 'After the entry of German troops into Bulgaria had brought to a head the long-threatened German invasion of the Balkans, His Majesty's Government in the United Kingdom, in full consultation with the Dominion Governments concerned, have sent an army to Greece comprising troops from Great Britain, Australia and New Zealand to stand in line with the soldiers of our brave ally in defence of their native soil. The British Air Force, which has for some time been operating in Greece against the Italians, has been strongly reinforced.'

9 Wednesday 23 years old today. Presents from Marie and Marjorie and Dora and the Estimates Group and flowers from Doreen. Present from Hilda waiting at home.

18 Friday At last – Promotion! Everything comes to those who wait! Today's thought!!

MAY

2 Friday Worst Air-Raid of the year. Gets the Office this time. Write letter No. 24.

3 Saturday All the windows out at the Office and some of the inner walls blown down with the land-mine which fell on the other side of Brunswich St. So cold that we have to work in our coats.

Air-Raid at 10.30 – literally hundreds and hundreds of planes! The roar of fresh planes coming in from the sea never wanes until about 1.30 in the morning. Nothing here, but I dread to think what has happened to Birkenhead and Liverpool.

Double Summer Time. Put clock on another hour.

1 Sunday Thick pall of smoke still hanging in Liverpool direction this afternoon. After bath, go to Barnston again with Fred and wander round the fields. We find six bomb craters in one of the fields and one of them is more than 25 feet deep. They chose the best place to land. Wish twice for peace on earth and my man after throwing a horse-shoe over my left shoulder and again at the wishing well.

Air-Raid again and swarms of planes. They must be trying to finish off Liverpool altogether.

2 Monday Go to the Office as usual to discover that there isn't any Office there. The whole of India Buildings, and all that therein is nothing but a charred cinder. Police direct us to Lancaster House, the only other telephone building left, as Bank and Royal and Central Exchanges are also hit. Organisation nil, and we help to carry a few unburnt files that are in the basement. Cable from Bill to keep my chin up. More fires at Liverpool.

7 Wednesday It would be easier to recount what damage in Liverpool HASN'T been done. Everywhere in ruins and blackened remains, and there are whole streets reduced to nothing but ruins.

Spend the day trotting up and downstairs in India Buildings carrying boxes and files. Have cup of tea and a roll from Mabel's Canteen which stopped outside and ate it on the steps in the street. Home at 4.45 with Streatie.

7th night of Blitz. More damage to the middle of the city. HPO hit again for the fourth time.

---

12 Monday ABBEY, HOUSES OF PARLIAMENT BOMBED Westminster Abbey, the Houses of Parliament and the British Museum were damaged during the Luftwaffe's mass attempt to burn London on Saturday night and early yesterday. But night fighters of the RAF made the Nazi Air Force pay. They shot down thirty-one of the record bag of thirty-three moon raiders. AA guns got the other two. These losses bring the total of raiders shot down in the first ten nights of May to 124. Assuming that each plane carried a crew of five, this means that the Luftwaffe has lost over 600 trained men, approximately 160 of them on Saturday night. Some of the German crews were burned to death in the fires they had started. One RAF pilot caught a bomber going home, and saw it plunge in flames into a fire burning on the ground.

LAWRENCE OF IRAQ Lawrence of Arabia's colleague in the last war is stated to be in charge of British forces which have driven back rebels in Western Iraq. The officer is named as Captain Abu Heneik, who seems to be Major J B Glubb, who is known as Abu Heneik ('Father of the Chins') because of an old war wound.

---

13 Tuesday HESS, HITLER'S DEPUTY PRISONER IN GLASGOW Nazi radio said he went mad and killed himself. Rudolf Hess, Hitler's deputy and 'dearest friend', has landed in Scotland in a Messerschmitt 110 and given himself up. This was officially announced from No. 10, Downing Street last night. It followed an earlier statement broadcast from the German radio that Hess had gone mad, vanished in a plane, and was believed to have committed suicide. Berlin radio added that Hess left messages stating his intention to kill himself. Then at 11.20pm the following message from Downing St. blew the German statements sky high. It read:

'Rudolph Hess, the Deputy-Fuehrer and Part-Leader of the National Socialist Party, has landed in Scotland in the following circumstances: On the night of Saturday, 10th, a Me.110 was reported by our patrol to have crossed the coast of Scotland and was flying in the direction of Glasgow. Since a Me.110 would not have the fuel to return to Germany, this report was at first disbelieved. However, later on a Me.110 crashed near Glasgow with its guns unloaded. Shortly afterwards, a German Officer was found with his parachute in the neighbourhood suffering from a broken ankle. He was taken to hospital in Glasgow. Here he first gave his name as Horn. Later he stated that he was Rudolph Hess. He brought several photos of himself of different ages, apparently in order to establish his identity.'

JUNE

1 Sunday Announcement that clothes are to be rationed starting from tomorrow. 66 coupons a year.

2 Monday COUPONS MONDAY Many retail store executives will spend today, Whit Monday, when their shops are shut, working out a new system of values for window tickets. For in future, all clothes, except hats, displayed in Britain's shop windows, will bear two marks, their price and their value in coupons – clothes coupons. This will be among the first results of the Rationing of Clothing and Footwear Order, announced yesterday.

14 Saturday Armistic year babies to register – that's me! If only they would call up ALL the female 23s! Go with Fred and Mum to Sports Gala in aid of the local ATS. I am the only one to enter for the Single Women's race, although there are heaps of entries for the Married Women. Perhaps I am the only unmarried one there!

JULY

1 Tuesday Meet Mum and go to Food Offices with ration books, identity cards.

12 Saturday Meet Mum at 12.45 in Liverpool and lunch at Owen Owens. This is the first time Mum has seen Liverpool since the last big blitz on the city in May. She is horrified. I feel like a guide showing visitors the ruins of Pompeii.

14 Monday BRITAIN AND SOVIET SIGN PACT Britain and the Soviet Union have signed an agreement whereby each will support the other in every way in the war against Hitlerite Germany, and neither will sign a separate armistice or peace except by mutual agreement. The agreement was signed on Saturday in Moscow by M Molotov and Sir Stafford Cripps. It was the result of negotiations between Sir Stafford and Stalin, who was present at the ceremony.

<u>RAF MEN FLEW THROUGH STORMS TO BOMB BREMEN</u> Flying through heavy thunderstorms, Bomber Command planes raided Bremen and other places in North-West Germany on Saturday night. Some exceptionally heavy bombs as well as incendiaries were used in the industrial areas and shipyards by our machines. Big fires broke out. One crew reported they could not see their own bomb bursts so heavy was the general strafing by our machines.

15 Tuesday <u>BOMBS</u> In the last few weeks alone we have thrown upon Germany about half the tonnage of bombs thrown by the Germans upon our cities during the whole course of the war. This is only the beginning ...' Mr Churchill said yesterday afternoon.

<u>WE SEND BOMBERS BY THE HUNDRED NOW</u> Some of the RAF bombers now penetrating night after night deep into the heart of Germany are carrying three times the load that our planes took over a year ago. In addition, while the raiders we sent over twelve months ago could be numbered by the score, they can now be numbered by the hundred.

<u>HUN THREAT TO USE GAS</u> Germany is preparing to use poison gas, judging by the Nazi-controlled Paris radio. Quoting Stockholm reports that the Russians have used poison gas on the Finnish front, the announcer said: 'Should the reports be confirmed, then it is clear that the German High Command will know how to take reprisals against that breach of international law.'

22 Tuesday Issued with steel helmets. What a sight some of us look!

AUGUST

23 Saturday Invasion Night (practice). Home Guards in action outside our house. Go a short walk with Mum pretending we are a couple of decoys.

27 Wednesday Buy box of sweets and a cake for Mum. Mum out for the day with Mrs Cotterall and Freda at Dyserth. Wash stockings. Now this is where the bombshell drops – Mum arrives home in a taxi having broken her bad leg whilst walking up one of the rough roads. Mrs Cotterall and Mrs Curtis help to get her to bed with her leg propped up, after giving her first a dose of brandy. Poor Mum sleeps not a wink all night and inbetween my slumbers I can hear her moaning.

28 Thursday Leave everything at Mum's bedside. Three hours overtime. On my return home, a great shock for me to discover that Mum has already gone to hospital – the bed is left just as she has lain in it with the shape of her head still on the pillow.

31 Sunday Meet Nunk at 1.30pm at Woodside and both of us go to see Mum at Clatterbridge Hospital. She is in Hut 7 and looks fairly comfortable.

OCTOBER

26 Sunday Go to hospital with Fred to see Mum. Mrs Borrows and Hilda also go and they come back with us for tea. They tell me that Bill has been in a military hospital suffering from fever. And he hasn't let me know about it!

28 Tuesday Letter from Joe to say he is coming home at the weekend.

NOVEMBER

7 Friday FINLAND GOING OUT OF WAR Finnish Radio this morning: 'Military operations are drawing to a close as far as our country is concerned. Even though the war goes on between the great Powers, Finland will not carry on any longer than is necessary for her own safety and defence, while it is realised that our frontiers cannot finally be determined until the coming peace conference.' According to a Helsinki message early today, the Finnish Social Democratic Party has asked the Government to find out the views of

Parliament in secret sessions before an answer is sent to the United States note calling on Finland to end the war with Russia.

9 Sunday <u>HEAVIEST RAF RAID EVER</u> Berlin hammered despite appalling weather; 500 planes – 37 missing. Flying in appalling weather conditions, with the temperature often 34 degrees below zero, the Royal Air Force has delivered the heaviest bombing attack ever carried out in Germany.

14 Friday <u>ARK ROYAL SUNK!</u> The aircraft carrier Ark Royal, which the Germans often had reported sunk, now really has been lost – victim of a German submarine – the British Admiralty announced today. The communiqué said the 22,000-ton floating airfield sank somewhere on some undisclosed date while in tow after having been torpedoed. She was the third aircraft carrier lost by Britain in the war and the newest of them all.

22 Saturday <u>ROMMEL SURROUNDED</u> Early today a Cairo military spokesman gave out the tremendous news that General Rommel's Tank Forces in Libya are surrounded. Broken into two groups, they are trying desperately to break out of the British rings, but all the time their position is becoming 'more unfavourable'.

24 Monday <u>BRITISH TAKE BARDIA, 15,000 PRISONERS</u> British forces enter the Italian desert stronghold of Bardia, Libya, after its capture January 5th 1941, yesterday made a triumphant return to the city which had been in Axis hands since April 13. The glory of recapturing the town went to the New Zealand troops.

Buy grey wool for Bill's socks coupon-free, carry it under my arm, no wrapping paper allowed. (War effort!)

DECEMBER

7 Sunday Take Mum some clothes for tomorrow. She is awfully excited about it – like a prisoner who has just heard of her release. Oh, it will be lovely to have her home again.

8 Monday JAPAN ATTACKS USA! Hawaii and Manila Bombed: Chute troops off Honolulu. At least two Japanese bombers, their wings bearing the insignia of the Rising Sun, appeared over Honolulu at about 7.35am (Honolulu time) today and dropped bombs. Reports say the Japanese bombers scored two hits, one at Hickam Field, air corps post on Oahu Island, and another at Pearl Harbour, setting an oil tank afire.

JAP PLANE CARRIER SUNK. U.S BATTLESHIP ABLAZE The U.S. President decided today after Japan's attack on Pearl Harbour and Manila to call an extraordinary meeting of the Cabinet for 8.30 o'clock tonight and to have congressional leaders of both parties join the conference at 9pm.

350 KILLED IN A SURPRISE RAID ON HAWAII AIRFIELD 7 Japanese airplanes attacked American defences bases at Hawaii and Manila, and President Roosevelt ordered the army and navy to carry out undisclosed orders prepared for the defence of the United States. The White House said Japan had attacked America's vital outposts in the Pacific … Hawaii and Manila .. at 3.20pm and that so far as was known the attacks were still in progress. These attacks, so far as is known now, were 'made wholly without warning – when both nations were at peace.'

10 Wednesday JAPANESE SAY TROOPS HAVE LANDED IN THE PHILIPPINES.

12 Friday US GOES TO WAR WITH GERMANY AND ITALY. 40,000,000 IN CALL-UP. 7 DAY WEEK ORDERED. Tonight, for the second time in a quarter of a century, this nation is formally at war with Germany.

22 Monday Post Xmas mail and parcels. Buy flowers for Mrs Borrows and go to her house in the evening. Spend an enjoyable evening just talking and exchanging presents. I receive a cut glass vase, and coat hangers. Sleep with Hilda and dream of other times when my beloved slept so near to me in just the next room. I look in at the sitting room where we used to sit and talk, and the bedroom where we kissed and the walls whisper back at me some of the words that he used. And then the cock crows outside and it is half past six and time to get up.

25 Thursday Pamper myself this morning. Have breakfast in bed with Mum. It is a beautiful expensive feeling – to sit propped up in pillows in front of a tray. Just think! Beef for dinner! On Xmas Day! But enjoy it just as much as turkey. Sew up some cami-knickers that Mum knitted for me. Darn stockings. Put on wireless to hear King's speech, messages from abroad. Sing-song to Fred's guitar. Shampoo my hair and bath.

31 Wednesday Thank heaven that this year is over!

1942

'This, above all, to thine own self be true'
Hamlet

JANUARY

4 Sunday Church with Mum and Fred – very, very cold. Sit by fire and read 'Gone with the Wind'. Once I start a book, it is impossible to leave it alone. Poor Scarlet O'Hara! She couldn't see what was under her very nose, and she only caught a glimpse of it as it was drifting away from her unwanted, and then it was gone – like the wind!

> **9 Friday** <u>JAPS PIERCE BRITISH LINE</u> Japanese heavy tanks forced a breakthrough on the bitterly-contested front north of Kuala Lumpur, British military sources said today, and the battle front has assumed 'a serious aspect'. The Japanese attacked in a general offensive with mechanised units heavier than the British defence and with great number of troops in support.'

Go to lunch-time Rumba Class with Marjorie H and Peggy. Learn more of the Tango than the Rumba. Seems to bring out the Latin in me, and can't settle down to work in the afternoon. Joe home on Weekend Leave at 1am.

10 Saturday Hilda gives me good news – Bill has got promoted, now Flt. Sgt. Send him a cable for his birthday and congratulating him. Air Raid, only a few guns, not many bombs.

11 Sunday Bill's birthday. Read Chinese torture book by P.C.Wren. Joe returns from Leave – still as secret as ever regarding his comings and goings.

12 Monday Telegram from Bill telling me about his promotion and new address. Go with Fred to Table Tennis and play as well as I'll ever play. Beat Fred once.

17 Saturday Bedford Dance Class with Marjorie.

20 Tuesday Step out of doors this morning and nearly vanish from sight in a mound of snow, snow! And still more snow!! – great high banks of it, long smooth drifts of it. Two Wrens with storm lanterns – feel as if we have slipped back a century.

22 Thursday <u>DAY-LONG BATTLE IN MALAYA</u> Heavily reinforced Japanese troops across the Muar river have turned south-east in an attempt to cut the railway and roads linking Singapore with our troops in North Central Johore. A major battle has been raging for 24 hours at Payong, where Australians holding hill positions are resisting an advance towards the important road junction of Yong Peng. Both sides have thrown all arms into this struggle. Throughout yesterday dive-bombers and fighters roared over the front.

<u>AUSTRALIA FEAR WAR 'AT DOOR'</u> The Pacific war may be at Australia's door at any moment now. With the appearance of fleets of Japanese aircraft over many parts of New Guinea, it is feared that a major onslaught is about to be made on this great sprawling island, possibly as a preliminary to the invasion of Australia. The south coast of New Guinea is less than 150 miles from the northern tip of Australia. More Snow. Buses only go as far as Arrowe Park. Roads blocked. Wind icy.

25 Sunday Have a whole day by the fire reading and chewing precious chocolates – a whole ¼ lb box! Nunk in bed all day – he's fast becoming a cranky old man. Wish I could go out with the boys …

26 Monday <u>NEW AEF LANDS IN N. IRELAND</u>   The second AEF has reached Northern Ireland less than two months after the SS went to war with Germany and Italy. Maj. Gen. Russel P. Hartle, the Commanding Officer of the disembarking troops, stepped ashore first and was warmly welcomed by British and United States army officers. A band broke into strains of 'America' as he reached the end of the gangplank.

29 <u>JAP SHIPS SUNK OR HIT IN 4 DAYS</u> United States and Dutch sea and air forces, in a great running battle with a Japanese invasion armada in the Straits of Macassar, have sunk or damaged as many as 33 transports and warships in four days, and may have shattered an attempt to invade Java, heart of the United Nations' defence in the south-west Pacific.

28 Wednesday Royal Court to see Ivor Novello in 'The Dancing Years' – colourful costumes, swinging waltz tunes, beautiful dancing.

30 Friday Wallasey for rations. Whilst waiting for the bus, got into conversation with a most interesting man who was in the Navy in the last war. Very entertaining and helps me to forget about the rain. Completely forget about being wet when I see THE PARCEL – good old Bill! Turned up trumps again! With five pairs of silk stockings, and lots of snaps.

31 Saturday Bedford Dance Class. Miss last bus home. Meet airman also wanting to get to Heswall and walk as far as Singleton Avenue with him, then taxi. Home around midnight. Very bad reception from Mum and Nunk!

FEBRUARY

2 Monday Write letter to 'Airman', send PO for 5/-, half cost of taxi.

---

13 Friday GREAT SEA BATTLE IN STRAITS OF DOVER. SCHARNHORST, GNEISENAU OUT. ENEMY DASH TO HELIGOLAND *Scharnhorst* and *Gneisenau*, the German battle-cruisers, and the cruiser *Prinz Eugen* – survivor of the Bismarck encounter – which have been bombed more than 100 times in their hiding place at Brest, escaped yesterday in misty weather and a fierce naval battle raged in the Channel.

SINGAPORE STILL FIGHTING ON Singapore is holding on. Singapore is fighting back. Counter-attacks on the Japanese left flank have been sucessful.

NAZIS SAY 45 DIE UNLESS The Germans have ordered the execution of 45 Frenchmen held as hostages unless the authors of two recent attacks against Germans in Occupied France are discovered within a few days. Twenty of the men are to be executed at Tours unless the person who attacked a German sentry is found by tomorrow. The 25 others will be executed at Rouen unless the people who threw bombs at Germans there are arrested before Sunday. The Germans last year shot several Frenchmen held as hostages for the killing of two German Officers at Bordeaux and Nantes.

Letter No.69 from Bill, a beautiful letter! Makes me feel as though I am still a very real part of his life. Details plans for future.

---

16 Monday SINGAPORE, SURROUNDED, FALLS TO JAPS The Imperial Forces in Singapore surrendered unconditionally to the Japanese at 7pm yesterday. This was announced by Japanese Imperial Headquarters. Mr Churchill broadcasting last night, confirmed the fall of the island. Mr Churchill said that he spoke under the shadow of a heavy and far-reaching military defeat. 'It is a British and Imperial defeat. Singapore has fallen. All the Malay Peninsular has been overrun. Other dangers gather about us out there, and none of the dangers we have hitherto faced successfully at home and in the East are in any way diminished. This is, therefore, one of those moments when the British nation can show its quality and its genius. This is one of those moments when it can draw from the heart of misfortune the vital impulse of victory. Here is the moment to display that calm and poise, combined with grim determination, which not so long ago brought us out of the very jaws of death.

Hilda says Bill has been taken off flying duties.

20 Friday <u>CHURCHILL CALLS IN CRIPPS</u> Mr Churchill has reconstructed the War Cabinet and reduced it from nine members to seven:
Prime Minister, First Lord of the Treasury and Minister of Defence, Winston Churchill (aged 67), Lord Privy Seal and Leader of the House of Commons, Sir Stafford Cripps (53), Lord President of the Council, Sir John Anderson (59), Foreign Secretary, Anthony Eden (44), Minister of State, Oliver Lyttelton (48), Minister of Labour, Ernest Bevin (60).

23 Monday Go to Dancing Class – Betty doesn't turn up but David does! Learn the 'open tallermark' in the waltz and the 'fish-tail' in a foxtrot (which follows the 'cross-swivel'). Explain to David about Bill (wonder if he'll still be interested!)

24 Tuesday Feel very depressed this afternoon – everyone talking about holidays and painting pictures of old-fashioned inns perched on the cliffs at entrances to bays. And the Battle for Britain is about to commence at any moment now!

27 Friday Mum has news of a furnished house to let in Tower Road South. Go with Mum to see it. Looks all right. Discover the only fish and chip shop in Heswall, and the 'fingers' are beautiful. Eat them on way home.

28 Saturday Go with Mum to see over furnished house, very warm and cosy-looking, but much too dear! The lady herself is VERY nice and we have a long chat with her in the sitting-room. Spend a few 'points' on tinned fruit and veg.

MARCH

4 Wednesday Airgraph from Bill, No.77. Airgraphs are very unsatisfactory. I feel very disappointed and very worried. The tone of the note is in the nature of a reproach, ie: dancing.

9 Monday Dancing Class – not so keen about it as I was (effect of Bill's letter?) Biggest shock of my life this morning when Peggy announces that she is getting married on Thursday, and not even engaged! Michael is going abroad.

---

11 Wednesday <u>REMEMBER HONG KONG!</u> Jap atrocities horrify world. Mr Eden's disclosures in the House of Commons yesterday of Japanese atrocities in Hong Kong have shocked and horrified the entire democratic world. These were two of the worst revelations he made:

> Fifty British officers and men were bound hand and foot and then bayoneted to death;

> Women, both European and Asiatic, were raped and murdered. One entire Chinese district was declared a brothel, regardless of the status of its inhabitants.

<u>JAPS MAKE NEW LANDING ON INVASION ISLAND</u> Japan has won another foothold on the vast jumping-off ground of the Indies by occupying Finschlafen, in New Guinea. Invasion grows nearer to Australia every hour.

Fred gets news of a house from Mr. Eades. Overjoyed – the house is ours! Now we can move, and that right speedily.

12 Thursday Peggy's Wedding Day! A dozen of us arrive at Church by PO van to see her – oh! how cold and forlorn it looks! These whirlwind marriages are not half as romantic as they sound.

16 Monday Furniture Removers don't arrive till nearly 2pm and we can't make a meal as everything is packed. Bit of a 'dust-up' with Mrs Curtis over the rent book! New Address – c/o Mrs Garnett, Telegraph Road, Heswall (Her husband a dental officer in the army.)

26 Thursday Three letters from Bill. Still on old subject of dancing! And outings with other men!

APRIL

9 Thursday Am I really 24? Kiss and a handshake from the family. Presents from girls at office – writing paper and envelopes, mending case, brooch and set of trolley cloths to embroider, china rabbit. Buy cakes to celebrate.

17 Friday Cable (at last!) from Bill for my birthday. Thought he was going to fail me this time.

20 Monday PETAIN HANDS FRANCE OVER TO PIERRE LAVAL
'Frenchmen, a new Government has been formed. Admiral Darlan, who remains my successor-designate, will take over the defence of our territory and our Empire. M. Pierre Laval will, under my authority, direct the home and foreign policy of the country. It was with him that, at the most tragic moment of disaster, I founded the New Order, which was to assure the rise of France. Today, at a moment as decisive as June, 1940, I find myself associated with him once more to continue the task of national reconstruction and European reorganisation. Frenchmen, your wisdom, your patience, your patriotism will help us to triumph over our trials and our sorrows. With one heart, unite behind the new Government, which will give you new causes for belief and hope.'

NEW 'LAWRENCE' WINS US BURMA ALLY An unnamed British Officer – Burma's Lawrence of Arabia – has won for us a new ally against the Japanese invaders. Living with the natives, moving through the Shan States, talking with the village chiefs and headmen, this officer has succeeded in rallying the wild mountain tribes to the flags of the United Nations.

HEAVY DAMAGE IN TOKYO While US official sources are still silent on Saturday's daylight raids on Tokyo and other Japanese cities, Axis reports indicate damage was considerable. A Tokyo report quoted by Berlin radio yesterday said that factories, a cinema and houses had been burned down in the capital, while similar damage was done in other towns.

NAZIS TAKING OVER IN TOULON Insistent rumours in Toulon and Marseilles say that the battleships Strasbourg and Dunkerque and the cruisers Colbert and Dupleix will soon be handed over to the Germans. It is reported that naval experts from Berlin have already arrived and are only waiting orders to take over the ships.

29 Wednesday Two books 'Gen' from Bill, very interesting reading. Strikes home to me very forcefully how every airman is just longing for a breath of English air and the smell of the woods after rain. (Poor old Bill! I wish I could do something.)

MAY

1 Friday THE WAR TODAY

<u>South Pacific</u> – Japanese reported concentrating fleet and transports in Marshall Islands for thrust against U.S Australia lines.

<u>Burma</u> – British withdraw to line 25 miles south of Mandalay to escape entrapment.

<u>Philippines</u> – Corregidor downs three Japanese planes, shells enemy batteries and supply dumps.

<u>Australia</u> – Allied fliers smash 30 grounded Japanese planes at Lae; pound ground installations and down three Zero planes at Salamaua.

<u>Western Europe</u> – Weather slows RAF offensive; eight Nazi planes downed over Britain; chemical factory at Tessenderloo, Belgium, working for Nazis, is blown up; 250 killed.

7 Thursday Fred has a notice to report for his Medical next Wednesday. Gosh, they are being very quick about it; he only registered about two or three weeks ago. I also receive a form to fill in from the Ministry of Labour. So poor Mum thinks that ALL her chicks will be leaving her now.

11 Monday <u>CHURCHILL WARNS HITLER NOT TO USE POISON GAS</u>
Prime Minster Churchill tonight warned Germany that any use of poison gas by the military machine would result in the RAF carrying gas-warfare 'on the largest possible scale far and wide against military objectives in Germany. We ourselves are firmly resolved not to use this odious weapon unless it is first used by the Germans.'

13 Wednesday Fred's Medical. Rings me up to say A1 and all right about going into Air Force.

20 Wednesday Hilda reports Bill's new address now East African Forces, somewhere in Tanganyika.

26 Tuesday Fred's Interview for RAF, but his boss says that he won't be released from his apprenticeship until he reaches the age of 21.

JUNE

1 Monday 1250 PLANES RAID COLOGNE: CITY IN RUINS.

6 Saturday Holidays commence today! Meet Marjorie and her mother at Lime St. Station in time for 9am train. Very hot travelling! Change at Leeds and have lunch there. Arrive Bolton Abbey at 2.30 where the heat wave proves to be almost overwhelming; our cases feel like lead. Meet the Aunt and the old Grandmother who is a regular tartar (Please God, save me from being too old!) Go a walk in the evening with the Aunt and Uncle Bob and find some mushrooms for breakfast.

8 Monday Leave early for Ilkley. Buy rations and do shopping in village first, then climb up onto the moor where we eat our lunch. Take some snaps at the mountain tarn, amidst the ducks and a swan. Weather very showery. Watch the shadows of passing clouds creep across the mountains opposite, one ridge called 'The Cow and Calf'.

9 Tuesday Walk along banks of the Wharfe, see the waterfall and the Strid. If I were able to write Symphonies, I would write them here. Continue on to Bardon Towers (in ruins), Burmsall, Appletreewick (never heard of AM stamps here), back along opposite bank of river through woods – about 18 miles.

11 Thursday Long journey by bus to Otley, then Harrowgate, then to Ripon. After numerous enquiries, eventually find Fountains' Abbey, a massive ruin dating back from 11th Century, set amid ornamental lakes, parkland and woods. See woman at work in Land Army. Queue system for 'buses in operation' all the way home, but land back to Bolton Abbey at 9.30. Wonder why half a dozen bus companies operate in close rivalry over same routes – confusing!

14 Sunday Arrive at Leeds to discover next train to Liverpool doesn't arrive till 10.15, too late for last bus from Woodside. Think up ideas about where to spend night and whether to send Mum a telegram or to phone. However, at Manchester I try Cheshire Lines Railway and find a train leaving at 8.10, arriving 9.10. Travel in same compartment as ATS girls talking about vaccination marks.

15 Monday Can't get up this morning – awful routine of office life begins over again.

26 Friday Marjorie phones up for me to visit her. She has volunteered for the Land Army.

JULY

---

1 Thursday CHURCHILL WARNS EMPIRE IN 'MORTAL PERIL' Prime Minister Churchill won an overwhelming vote of confidence in the House of Commons today at a moment when he himself admitted 'the British Empire is in 'mortal peril'. By the resounding tally of 475 votes to 25, the House threw out a motion of non-confidence in his conduct of the war, introduced by Sir John Wardlaw-Milne. The Parliament and the nation once again entrusted their future to the Prime Minister, accepting his disheartening disclosure that 50,000 men have been lost in Libya, and his grave warning that instead of ending in 1942, as many wishful thinkers hope, the war will be a long one.

---

5 Sunday ATC Parade Text – 'They that wait upon the Lord shall renew their strength, they shall mount up with wings as eagles, they shall run and not be weary, they shall walk and not faint'. Disraeli once said: 'Youth is a blunder, mid-life is a struggle, old age is a regret'. Not quite true.

6 Monday Letter No. 89 from Bill. Mum giving piano lessons.

15 Wednesday Matters have definitely come to a climax today between Mrs Garnett and Mum. We'll be moving again before very long. I can see that. Oh, to have our own home again! We feel like little orphans of the storm, buffeted about from place to place by every selfish whim and caprice. Talk it over with Fred.

17 Friday Auntie Bessie calls – Jack won't come back. A letter from Col. Newman, a prisoner of war in Germany, states definitely killed.

20 Monday Egyptian ship 'El Nil' in the river carrying Japanese diplomatic internees to Portugal for exchange with some of our men.

22 Wednesday High spot of evening – talk (?) with the Garnetts!! Don't have it all their own way though. Quiet 'Little-Mouse Girl' speaks her Mind! Must have been a big surprise!

25 Saturday First office dance of the war held in the canteen at Lancaster House, 7 – 10.45pm. No band! Two players eventually turn up, but the pianist very versatile, has to be! Excitement runs high when two rats scamper across the beams in the ceiling.

27 Monday First air raid warning for ages goes tonight.

31 Friday Pay-Day! Plus arrears of War Bonus - £17.18.0d. (£6 in the Bank, more than I've ever put in at once before).

AUGUST

9 Sunday Double Summer Time. Go a short stroll with Fred to the Beacons and watch the sunset, earlier tonight, because of the clocks being altered an hour. First sign of Winter. Feel very sad tonight somehow. It seems as though Life will never be happy again. I want to cherish every poignant moment before it is snatched away from me, like when Fred and I stand shoulder to shoulder looking out to sea … and a dog barks emphasizing the silence.

13 Thursday Nunk brings home 'World News' books, with very good pictures of St Nazaire Commando raid (scene of Jack's last stand).

---

17 Monday <u>**CHURCHILL AND STALIN MEET**</u> Prime Minister Churchill, who was in Moscow from August 12-15 with Premier Joseph Stalin, arrived at a number of decisions on the conduct of the war, and reaffirmed the alliance of their nations against the Axis. The four days of dramatic negotiations brought Mr Churchill and Stalin together for the first time.

FLYERS BAR JAP AID IN SOLOMONS **LONDON HEARS OF GREAT US VICTORY** Gen. Douglas MacArthur's airmen maintained ceaseless vigil over the waters northeast of Australia to prevent Japanese reinforcements from reaching the Solomon Islands as the battle for control of vital bases there entered its eleventh day today.

Mum out giving piano lessons.

18 Tuesday Post 'Neptunes' of Commando raid at St Nazaire and postcard and letter to Bill. Go a short walk with Mum – lovely evening, wind like a caress – and take blouse pattern down to Ann. While there, heard of houses to be let from adverts in Echo. Write after two of them on return home. Don't expect too much!

20 Thursday **BIG HUN LOSES IN 9-HOUR DIEPPE BATTLE** After the nine-hour battle around Dieppe yesterday, in the biggest Commando landing yet made on occupied territory, Canadian, American, British and French troops were last night returning to England. Some indication of the size of the engagement may be gained from the Nazi report that 400 landing barges were used in one wave, and from the fact that about 300 planes --Nazi and British – were destroyed or damaged in the greatest air fighting since the Battle of Britain.

21 Friday Do some sewing, and then abandon it in favour of going with the boys to see Laurel and Hardy in 'Great Guns'. Have seen it before, but still think it funny.

22 Saturday **800,000 NAZIS MASSED AT STALINGRAD** Dispatches from the front today said the Germans have massed 50 divisions – possibly 800,000 men – on a 60-mile front at the Don river elbow in an attempt to crash through to Stalingrad. The bloodiest fighting of the war was reported going on along the west bank of the Don and at points on the eastern shore where Nazi automatic riflemen managed to cross the stream. Two parties of German store troops, which reached the east bank, were said to have been destroyed.

26 Wednesday <u>DUKE OF KENT DIES IN CRASH FLYING TO ICELAND</u>
The youngest brother of the King, the Duke, who was in his fortieth year, had been closely associated with the RAF since early in the war. He was the first member of the Royal Family to fly the Atlantic. He had flown thousands of miles under war conditions in a plane equipped for battle with enemy aircraft.

SEPTEMBER

1 Thursday Three years ago today! The 4th year of War begins. National Day of Prayer. Short service held in the office round a wireless set and everyone joins in the hymns and prayers. Experience feeling of being very near to all those I love – Joe at camp, Fred at work, Mum at home, and Bill miles away across continents and oceans, yet all together in spirit.

7 Monday Post parcel and letter to Bill. Week's holiday at home. Mum receives letter from solicitor for notice to quit by 14th September. Glad I was home. Go out with Mum on a picnic. A training plane comes down so low that we see the pilot wave back to us as he passes.

9 Wednesday Letter for Fred, calling-up papers for the Army. Take bus to West Kirby where he is working to give him the news. Ring up the firm and position seems hopeful.

10 Thursday Fred informed by firm that no reservation can be made in his case and that all apprentices are now being called up. Feel very sore.

13 Sunday Rather sad in view of the coming separation. This will be Fred's last Sunday at home: so another chapter closes in my life.

18 Friday Joe home again on day pass. First time that Fred hasn't been here with him. Saw Fred off at station yesterday with a large lump in my throat.

22 Tuesday <u>EVERY FIT MAN IN STALINGRAD IS NOW FIGHTING IN THE STREETS</u> Stalingrad's defenders have begun to launch strong counter-attacks in many sectors. As a result, the German troops which penetrated into the north-western suburbs are being thrown back street by street. During the past 24 hours, the Germans have made no appreciable advance, despite their terrible losses and the fact that they constantly brought up reinforcements.

26 Saturday <u>RAF HIT OSLO GESTAPO HQ</u> 'During the rally of the Quisling Party in Oslo yesterday afternoon, a flight of four RAF bombers attacked the Nazi headquarters in the city. At the time of the attack a meeting of the party leaders was being held nearby. Bombs were dropped from about 100 ft. and hits were seen on the Gestapo buildings. One of our aircraft is missing.' Agency messages today said that Quisling was in the middle of a speech when the RAF dropped their bombs. He, his bodyguard and his followers raced to the cellars.

<u>NEW ELECTRICITY CHARGES ORDER</u> Electricity companies' peacetime practice of making a minimum quarterly charge, by arrangement with the consumer, is to be abolished. Major Lloyd George, Minister of Fuel and Power, made an order prohibiting undertakings from making these charges this afternoon. As an alternative, electricity companies will be allowed to charge up to 6s 3d a quarter, including energy used up to that value. Extra units of electricity will have to be paid for.

28 Monday Have lunch with Jack and Dorothy. Watch Americans eat – using a fork and no knife, chips they eat with their fingers. Gives a delightfully casual effect to a meal. Furniture van still outside door when I arrive home. Mum and Nunk have had a fearful row with the landlady. This then is it! What a mess! Unpack at new lodgings and sort clothes. New Address: c/o Miss Wright, Mon Repos, Pensby Road, Heswall.

OCTOBER

1 Sunday Church with Mum – communion service. 'Peace I leave with you – my peace I give unto you'. I could have listened to him for hours. Come home the long way round by Barnston, loitering and chatting on the way. If we had known that someone important was waiting for us at home, Fred on his first visit from the Army; we couldn't have got home quick enough! He has taken to it like a duck to water and looks fine.

7 Wednesday The much-longed for Parcel from Bill arrives this morning – not one parcel either, but two! Contains tea, sugar, butter, cocoa, jam – very thrilled with them! Bill is good. What a very pleasant place the world looks today! Send cable to Bill giving new address and – '2 parcels arrived today'. 25 words = 10/5d.

11 Sunday Grand Family Reunion. Everybody at Home!

18 Sunday Joe's 21st birthday. Fred home for the day. Mum makes a very nice birthday cake and decorates it with a Spitfire. None of us can think of a suitable present for Joe, so we all give him money - £21 from Mum, £21 from Nunk, £1 from Fred. Tea is a hilarious affair, with Fred giving demonstrations of anti-tank warfare and bayonet practice. Very grim and very gory. But he loves it!

25 Sunday Church with Mum, very cold and no heating allowed till 1st November. Fred home on day pass. Thinks he will be posted to a unit next Wednesday. Play parlour games with him – I was always the mug: I am the German. Then, when I am lying wounded, he demonstrates how he'd carry a pal back to the base out of danger. Very good.

29 Thursday Sybil's last day at the office before joining ATS. Marjorie now in the Land Army at Gloucester.

30 Friday Parcel from Bill – one tommy skin bag, a beautiful thing! Much too good for a knitting bag. Shall use it as a 'hold-all' if I can get it fitted with a zip, perhaps lined; the fur is lovely, so soft.

31 Saturday Take the Bag to the office to show Hilda, and everyone gives it their emphatic admiration: 'Most unusual'. 'So expensive-looking', etc. It is rather wonderful to think that Bill actually shot the rhino himself. Very proud of it.

NOVEMBER

1 Monday Unexpected phone call just before 12 to go out to lunch. It is from Frank McGinty, arrived in port this morning until Thursday. Go to Reece's and do more talking than eating. Shampoo hair this evening in case Frank rings up to go places tomorrow night.

2 Tuesday Buy two pairs of shoes, one a 'Utility' style for real hard wear, and the other a crocodile-skill for best. So busy using my coupons I forget to have lunch. Phone call from Frank to go dancing tonight – a real thrill for me! –

and Elizabeth offers to accommodate me for the night. Dash home, pack my nightie, and meet Frank at 7pm – and first stop the Rialto! Have a wonderful time, and our steps surprisingly enough fit just nice! So many men! And 'nary a one could we get to our PO Dance! Meet a friend of Frank's named Ken Roberts, a glider pilot. Leave at 10.45 in thick fog and arrive at Elizabeth's just after 12.

3 Wednesday Frank stays for a while and Elizabeth makes us a welcome drink and he leaves for home about a quarter to one. He said the walk would only take half an hour. He is rather sweet.

---

11 Wednesday <u>NAZIS OCCUPY VICHY FRANCE</u> Hitler sends his army in at dawn. 'I had to act before British and American troops invaded Corsica and Southern France.' German troops marched into unoccupied France at dawn today to take over the whole country. The news was announced to the French people by Paris radio, which quoted letters from Hitler to the French people and to Petain, giving his 'reasons' for the decision to march.

---

12 Thursday <u>ALLIES RACE TO MEET TUNIS NAZIS</u> A combined British and American army is driving eastward at top speed from Algiers to meet Axis airborne forces who have landed in Tunisia. The 'Cease Fire' came at 8am and seems to have been obeyed in all the chief coast towns, including Casablanca, which is occupied by American troops.

<u>**BIGGER PENSION EARLY IN 1943**</u> Increases in the weekly payments to old age pensioners and widows will be made in the early weeks of the New Year. The statement in the King's Speech yesterday that 'renewed consideration' will be given to the position of old-age and widows' pension and further measures will be laid before you' is a specific Government pledge to make further improvements.

Go along to Ministry of Labour office in Leece Street. Made a momentous decision this afternoon – put in application for release, for service with the WAAF. Feel almost repentent about it on the bus coming home.
Write letter No. 63 to Bill.

DECEMBER

8 Tuesday Official notification of release from the office. Gives ME rather a shock – can't say whether I am glad or sorry. Tell Mum all about it.

9 Wednesday Go with Margaret at lunch time to Ministry of Labour and WAAF Recruiting Depot. Margaret's release has been deferred for at least two months

10 Thursday Write letter No.66 to Bill, giving a first intimation of my new spring outfit being Air Force blue!

15 Tuesday Letter from Bill No.122. Also a notice from Labour Office to attend for a medical exam next Monday. (Gosh, I've started something now!)

21 Monday Medical Exam at 12 noon. I am now satisfied that all my parts are in good working order. Rather enjoyed it once I got going. Passed Grade 1 and recommended for Clerk Special Duties. The only thing that worries them is my temperament, whether I might be inclined to panic in an emergency – all according!

25 Friday Christmas Day. Two letters Nos 125 and 126. Not a bit seasonal, instead very warm and very wet. Have a truly wonderful dinner of roast chicken and pork, peas, sprouts, stuffing, apple sauce, pots., and gravy; then Xmas pud and custard. Nunk got the 6d this time. Start to read 'Jane Eyre'. Tea at eight, just Mum, Nunk and me – pears in jelly, mince pies, Xmas cake. Play games after round the fire. Bed at 12.30. Joe home 2am. Mum moaning all night with pain from her leg – not much sleep.

30 Wednesday Write Air Mail cards No 59 and 60. (Not having a wireless, unaware that this service has been discontinued, until after the cards are printed.)

31 Thursday Have lunch with Sybil at Ridgeway's Café, Lord Street. She is in civvies this time. Tells us about her lightning proposal from a boy of 20. Go to see 'This Above All' at the Troc with Pat and Jean – just a last minute arrangement and very enjoyable. Did not realise that the title is part of a quotation from 'Hamlet':

'This, above all, to thine own self be true;

and it must follow, as the night the day,
thou canst not then be false to any man.'

Have grave doubts that if I were the WAAF in the story, I should feel as
though I had been to mine own self true.

1943

'LIFE and DEATH
is but an END and a BEGINNING,
and it matters not whether we live or die,
but HOW WE LIVE and WHY WE DIE.'
The Silver Fleet: 'I shall not die'

FEBRUARY

3 Wednesday Airgraph No 138 from Bill – the first since hearing about my joining the WAAFs. I wish it didn't have to be like this – and THE LETTER! Sealing my fate. Report to Gloucester next Thursday! Have a feeling in my tummy like I used to have at the start of an air-raid. So many things to do.

11 Thursday THE DAY – Adventure calling! Beginning at 9.20am. Margaret and Dora wave me goodbye at the Station and give me a present from the office. Proceed from Woodside to Shrewsbury, then Hereford to Gloucester. Herded into a lorry and drive to a maze of huts, have our hair messed up, and medically examined. Our first meal at the cookhouse – memorable! Then a lecture on the duties we have to do tomorrow, scrubbing with no soap, dusting with no duster. I've not the least idea what to do.

12 Friday Make beds and wash floors according to orders. Parade at 8.15. Eyes tested and then sit around all day giving and receiving forms and having interviews with bare intervals for meals. I've never felt so miserable before in all my life, just sitting around all day and being shepherded from one place to another. And then, the crowning disappointment of not being able to Clerk S.O. as the Grade is closed. Decide to wait and be remustered.

16 Tuesday 8.30 Exchange Parade and this morning it is our turn to do the passages as well as our own floor space. Exchange corsets, brassiers, and slacks. Terrific queues at the cookhouse for morning break, but we get our cake. Lecture on 'How to be Happy in the WAAF' – and play 'silly-beggars' to the NCOs. Clean windows for inspection tomorrow and Parade at 2.45 that brings our spirits down to zero. Vaccination and Inoculation together and not an ounce of sympathy, just so many guinea-pigs. Everyone moaning and fainting.

17 Wednesday Wakeful night. Arms still stiff and wooden. Kit Inspection. Issued with Service Identity Card. Pay Parade, a real heel-clicking high-stepping business all for 10/-. Light fire in hut, sit round it and talk.

24 Wednesday Go through Gas Chamber. Unexposed parts of face and neck sting when gas is present. One girl takes off her gas mask in the Chamber and has to be carried out. Cinema show on the Dangers of Careless Talk. Pay Parade for 14/-.

27 Saturday Route March, only a short one, about a mile and a half each way – down a country lane at the back of the camp. Lecture on 'Discipline and Morale in the Services', then doling out of Fatigues and Drill.

MARCH

3 Wednesday Feel ghastly this morning, sick and faint and giddy. Can't touch breakfast, just have tea. Won't report sick, because I must remember 'that I am in the WAAF now'. A familiar saying! Could weep on the parade ground. Lecture on First Aid and War Bombs and War Gases.

5 Friday Parade in Anti-Gas equipment, what a sight we all look! The raid will be over long before we get into all this clothing! Lecture on King's Regulations. Lecture on Security. Rush teatime because the Group Captain wants to see what the NAAFI looks like with 500 girls in it!

8 Monday Parade in full anti-gas equipment – many more faintings. Route March. Lecture on 'Care of Clothing'. Rehearsal of 'Passing Out Parade'. Squadron concert at the NAAFI. Turns out very well. The rendering of two songs: 'I'll Walk Beside You', 'Two Eyes of Blue' make two little rivers trickle down my cheeks. No right to be in the WAAF.

10 Wednesday Polishing and brushing of buttons and shoes in readiness for the great occasion of the 'Passing-Out Parade', (which proves to be far less of an ordeal than it is made out to be). Congratulations and Final Lecture. Pay Parade: 14/-. Subsistence Parade: nil. Posting Parade, a very exciting event this. Going to Shrewsbury, which is a little nearer home. Some disappointed because of staying, some because of leaving.

11 Thursday Arrive at Shrewsbury camp via Birmingham and Wolverhampton with three others in time for tea and given sheets and a mug. We live in little houses, four in a room. Visit the NAAFI, nearly all men.

12 Friday After breakfast, go to see WAAF Admin Officer and Accounts. Arrange about Voluntary Allotment of 3/6d per week. Then they tell me that I and another General Duties are to be posted to Wheaton Aston, a satellite camp, and that we shall be billeted at Perton.

---

13 Saturday <u>13 HIT-AND-RUN RAIDERS DOWN IN 24 HOURS</u>
Germany, stepping-up sneak raids over Britain, in the 24 hours ending at dusk last night made four attacks on this country with 74 bombers and lost 13 of them – the highest proportion of 'kills' for months. The four attacks included a night raid on the North East (the Germans claimed that Newcastle-on-Tyne was their target), a dawn raid on the London outskirts and an afternoon attack on the South-West.

COMPLETE BREAKDOWN A report has been received by the U.S State Department that Hitler is suffering from a complete breakdown, says the Reuter message from Washington yesterday. There have been reports from neutral sources that a mental specialist had been called from Sweden to Berchtesgaden.

At 7am I am told to be ready for 7.45am bus to Wheaton Aston, a journey of about 15 miles. Report to Guard Room and Accounts and then begin work in earnest – in the cookhouse! Wipe and scrub and brush and mop and then attend to dish-washing. Oh God, I hate it! Return to Perton by service bus at 5.15.

14 Sunday It has suddenly come over me that I must go home. Decide to try it on a day pass. Go to see about a 295 Form as soon as I arrive at Wheaton Aston. Do exactly the same sort of work as yesterday, only more of it! Alight from service bus at Codsall Station and take train to Wolverhampton and then to Liverpool (12/3d single) arriving at 10.10. Walk home to Birkenhead – Home! Home to see Mum, and Fred too. Talk till 4am – so much to say!

17 Wednesday I'm in the middle of mopping the floor when I hear from the Sgt to report to Orderly Room after lunch. I don't need a second telling!

Report to P/O Hamilton who is in charge of Crew Room and I am to be the other time keeper. Seems quite easy, but at least it is better than the cookhouse. Ring up hospital – Fred very poorly. Write letter to Mum in reply to the one I received from her today to say that poor Fred was taken to hospital with pneumonia, temperature 101.

APRIL

1 Thursday RAF 25 years old today. Talk by CO.

4 Sunday Summertime begins – one hour less sleep. My first day in the Orderly Room. I manage to type a letter properly on my third attempt. It seems very much the same system as in our old office, but better than the Crew Room. I appear to be doing things today that I have not done for a long time – I play hockey, a practice match between Perton and W/Aston mixed teams. Win: 3-1. Go to cinema show: 'Ship Ahoy', with Eleanor Powell. Life seems very much more interesting.

8 Thursday Two birthday cards from Mum and Florrie, also two parcels from Mum – one containing egg-box, letter from Bill and Income Tax, and the other containing holdall and two handkerchiefs. Have only just realised that it is my birthday tomorrow.

18 Sunday 10.15 train to Trentham, but no Fred to meet me and on arrival at camp I find he has been posted to Heath House Red Cross Hospital. Fred is very surprised to see me. We have tea there, travelling back with two soldiers also visiting the hospital.

22 Thursday Go to Civic Hall for dancing at Wolverhampton – a magnificent place. Very generous escort (Bernhardt) who buys me tea and cakes and another shandy. Apparently his people are rich and own a diamond business; his income tax for 6 months amounts to £353 (I saw the letter). Emile is also here and I dance with him quite a lot. Apparently he is one of Bernhardt's employees.

30 Friday Up early and pack ready for week's leave. Collect eggs from farm. Leave camp at 1pm. Buy some pink tulips for Mum. Joe gets home every night now on 'living-out' pass. Letter from Bill No 159 containing most startling request. He asks to become engaged!! And on my next Leave!!!

Telegram also giving new Squadron address. Can't sleep, too busy planning wedding.

MAY

3 Monday Go with Mrs Borrows and Hilda to buy engagement ring. Meet Mum in Liverpool. Call at numerous shops and try on literally dozens of rings of all shapes and sizes, and costing anything from £20 to £150. I want an emerald very much and I finally find one that I like at Boodle and Dunthorne's costing £37.10.0d (no purchase tax). Lunch at Lees. Send cable to Bill, and Mum cables Congratulations. 'Echo' office to insert announcement in local papers (18/-). Tea at Sisson's.

7 Friday Go by bus to Saughall Massie to have ring officially placed in position. 'Pop' in Bill's absence, plights me his troth. Gives me four eggs and flowers.

8 Saturday Weather very much in keeping with my mood and thoughts at going back, and not at all in sympathy with good news that Tunis and Bizerta have fallen. The whole of North Africa is now 'in the bag', only six months from start of campaign! Send 'Echo' to Bill.

---

21 Friday 'BATTLE OF GERMANY' IS ON – NON-STOP AIR WAR PLEDGED The great Allied air offensive, now described as the 'Battle of Germany', gathered momentum today as American air power heavily raided the Nazi U-boat installations at Wilhelmshaven and Emden, destroyed 113 Axis planes off southern Italy and bombed a huge dam in Sardinia. The RAF also hit hard at Fascist Europe. Speedy Mosquito bombers of the RAF last night raided Berlin for the second successive night, while other planes struck at Nazi communications and industrial targets on a broad front in Northern France and northwestern Germany.'

---

23 Sunday Take telegram into Signals to recall airmen from Leave. First lesson in cycling with Cpt. Thompson. I come off a number of times, but manage to ride halfway round perimeter track to SHQ on my own after half an hour. Never knew that cycling hurt so much.

26 Wednesday Assisted Capt. Thompson during Parade – 90 offenders. Go on first bike ride on the roads with F/Sgt Foster and Cpt. Thompson to Church Eaton and back. Arrive at Wheaton Aston Dance at 9pm.

JUNE

10 Thursday Letter from Bill, No:166, also one from Mum, and one from Hilda. Quite a rush afternoon – making out my documentary evidence as witness for a charge (my name will be 'mud), and telling the Adj. What to do when a RAF pigeon is found. Wheaton Aston Dance – go to NAAFI first with Lorna and Marjorie and meet Capt. Bolus there, then go to the dance about 8.30. Talk and talk, very stimulating to be with, till 10pm when he has to go night flying.

20 Sunday Hear Peg's life story. A real human document. One doesn't need to read novels in the WAAF.

JULY

<u>**SICILY INVADED**</u> Allied forces under the command of General Eisenhower began landing operations on Sicily early this morning. The landings were preceded by Allied air attack. Allied naval forces escorted the assault forces and bombarded the defences during the assault. Allied pilots returning from flights over the Sicilian battlefields today told most graphic stories of how the invasion of the island looked from the air. 'A chain of smoke and flame ten miles inland from the coast could be seen from the air. Allied warships shelling without interruption as our forces landed sometimes dashed in close to the shore, fired salvoes and then swooped out again. I have never seen so many ships in my life.'

26 Monday <u>**ITALY UNDER MARTIAL LAW**</u> Rome radio this afternoon announced Martial Law throughout Italy before phone communications between Italy and Switzerland were cut. Fighting between Italians and Germans and great demonstrations throughout the country were reported. Mussolini is under house arrest, and Scorza, Fascist Party secretary, and the entire Italian Cabinet are detained under a strong guard at a place outside Rome, according to Berne reports.

THIS IS WORTH REMEMBERING The paper 'Schwarze Korps', official organ of the Nazi SS says that if the war is lost by Germany, a new world war must be envisaged in 1963. In another issue, the same newspaper says that 'young Germans should marry as soon as possible, for prudent people must know that life goes on and that our grandchildren must accomplish the task if our children are not able to do so'.

Letters at last! from Mum (Notice to quite lodgings), and two letters, Nos 165 and 167 from Bill.

AUGUST

1 Sunday Wheaton Aston now a parent unit. 50 ATC boys invade the Camp today for a fortnight. Little fellow called Billie Bunn reports to Orderly Room to be the runner and general help: he's only fifteen. Most of them in the NAAFI during evening smoking pipes and drinking beer. Ye Gods!

8 Sunday Read book of Marjorie's called 'The Ideal Marriage', and have to leave off every so often to do a spot of embroidery to hide my blushes. It fascinates and yet repels me. But I'd like Bill and I to develop our new technique! in our own way!

9 Monday Poor Mollie's bad day. Apparently took down a lot of letters yesterday from the CO and now can't read them back. I am detailed to do them in her place. Rather proud of that (although I do feel awful about it). Stay late till after 8pm finishing arrears of typing.

17 Tuesday Letter from Mum (Fred home on another seven days). Decide to try for a 48-hrs from tonight to see him before he sails. No Liberty bus and no transport during afternoon. Last minute dash to get PO van going into Stafford. Talk with motherly woman about the War and Our Men and Folks in General. Get off bus at new address: 396 Pensby Road, Barnston, Wirral, Cheshire, and give them all a surprise. Shown over the new abode and explore all the little nooks and crannies. It's a house to discover.

21 Saturday Meet Sgt. Pilot (Arthur Gwyn Jones) and go cycle ride as far as Royal Oak. Like him till on way back – then! Then! ¾ beast!!!

22 Sunday Interview with WAAF Officer. Write letters to Dr Carlisle and Mr Eades regarding my application for 3 months temporary release from the WAAF.

23 Monday NAAFI for coffee. Sit talking with Lofty and fellow called Cullen who gives me some very fatherly advice. I take it in the same spirit it is given; only hope it isn't too late. It has taken me all this time to learn the lesson that men don't go out with girls just for company any more – not in the RAF anyway.

31 Tuesday Another informal talk with CO, who seems very keen on the idea of taking leave first. We discuss it in every detail and I find him most helpful. One thing he says that I'll never forget – 'I am sorry there has to be a break in your service. You are a good shorthand typist.' He arranges an interview with the WAAF Officer, and W/Cdr signs my leave form. Do Duty Clerk for Jean.

SEPTEMBER

3 Friday War Started Four Years Ago Today!

BRITISH TROOPS AGAIN FIGHTING ON EUROPEAN CONTINENT
Today, four years after Britain entered the war, British troops are again fighting – in Italy itself. Two hours before dawn this morning, British and Canadian units of the Eighth Army, protected by the most powerful naval and air bombardment of the Mediterranean campaign, crossed the Straits of Messina and landed on the beaches around Reggio on the toe of Italy.

HEART OF PARIS BOMBED TODAY Huge Anglo-American air armada strikes in daylight.

Pay Parade £1.16.0d. Leave just before 5pm in PO Telephones Van. 5.27 train from Stafford to Liverpool. Home by 8.30. Mum so glad to see me again. Nunk busy in the garden. Letter No. 184 from Bill.

8 Wednesday Good news tonight – 'Italy's Unconditional Surrender!' Can hardly believe my ears. The news is too much for Mum, who has one of her bad attacks, the only cure: Sal Vaolatile.

9 Thursday <u>ITALY IS OUT</u> Italy has laid down her arms in unconditional surrender to the United Nations – utterly defeated on land and sea and in the air. The birthplace of Fascism is the first of the Axis pillars to fall; the fate of the others is now beyond all doubt. Seven million Italian soldiers have ceased to fight the allies, and last night Marshal Badoglio himself broadcast a surrender proclamation, which warned the Germans: 'We will oppose attacks from any other quarter'.

12 Sunday Visit from police to say 48 hours extension granted. It's like living on the edge of a volcano, this waiting for hourly extensions. Terrific thunderstorms during night – too much like an air raid for my liking – ALMOST frightened.

13 Monday Telegram confirming '48 hrs. extension, pending receipt of letter. Chocolate ration from Wheaton Aston sent by Cyril with short note. Another storm, and rain in a huge deluge, so that water butt overflows and floods the yard almost to the doorstep. Two kiddies – Fred and Eddie – in boots and macs soon get the water moving again. Write letter No.29 to Bill.

16 Thursday <u>LONDON RAID</u> 4 out of 15 Nazis down. Four aircraft were shot down during raids on Britain in the night. Fifteen bombers crossed the coast; two or three reached London, where there was a warning lasting an hour.

Make cami-knickers out of old slip. Transforming green coat to make it fit Freda! As I sew, I can see it slowly beginning to fit the child – only snag, the armholes. Telegram granting 7 days extension, with a footnote 'to return to Unit on expiration', meaning – 'That's all!' Write note to Cyril, enclosing cigarette coupons.

22 Wednesday Orderly Room move to new building. Typists now have a room of their own. Talk with CO who is very apologetic and wants to know all the details about how Mum is managing. Offer to allow another week's leave, but says how pushed he is for a competent Shorthand Typist. Then the wonderful surprise – recommends me for ACW – Aircraft Woman Class 1! – and immediate remustering to Clerk CO! He says I must gain at least 60 – 80 percent (IS the Sergeant mad! – HIS promotion was turned down). Very busy!

23 Thursday My ACW1 (Aircraftwoman Class 1) has already been promulgated, on PROs (Personnel Routine Orders). A quick worker is our CO! Backdated from 1.9.43. Write letters No. 32 and 33 to Bill. Swot up some shorthand – 'genned' up on gramalogues, contractions, etc.

OCTOBER

13 Wednesday ITALY DECLARES WAR ON HITLER Churchill and Premier Stalin today announced that Italy had declared war against Germany. The White House said Marshal Badoglio had communicated Italy's declarations against her former Axis partner to General Eisenhower, Allied commander in the Mediterranean theatre. In his message to the General, Gadoglio said that 'by this act all ties with the dreadful past are broken and my Government will be proud to be able to march with you on to the inevitable glory.'

Welcomed home by a kiss and a whispered endearment, followed by the strains of the old guitar, and a voice 'All our tomorrows will be sunny days'. Cycle ride with Fred round Thurstaston and Arrowe and Barnston. Moonlight ride back to Camp from 7.5 train to Stafford and Gnosall.

22 Friday 'DON'T RESENT MY DEATH' – RAF FATHER When the two sons of the late Sergt. Pilot Eric Victor Durham, RAF of Liverpool, become young men they will read a letter written by their father to the eldest son, John. Sgt Pilot Durham died in action over Germany in 1941, when John was one year old. His second son was born after his death. 'Respect all women', says Sgt Durham in the letter. 'If ever a woman is found to go wrong, or gets into trouble, the cause can usually be traced to a man. You were born while the guns were firing at enemy planes, an enemy which took your Daddy from you. Live a clean life, help the weak, despise the bully, be proud of your ideals, don't feel resentful because your Daddy was taken from you. He felt it his duty to fight for the right. You can be proud your Daddy belonged to the RAF. I am proud to have belonged to a great Service.' Sgt Pilot Durham's father is Rev G.E. Durham, known on the Merseyside as 'the fighting parson'. He was a sergeant-major in the Royal Marines and was ordained after the last war. Mrs Durham said today: 'My son was 27. He was a great sportsman. His widow is doing a grand job of work at a Windermere war nursery, and she has the two

> boys there with her. I feel that they must reach years of discretion before they read their father's letter. Fourteen would, I think, be a suitable age.'

I reign alone in the Typists' Room. My job to do SROs. CO returns this afternoon. In with him for three solid hours going through his correspondence. Stay late till 8pm. Cinema Show at 9pm – John Garfield in 'Air Force'. It gets too monotonous altogether seeing Jap planes crumple up in mid-air and Jap ships break in half – American film, of course!

25 Monday Up early in time for 8am transport to Thernhill for Trade Test Board. Travel by car with S/Ldr Walker. Written test (3 hours) and Oral not too bad. 98% typing – shorthand easy. Have lunch at Thernhill. Back at Orderly Room at 15.00 hours.

26 Tuesday Letter from Fred. CO asks for report on how Trade Test went yesterday – says will be quite satisfied if I get ACW1 Clerk CO; but I SHOULD get over 80%, which is LACW. Approached by S/Ldr. Semple to be 'Receptionist' at Officers' Mess Party next Friday.

29 Friday Officers' Mess Party at 7pm. Clad in very nice Spring overalls, perform duties of Receptionist, dancing attendance on all and sundry. Introduced to CO's wife, and Lt. Col Gressang (US). Sell tickets for cake, and make £8 for Ben Fund. Taste delicious concoction called 'Punch'. Have choice of escorts to see me home, choose Irish boy called Tommy.

NOVEMBER

7 Sunday Result of Trade Test – ACW2 Clerk CO!!! Can't understand it, when total percentage was 86%, sufficient for LACW!! If my marks had been divided by half I should still be exactly the same, ACW2 CO. Going to ring CTTB.

10 Wednesday Letter from Mum. Letter from Gerry. Meet Gerry at 6pm on way from Guard Room, where he gives full expression to his powers of oratory. Takes nearly an hour, even so. Drive to Newport and acquire a new personality. Dine at Royal Victoria Hotel – believe it was chicken. See a film, can't even remember the name of it after. Unable to sleep much … xx … (Bill, Bill) xx .. act of homage.

11 Thursday Drive to Hinsbock (Fleet Air Arm Station) via High Ercall. Then to Shrewsbury, first calling at farm where Gerry's brother stayed just prior to crash. Smoke first cigarette. Lunch at Honeychurch Café. Wander around town while Gerry visits TM's office – coffee at WVS, etc. See a film 'Five Graves to Cairo', featuring Afrika Korps and General Rommel. Tea in Cinema Café – mixed grill. Beautiful night. Lorry back to camp with many wrong turnings. Almost irresistable – almost! No, no, no.

12 Friday Long session with CO this morning, and tell him about my day off and my plan to transfer to AMGOT with Gerry.

15 Monday Letter from Mum to say Fred has gone abroad.

16 Tuesday Letter from Joe – wants to get posted to Wheaton Aston. I wonder why. Asked to help at Officers' Dining-in-Night' tonight, which I don't enjoy much as I feel as if I am here under false pretences. I don't know why the CO asks me to go (there's nothing to do) unless he thinks I enjoy a good feed!

26 Friday CO sick with flu – sends a message for me to go to his quarters to take some personal letters, to wife, etc. He does look ill. Specialist coming to see him tonight.

27 Saturday Letter from Gerry. CO in hospital with pneumonia. Airman died in his bed this morning.

DECEMBER

1 Thursday <u>CHURCHILL, ROOSEVELT, CHIANG HAVE MET, AGREED ON PLAN TO BEAT JAPS</u> Plans for the defeat of Japan and the stripping from that country of the territory it has gained by aggression have been decided at an historic conference in North Africa between Mr Churchill, President Roosevelt and Generalissimo Chiang Kaishek. There are four main points in the communiqué issued this morning:

> *Military operations have been agreed upon: unrelenting pressure will be brought against 'a brutal enemy' by sea, land and air;*

> *Japan will be stripped of all islands in the Pacific seized or occupied since August 1914;*

> *Manchuria Formosa and the Prescadores will be returned to China;*
>
> *Korea will 'in due course' obtain its independence.*

The Conference lasted five days.

2 Friday Visit from F/O Vinnell during afternoon, who has made this his HQ – 'warmest place on Station', apart from bed.

18 Saturday Letter from Gerry. Trade Test this morning, now ACW1 Clerk CO, CO follows this up with short talk designed to boost my morale, that I, as his Confidential Secretary, should be the 'Big Cheese' around here. Altogether, something to think about. Promise to get LACW next month.

24 Friday Phone call from Gerry. Xmas Eve Dance. Dance with red-haired Sgt. and Cpl. Bolus and F/Lft. Buckley, before being claimed by CO. 'Excused' twice by F/Sgt., but CO refuses quietly and firmly. Also excused twice by Vic (F/O Vinnell) who grumbles at my elusiveness, but manages to see me home.

25 Saturday Christmas Day **Xmas cards** from Jean and Frank, Mollie and Jim Hoyland. Real eggs for breakfast. **Xmas Service** at 9.30. Only 20 there. Make up presents for Xmas tree, which I help Vi to dress in afternoon. **Xmas Dinner** served by Officers and Sgts. who sign my menu. Afterwards, help to serve cooks. **Cinema Show:** 'Mr Wong in China Town'. **Xmas Party:** with Vi. Dance with F/Lt. Buckley and F/O Vinnell, and several others with whom I play party games. Win prize from Xmas Tree for being first to produce man's suspender (Vic's).

27 Monday Report sick with burnt finger (cigarette). Make a foursome with Helen and Dennis and Vic, and cycle to Bradford Arms. We are the only ones there and have a lovely cosy talk around a log fire. Sgt's Mess Dance – spend most of the evening with Vic, teaching him dance steps.

28 Tuesday Go to Stafford on Liberty Bus with Vic. See film: ''Sing, You Sinners', with Bing Crosby.

29 Wednesday Cycle to Gnosall for 1pm train, arriving in Liverpool 5.15. It is a hard push home on the bike, which needs cleaning and oiling and pumping and everything else. Hoping Joe might oblige while I am on Leave.

1944

'May this wing and my prayer bring you home – always.' *Nina*

JANUARY

4 Tuesday 'WHY WAS I BORN A GERMAN?' Nazi's heartcry. One of the most illuminating documents taken from a captured German in this war is a diary kept by an ex-Hitler Youth Storm-Trooper leader who was made prisoner by the British in Italy.

The writer is a very young man. His entries begin on a note of high pride and end in horrified disillusion. His first entry is made on January 23, 1943, when he joined the German Army proper. It reads: *'Fitted out for uniform. Feel and look fine, if a little odd.'* A month later he writes: *'Gradually I am beginning to feel myself a real soldier.'* He arrives in Italy on 10 September 1943 and records his feelings of *'pride and honour because I am fighting for our great and well-loved Fuhrer'*. This entry, clearly written in a state of high Teutonic emotion, conflicts with this verse from 'The Song of the Panzer Grenadiers':

> *'We have battled and fought:*
> *No pain laid us low,*
> *For death cared we nought,*
> *We triumphed o'er the foe:*
> *For always we lead, and when danger nears*
> *It's – 'Forward the Panzer Grenadiers!'*

The change comes towards the end of November. By this time the diarist has had his fill of fighting on a British sector of the front. Early in December, he writes bitterly:

'I wish I was an Englishman! All this retreating does not agree with me.'

The last entry in the diary is dated December 22, the day before the writer was captured:

'Yesterday night, during the retreat, I finally broke with my old life. Gone are the old values, all that was precious to me. In my soul only one thing remains – a hatred of the bestiality of the German Army. At the least, one is a human

being. Everyone curses the Nazi Government, but few have the courage to turn against it. The brutality of oppression is still so strong. I would like to help strengthen the thousands who long for final collapse. Why was I born a German? I feel myself always a slave.'

CO not back from Leave till late afternoon – thanks me for Xmas card and warns me that he may soon be posted, hope I am too! Meet Vic at 7.30 (prompt for once) and cycle to Bradford Arms. Neither of us is short of inspiration for things to say, very happy time! Stopped by policeman on way home for having no back light.

13 Thursday Station Dance with Vi. Dance with Vic (who has had a 'prang' on his cycle necessitating bandaging of his thigh) till excused by CO for last dance together before his Posting.

16 Sunday Bid farewell to dear old 'Brownie'. 'Gone are the days – ' I do feel sad. Grants me a last bequest of Supr' as my Annual Assessment after showing him AP.837. The G/C dictates his first impressions of the Station; all critical. Meet Vic at 7.30 and cycle to Bradford Arms. Tells me of differences between himself and Pauline, his fiancée. Show him snaps of myself in civvies.

18 Tuesday On first charge this morning for 'riding cycle without lights' last night. (10 yards I rode before realising dynamo was not switched on.) SP Tinsley. Go to Stafford with Vic per new bus service. Very comfortable person to be with. Dine at Station Hotel, exchange confidences over soft drinks.

20 Thursday On another charge this morning for not finishing some typing for MT Officer last night. Given 4 days CC. Oh, I must get away from this! Two hours jankers in Cookhouse, tearing labels off salmon tins.

21 Friday Pay Parade - £1.14.0d. Vic calls in to see me, and very surprised to hear why our trip tonight is off. Report at Officers' Mess to peel spuds for two hours. Stay for supper with CO's batman. Write letter to CO.

22 Saturday BERLIN'S WORST NIGHT OF TERROR Berliners are today convinced that last night's 2,300 ton attack on the German capital was more terrifying than all the assaults that have gone before, Swedes who experienced the raid and who have reached Malmo, reported late tonight.

The raid, they say, was paralysing despite the fact that a 'sixth sense' had warned many Berliners that it was 'just the right night for an attack'. People queued at the entrances to the capital's deep shelters long before these were opened at five o'clock and most of them stayed underground until the early hours of this morning – though Berlin's final 'All Clear' had sounded about midnight.

OUT HITLER ARMY PLOT A warning to Nazi leaders that the German Army is planning a putsch to overthrow Hitler and make peace has been circulated by Gauleiter Erich Koch, one of the party's chiefs. The letter says: 'The Fuhrer is in danger. Parties of reaction are trying to displace him and establish a military dictatorship under which Germany would immediately start peace negotiations against the will of the people'.

8 DOWN LAST NIGHT London Barrage in Full Action. Eight German raiders were destroyed last night, it was officially announced early today. Fiercest barrage Londoners have heard for many months

FEBRUARY

1 Tuesday Jim reports some more developments regarding this queer underground movement that is being conducted against me and my friends. Says he received message from Adj. (via Hobby) to keep out of Typists' Room – he has not been in for ages! Why SUDDENLY say that? Go for a walk to discuss full implications.

2 Wednesday Write Airgraph to Bill. Type letter to Mum. Write letter to Vic. Phone call from Vic at 00.15 hours, just finished night flying, so walk up to the Mess with him, and deliver letter personally.

Tuesday morning

Vic my dear,

I have scrapped the other letter I started to write to you last night, because most of the things in it we had already discussed. Thanks a lot xxx I am glad you didn't allow me to waste time by going to sleep, and probably dreaming of good times with you. It is the contrast I don't like, when you wake up to smile into waiting blue eyes, and stretch up your hand to touch a stubborn chin, and you find nothing but blackness and an empty void, where once was you – dear you. Contrast indeed!

Vic, I know exactly how you must feel about the way they are trying to make our relationship into a 'hole-and-corner' affair, hedged round with deceptions, and shunning the light of day. We ought to feel so proud and happy about it – about this lovely precious thing we have discovered, how could they try to hurt it? – and instead, you feel hurt and angry and resentful, don't you? It seems doomed almost from the start. But they won't succeed. They don't know very much about human nature, or they would realise that difficulties such as these are only going to toughen our determination. And I am quite determined, Vic, about 'Our Day'. I haven't changed my mind.

You are very keen to see me in 'civvies' aren't you? And it occurred to me suddenly that you wanted to see me so clad to help you in your work of comparisons. After all, this RAF life and inevitably the uniform are very unnatural, and so you want to see what I look like as an ordinary normal person living a normal feminine life – in short, you want to discover if Nina the woman falls very far short of Nina the WAAF. She won't if I can help it, Vic, because what you think of me seems to matter so tremendously. No-one else's opinion matters much (outside my mother and my brothers). Why should yours? I think I'll leave that as an open question.

We HAVE had good times, Vic, I have enjoyed every minute of them. And 'Our Day' is going to be no exception, except that it is going to be better than every before. I AM promising a lot, aren't I?

Now it is your turn to be 'the damned elusive' – I am duty clerk tonight, of course and alone. I have phoned the Mess and Ext. 54 – 'not in' at the former and 'no reply' to the latter. There are obvious signs outside my window that there is night flying. I wonder if that means you are not available. I wish you were here. Till Saturday, then – when I'm hoping you'll dance with

Your partner in crime

xxx Nina

Nina, my darling,

I wonder if you have any idea how lonely I feel. This night which was to have been OURS. How I've longed for Saturday night to come round after this past week of a forced parting. Tonight, I could have held you in my arms.

Instead, here I am cooped up in Sick Quarters with a face too painful for words. And you – well, I guess you're dancing with some other lucky fellow, Nina. And I don't blame you for it should be a good dance. Last night when I was in bed, I cried from sheer loneliness. It seems ages since we had an evening to ourselves, dear Nina. Why should Fate rob us of the few precious hours that should be ours? If only you knew how much I look forward to being with you. Your company gives me a warm glow of companionship such as I've never known before. Life is indeed pleasant with you, my dear.

Yes, Nina. I too have my dreams. I dream of a smile that touches my very heart. A smile that would make light the darkest possible moment that life could hold for me. A smile that takes me to paradise. Indeed, the waking is hard and cold, for often in my dreams that haunting smile is only a few inches from my own lips and those sparkling eyes so very close to mine. Why must such dreams ever fade unless they are to be replaced by sweet reality?

Believe me, Nina, our relationship will not suffer because of the people around us and their bickerings. It's too fine to suffer because of them. It will grow even more beautiful with time because I am determined to cultivate it. We are fighting right now to preserve the beautiful and decent things in life and if necessary I'll start my private war that you and I might keep our very great happiness.

Nina, the Woman, Nina the WAAF. You make them sound like two different people, my dear. Why? To me there is only one Nina. You could never be anything but the sweet, loveable person you are. I want you in civvies, Nina, because I want no train or convention on 'Our Day'. We can be just an airman and his – well, I'll leave you to fill in what you wish. We can be man and woman together, instead of just a couple of numbers. I feel very excited about seeing you in civilian clothes because I feel certain I shall find a new and exciting side of your nature. Who knows, you may find some new things about me. I hope you will!

I too think Shrewsbury is a good idea, Nina. But what the hotels are like I know not. I guess I'll have to book in advance and hope that the place is a good one. Perhaps I can see you tomorrow night (Sunday) and we can talk it over then.

Goodnight, my dearest,

Your Victor xxxxxxxxx

7 Monday Visit Vic in Sick Quarters and go a walk to Wheaton Aston in moonlight.

14 Monday Late Night Pass. Now 'all set' for Grand St. Valentine's Ball at Gnosall Village Hall. Go with Vic and have a grand time doing slow foxtrots. Excused by a couple of Sgt. Pilots, much to Vic's annoyance, who is in the middle of saying 'something important'. Shows me the stars, and says he'd pull one down for me, if I wanted it. Vic very daring tonight – x – slap in the middle of the dance floor, during no lights and a waltz.

18 Friday Cold? – not 'arf! No fire in the billet. No soapflakes to do any washing. No fuel or boot polish. No anything

The Mess, Friday evening

Nina dearest,

I shall be seeing you tomorrow and spending a few all-too-brief hours with you. But at the moment tomorrow seems such a long way off and I am very lonely. Strange that one can feel lonely amongst so many friends, for there's no lack of company in the room at the moment. And yet my spirit is not in the room. It is living past happy occasions. Dinner at the Station, a day in Birmingham, the comparitive seclusion of the lounge of the 'Bradford'.

Yes, Nina, you can curb our activities for you know I'm at your command, but you cannot stop me dreaming and you cannot stop me committing my feelings to paper. If I had my way I should have been with you this evening. That cannot be., but I can be with you in spirit and that is some small consolation.

When I saw you this afternoon it took all my control to stop myself kissing your smiling lips. It's very hard to put on a casual offhand air when I see you in 'business hours', Nina. But it seems that control is a thing that I must exercise quite a lot these days.

On Monday I go on Leave and to me it seems to be just the beginning of ten days loneliness again. It seems that this Leave is not going to bring me a great deal of pleasure because my heart won't be in it. After all, we only have one heart apiece and if mine is in Wheaton Aston I cannot be expected to be very happy in London. In fact, it seems like a waste of ten precious days.

Nina, you would have probably stopped me from saying this had you been with me, but right now I'm free to write what I like. Please read it carefully, my dearest

Goodnight and God bless you,

Your Victor xxxx

98 Brighton Road, South Croydon, Surrey
22 Feb 1944

Nina , my darling,

My first day at home and I feel dazed. I feel out of my element. The weather in London is pretty poor and there is a cold wind blowing but the wind doesn't account for the chill inside me. I'm lonely, Nina, lonely for you. The hours seem to drag by and all I can think of is next Thursday week. If you only knew how I felt I'm sure you would get that 48 by hook or by crook. I miss everything about you, Nina. I miss your smile, your voice, your eyes. Your lips and oh! how those lips haunt me. I pray that the day may come when I shall know that you are mine completely, the day that you tell me to reach for that star

Oh Nina, life is so sweet with you. You have given me all I could desire. Companionship, laughter and as far as you can at the moment, love. I read an article the other day by a psychologist on *'Why we love'*. He said that love brought a spiritual completion, that the two spirits are the compliment of one another. Nina, I do feel complete with you. It is hard to describe except to say, perhaps, that it IS a spiritual completion.

If by chance you cannot get the 48, I shall come back to W. Aston. Believe me, it's no good to me unless you can come to London. In spite of the way I have opened my heart to you in this letter, Nina, I'm still remembering all you asked of me. Not to cross bridges before I come to them; I'm not asking that you should commit yourself in any way until you feel that the time is ripe.

But this letter is an honest statement of my feelings for you. I know you will treasure them, my dearest, and I pray that when the day comes for you to decide, you may not find me wanting.

And now I must have some lunch and visit the West End for some soap and a bag. I'll write again soon, Nina.

Good bye for now and God bless.

Your Victor

479352. ACW1 Chessall N.
SHQ, RAF Wheaton Aston, Little Ormond, Staffs
Wed. 23rd Feb '44

Vic, My Dear, xxx xxx xxx

There you have an official address, but I hope to lose this person a week tonight when – 'just Nina' will meet – 'just Vic'. Lovely, lovely thought! I am counting the days.

No letter was ever so eagerly awaited as the one that arrived from you this morning. Thank you for that, Vic, and for the sweet words of love contained therein. The day doesn't look quite so grey now or the outlook from my window so bleak. But even your letter can't do anything to brighten the gloom of an empty grate and a room that feels like the inside of a refrigerator.

I remember you saying once that this was the warmest spot on the Camp – but not today, Vic. There is apparently no coal or fuel on the Station, except for cooking purposes. Now, aren't you glad you are not here? I can imagine you curled up on an armchair in front of a crackling glowing fire, pipe in mouth, blue smoke curling ceiling-wards, and perhaps an interesting book. What comfort! There is maybe just one small item missing from this picture, Vic – your left arm doesn't seem to be doing anything. Don't you think it would look more complete if you put it round someone? – someone who feels rather cold and very very lonely? – me, for instance. I wouldn't disturb your reading, and I'd keep very quiet xxx I promise.

I shall do my utmost to get that 48, Vic, so don't worry. I want it just as much as you do. By the way, do you want me to get you a ticket for the last bus back on 4th March?

I wear your chamois gloves every day, and I am hoping that they won't be worn out by the time you return – sorry, WE return. It is like a keepsake you have left me, not that I require anything to remember you by. So many things do that – a table for two in a café, a brown paper bag containing shopping (OUR shopping), the cracked cup you wouldn't let me have, and two eyes gazing into mine. My dearest, you've meant so much.

Do try to have a good time, Vic, please. You will be working hard enough when you are posted, as you expect to be soon. And Vic – you asked me 'to trust' you. I didn't quite understand just what you meant by that remark; but look, Vic – I want you to give Pauline a chance. Don't shut your heart blindly, irrevocably, and then regret it to the end of your days. Why not take what the gods offer? Or at least, sample it, and then choose. Don't let me prejudice you, Vic, it was never my intention to 'cut in', you know that, don't you? I don't come for you in a jealous possessive way. I simply want you to be happy, and I want you to choose the way that will give you most what you want, what you need. Choose well, my dear, because it is for a lifetime. It would be a most terrible thing to learn that one's husband had discovered he'd made a mistake – too late.

London's having its share of raids again, I see. Please, my sweet, look after yourself. Till blue eyes meet hazel, I am

A Very Impatient, Nina.

PS I shan't be angry if you write again. Like young olives, I want 'More please'.

C/o Wings Club, 11 Grosvenor Place, London SW1
24th Feb 1944

Nina Dearest,

Perhaps on second thoughts the address above would be the better one to use. It's a club for Air Force Officers in London and I can always call there and pick up my mail.

Today you put in your pass and I'm really crossing my fingers hard. It just must be, Nina. On Tuesday, I bought your bag in London and the store posted it on to you. No doubt you have received it by now. Also, I have booked two rooms at a quiet hotel in Kensington, just off the centre of London, so it's up to you now, my dear. I'm going to 'leave' London about midday next Thursday, which means early in the evening to dump my luggage at the hotel which is called 'The Rembrandt', just in case you need the name. Your train is the 5.48

from Stafford, which is supposed to reach Euston at 8.50 but I guess it won't be in until about 10.30 and perhaps later if there is an air raid in progress. If the 3.32 from Stafford is very late you may be in time to catch that train. I shall be at Euston at 8.50 sharp to meet your train.

Nina, have you got two tickets for the bus on March 4th? If not will you please do so as I forgot them before I left.

We have had some pretty hefty raids since I've been home, well, when I say raids, it's not the number of aircraft as the amount of gunfire that's rather disturbing. It's really a terrific barrage. Last night when I left the Wings Club, I was just in time to get best part of the windows about my ears. A bomb fell not so very far away and that accounted for best part of the windows. Never a dull moment, Nina.

I've been longing to figure out a programme for our two days and I can't quite make up my mind just how you would like to see London. Would you like to see places of interest, such as St. Paul's Cathedral, Buckingham Palace, Tower Bridge? Or would you rather hit the high spots such as theatre land?

Actually, it's best to carry out the first suggestion on such a short visit, but perhaps we can see the sights on Friday and squeeze in a show on Saturday. But whatever we do, Nina, I know I shall be completely happy because I'm doing it with you. I'm longing for Thursday to come round and I'm praying that your pass goes through without any snags. If there is any hitch, Nina, you will let me know, won't you? Then I can return to W. Aston and at least we can have the evenings together. Write to me at the Wings Club as soon as you know that you are coming to London or otherwise and then I can relax.

Believe me, dear Nina, to see you smile once again will make me feel years younger. I guess that smile of yours has bewitched me; it certainly has done something to my heart. In other words, my dear, the morale is falling a bit low once more and I need you to boost it up. I'll write again soon, Nina, and in the meantime, I'm thinking of you often and wishing all the time that you were here with me.

Au revoir for the time being and write often, please.

God bless

Your Victor xxxxxxxxxxx

The Waafery, RAF Wheaton Aston, Little Onn, Staffs

Saturday night, 26th Feb '44

Vic, You are a darling xxx –

Sorry, that should have been a capital letter – DARLING! xxx The bag arrived yesterday and such a fine one too. I hadn't even visualised one quite so nice. I really must compliment you, Vic, on your good choice – and your sound judgement! (Everything fits in perfectly. I've just tried it out.) I think you must always do my shopping for me.

I put in my application today, Vic, which will be time enough. The ruling is to allow three whole days before the commencement of a 48 hrs. pass, so there is ample time. Another item in my favour is – 'Hobbie is on Leave, to get used to the idea of being a father. Aye, it's come! The world is to be saddled with another little 'Hobbie', boy too. By the way, do you think I should bring my respirator with me, for getting past the SP's at Stafford? I don't want to, but perhaps I should. I couldn't leave it at the Left Luggage Office? I needn't bring my steel helmet though, need I?

So you see, Vic, everything ought to be 'hunky-dory', that is, everything except - . There is just one thing that worries me and that is money. I suppose I could write home for my bank book but it is going to be a bit difficult to explain why I want it, and if I don't give any explanation it will sound all the more suspicious. I have exactly £4, not counting next Friday's pay which I hope to get on a casual payment parade next Tuesday. I don't want to be in your debt, Vic – not any more than I am already, not any more than I can possibly help. Do you think I ought to come to London?

I have mentioned in my letter home, by the way, that I am contemplating a visit to London to stay with a girlfriend – (ACW Smith? – the same girlfriend for whom I have booked tickets for the last bus on Saturday night?) I did this following a dream I had the night before last. I was alone in a large badly lit Railway Station, presumably in London, and there was an air raid in progress. (It is still very easy for me to remember what they are like.) And I couldn't find you, Vic, anywhere. The place was deserted and the lamps shook, and I was crying with loneliness and anxiety for you – and then crump! – I was winging my way to where you beckoned from Our Star. You were there waiting for me! We looked down together from our 'rendez-vous' up aloft to watch the sequence of events – I was two days overdue from the Leave and a telegram had been sent home. No-one had seen me; no-one knew where I was; no-one had the slightest idea where to look for me. And the body of an unidentified female lay in a London mortuary! Now, isn't that a nice cheerful little dream, Vic? Yes, I know, I cried about it myself. So, I thought, well someone had better have some idea where I am.

This is going to be a Grand Adventure, my Victor, and whatever else it may prove to be, I don't think we'll complain of boredom. As for the programme during these two days, I think you'll know how to arrange that. But in case you'd like confirmation of my ideas in this respect, here they are – I want to see places and things and people I can't see anywhere else at any other time, and when it is too dark to see, I want to do the kind of things we CAN'T do at Wheaton Aston. It would be a pity to spend all our time inside a theatre or cinema, wouldn't it? (except perhaps once) when there was a great big world outside waiting to be discovered. Let's go dancing one night, Vic. We have often promised ourselves we'd do that, but never yet had the opportunity. I want to go to bed very late and get up very early, so that I won't be wasting any more of the precious moments with you than is absolutely necessary, so that I won't be missing any of the delights that seeing London with you has to offer.

This sounds a very tall order, Vic. Do you think you'll be able to cope? You had better get some sleep in now while you have the chance, like I am doing, or else we'll both be returning to Wheaton Aston on our knees. And then what will they think? – You don't care? No, my sweet, and neither do I.

Wings Club, 11 Grosvenor Place, SW1
Saturday afternoon, 26.2.'44

Nina, my dear, xxx

Thank God for your letter, which I found waiting for me when I returned home last night. I've been waiting so impatiently for it ever since last Monday. It made me feel a new person and that chill in my heart has been partially thawed. But only you in person, my dear, can bring me the true comfort and happiness that I have known these past three months. I feel that I need the warmth of a pair of hazel eyes looking into mine to thaw out the icy glint that I'm sure must be very obvious to everyone.

Nina, you must believe me when I say that I am giving Pauline a chance. I'm not trying to force an issue for I know you would not want it that way, but my darling, I just cannot forget you. We have been so completely happy together that I am certain that I cannot find its equal anywhere. I won't make a mistake, Nina, the future means too much to me, especially in view of a not too happy past. If you ask me to reach for that star you will know that I am doing so with full confidence in myself and in YOU. That's what I meant by 'trusting me', Nina. There will be no mistakes = too late. You must believe me when I say that you did not 'cut in'. There is a terrific contrast between your whole build-up and that of Pauline and I could not help but draw my own conclusions, my dear.

Nina, my left hand IS cold and what is so terrible is that I can do nothing about it. I have come out for the day on my own and am sitting in the Club at this moment having just finished lunch. Plenty of time to think about the 'Bradford', a day in Birmingham, the village dance at Gnosall. I can close my eyes and see your smile and no-one can interrupt my beautiful daydream. As Thursday draws near, I can feel my heart beating faster, my first glimpse of Nina dressed as I would always have her be. Nina as a woman, instead of regimented person. Roll on March 2nd, happy happy day. If I can get away early enough on Thursday morning, I will come all the way to Stafford and travel back with you, but at the moment the train times are a little vague to me. I shall be waiting again on Monday and I'll let you know definitely then. The enclosed card is OUR hotel, my dear, and I can see nothing to stop us having a heavenly two days together.

Goodbye for now, Nina. God bless and – write often.

Yours in anticipation,

Victor xxxxxxx

479352, ACW1 Chessall, N.
SHQ, RAF Wheaton Aston, Little Onn, Staffs
Monday, 28th Feb 1944 (Duty Clerk night)

Vic, my dear, xxx

I have just finished speaking to you on the phone, and fact that I should have spoken to you at all tonight is a most delectable surprise. There was I expecting some dull routine call about a posting or a signal, and instead – it is YOU.! I could hardly speak for the wonder of it. One never knows what the gods will have to offer us next. So, let's away from dull care, Vic, and let's live as life was meant to be lived, enjoying what we have, forgetting what we have not, and who knows? – the 'have-nots' may suddenly be transformed into 'haves'! Tonight I am living in a sort of waiting expectation. I feel anything can happen.

This morning I awoke to a world of white. The hedgerows were intricate lacey patterns threaded with jewels that sparkled and shone in the light from the pale wintry sun; the ground was a thick white velvet carpet into which one's feet sank to a depth of almost six inches; and SHQ looked like the entrance to some faery grotto – I almost expected Father Xmas himself to come out and greet me. Now, the snow has turned to ice, and there are hard sharp ridges everywhere that make cycling a work of art. I am ruefully caressing a bruise on my leg at this moment where I came off my bicycle and then slipped on the glassy surface I managed to choose for the scene of the accident. I do hope it isn't quite so cold as this next weekend, as my civilian clothes will be a trifle inadequate. However, one day at a time. If it is cold, then nothing will alter it? – we should probably discover SOME delights, which would never have come our way if the weather had been warm.

Tuesday morning

Your letter has arrived xxxxxxxxx I hope mine has too. And now we are probably reading each other's letters at exactly the same moment. I am thinking of YOU – exclusively, and YOU are thinking of ME – Wheaton Aston to London, London to Wheaton Aston, two hundred miles there and two hundred miles back? – nothing at all to the loving spirit! Wings have we?

I still feel, Vic, that you are being a little unfair. After all, two persons can never be exactly alike or appeal in the same way, and if you are going to keep one picture constantly in your mind's eye and make comparisons, the other person isn't getting much of a chance, is she? I should probably fail hopelessly if you judged me by some of Pauline's best points, and in the same way, it is hardly fair to judge Pauline by some quality that you think I possess in a greater measure. Of course, my dear, it all depends on what you yourself desire most. And again, Pauline may be a woman still in embryo. It may be that she has not yet 'found' herself, her personality still only half-formed, but that when the flower of her true character reveals itself, you may be very agreeably surprised. So, you see, there again I have an advantage.

That would be a grand idea, Vic, to travel down with you all the way from Stafford – and another way of making the best possible use of all our available time together. It would also mean that there would be no likelihood of my losing you, or missing you, in the big strange city, just when I should want to cling hold of your hand all the tighter. Isn't it an awful lot of trouble for you though, Vic? Don't do it just on my account. I should be all right, you know, and I should have the feeling of anticipation, of something exciting going to happen, to busy me up during the journey. Anyway, I shall try to get the 3.15 bus from Camp and I'll wait for you at the Station. If you are not there by the time the 5.40 train arrives, I shall not wait longer.

I must get this afternoon's post, Vic.

Till The Day – You couldn't be as excited as I am, or as impatient –

Love, Nina xxx xxx xxx

PS Hotel Rembrandt, here we come! I shan't forget my bath towel.

Officers' Mess, RAF Station Wheaton Aston, Staffs

Monday evening

Dearest Nina, xxx

I find it a very lonely evening, the first that we have spent apart since I met you in Stafford last Thursday. Sitting alone in my room I cannot help but marvel at the events of the past three days. The joy and complete happiness that has been ours has left me dazed. I never realised that life could be so beautiful as it is when I am with you. Never, dear Nina, has anyone ever given me so much to live for. Somehow it doesn't seem possible that you can ever be taken away from me, that you will one day cast away our love and happiness. I believe that one day all our dreams will come true, and we shall belong to each other for all time.

Our two days in London made my happiness complete. In my dreams I shall stand by the lake in St James Park a thousand times over. Remember how the sunlight shone on the water, turning the lake into countless diamonds?

Regent Street and Piccadilly bathed in Spring sunshine, the wind blowing on Tower Bridge and the view of the city's heart gleaming in the sun, that hushed moment when we stood beneath the mighty dome of St. Paul's cathedral. Did He see us there, my darling, and bless our happiness?

I shall never forget that moment when in the darkness of the cinema, I felt your very soul embrace mine, and I shall treasure for all time those warm, intimate minutes in your room when your body was so close to mine that it seemed our lives must indeed become one for ever and that Nina and Vic would cease to exist as two separate people.

Last night, my sweetheart, I poured out my love to you because my heart was so full that I could hold it no longer. And why should I keep it back, Nina? I know that all our happiness and love will not die with my posting. We would be fools to lose heart and despair. We can keep it fresh and lovely for ever by faith and trust when we are parted, and when we can meet then we must live this life to the full.

I have no greater gift to offer, Nina, than a heart that loves you well. It's yours to make or break, my darling. I have not a great deal of money at the moment but life and warm love I have in abundance.

Remember all these things, dear Nina, remember all our grand times together (there will probably be additions before the critical time) and when the time for you to choose comes round, choose well and may your happiness be complete.

Goodnight, my darling, God bless.

Your lover,

Vic

MARCH

7 Tuesday Vic is so serious, he makes me afraid for him.

Officers' Mess, RAF Station Wheaton Aston, Staffs
Wednesday evening

Nina darling,

You probably wonder why I spend all my evenings writing to you, but there is a very good reason for it. I've had quite a busy day over at Tatenhill with two unpleasant rides, there and back and a few moments ago I was sitting in the Mess smoking my pipe and thinking and relaxing a little. Suddenly someone started to play softly on the piano the 'Warsaw Concerto'. A lovely melody which seemed to reach down into my heart, but oh Nina, how lonely it made me feel. A beautiful melody reminding me of a very beautiful woman. Every day that I am away from you I realise just how much your companionship and love mean to me. In my heart I feel the pain of utter and complete loneliness and there is nothing in this world that can cure that pain, Nina, only you.

I wonder if you realise how happy I am with you, darling. I cannot find words to describe it for words have not yet been formed that can do justice to such deep and profound emotion. It's a sense of completion, a feeling that all's right with the world. I pray that one day you will be free to give yourself to me completely, Nina, for there are so many joys that could yet be ours.

I am very tired at the moment and feeling the effects of a day spent in the fresh air. I'm thinking now of last Friday night for it was about this time that I came to your room to say goodnight. If only you were here now, my darling. The thought of having you close beside me at night makes my heart beat very fast. The thrill of your warm, soft body close to mine is something out of this world, and something that I desire very much. It seems to me that my love for you is complete, Nina. I don't mean that it cannot glow any more for I know it can and will do. What I mean is that it embraces every sphere. First of all we found friendship and learned to open our hearts to one another. That friendship has grown continuously and has become love. And then came last Friday night, and in those sacred moments in your room I knew that I really did want you, Nina.

No wonder I am lonely when we are apart, and yet it looks as if I have a whole lot more loneliness to come. Circumstances decree that it shall be so, but it will only make me all the more determined to win through and gain the other half of your heart. I have an unshakable faith in this bond that holds us together, Nina, and I believe the day will come that will prove that my trust was not misplaced.

Faith in another person gives you something to live for and now I have everything to live for, now that I have faith in you. Death is an easy thing to come by these days, Nina, especially for men in my job, but death has lost its sting for me. I'm not afraid of it any more. But if it should come my way I'm sure that my last thought or feeling would be one of sadness. Sad that I had not been able to stay on for all the beauties of a world shared with you. That would be my greatest loss. I'm afraid that the world would lose nothing.

Goodnight, my darling.

For ever your

Victor xxxxxxxxx

Officers' Mess, RAF Station Wheaton Aston, Staffs
Saturday evening

Nina darling,

Who should I be writing to? Or I should say, to whom should I be writing? Whichever way it's said it boils down to the same thing. I've plenty of duty letters on hand. But there's only one person I really want to write to and I am doing that right now. I want to write to you, Nina, because it helps to fill in the lonely evenings when I cannot see you. And they are lonely, very lonely. God knows how I'm going to feel when I'm posted. I guess I shall be living from day off to day off.

Last night was very sweet, my darling. A warm night, friendly stars, a quiet country road and the beauty of it all was that I was able to share it with you. I appreciate those sort of things always but my happiness is doubled with you. We pause and kiss, and new life seems to flow into me when your lips touch mine. The stars wink happily, they know when two hearts beat as one and love reigns supreme. And probably a wise old owl will smile (if owls do smile) when he hears my stumbling, awkward phrases as I try to express the feelings in my heart, and in trying, fail miserably. I always feel that the words I say never can do justice to my love for you, Nina. I love you so deeply and warmly that only actions can come anywhere near to a complete expression of that love. Walking along with my arm about your shoulders it seems fantastic to think that I could ever lose you. Our spontaneous, happy conversation tells me that I have found happiness that money could never hope to bring me. Those tender moments when you are in my arms make me long for our honeymoon, that we may give all in that sacred moment when we are literally one body. What chance has a poor man to express all his feelings in the limited scope that words offer? Perhaps after all the most poignant moments are those when our eyes meet and no words are spoken. Remember that moment in the 'Carlton', Nina? I don't think you are likely to forget it.

If God answers my prayers, and I believe he does, then one day not so very far away you will come to me, never to leave again. And I shall be waiting with open arms, beloved, ready to live OUR life to the full. Always remember that when we are apart, Nina. Remember that I am waiting for you no matter where I go or how long we may be apart. It may seem strange that I have so much faith in a love which you are not free to tell me about. But life is so full and lovely with you that I cannot see how I can lose. I've built a dream around us, Nina, and soon these dreams will become reality. One day there will be no more lonely evenings for me. No more aching hearts and no more waiting. You will be my wife and for us life will begin anew. Gone all the dark days of poverty and want, gone all these lonely evenings and weeks of uncertainty. In their place will be undying love and companionship. Never again will those blue eyes turn to ice because a pair of hazel eyes will take away all the coldness, and a smile like the sun itself will warm a heart that now can feel so cold with loneliness and longing.

Nina, you will be mine for all time and I will treasure you beyond all other things. God bless you my darling, and keep you for me.

Your lover for all time,

Vic xxxxxxxxx

Officers' Mess, RAF Station Wheaton Aston, Staffs
Sunday evening

Nina darling,

I am sitting in the Mess at the moment beside a fire which looks as if it's just on its last legs. I've been waiting all evening for you to phone, but I guess you are stronger than I thought. I suppose that right now I should be sitting down writing those hundred and one duty letters that are hanging over my head. But instead, I pen a few lines to the person who is nearest my heart, and always in my thoughts. You, my darling.

The time is now twenty minutes past ten and so far this evening all I've done is to play one game of snooker. A very successful game too, and natter the time away with a couple of navigation types.

It's so very easy to sit down and write to you, Nina, and so very hard to write to other people. The words just seem to flow from my pen because between us there is an invisible bond stronger than steel. We have love, companionship, sympathy, mutual understanding and a thousand and one other things besides, and life flows smoothly and easily along the right path when we are together.

I dreamed of you last night, my darling, a dream so beautiful that when I realised I was waking, I tried to go back again and recapture its beauty. We were married but as we set out on our honeymoon innumerable difficulties arose. We couldn't get a train and when we did it was terribly late. We couldn't find a conveyance at our destination and had to walk miles to the sweetest little honeymoon cottage you ever saw. But we laughed all the time and there was always a humorous side to the most trying moment. Then came that moment, the start of our first night. In my dream I knew the joy of your arms about me and the warmth of your nearness. Your kisses, hot and passionate bringing me an insight into paradise itself. Then the time was ripe for the consummation of our love. The time when companionship, understanding, physical desire, in fact, every emotion that is summed up in that brief word, love, is expressed in a practical form. Why did I have to wake, Nina, into this cold, hard world only to find that I was alone after all? Where were those loving arms that only a few moments before had held me so tightly? I asked myself 'Is my life going to be made up of dreams? Am I never going to know these joys that so far have been mine only in the mists of a vision?'

The answer, my darling, is that one day I shall know all these joys and find my heart's desire. You will be mine, of that I am certain because it is one of those things that I want so much that nothing can stop it from coming true. And in my heart, Nina, I believe that you want it too. Our love is like a beacon in this dark world of trouble, a guiding light to both of us. If we turn our backs on it we shall stumble off into darkness and who knows what unhappiness.

Remember, Nina, that my leave is due in May. Even if I leave here I shall still be due for some about the same time and Devon can be very lovely in early summer. It rests with you, sweetheart.

And now I must wend my way towards bed. Who knows, I may dream again tonight, Nina, and what more could I ask for what I cannot have in the flesh.

Goodnight, beloved. God bless you.

Your lover,

Vic xxx

26 Sunday Vic on a week's attachment to Seighford for decompression tests tomorrow! Gives me a letter to read:

Officers' Mess, RAF Station Wheaton Aston, Staffs

25th March 1944

Nina dear,

This evening I feel very lonely because flying has been scrubbed and I cannot make contact with you. I've tried the picket-post and the orderly room but to no avail. I would like to have a walk with you for an hour or so. To put my arm about you and know you are mine.

Thank you, Nina, for the tunics, sewing on the 1939-1943 Star and moving up the Nav badge. They are perfect. The note you left me made me feel rather sad. In a few short lines you expressed a wealth of emotion:

'Vic Dear,

I hope this will please you. I enjoyed doing it for you.

May this Wing and My Prayer bring you home – always.

Nina'

Now more than ever it seems important that I should always get back safely. Your prayers will bring me home, my darling, home to your side where I belong. When I fly operations once again it will be with a different outlook from that of my last tours. Always I will have the feeling that all dangers braved will be for OUR benefit. I will know that your prayers guard my aircraft and that your spiritual faith will be doing all within its power to overcome any material disaster. I will have no fear, for I know that if I meet death early in life I have died for a great faith, that faith I have expressed to you so often, that one day we shall find happiness together. That happiness means so much to me, Nina, that I will willingly die defending it.

Into these three months since Christmas we have packed years of love, sympathy and mutual understanding, so much so that I believe you are the woman who can make my life complete. 'Tis said that love beautifies and in my eyes, Nina, it has made you indeed a vision. The brightness of your smile was always apparent for was it not that that first warmed me to you? That brightness has increased and other things added to it. To look into your eyes brings me peace and calm confidence. I've known the thrill of your lips to mine and, just recently, I've known that Eden can be mine when I hold your warm naked body close to mine. I've known too the ache of a lonely heart. Yes, it is indeed a pain for there is no-one who can cure it except the person you love. But the pain makes the joy of meeting indescribably beautiful Nina. Nature always balances itself.

How glad I am that we did not let the uncertainty of last Wednesday morning and afternoon discourage us. Wednesday night and Thursday seem just like a dream. Every time I close my eyes we are walking beside the Dee again, talking and laughing in the way that only lovers do. Then it is the early morning again and I am holding you in my arms, fresh from sleep and looking very desirable. It is terribly hard to resist you, Nina, and although you may not know it, I am always completely at your mercy. My love and my body are yours, dear mistress, to take when you so wish it. And now I am wishing hard that nothing will interfere with next Saturday. When I see you tomorrow night we can make all the necessary arrangements for my contacting you while I am at Seighford and as soon as I find out what the score is there I'll let you know.

Goodnight, my Nina, and God keep you for me.

Your lover,

Vic xxxxxxxxx

Officers' Mess, Royal Air Force Sighford, Nr Stafford
27th March, Monday evening

My sweetheart,

I feel utterly and completely lost. It was bad enough at Wheaton to spend an evening away from you, but it makes me feel hopeless to be on another Station. Thank God I can see you for a few hours tomorrow night, for only you Nina, can take away this loneliness. I really need you now that you have become so much a part of my life. Well, Nina, I phoned the Queen's in Chester tonight, but they could not change the rooms on Saturday, so I switched them to Thursday night in the hope that you can manage Friday off. After all, Stuart Harris did suggest last week that you book Friday. I guess this will be stale news when you read this, but I feel I must get it off my chest, and as I cannot talk to you I must write. Nina, please try hard for Friday. We may not be so lucky if we go on spec on a Saturday evening and of course Friday has all the added advantage of having all the shops open. I'm sure you can manage another mushroom omlette or a chicken lunch!

I'm not quite sure what I'm going to do with myself all day Wednesday. You see, I have tomorrow afternoon and Wednesday off and take my next test on Thursday morning. Quite a big blank to fill in, isn't it? It seems terribly important to me that everything works out OK this week. I would like nothing more than a home posting and to keep that date for two days every quarter. Who knows Nina, you may relent and extend my happiness. How I long to spend a complete leave with you! I know that we could be so very happy, my darling, that it seems a sin to waste nine precious days. Perhaps one day you will give me a chance to prove that I can make you sublimely happy. Think of nine days of greeting the dawn in my arms. It doesn't seem so shattering to be kissed gently out of dreamland into the world of reality, does it? Nine whole warm, sunny days with Spring in the air and you by my side. It sounds like paradise Nina! Won't you ever step into paradise with me? Of course you will, darling, and I know you'll do it soon. I'm waiting for you, ready to give you all the life and warm love that is mine to give.

Goodnight, my dearest. God bless you, and – sweet dreams, beloved mine.

Your lover for all time,

Vic xxxxxxxxxxxxxxxxxxx

Orderly Room, Wheaton Aston
27th March 1944

My Dear One,

I have just finished speaking to you over the phone. You probably thought how cold and calm and restrained I was, yet could you have known of my spirit's sudden uplifting, and my heart's strange yearning at the sound of your voice – could you have known how despairing I felt at the thought of another twenty-four hours spent away from your side – you would indeed have been very surprised. I surprised myself, Vic! I was surprised at how matter-of-fact my voice sounded, when inwardly I was a seething cauldron of emotions.

I forget what I said; I almost forget what you said – that didn't seem to matter, so long as we said something, so that the sound of our voices would carry a little of each other across the intervening space to give us comfort.

Oh Vic, I wish I could be sure of which road to take. I seem to have been dithering about at this crossroads for a long long time, and I still haven't been able to unravel the tangled muddle of my thoughts and feelings. And it is myself I am not sure about, Vic – be very certain of that. Strangely enough, you are the only person I do feel sure about. No wonder I have come to rely so much on you, so that to give up all that you have come to mean would hurt me just as much as it would hurt you.

Try to be patient with me, Vic. Try to understand. Please try to help me – till I get back a faith in myself. For nearly four years (you will know that is a very long time), I have been telling myself: 'This is it, this is the man you are going to marry; his is the face you will see last thing at night and first thing in the morning and who will play a principal part in all your dreams of the future." For four years I have believed that, and now – in three months, I am not so sure; I am not sure at all. I have been going through a very painful transition stage, whereby a different man now plays the leading role in my dreams, and that face is replaced by another. Is this merely a phase? Is it just that I want to translate these dreams into reality so much that I cannot wait any longer for one elusive male? I do not know. I am tired of thinking. My thoughts go round and round in circles and I get no further. How can I be sure of what I feel under such conditions?

All I know is that tomorrow I see you again, and my thoughts will be quieted and I shall know peace for a little while. All I know is that nothing else in this life could give me greater joy than to know that peace always.

Goodnight sweetheart. Bless you.

Nina xxxxxxxxx

APRIL

My darling Nina,

Outside, the night is stormy. Black clouds lower in the sky and rain has been falling. Even the weather is in keeping with my mood, Nina. How I miss you on the evenings we spend apart. The black clouds are akin to my heavy lonely heart and the rain to my heart's tears. I long for a home of our own, Nina, somewhere where we two can find a haven from this interfering world and share our glorious love.

These are not easy times to get married in, I know, but I want more than anything in the world to marry you, darling. To make you mine for all time and to know that I belong to you for ever. I'll treasure you always and do all in my power to keep our love as beautiful and as fresh as it is today. I dream and plan for our future and in my dreams I see it bright and hopeful. Full of laughter and happiness, mental harmony and physical harmony, happy sharing that 80% and the 20%. Nina, how can we go wrong? All our days will be happy because our moods are one.

Since last Thursday night, darling, something has happened to me. A new emotion, nay, thousands of new emotions have been aroused inside me. We gave ourselves to each other because we love so fiercely and in doing so we found unbounded joy. Now we take a part of each other with us wherever we go for all time. One night, and I pray it be soon, we shall find the sequel to last Thursday the first night of our honeymoon. A honeymoon spent far from crowds and towns in a soft pleasant countryside, the only possible surroundings for us, my Nina. We both find crowds irksome. The stars and the moon are our friends and the warm sunlight our altar to worship God. I cannot think of life without you now and what's more, I have no intention of entertaining the thought. I am going to fight to make you mine with every ounce of strength in my body, and there is plenty of strength in that warm, slim body that you held so close to you but a few nights ago, Nina.

My Nina, my friend and comforter, sharer of my joys and my sorrows, my sweetheart and wife-to-be, and forever my beloved mistress, keep yourself for me, darling always, and never forget that you have only to say 'Yes' and I'm yours. God bless you sweetheart. I love you with all my heart.

Your lover,

Vic xxxxxxxxxxxxxxx

6 Thursday All leave cancelled – must mean only one thing, the Second Front. Meet Vic and go on usual cycle ride to 'it-doesn't-matter-where'.

9 Sunday My birthday – only Vic wishes me 'Happy Birthday!' Very annoyed – 60 pages of typing supposed to be so very urgent still lying where I left them on Friday night untouched – waiting for me, I suppose, to work late on them again! And so I complete them – at the expense of Hockey! Meet Vic. Cycle to Blymhill. Visit quaint old Church there and side by side make our vows and pray for light in our darkness.

22 Saturday Meet Vic at 7.30 and cycle to 'Spreadeagles Hotel' the long way round. Country looking more beautiful than I have seen it for a long time and always there is Vic. Gives me birthday present of brown lizard-skin powder compact, with sweet little note inside:

'To my Sweetheart,

May your future be full of happiness, Nina, and may I have the honour of sharing that happiness?

Your lover for all time,

Vic xxxxxxxxxxxxxxxxxxxxxxxxxx'

Officers' Mess, **RAF Station** Wheaton Aston, Staffs

Sunday evening

My Nina, xxx

Here it is 10.45pm and I promised myself an early night in bed. Right up until the last minute I hoped you were going to phone, but when half past ten came round I knew it was not to be.

I feel tired and dispirited, Nina. All night I have been walking about the Mess like a caged animal, unable to rest when the phone rang in case it was you. How I would have welcomed the sound of your voice! After supper tonight I felt lost. I longed to cycle out to meet you and know once again the pleasure that your welcoming smile gives me. If this is only one evening apart, God knows how I shall feel if we have to part for weeks.

I feel sick with loneliness. Nina, I would rather stand any amount of physical pain than this heartache. Believe me, I would rather be tortured for a whole hour than miss being with you for one single evening. And what a glorious evening it was too. Warm and sunny with the birds providing the incidental music to a lovely scent. I stood outside the Mess for a few minutes tonight and lived again the time from Xmas until now. Place names crowded their way into my memory and each place bringing its own particular beautiful, thrilling moment. Chester, Stratford, the 'Bradford', the 'Spread Eagle', Wheaton Aston and oh! a thousand more and about each I could write a book and dedicate all the books to – Nina.

Life has seemed very wonderful to me these past four months. We have watched the cold starkness of winter turn into the gentle warmth of Spring. With Nature has our love grown, my darling and now it has blossomed into a flower more beautiful than any known on this earth before. We have both asked Him to bless our union, Nina, and our prayers have not been unanswered. With you have I known the golden warmth of true love and companionship. In your arms last Thursday night, Nina, I experienced a sublime happiness that I can only find within the dear circle of those arms. To attempt to describe the fullness of those moments in written words would be nothing short of stupidity. I am no master of words. No flowery phrases flow from my pen at will. When my feelings are beyond words, Nina, I say nothing, and last Thursday night I experienced thoughts and emotions out of this world. A paradise, an Eden of Edens. Only with my whole body can I worship you in the way I feel most fitting. I am confident enough to say that we found our happiness together, darling, and on the strength of that confidence I am asking you to marry me just as soon as you possibly can.

Please, Nina, don't keep me waiting any longer than you can help. Remember always that I love you with my whole being. No-one else has taken from me the things that you have and now that I have found my love I give everything and give so very willingly. Have faith in our love, Nina, and find strength in that faith to meet all difficulties. Lose none of the joys that our life together can bring just because one moment of faintheartedness made you take the line of least resistance. Know the things that you love and treasure, be honest with yourself always and remember that it's better to hurt a lot of people a little than to cast two hearts for ever into a pit of misery, especially if one of them happens to be your own. In fact, to quote you, Nina: "To thine own self be true".

Goodnight and God bless you, my sweetheart,

Your lover,

Vic xxxxxxxxxxxxxxxxxxxx

MAY

2 Tuesday Wave 'Au Revoir' to Vic till Wednesday night – on his way to Air Ministry for interviews regarding Special Signals Duties. Read 'Men Only' – asleep early.

3 Wednesday Meet Vic in Stafford from London train. Have dinner at Station Hotel, and told all the details – nothing about the job, of course, except that he thinks he's got it. Gives me his ring to reassure me.

9 Tuesday Letter No. 217 from Bill – chooses to remain overseas another year! (in view of shortage of mail from me) – and chooses not to marry me -! Because I won't be available in another year! - !

11 Thursday Vic is posted to a Squadron in Norfolk as from Tuesday.

15 Monday Vic brings me half a dozen duck-eggs and leaves me his cycle lamp and pump in exchange for mine. Also leaves me book of poems. Seems like a general 'last will and testament'. Beginning to feel now that something drastic is happening. Sew his gloves. Cycle to Blymhill with Vic for last time and pray together in the old Church there for strength and courage and eventual reunion. Last kisses at five-barred gate. 9pm strikes!

479352, ACW1 Chessall, N.

SHQ, RAF Wheaton Aston, Little Onn, Staffs

Tuesday (lunch-time) 16th May, 1944

My Love,

That train is carrying you further away from me. I can almost hear the rattle of its engine and its steady de-de-de-donk, de-de-de-donk as it eats up the miles. (What was that tune you said it reminded you of? I can't think of it now; I wish I could remember. All I can think of is the opening bars of 'The Wedding March', but that is silly, of course.) Every moment now means that you are taking my heart with you, and every jolt tugs at my heart-strings – that slender cord that has woven itself around us with such strong and tender ties. It is being tried to its uttermost, and yet I know now it will withstand the test.

You have given me courage, Vic – your courage; you have inspired me with your confidence, and you have warmed the chill in my heart with your love. That was last night. Today, there is a cold hollow place where my heart used to be, and as I look from this window, all the world is in agreement with me. Vic, our lives lately have become so much a part of all this glory around us that even the elements reflect our mood. Have you noticed? We said it would rain, and this morning the sun looked very pale and sorrowful, I thought, as I looked through the dividing mist and saw its tear-washed eye. It comforted me to know that it cared too. Dark brooding clouds, (so like the thoughts that come unbidden to taunt me 'Vic has gone, your love, your life') hang in a heavy storm-tossed sky, (so like the surging turbulence of feeling that comes to me with the realisation of how much you have meant). Oh lover, come back to me, and put the sun back in the sky, xxx xxx xxx soon.

Tuesday evening

We couldn't have seen each other tonight in any case, Vic. The sky is still crying, and the wind hasn't any love to keep it warm – either! It is teeming with rain. Or perhaps I am writing this only to comfort myself, because if you were here still, I know it would have been a lovely evening and, of course, we should be seeing each other. The weather has never prevented us yet, has it, sweetheart?

At least three people have asked me today for the loan of my cycle. I have been never been asked previously, except very occasionally and only for short periods. They must all know I shan't be needing it tonight, or most nights.

I have just asked the time from the girl in the next bed to me. It is nearly nine o'clock. Soon, very soon the old clock at Blymhill Church will strike out the hour – nine deep booming notes, and this will be our signal. Perhaps you will hear them too, Vic, wherever you are and whatever you are doing and in what strange company you find yourself. High above the clamour of the outside world, perhaps the call of the clock will reach you, and at the sound our thoughts and our spirits will go winging out to each other across the distance that separates, guided as if by instinct, like a homing bird to its nest. Vic, my love xx please answer the call –

'B.B.b-oooommm!' – Take my hand, Vic, and tread softly. We are standing just inside the porch and you are taking off your hat. The sun is shining now and its dying rays alight on your bared head, turning your crisp curls to threads of gold, and illuminating your face with a soft glow. Darling of mine, something always stirs within me at sight of you.

'B.B.b-ooommm!' – 2. The heavy oaken door is before us, and we gently push this open and pass into the cool darkness beyond. We blink a little after the bright glare of the sun, and then hand in hand slowly tip-toe past the stone statue to our low wooden pew at the back of the Church.

'B.B.b-ooommm!' – 3. We look at each other for just a moment and smile. I feel again the strange quickening of my heart and the pulsing warmth that flows between us at your touch. Is it your heart I can feel throbbing at the end of your fingers, Vic, or is it my own?

'B.B.b-ooommm!' – 4. I look towards the altar at the other end of the Church, and in the dim uncertain light I can see nothing. Your clasp on my hand tightens and we are both suddenly conscious of a Presence. We bow our heads in prayer.

'B.B.b-ooommm!' – 5. I thank Him first of all for every good thing He has given me, for all the beauties of this earth on which we live, for health and strength to enjoy them, and the insight to appreciate them; for the love of family and friends, and also for this dear person at my side. At this I snuggle closer, to make quite sure you are still there, My Vic.

'B.B.b-ooommm!' – 6. I tell Him about you, Vic, and those dark and lonely places you must tread, where I can never go. But He can go with you, my dearest, every step of the way, and I ask Him to uphold you, and give you courage, and to whisper in your ear as He did in days of old: 'Be not afraid.'

'B.B.b-ooommm!' – 7. Whenever you feel His presence, Vic, just when you need it most, you will know that I am there too, and through Him we can be one, always.

'B.B.b-ooommm!' – 8. Last of all, Vic, I pray for our early reunion, for that meeting from which there will be no more 'Goodnights' and never any more partings. I want to be with you and to be always a part of you. Please God, bless him and keep him safe.

'B.B.b.b-ooommm!' – 9. I look up and see that you too have finished. I am so happy, my sweet, but forgive me, I cannot help smiling at you through my tears. Oh Vic, Vic, Vic. I love you so. x – x – x – x – x (slow dragging kisses, demanding my life, my love, all.)

Nine o'clock has just finished striking. I rub my eyes and look about me and sigh for the departing glory of the last few minutes with you. I reach for my hankie in the pocket of my greatcoat (yes, another fly in the eye), and my hand encounters - ? something hard and long? – Oh Vic, do you know what it is? – the rusty nail from the old wooden gate at Blymhill Church. So we have really been there tonight. Vic, you and I, - leaning on the gate as usual, and staring into the churchyard and seeing nothing but each other – and it was not just a dream xxx.

Good night my Love.

Wednesday night

Hello Cherub, xxx xx

Tonight, as you know, is domestic evening, and it appears that I too have become smitten with 'the painting fever'. You see, Vic, I felt so ashamed of my bit of wall, as it was the only panel left that was completely unadorned. The difficulty was deciding on a subject. There was already an assortment of tulips, croci, iris, poppies, etc. and one girl, obviously suffering from the pangs of unrequited love, had painted the picture of her own heart (as she said) blood red, with an arrow quivering through its centre. Someone suggested I should paint a picture of a passion-flower, but I ignored this. It had to be something mauve or purple to preserve the general colour scheme, and I thought of our cycle rides together, Vic, and how we had admired the blossom on the lilac trees. So a spray of lilac it was, and looking now at the finished effect, at least you can tell what it is. The general verdict was that they didn't know I was an artist – and neither am I, but I have still got the contract for painting and decorating the Sgt's bunk!!!

It is the Sergeant's Mess Dance tonight and there are only a few of us staying in. Somehow, Vic, it is the last place I want to go. And anyway, it is still raining outside – so you know how I feel too, darling! By the way, I want you to do something for me, if you will. Have you a piece of string handy? And a pair of scissors? Or a penknife? Well, I want you to measure the width of your upper-arm with the string and then cut that length off. Ah, come on, Vic, play with me. Have you done that? The piece of string you now have in your hand is the exact size of your upper arm? Then now, I want you to post it to me. No, Vic, I mean it. There is a reason. Humour me, please?

Thursday, 18th May 1944

There was no letter from you this morning, Vic. I thought there might have been. I expect there will be one tomorrow though.

I typed the covering letter for your Conf Report today, but can tell you no more than that. I am Duty Clerk again tonight. It shouldn't be my turn really, not so soon, but one of the girls wanted to go to the Dance badly tonight, so I have swapped with her. It is very late, Vic, and I have been very busy doing another Court of Inquiry, well, it is the one for Zanzottera. He pranged very near to where we saw those WRNS the last time we were on the river.

I wish you were here, Vic, to share my supper. The toast is just made, and the tea, and also I have cooked one of those eggs you left me. They taste delicious, and the flavour doesn't seem to be any different from ordinary hen-eggs. (Doing okay, Vic?) I didn't have your watch to time it by, but I must have made a good guess.

Won't you come to me tonight, like you did the last time I was on duty? I cannot promise to stay awake until you come, but you can always wake me. You won't have any compunction about doing that, I know. Oh darling, I wish – I wish – I wish - . No, you know it all, and perhaps you are wishing exactly the same. Meet you in my dreams, Vic. I shan't be long getting there.

Nina

PS I saw Peter this afternoon. He asked me if I had heard from you, and I couldn't think of anything to tell him. I remember you said a few days before you left that there was something you wanted me to tell, or give, to Peter. What was it, Vic?

Officer's Mess, RAF Station Foulsham, Norfolk
17th May 1944

My Nina xxx

Installed more or less safely in my new abode. My first thought when I reached Fousham Station last night was 'Well, I've finished travelling away from Nina. My next train journey will take me back to her'. And so it will, my darling, as soon as I possibly can.

Before I left Wheaton yesterday I left the tin of Horlicks at the WAAF picket post. Did you receive it okay? The journey here yesterday was quite uneventful. It was quite tedious and I have found out that I could have come via Rugby and Peterborough more quickly.

On the way down to London I all but finished the adventures of Tony, and took some comfort from the fact that he did find Kathe eventually even if it was slow work. Believe me, Nina, it will not take me as many weeks to find you again and we visit our Acacea – the banks of the Dee.

In London, I had a couple of hours to spare so I lunched and paid a short visit to the company for which I used to work. Just enough time to answer all their kind enquiries. I left London at 3.40pm and finally arrived here very dirty, tired and hungry about 8.30pm.

This place suffers from isolation perhaps even more than Wheaton does because there is no main line within such easy reach. From what little I've seen of the food it seems quite good and a glass of fresh milk with lunch each day has its points. This morning I spent paying the usual duty calls to SHQ and filling in the necessary if rather morbid details of the people to be informed in case of my decease. I had to put your relationship as a friend. That is indeed very true but oh Nina, how much more are you besides! Soon I hope I shall be changing the name and address of my next of kin! Keep your promise, darling, and say 'Yes' as soon as you can.

Today started off cheerfully enough and if it was intended to deceive me then it certainly succeeded. I left my raincoat in my room and set off to walk around to my various ports of call. Needless to say it was soon raining and I was soon soaked and my spirits were somewhat dampened. Not even drawing ten and six for yesterday travelling raised them.

And this evening has been my first evening here. No Nina, no triangle, top or bottom to meet her at, no sunny lanes, no happy laughter and carefree conversation. No life, my Nina, without you. A dark, overcast sky is very appropriate just now. Read the inscription on my photo, Nina: 'Take care of my happiness'. Please darling, take care of it. I'm longing for our next meeting and praying that it will not be too far distant and hoping too that we may be able to go home when I see you next.

My letters may take a few days to reach you as they have to go by a rather devious route, but I'll write often to you. I'm looking forward with all my heart to your letters with their surprises and holding my breath in anticipation of my first 'parcel from home'.

I've thought of you at nine o'clock as I promised I would and I KNOW you thought of myself for, for a minute or two, you seemed beside me once again. But you are constantly in my thoughts all day, Nina. Soon I hope to be able to tell you when we can be together once more. I love you, dear, with all my heart.

Until Acacea,

Your own,

Vic xxxxxxxxxxxxxxxxxxx

Officers' Mess, RAF Station Foulsham, Norfolk
19th May 1944

My darling,

I'm just beginning to realise the truth in the line of our song: 'No joy I find when we're apart'. At the end of my fourth evening away from you I feel very depressed and lonely. Our times together were so very lovely, marked all along by continuous happiness. This seems very much of an anti-climax. But we must try not to be downhearted, and look forward to the future which we will try to make even happier than the past five months to compensate for our enforced parting.

I shall have some leave in the near future (we get about seven days every six weeks) but days off will be vague until I get crewed up.

Today has been interesting enough, my first real day of getting down to brass tacks, and I shall like it even better when I start flying. I have not been able to procure a bicycle as yet and I mutter to myself as I walk about, rude things about dispersed aerodromes! As I sit here writing to you I wonder what you are thinking. Will I be able to come home with you in the near future? Will you say 'Yes, soon'? I hope you will, my Nina. All these things are terribly important to me, perhaps even more so now. Do I worry you, Nina? I don't mean to, but I know you will realise that these things are seldom out of my thoughts. So very often I live again precious moments of Chester, Stratford, Birmingham. In my imagination I am cycling down sunny lanes again with you enchanted by your smile, the smile that first brought us together. No, it won't 'go up in smoke' darling, of that I am confident for I know you love me as much as I love you. But I AM lonely, Nina, and if you said: 'Yes', in your next letter I know it would lift me up to those clouds again.

There are so many things that I want to say to you, Nina, but letters are a very unsatisfactory medium of expressing such powerful thoughts and emotions. I know you won't have forgotten all the things we have said and done together, and don't forget, darling – just say the word and we can go ahead. All my letters to you will probably be censored. We cannot post them in a letter box but they have to be handed into SHQ which accounts for my name and number on the flap. This all takes time, but after the first one you should receive a steady flow.

Goodnight now, sweetheart. God bless, and – I love you,

For ever your, Victor xxxxxxxxxxxxxxxxx

Officers' Mess, RAF Station Foulsham, Norfolk
21st May 1944

Nina darling xxx

My third letter to you since arriving here. I hope you received the other two safely. Each day I look hopefully at the letter-rack but of course so far it has remained empty. Tomorrow being Monday I hope for a letter from you, dear. It seems such a long time ago since I said au revoir to you last Monday. Precisely seven days that have seemed like seven months.

It remains very cold here and I am beginning to doubt if this really is May. Has the sun forgotten how to shine? Did I dream that sunset as we cycled home from the 'Spread Eagle'? Truly this seems like another world and I'm longing to get back to you and true happiness.

Do you remember reading to me a passage from our book that started:

'Tony thought of Plato's myth of the man-woman who had once been a single complete living thing, and then had been severed, so that the half, man,

and the half, woman, must always go seeking the other lost half for completion.'

It finishes: '*Love then perfectly that the flesh you make of your love may be perfect.*'

I've read that passage over and over again to myself substituting Vic for Tony and Nina for Kathe. At nine o'clock each night I've thought of you extra hard. In fact, any memory or thought that brings me a little closer to you is indeed precious to me.

I suppose it must be really silly to get depressed as I do at times, but Nina, you must know that in you I have found true peace and happiness that can only come with mutual love and understanding. Is it not natural then that I should feel lonely and incomplete without you?

Perhaps you have already decided to say: 'Yes', while I am writing this. I'm always hoping so Nina, and I shall open all your letters with a heart full of expectancy.

To come down to the material side of life. Yesterday I bought another pair of pyjamas, a dusty pink shade like the ones we saw in Chester. I hope you like them. I haven't forgotten the burnt orange colour but I have no means of getting them yet. I've also managed to get a bicycle, which makes life a lot pleasanter besides giving me an extra couple of minutes in bed of a morning.

I intended phoning you this evening about 4.30pm, but then I realised that you would be at home. How I envied you! But perhaps soon I shall be there with you, Nina. Will it be OK if I phone you on Saturday next at 7pm? Write and let me know if that will be OK.

This is all for tonight, darling, except to say that I'm longing for your letters and – I love you with all my heart.

Your sweetheart always,

Vic xxxxxxxxxxxxxxx

479352 ACW1 Chessall, N
SHQ, RAF Wheaton Aston, Little Onn, Staffs
Tuesday 23rd May 1944

My Darling,   XXX x XX x Xx

Nothing could have pleased me more yesterday morning than to receive that very first letter from you. I seemed to have been hungering and thirsting for it for days. They do take rather a long time, don't they, Vic? This is dated 17th and I receive it on the 22nd – five days! Your second letter, which I received this morning, is dated 19th May – a little quicker, only four days! But I have heard from you, that is the main thing and thanks a lot for them, Vic. xxx xxx xxx xx x

Oh yes, the tin of Horlicks, Vic! I did not know what arrangements you had made regarding this until I got your letter yesterday, and then I made my way to the WAAF Picket Post to collect the same. I – er – collected the TIN all right, and there was still a little label stuck around it 'This tin of Horlicks is for ACW, Chisle', but there wasn't even a spoonful left in it. So I thanked them for saving the tin, and left it with them as a gift.

So you kept your word, my dear, and filled in my name and address as your second next-of-kin! I can understand how strange it would feel to put down our relationship as 'friend'. You WILL remember to see whether Clerks G.D are in short supply down there or not, won't you, Vic? I should like, more than ever now, to be stationed with you, just as soon as you can arrange it.

You see, I think I told you that I had a letter from Bill yesterday – well, the news it contained shook me considerably. At the moment, I don't know where I am. I feel as though I am sitting with a sword hanging over my head, waiting for the damned thing to drop at any moment. I didn't think I should have this crisis to face quite so soon. The words that leaped out of the page at me as I looked at it were: 'I am waiting for my relief then I'm coming home, and I decided that to come home was the best thing for the sake of us both, because even if I did think things were going wrong I do want to and must see you ...' etc. and more: 'in June at the latest you will be in the arms of ...' That last sent a cold chill down my spine. Vic, don't you see why I want to be near you? Oh, Vic, what am I going to do? I need you now. What comfort there is in the touch of your hand! What sublime confidence you give to me in its strong clasp! Vic, Vic, I too am frightened. Give me courage, please.

Another thing, Vic, I want you to come home with me on your next day off, as soon as you can make it. There isn't very much time. It is nearly the end of May now, and next week is Whit week, and we have only got till the end of June at the latest. It would be terrible, wouldn't it, if you and Bill both arrived home together? I just couldn't cope with that at all.

Oh, by the way, I told my mother all about you – well, the most important things, anyway, such as having fallen in love with you and never having felt like this about anyone else. It was very easy. Somehow, it all came tumbling out and now I feel tremendously eased. She didn't turn a hair at the difference in age and said that love knew no barriers in that respect. I showed her your photograph too, the one stuck in my diary.

Getting home on Saturday night had its complications. The Adjutant issued verbal instructions that there was no rail travel on day passes – none at all. However, nothing daunted, I set out, quite prepared to change into civilian clothes if need be, to get home. F/O Boden was on the bus going into Stafford and he advised me to hitch-hike. He said it would be easy, and even volunteered to do the 'thumbing' for me on the corner by the Odeon. He was very kind and I did appreciate this, because that is the part I didn't like. Within five minutes, I was sitting between two lorry drivers on the front of a wagon bound for Warrington. Two more lorries took me to Liverpool, the latter being driven by a Yank with a negro as his mate! I daren't look sideways and meet those rolling eyes. I was home by 9.30.

We had your duck-eggs for breakfast next day. I told Mum they were from you. Dinner was a succulent affair of lamb chops with mint (from the garden) sauce, spring cabbage (also home-grown) followed by rhubarb (hand-picked) tart and custard. It tasted even better than lunch at Bollard's, Vic. As well as the contents of your parcel, I also brought back with me a pot of jam rhubarb. I should have liked to send you this also, but discovered that the bottle leaked a little, so I have kept that – but I wish you could share it with me. It tastes delicious; I had some for breakfast this morning.

The garden shows a vast improvement to when I saw it last. The apple blossom must have looked a picture, but during the recent high winds, most of the blossoms have fallen off and now look like scattered confetti. (Did someone get married here recently? – next apple-blossom time, Vic).

The time came all too soon for me to return to Camp. I left at the usual time for the 7.5 train to Stafford from Liverpool, as I knew it would be hopeless to attempt to hitch-hike back. Would you believe it, Vic, there wasn't an S.P in sight, and there were loads of Services people travelling? When I spoke to some other airmen on the train, they all said there was no rail travel ban at their Camp. Apparently it is only ours! – Phooey! So as soon as you can possibly manage it, let me know, Vic, won't you? HOW I miss you, my Vic. It seemed terrible to have to travel by train alone, without you to guide me and arrange things. This is the first time, you must remember, for quite a long time, but I'll learn.

Au revoir, dear Vic.

Nina

Officers' Mess, RAF Station Foulsham, Norfolk
24th May 1944

My Nina,

A letter from you today. I almost sobbed with relief when I saw it and I think my hand must have been trembling a little more than usual because I found it difficult to open.

When I read it, there they were, all the same hopes and longings that have been in my heart ever since I left you. Isn't it a wonderful feeling to have someone who is in complete harmony with you?

Darling, I feel that I should explain my telegram. I was worried that my letters may not be reaching you. I know really that's a silly thing to think, but I didn't want to leave anything to chance. So, just in case you didn't hear from me I thought I would make doubly sure. Can you understand Nina? I get all sorts of little panics going on inside me where you are concerned. To me you are THE most important person in the world. So you see I just cannot afford to take chances.

Nina, please don't think that I have gone. Just think that I am away but for a little while. This past week with no contact with you, not even a letter, has made me realise just how utterly lonely I can be. How much I depend upon you, and how much our lives have very surely become one. But now I must turn from my own aching heart to comfort you. Nina, I have no fear. Our love is strong, perhaps one of the strongest things in a changing uncertain world. In my own heart I know I can never change and I am as confident of you. It has stood so many tests so far and has grown and flourished in circumstances that were nearly always adverse; we never did look back, Nina. Know now that this parting will only make it stronger still. Know too that I am ready to marry you as soon as you give your consent. I have been sure of this for a long time now, darling. This past week has been confirmation if any had been needed.

Blymhill Church bell striking nine!! Oh, Nina, He must see us in our loneliness. With bowed heads, hand in hand, we prayed that He may protect our love and bring us together again soon. Forgive me Nina, that if, before giving thanks, I prayed that one day we may find a haven of our own, our own little world. I am thankful for all the goodness around us, but if only, if only I can keep you always. No more years of loneliness. No more pondering troubles in my heart until they assume the size of grievances and I see the world through the distorted eyes of a bitter person. What a contrast to the rest of my life these past five months have been! Thank you for them darling, and thank you in anticipation for the rest of our days together, both in this world and the world to come.

So, my Nina is an artist. I am not surprised really, for I am sure that anything touched by those hands must assume a beautiful form. I've seen no lilac here, Nina. My days and evenings I spend studying for I have plenty to do. Only when I sit down to write to you is there beauty around me. As I write, then once again is there blossom on the trees. Apple, lilac, cherry blossom. 'Cuckoo' flowers are in the hedgerows again and Ring-cups beside the lake and I am 'Commando' once again to gratify my lady's wishes (God keep her).

And enclosed is your piece of string. Treasure it for I nearly broke my neck trying to hold one end between my teeth and put the rest of it round my arm. But I know it's for a good cause, Nina. Your parcel should arrive tomorrow with its homemade? inside. Life is indeed full of pleasant things now and they can all be traced to one person. My Nina. Yes, mine, all mine.

Originally I wanted you to give Peter the frames for the 'Polyfotos' but I posted them on to him. It seems that he did not receive them after all, or my letter. I never dreamt that he and I would tread so vastly different paths after leaving Wheaton.

And now I'm wondering what your next letter will hold for me. You say you have lots of things to tell and they all have a bearing on your going home and a letter from Bill. Can it be that you are going to say: -. Oh, Nina, if only you would say 'Yes'. But patience, Vic, everything comes to he, who waits. Soon, Nina, I hope we shall be together as I shall have some leave coming along. Oh what a meeting we shall have. Forgive me darling, if, when I see you, I seem overwhelming. But you see the cork will be well and truly off. I'm longing for it.

Till we meet Nina, I'm learning to love you more every day and longing with all my heart for our wedding day. Take care of my happiness as I shall always take care of yours. God bless.

Your sweetheart for all time

Vic xxxxxxxxxxxxxxxxx X

In bed

10pm Wednesday 24.5.1944

My Darling,

It is a beautiful evening, and it seems almost a sin to waste it so. But what else is there to do? I begin to understand now why people dislike this Station so much. My cycle is leaning against our billet outside, looking very forlorn and forsaken. It hasn't been used once in the evenings ever since you went away.

To prove to you how lonely I am, Vic, I go to all the Shows it is possible to go to on Camp – good, bad or indifferent. There was a good one last night, a play entitled: 'Without the Prince'. Every member of the cast was superb, and I was able to get a seat, which was a bit of a change to the Show on Monday night. I wonder why plays are never so popular on this Camp as Variety?

The Show on Monday night was put on by the WRNS of HMS Fledgling. (You went to a dance there once, didn't you?) There were a lot of cracks about the RAF, of course, but it was very mediocre, I thought – possibly because of having to stand the whole two-and-a-half hours on a form at the back. You might have appreciated one item, Vic, when old Jenny was dragged, literally, up on the stage and took the part of 'Sadie', a gangster's moll. S/Ldr Grovenor was the gangster. Here are two gags I hadn't heard before:

> *'Here's to you and home and Blighty,*
> *You in pyjamas, me in my nightie.*
> *And because we'll both feel flighty,*
> *Why the pyjamas? – Why the nightie?'*

Oh, you are not laughing, Vic. Heard it before, I suppose? I'll try again:

'We see Americans everywhere now and it is getting very difficult to find a place to lean. One day a WAAF went into a chemist's shop and asked the American who was serving behind the counter: 'Have you any lifebuoy?'

He took one look at her and said: 'You set the pace, baby'... (pause for laughter) ... she wore the sort of dress – well, one Yank and it's off.'

I can't remember any more.

Thanks for the telegram, Vic, which I was told about last night when I came out from the Show. I could hardly breathe while I rang up Signals for the content of the message, for fear Bill was already here. I was glad it was from you. Have you been worrying, my sweet, because you haven't heard from me? You will know now that I wrote as soon as I received your address, which was on Monday. By the way, Vic, when did you send this telegram? From all the numbers and letters across the top, it looks to me as though it was sent on the 19th. That is four whole days, before I receive it! If that is true, why, you might be the other side of the world. And heaven alone knows when you will receive my telegram reply! I telephoned it from the NAAFI at lunchtime today, and just in case you receive this letter before the telegram, I'll tell you what it says:

'Letters on the way also parcel. Remember Blymhill.
Nina.'

Peter goes tomorrow evening. He came in to see me yesterday to collect my cycle lamp, which I had completely forgotten originally belonged to him. I am sorry, darling, that I gave you all the bother, because in the end it has been given in. However, I still have the pump, but one doesn't get fined for being without that!!!

I think I'll go to sleep now. The lights will be unceremoniously switched off soon. I wish I could snuggle up in your arms so that you were as close as possible to

Your Nina.

Soon? Xxx

JUNE

Foulsham
2nd June 1944

Nina darling,

Such joy to hear your voice tonight. Whilst speaking to you I closed my eyes and imagined you were whispering in my ear. That all I had to do was to turn my head and find a pair of warm, kissable lips on mine thrilling me with life anew. Don't laugh at my dreams, Nina, they are all I have to comfort me 'til we meet again.

As I told you tonight I am on the deck for two days owing to a damaged ear. I failed to keep them clear by pinching my nose and blowing hard whilst descending from a considerable height a couple of days ago. Now, I have a hell of a pain in my left ear and it's making me thoroughly miserable. The Doc is giving me inhalations and nose spray but the pain seems to be local to the ear. But he tells me it's not serious so I guess I'll live to fly again.

Tomorrow I am Orderly Officer, a job that would have been most unwelcome at Wheaton, but now, well, what does it matter. I accept it almost gladly. The film 'Fantasia' is showing at the Station cinema tomorrow and Sunday so I think I'll pay a lonely bobsworth and see it. The music is provided by the Philadelphia Symphony under Stowkoski and all I have to do is close my eyes and dream that we are seeing it together. If only your gentle hand would take mine what a difference it would make. No wonder I consider life very incomplete without you, my darling.

We must always strive to find each other, Nina, and how well I have realised that truth since we parted. I know now that there is an Acacea to which we must always return. A feeling of being incomplete when we are not together. Only you for me, Nina, and only myself for you, and to find life-long happiness we must adhere to this. Tony was foolish enough to think the passing years had erased his love for Kathe. How wrong he was and what misery of spirit it cost him!

Nina, the smile has slipped a little in the past weeks. Don't blame me, darling, please. You teasing about the 'other fellow' who was useless with dynamos soon pushed the smile back in its place. Remember the day when I found your bicycle after the S-Ps had failed miserably? Oh please, Nina, let me blow my own trumpet sometimes.

'Did you think of me a little?'

Dear God who knows all, please tell her I love her and think of her ALWAYS. A quote from your letter and a verse from my prayers. A question from you and an answer from me, Nina. Please, darling, know that you are always in my thoughts. I can remember no life before last Christmas and I can think of no future without you. I treasure our love beyond all worldly things and I will keep it whole and pure so long as there is breathe in me. That's how much I think of you, Nina, as far as words can describe my feelings. I hope soon to let my actions speak for themselves.

Trust in our sprig of white heather which you carry with you in your diary, darling, and have faith in our love. God bless you always and keep you for me.

For ever your, Vic

PS A date on Sunday night at nine, Nina xxxxxxxxxxxxxxxxx

4.6.'44
Sunday aft., SSQ

My sweetheart, xxx

As if it wasn't bad enough to bear a heartache, the pain of being parted from you, Nina, it has to be added to by a pain in my ear that at times makes me feel desperate. As you can see from the top of the page I am in Sick Quarters and I don't think that I can feel much lower than I do. I reported sick on Friday morning and was grounded for 48 hours. On Saturday (yesterday) the pain became almost unbearable and when I reported sick again this morning I was told to fetch my small kit. In other words, 'Inside, brother'. The cause of all the trouble is a boil inside my ear and they say I am run down. Only you can know how much I have been pining these last three weeks. Just now, Nina, I would sell my soul for one smile from you. A kiss and the feel of your arms about me are things that I long for and dare not hope for.

I have asked F/Sgt Foster, a brother navigator, to phone you at nine tonight. I know you won't like this, darling, but it will save you worrying and a promise is a promise even if I cannot fulfil it in person. I can say almost for certain that I shall be with you on Monday, the 12th as arranged so please don't worry on that account. I hope you can read my writing, darling, but I find bed is not the best place for wielding a pen.

After tea

Don't wonder at the strange postmarks on my letters. I will explain when I see you. It's surprising what new hope you can gleam from little things when you feel down and out. Lying here in bed I look at the second hand of my watch ticking its slow but sure way around each minute. Each movement bringing me another second nearer to you, my beloved. Since last Christmas life has been made up of living for those all too brief hours spent with you, Nina. At Wheaton I existed during the day and lived in the evenings. Now my period of existing has been lengthened into weeks, with each minute of parting making me vow that one day we SHALL both find complete happiness, the other half of ourselves. I sometimes wonder if the passing years that have brought this great civilisation, this great cultured civilisation with its social order, has it brought us more happiness? Was not man as happy when he found his mate and made a home for her in his own cave? But that is wishful thinking, I suppose.

Dear Nina, have you decided to say: 'Yes' yet? I know you don't think now that I am trying to force a decision. I only needed one lesson like that and the cold fear that your answer planted in my heart will be remembered by me always. You brought me to my knees that night, Nina. Thank God you didn't kick me whilst I was down. Now I ask the question longingly, always hoping the honour of your 'Yes' will be mine.

The pain in my ear has eased a little during the past hour or so thanks to some codeine tablets and I'm hoping for a decent night's sleep tonight. I would that I could sleep with my heart touching yours, my love, a sleep that would ease all pain, both physical and spiritual. Deprived of expressing my love with my body, the temple of my soul, I feel stifled and suppressed. I try to write of my love for you but the words seem to mock me from the paper. All the feelings and emotions are there in my heart, Nina, just as they have always been, with the safety valve clamped down tightly. Can you remember my kisses, darling? Can you remember what it feels like to be held so tightly that it feels as if you and I have become one body? Do you remember those nights as Vic and Nina? It's all there, my love, bottled and maturing until we meet again. No-one can ever take your place, Nina, no matter where I go in this world. 'For what I am worth, I am yours.'

Outside it is bright but not sunshiney. The wind would seem to be from the nor'west, probably the same wind that has blown across Wheaton. Say something to it, Nina. Tell it you love me and it will bring me your message. How I long to hear those words again. 'I love you, Vic.' To me they mean life. They mean at last I am no longer alone, that there is a new world for me. This is life, Vic. Remember the lessons of the past, let it teach you patience and sympathy towards the unfortunate, and with these things at heart live your happy future. I love you, my Nina.

Yours sweetheart,
Vic
Remember Blymhill xxx xxx xxx 'Will thou take me .....'

Sunday night, 4.6.1944
10pm. In bed.

My Love xxx xxx xxx

Once again we are doomed to disappointment. I wonder why this time? I was in the NAAFI from quarter to nine till half past, waiting for the telephone to ring – and the greater part of that time it was disengaged. At half past nine, I dialled the Operator, intending to ask whether a call from Fakenham had been received, but although I tried again and again for at least a quarter of an hour, I could get no reply from the Operator. I could hear it ringing through all right, and the line wasn't engaged, so I can only conclude the Operator was asleep.

Well, now I must write you what I would have told you tonight. First of all, Vic dear, I miss you terribly – and Vic, I love you.

Secondly, I must tell you about my day at Stafford yesterday. Well, actually, I didn't set off tell after lunch, and I cycled there. It took me less than an hour, and I only went slowly. I didn't want to get to Stafford too soon, you see, or its limited number of attractions would be exhausted too quickly.

My first port of call was the Station Hotel, where I spoke to the delightful (?) Mr Smythe himself. (He's the proprietor, by the way – just the sort of person who would spell his name with a 'y'.) He told me that no bookings would be made except by post. I made sure, however, there were vacancies for the two nights in question, before proceeding to the Post Office to write a nice little 'billet dous' to Mr Smythe from a person named HVA Vinnell. You will, no doubt, be receiving confirmation of the booking direct, as I put your address in the letter.

After that, I just did a little shopping for such things as soapflakes and birthday cards (it is my mother's birthday on the 18th) – oh, and another shampoo! Then I had tea at the YMCA with one of the Signal's Corporals I met there, and finished up at the Cinema (not the Odeon) where I saw a George Fornby film 'Bell Bottom George'.

You know, Vic, it seemed the strangest thing to me not to be meeting you somewhere first thing in the morning, at one or other of the triangles, and cycling for dear life to Gnosall Station for the 8.43. It was the funniest day off! – not 'ha-ha', not a bit 'ha-ha', but very very peculiar. And to sit in the Cinema alone – no, Vic, no-one to turn and look at, no hand to hold, no-one to laugh with – I didn't like it!

Yet even this wasn't really painful, not compared with the ride back from Gnosall. It was raining when I came out of the Pictures, and so I got the 9.20 train from Stafford, and cycled to Camp from Gnosall. This really was painful, Vic. It was here, where by mutual consent, we had descended from our cycles and you had drawn me close – here, in the middle of the lane, as though time itself had stopped and the world was holding its breath. I closed my eyes and remembered it all, your whispered words, your kisses that gave as much as they demanded. Oh Vic, Vic, Vic, please come back again and make me live – this yearning for you, no-one else could do this. Then into the vortex of my thoughts intruded the note of a shy little songster perched on the bough of a tree just above my head. 'Vic' – 'Vic' – 'Vic', it said, its head on one side, 'you can't forget him, - you can't forget him,' and I smiled in spite of myself, because I knew it was true and I knew I didn't want to forget you.

This letter to you is very much overdue, Vic. I seem to have been carrying it round with me inside my head for days, until it will be almost a relief to transfer it to paper. Let me see, after referring to my diary, the last time I wrote to you was last Monday. On Tuesday, I made all arrangements to play tennis, and then Sgt Hoyland missed the bus to Stafford complete with all the gear for the other two players. Having missed tea, the messing Cpl gave us tea in her office, and we spent the evening there having a good long 'jaw' – while a thunderstorm raged outside. So it was a good job in a way that we weren't getting soaked on a tennis court!

However, we all made it on Thursday night, and I thoroughly enjoyed the game. Vic Hermolle is quite a good player. We didn't pack up till just before ten, and then followed a terrific dash to catch the 10.20 bus back. There was no time to get a drink and we all felt very thirsty, so we called in at the Station Dance – for food and drink principally, certainly not to dance. There is nothing to go to a dance here for now, Vic. It seemed such an awful waste of time even to go for an hour.

Then, on Wednesday – oh well, you know what happened on Wednesday. Tonight was a repeat performance. There appear to be quite a lot of things I do now that I had neither the time nor the inclination for when you were here – not the least of them being my frequent visits to the NAAFI, where I sit at the table next to the telephone box with my ear glued up against it for fear I should miss its ring amid all the noise.

I was so thrilled on Friday, Vic, when I spoke to you – almost too thrilled to be able to collect my thoughts sufficiently to tell you. It was like a suffocating feeling in the region of my chest, and it seemed as though my heart were beating in my ears. Is that love, Vic? I sometimes hesitate to think of what your telephone bill will be this month. How many minutes did we have on Friday, Vic? We must try not to be so extravagant next time.

By the way, darling. I hope that you will have noticed the enclosure. You see, it is magic. I took one small piece of string – you will remember it was a very ordinary piece of string? – and now, by waving my hand over it sew, and sew, and sew, it has changed to a circle of elastic, and not one circle, but two!! Not even the great Vinnellski himself could do better than that! Even his world-famous match-trick has nothing on this! And it works! Just try it, Sir, hif you please. Slip the circle over your hand and up your arm – and lo! doesn't your shirt sleeve stay put?

Darling of mine, how impossible it would be not to be profoundly moved by the power of your love as expressed in your letters. I wish I could write letters to you like that, that would convey to you in some measure what I am feeling, and that would make you feel the same. I stare past the handwriting on the paper in my hand, the room round about whirls and fades, and instead, my eyes are caught and riveted by the steady gaze of two very wide intensely blue ones, eyes that would look into my very soul and from whom nothing is hid. I see you Vic, so clearly. And yes, I am strong again. I feel your life, your confidence, your love, flowing into me.

One sentence in your letter caught my eye, Vic: 'Anything touched by those hands' you write, 'must assume beautiful form'. Are you thinking of the same thing, my dearest? Oh, if only I could practice my act with you now. What sheer heaven-sent luxury to we poor earth-bound mortals!

Soon, darling, soon, with

Your Nina

5 Monday ROME FALLS – ALLIED TROOPS IN CITY'S CENTRE

The Fifth Army reached the heart of Rome at dusk last night after a resistance in the outer suburbs by the German rearguard. And so – ROME, SUNDAY NIGHT – was the proud date line on the war correspondent's cables as they flashed their stories across the world. The German main army is apparently retreating fast north of the city. Highways fifty miles beyond Rome are jammed with Germans and transport, indicating that the enemy is making a big withdrawal to far behind the capital.

6. Tuesday – INVASION!

Churchill announces successful massed air landings behind enemy in France. 4,000 ships, thousands of smaller vessels. 'So far all goes to plan – 11,000 first line airplanes. An immense armada of more than 4,000 ships, with several thousand smaller craft, has crossed the Channel', said Mr Churchill today, announcing the invasion. 'Massed airborne landings have been successfully effected behind the enemy's lines, he said. Mr Churchill described the landings as 'the first series in force on the European continent'.

News of Invasion!! Began last night. 2 confirmed telegrams and 2 letters from Vic. Letter No. 220 from Bill. Letter from Fred. Letter from Mum.

The whole Station is now becoming defence-minded. Guns are installed in the Adj's Office. General test of gas equipment. Work for LDA on Operation Orders. Never known the Mess to be so quiet during reading of The News!

Officers' Mess, RAF Station Fousham, Norfolk
5th June 1944 (I think!)

Nina, my darling xxx

Another day of soul-shattering loneliness ... Well, it sounds impressive anyway and quite honestly I am well and truly cheesed with being alone in this room. As nobody known me not unnaturally nobody has been down to see me and if I 'lick the bucket' they'll probably bury my bones, without any fuss or ceremony very close to the salvage dump. (Next of kin of Casualties have been informed). Ain't it romantic being an airman!

But I was in on one good thing today. A lady from the YMCA van brought the patients two eggs each and I really did appreciate that gesture. There must be a lot of people like her who are doing good in a quiet, unobtrusive way.

I have now got out of bed and am sitting at the table writing. Yes, you can almost read it now, can't you?

I could shoot a horrible line just now if I was that sort of a fella. I've got a roll of bandage around my head and a pad over one ear that looks as if it is holding my brains (?) in. The 'thing' inside my ear has broke which has relieved a lot, if not all, of the throbbing and I hope it will only be a matter of a day or so before it decides to heal up.

I was hoping for a letter from you today, Nina, as I have not had one for four days. But my luck was out. A horrible thought struck me at lunch-time. Supposing you were in Sick Bay too. We have a habit of doing these things together, haven't we darling? But I believe you would have let me know if that was the case. Please do let me know as soon as you can if anything ever does go wrong.

Nina, I don't know if you are going to approve of this, but the moustache is on its way back and has nearly regained all its old glory. I'll tell you why I did this when I see you.

Being all alone for two days has given me plenty of chance for meditation and not unnaturally ninety-nine per cent of my thoughts (allowing one per cent for meal times) have been centred, or rather, have had their centre as you, us.

In my imagination I have lived again all those golden hours of those precious five months God granted us together. And when the pain of being parted from you has tortured, yes, tortured, Nina, me I have prayed hard that we should not be parted ever for very long. I have prayed for next week, that we may be granted time together, that for a while the heartaches may be banished. And I said the 'Lord's Prayer'.

Nina, tell me, when you say: 'Thy will be done in earth as it is in heaven', does it mean that God can have planned our parting? It seems very hard for a mortal soul to sit back and say, 'God wishes it'. I find it hard to find comfort in that thought when my whole heart and body are crying out for you. Perhaps it is easier to believe that, 'He moves in mysterious ways. His wonders to perform'. When He gives us our happiness, when He has blessed our union, perhaps He will look down and say that we have suffered enough and the reward of our patience shall be great indeed. We agreed not long ago that we had finished 'skimming the surface'. Do you remember, Nina? We delved down into our souls and found beautiful things that brought us happiness we had never experienced before. Now it is bringing us pain, but I would not change it.

To our future, Nina, to peaceful days rich with love and understanding.

God bless, my dear,

Your lover always,

Vic xxxxxxxxxxxxxxxx

SHQ

(Lunch-time) Thursday 8th June 1944

My Dearest,

I have just returned from the NAAFI Telephone box, from which I have sent you a telegram. This morning, Vic, I received two letters from you and you sounded so utterly miserable and forlorn in the latter one that I decided I must telegram you to let you know everything is 'hunky-dory' and that you are still the only man in my life and that I love you very much (x - - - x - - x) Are you feeling a little better now, Vic darling?

Today I am Duty Clerk again, and as this may be the last opportunity I shall have of writing you a letter that you will receive before I see you next Monday, it will only be a short one, because I MUST catch the four o'clock post just to make certain. But I promise you a longer letter tonight, when I will endevour to answer this collection of mail I have here from you. Please teach me how to write such heavenly letters, Vic. Each letter from you contains a few of those episodes we have shared together: you must have found the secret of preserving them – of capturing them and bottling them to produce a delightfully fragrant essence, so that when needed you can remove the cork and relive them all again at will. And when you write to me, Vic, you must spill some of it over the pages – strong and vital and heady stuff, that carries me away to a flowery arbour midway 'twixt earth and heaven where you are waiting. Oh darling – my love – sometimes it is too big for me to think of, this love of ours. I have been caught in its current, and it is inexorable; I feel that its destiny must be fulfilled. To turn back now would be to fight upstream, against the tide, for the rest of my life. And what of you? – where would you be? – cast up on some deserted beach, or clutching desperately to some boulder at the water's edge, in the hope that some day I would give up the unequal struggle and pass that way again? - ? - ? 'Vic - - - darling – ' If you could only read those words as I have just said them, with a world of unsatisfied longing in them, and a sigh, and a prayer, you wouldn't feel lonely any more.

I am wondering if this invasion business will make any difference to our plans. For one thing, we are still not supposed to travel by train. Will you be able to get here all right on Monday? I have written home to tell Mum when to expect us, but, of course, if we can't make it she'll understand. This is Vic I am speaking to – a man to reckon with, a man who bends Fate to his own will. Of course, you'll be in Stafford on Monday!!! 'Master of your Fate and Captain of your Soul'.

I love you, my Master.

I adore you, mon Capitaine.

And so for the present, Love, (till I can give it to you)

Nina X (adoration kiss) xxxxxxxxxxxxxxxxxxxxxxxxxxxxxxx

SHQ

(Some time later) Thursday 8th June, 1944

Vic, M Dear, xxx xxx xxx

Here I am again, with another long day nearly through and the quietude of evening settling on the world outside. The time is – need you ask it? – nearly nine o'clock, that part of the day I look forward to most, and Headquarters' staff are beginning to desert now they have all had a cup of tea. Before me on the desk, Vic, believe it or not, I have five letters of yours to answer – two that arrived this morning, one yesterday morning, and two on Tuesday morning. No wonder I woke up from my sleep and sent you a telegram toady to calm your fears on my behalf.

I remember writing in the letter I sent you from home that I hoped your ears were not burning. Little did I know that when you received that letter your ears would indeed be burning – with pain. Forgive me, Vic, but when I spoke to you last over the phone I evidently did not hear your mention of that damaged left ear. It was only when I read it in the letter you wrote to me immediately afterwards that I knew you had told me, or thought you had, but I didn't hear. You must have thought me horribly callous not to sympathise with you at all. I shouldn't be surprised if the cause of it was holding a telephone to your ear for too long at a time. I didn't use any bad language did I, Vic, when I was talking to you? – oh well, you couldn't have got it through talking to me. By the way, have you heard from Pauline lately? She does know your new address, I suppose?

(Sh-sh .... Nine o'clock is striking at Blymhill ..... come away with me, darling, away to the mountain-tops ..... let us soar away together ...... our spirits one.

(xx ----------------- I – l-o-v-e – y-o-u --------------------- xx)

Did I tell you what really beautiful letters you write, Vic? I love your sense of humour. It is presumption on my part to even thing that I could answer them, but I can only try; and if I fail miserably, Vic, please be generous and forgive, and think only of the spirit that prompted the deed.

I don't seem to have done you much good since I have known you, Vic, do I? You have had nothing but boils and misfortunes ever since. You didn't suffer with such things before, did you?

The two telegrams arrived here all right on Monday morning. I hardly dared open the second one, following so soon after, for fear that you were no better. Is F/Sgt Foster the fellow called Dick with whom you went the cycle ride? Did you not know that he had sent a telegram when he found he could not get through to me? It really sounded pretty bad when he said you were in hospital.

What do you think of the news, darling? I think it is grand, and I am glad it has happened at last, but how is it going to affect you and me and our week, commencing on Monday! Oh, I know, I am a selfish creature – always thinking in terms of how it will affect me and mine and those whom I love. But at heart I think everyone is like that. We were not meant to embrace the whole world in our affections; for me, that IS my world; and if I should lose one of the few who constitute it, then for me the war is already lost.

You would have smiled at the panic that took place here after the announcement. Less than two hours afterwards, there were little guns being erected in the Adjutant's office – for defence purposes, they say, but I think Stu. has probably got them trained on us when he doesn't hear the clicking of the typewriters next door. The main reason is, of course, so that Jenny can protect the CO. The LDA has been busy too and I have been working late on his stuff.

On Wednesday morning there was a grand Parade at 08.00 hours, that not even you could have wrangled out of. Because why? – because even the MO was there! The SPs blew little whistles and hoisted the Union Jack, and I couldn't tell what the CO was saying – the wind was blowing in the wrong direction – and so I had to make up my own words, as I knew it was some kind of prayer.

An officer's life isn't worth living at Wheaton Aston now, Vic. I typed out a notice a couple of days ago to the effect that 'All Ranks' Dances are cancelled as far as officers are concerned and they are forbidden to attend'. So that's that. Oh, and they must now notify the Adjutant when they are having a day off.

'The Duchess' is now concerning herself with the breaking-up of another promising romance, with more results than she had in our case. It concerns Ding and a girl from Accounts called Edna. The girl of course, was put on a charge for some trifling offence and was afterwards subjected to what 'The Duchess' fondly believed was a motherly talk. Do you know what she said to her, Vic? She asked her if she was in love with Ding? And whether he had ever told her that he was in love with her? I don't think I could have answered her civilly if she had said that to me. She is the wrong person to play 'Auntie Peg' and the last person I should go to if I needed advice. Not content with that, Vic, she has even extended the field of her activities to Din, and according to

Edna, has gained some ground. It is funny why she never treated us like that – at least, she had that much sense!

Oh, I have another joke for you, culled from another Camp Show. Tell me if you have heard it before. It concerns the Padre, and it is a terrible joke. I don't know whether I have got the nerve to tell you, because it is one that I could see without anyone explaining it to me – most unusual. Oh well, here goes – he was having a bath and two WAAFs were peeping through the keyhole. Heaven knows why or how they got there, but for the sake of the joke that is what they were doing. Then one said to the other: 'There you are, you see, I knew he had more than five inches there'. Oh, perhaps they were Orderly Sergeants or something, but why should they be patrolling the baths? Oh, I give up. Have you blushed yet, darling? Mmm, yes, it HAS gone suddenly rather warm in here. Aren't I daring?

Look, Vic, suppose I can get one day off next week (which seems very likely), will you return to Foulsham on Thursday night? It seems such a pity to waste the rest of your Leave. Why not spend the rest of it at home? I know that I still shouldn't be able to see you, but at least it would be away from Camp. That is a good idea of yours to bring your cycle with you to Stafford, and will simplify the transport question considerably. Besides, most of our favourite haunts would be totally inaccessible to us without bikes, wouldn't they?

Has the wind changed yet, my love? Well, when it does, when the wind blows in a south-easterly direction, will you listen for the words it will whisper to you, very gently, in your good ear? It will say: 'V- i – c, V – i – c, she l-o-v-e-s you. N-i-n-a told me so – o' and then with a long shuddering sigh it will vanish but the echo of those words will remain.

Vic, I do love you. And if I were to be granted only one wish, I should say – Let me keep your love like this always. 'Can you remember your kisses?' What a silly thing to ask me! Vic, the night flying aircraft are just being started up and I am alone at HQ. If I put out the light and lay in the darkness waiting, do you think you would come to me as you came once before? I know I can still taste the sweetness of your kisses upon my lips, and I can remember as if I had just been released from your clasp the wish I made that I could disintegrate and lose myself altogether, so that I could be free from the shackles and limitations that bind me to my mortal flesh. I want to be free; I want to lose my bonds; my spirit clamours inside me to be released from its cage, away from the chains that hold me. I have never been so conscious of the immortal part of myself, Vic, as I have been since knowing you. I certainly have no doubt now that I am really two persons, and the innermost one, the one that is really me and which is unbounded by customs and routine living and codes and conventions, is by far the more important. Have you had that experience? I feel I want nothing better than that your spirit and mine should one day escape our earth-bound fetters, and cleave and soar together into eternity. That would be the Death Triumphant. Would you be afraid of that? I know I wouldn't.

No, Vic. I don't think that the lines 'Thy will be done on earth – 'are as passive as all that. We weren't meant to sit back and say anything. I think this is a more positive prayer, that when we are shown what His will is, we may be granted the power to carry it through, no matter how hard and difficult the doing of it may be. I think it is because 'thy will be done' is often detached from the rest of the sentence, that alters the meaning entirely. People are fond of doing that with quotations from the Bible, so that they can make them mean almost anything that they want them to mean. We can only trust in Him; He can see the End and all the long road to it, whereas we can see only the Beginning. We can only believe that 'Everything works together for good to them that do His will'.

I am wondering why you have grown that moustache. Luckily, I don't really mind either way, and it will just prove an added point of interest.

Y – aw – aw – nn! Oh, darling, I think I will make my bed and do some dreaming now. The time is nearly one o'clock in the morning.

God bless, and hope to see you soon.

Your very own, Nina

---

9 Friday BRITISH GO FORWARD British and Canadian troops are continuing to make progress, against Rommel, whose reserves are now in action along the whole Front in Normandy.

Officers' Mess, RAF Station Foulsham, Norfolk
7th June, 1944 Still SSQ

Nina dear,

Where have your letters gone to? Are you well, darling, or has something gone wrong either with you or at home? I received your two packets of cigarettes this morning and thank you, Nina. I knew you wouldn't forget. I tried to imagine you handing them to me but there was no gentle hand to take in mine and feel reassured by its touch. Oh for a letter from you, my darling. Perhaps 'D' Day has put a spoke in our wheel. I also received a letter from Pauline this morning and my laundry from Wheaton. The letter brought a feeling of anger to me and a sense of frustration. I know I shouldn't feel that way, Nina, but you know, don't you, how much happier I am with you and how thankful that I am that certain fatal plans were not put into operation. When all my thoughts are of you and my love for you, this letter came like a blot on a beautiful landscape.

I have been reading a lot these past few days (there is nothing else to do) and a lot of the things I have wanted to write down and let you share them too. The moment I think of something beautiful or read a page that is full of meaning and beauty I want to turn to you. I think to myself: 'I know she would feel the way I do about it, the beauty of it would appeal to her too'. So often I try to get my feelings over to you and even though we are parted in the flesh somehow I think I succeed because for a moment the pain eases and for a brief moment the loneliness is gone.

Well, things have been happening in the past half an hour or so and I have got some more mail, but, oh Nina, still none from you. I had a card from the Station Hotel confirming my room for the 18th and 19th. Thank you, Nina. A letter from my bank telling me I am now a Flight-Lieutenant, and, oh dear, another one from Pauline. God, Nina, this is indeed a bitter trick on the part of Fate. I am really worried about you, my darling. I know that if I get on the telephone tonight I shall not be able to contact you. Life certainly seems to be running in one of those dark valleys right now. Very seldom does my spirit run at a so-called 'happy-medium'. I am happy with you and nobody can hope to reach the cloud-capped heights that we attain. Neither can anybody descend into our darkest valleys and we must walk then alone but never forgetting to look up. There is always the thought that on being down any further vertical movement can only take you up. Tomorrow – a letter, on Monday – your lips. D.V.

Although my head is still swathed in bandages I am going to ask the MO if I may go on Leave on Monday as I've arranged. I am practically sure it will be OK, but any adverse decision will require frantic telegrams. Talking of telegrams, there is something I should explain. I've found out today that you probably received two telling you of my retirement from service life into the confines of SSQ. Explanation: I sent one, F/Sgt Foster, the other of course, neither of us knew the other's intentions and as he has gone on Leave now I was in the dark until this morning. This is in danger of becoming complicated so I think I will elaborate when I see you, Nina. I'm sorry it occurred.

You know, darling, if only I could satisfy myself that you were not ill or in any kind of trouble I shouldn't worry so much. If you don't write I know you have a good reason and I trust that reason implicitly. Believe me, I have never pinned my faith on any one so much before. After all, when I look at your message on your photographs I know I have no reason to worry about us. You ask me to take care of your heart and in turn you have mine. It's very simple really. But if you were in trouble I want to be the first one at your side to help.

Enough of this worrying, though. Do I trouble you unduly, darling? Forgive me if I do, but I think it's excusable when I confirm once again that you are the only person I have in this world. The only one I can turn to and hope to have my thoughts and feelings understood. God bless you for it Nina.

In just under two hours from now it will be nine o'clock and for a few moments my spirit will walk with yours through the churchyard, into the peace of the darkened church and we shall pray together once more. I'll say 'thank you' first this time, Nina.

There's a kiss for you down the bottom of the page in the right hand corner, and a heart full of love wanting for you in my breast.

Your devoted

Vic xxxxx

Xxx

My Nina, my darling xxx

A letter!!! Oh Nina, can you realise how much I've wanted it? Do you know how heavy my poor heart has been these past few days? But that's all gone now. Out of the valley into the sunshine and once again I can see those cloudy peaks above me. Soon, soon, my Nina, we shall be there together. And the last words on the bottom of the first page, 'and Vic – I love you'. Joy, oh joy unbounded!!

My darling, I will be with you just as fast as the train can carry me and I hope it will be on Monday. So far the Doc won't make any promises and he says I may have to see an Ear, Nose and Throat Specialist which is a day's job at least. But I refuse to be pessimistic and am waiting hopefully for his permission to put in my Pass.

Nina, were you alone in the lane from Gnosall? Are you ever really alone, my dear? I doubt it, for always, during the day and often during my dreams, my spirit wings its way to you. My lips still demand your all and they are always willing to give as much in exchange.

Last Friday, when I was speaking to you, I felt pretty desperate. To hear your voice in my ear, so near and yet – so far. Somewhere your lips were speaking those words, (Two very kissable lips) and with those lips all of Nina that I have come to love and worship and call – mine. I wanted to say 'I love you' but the phone was slap bang in the middle of the Mess and I'm afraid I'm a bit shy, darling. But you knew it, didn't you? You must know that I'll love you always. What a lucky fellow Vic Hermolle is to be able to play tennis with you! I'd give a large portion of my allotted span of life for that pleasure now. But soon, Nina ....

Your work of magic, the result of your delving into the mystic depths of the unknown, those two arm bands are now performing their allotted task. Namely, keeping my 'shoit' sleeves up. I put a kiss on each of them for I felt certain you must have done the same. Incidentally, if ever the elastic is required for 'urgent reasons' in the future at any time, I will relinquish same without batting an eyelid. Only to you, of course. The great Vinnellske, I'm afraid, has now procured a steed, appropriately named 'The Flying Bedstead', which cramps his dramatic style no small amount. In fact, it doesn't even approach old 'DEF 30'. I wonder who's riding that bicycle now, Nina. Do you ever see it around!

Darling, you must believe that your letters DO carry your love to me. I feel that I cannot express myself fully in my letters and I guess we both feel that written words or even any words, written or spoken, can never hope to come near the full expression of our love. It will always be thus. But we have beautiful, never-to-be-forgotten memories. We have given ourselves completely to one another, an act which I honour and cherish above all else, an act which makes me for ever your Vic and you for ever my Nina. Remember this, my dear, and always have faith in it. Please know that you can never lose me and that covers all circumstances. I'm glad of that indestructible bond, Nina. We always said it would be all or nothing, didn't we? Thank God it was all.

Nina, there is just one complication I have thought about in case I cannot get away from Sick Quarters in time for Monday. I cannot write to the 'Station' for the obvious reason that my writing will not coincide with that of my last letter. Get me? Therefore if I have to let you know I cannot make it will you contact them and make necessary cancellations and re-booking if any. You see darling, I don't want any trouble to arise from that 'billet dous' you sent to Mr Smythe.

And now, Nina, as they will be interrupting me with my feeding trough any moment I'll bid you au revoir. I'm crossing my fingers oh so hard for Monday and say Fortune smiles on us. Pensby, here we come.

All my love to you, dearest one,

Your one and only

Vic xxx xxx xxx

SHQ (Sunday Morning) 11th June, 1944

My Dearest Vic,

Welcome to Stafford! This is to greet you upon your arrival here, but I promise to do the job much more thoroughly when I am in your arms and your lips on mine. Congratulations too, Vic, on your Flight Lieu! I hope it is in order to address you as such now, but at least I shall during your stay under Mr Smythe's roof. When you twirl that fair moustache and flash those rings in his eye, he will be as meek as a lamb to do your bidding. I am not sure that

I shan't be too. Don't overwhelm me too much, will you, darling? Let me feel that I still have some shreds of will-power left, however feeble and ineffectual they may be.

It is strange that if ever I ask you a question in one of my letters it always seems to be answered in your next letter, long before receipt of my original letter containing the query. Have you noticed that? So if ever you suddenly get a letter from me with a question you have already answered in a previous one, just ignore it, will you? It is just my lack of faith in this telepathy business.

In the post yesterday morning was a very bulky package from my mother, which upon viewing its contents caused me to give a whoop of delight. We have waited for these, Vic, for over two months – six little ones and one big one. The coloured miniature has still to come. Oh, by the way, I am talking about photographs, perhaps you guessed. I just can't tell you how much I like them, darling; they just couldn't be better. Your dimple has come out beautifully. I'll bring them with me on Monday evening. There has been no telegram from you so far, so I am taking it that our arrangements stand.

I had a bit of a panic in this connection, Vic, when Hobby announced a couple of days ago that every Monday and Thursday there was to be a lecture on Orderly Room Procedure, etc. and that all Headquarters staff must attend, commencing next Monday … ??? .. ? - ? However, Hobby and I are getting so fond of each other now that, when I asked him about it, he said he didn't want to cause any hardship and yes, I could be absent on Monday. I don't know what he is going to say when he knows that I will be absent on Thursday too on day off, because it is principally for my benefit, and a few others who still have not attained the exalted LACW rank.

I am thinking that I might be able to wangle that extra day this week, after all. You see, I was detailed yesterday for a 'Salute the Soldier' Parade at Penkridge, and so this week I haven't had a day off at all. I think I might make a judicious mention of this to my friend Hobby. You never know, he might play. 'Hope springs eternal in the human breast …..'

The 'Spreadeagles Hotel' was looking very well, Vic, and also Cuttlestone Bridge. I saw them yesterday on our journey to and from Penkridge for the first time since we bade them adieu for a while together. They looked a little wistful, I thought, but the next time I see them they'll smile, gladly – and so shall I. I left the Camp at 17.00 hours, along with 29 other WAAF and 40 airmen in buses. There was a very long march, in the course of which I was touched quite often by a lot of grubby little fingers. There were also a few sniffs from some women with folded arms at their garden gates, and some rather strong criticism of the WAAF as a whole. However, we survived! – and then, at the end of it there were some very long speeches by the village schoolmaster and the vicar and the local politician, in the middle of which one of the ATS girls fainted, falling with a heavy smack on her face. She had to be taken to hospital, her face was so badly cut. Then, not to be outdone, one of the WAAF fainted. She soon recovered though and marched with us back to the Church Hall for refreshments, served by the WRVS.

I have had an egg too this morning, although it probably didn't taste as nice as yours did. Do you think we could get any more eggs from Dan to take home? He came in here one day recently and asked if I had heard from you.

I have just taken another peep at your photograph, and I study every line and contour and expression. No wonder I love you, darling. You seem such a strange mixture of strength and tenderness, of power in reserve, and kindliness and humour.

There is some work to be done, I see – so I will bring this letter to a close.

Till your flesh joins forces with your spirit, - (that will be only till tomorrow)

I am – always,

Your Nina

PS And here are the lines you wanted:

    '*When in disgrace with Fortune and men's eyes,*

    I all alone beweep my outcast state,

    And trouble deaf heaven with my bootless cries,

    And look upon myself, and curse my fate,

    Wishing me like to one more rich in hope,

    Featured this man's art and that man's scope,

    With what I most enjoy contented least;

    Yet in these thoughts myself almost despising –

    Haply I think on thee: and then my state,

    Like to the Lark at break of day arising

    From sullen earth, sings hymns at Heaven's gate;

> For thy sweet love rememb'red such wealth brings
> That then I scorn to change my state with Kings.'
>
> **PPS** An extract from 'The Loving Spirit':
>
> *'Someone who knew that restlessness came from a rebellious mind, that fancied loneliness was the outcome of an awakening heart, that sleeplessness was due to the hunger of instinct, that dreams were the prelude to fulfilment, that fear was the tremor of a spirit craving completion.'*
>
> Restlessness? Vic – loneliness? Sleeplessness? Dreams? And fear that we may lose what we love most? Do any of these find any echo in your heart, darling?

12 Monday Vic has arrived! Talk together on the phone at 7pm and in the lounge of Station Hotel for a long time, and then have dinner. Never before seen anyone quite so glad to see me!

13 Tuesday Divisions Parade – in the rain! What could be more inspiring! Everyone's hair down their backs – mine included. Return to SHQ after Parade to rectify damage. Darn and mend. Vic calls at office during the afternoon. Meet him on 6.30 bus (only just squeezed on) to Stafford. Dinner at Station Hotel, then go a walk across the fields to the castle on the hill. Wallow in the sense of freedom – the wind in my hair, and Vic's voice in my ear.

14 Wednesday Meet Vic at Station Hotel where we have tea. 5.29 train to Liverpool. Home at 8.20! Introductions over, it seems that Vic belongs. Show him round garden and house. Nunk not well and in bed.

15 Thursday Letter No. 222 from Bill and postcard of Bombay. Day off. Vic up first. Go shopping after breakfast and (thanks to Vic) acquire some tomatoes – Mum's first this year. Also buy her some roses. Go a long walk through Irby, Thursaston, Heswall, and bus back home for dinner. Not a sound to disturb peace of country lanes, and walk across the fields without encountering a soul. Only uniform in Heswall! Mum plays the piano while I iron, and then comes to Liverpool to see us off.

16 Friday Phone call from Vic from Mess. Send birthday card to Mum with a note enclosed. Bus to Stafford and meet Vic at Hotel where we have dinner.

Sit in lounge afterwards and talk, oblivious to everyone and everything else except ourselves. A golden haze surrounds us. Raining, so Vic becomes a modern Walter Raleigh (in spite of onlookers). Au revoir to LIFE - !

---

17 Saturday 'PILOTLESS' ATTACK MAY NOT LAST At least three people were killed and several badly injured by a pilotless plane which crashed on some houses in Southern England during the first of two attacks last night. Houses were wrecked and an adjoining shopping centre was considerably damaged. Before it crashed, the plane was seen streaking across the sky with AA shots bursting around. Then it died and there was a terrific explosion.

In their mad quest for both a military novelty and a substitute for the Luftwaffe, it is believed, from the nature of the pilotless planes used against this country, that the Germans have prejudiced other forms of vital war production to produce these weapons. They are extremely costly **devices**, and have absorbed many thousands of man-hours, both in their production and in their launching.'

LUFTWAFFE TOLD 'DIE FIGHTING' Goring has issued an appeal to the Luftwaffe to go all out to smash the invasion which, if it succeeds, 'will mean the death of the German people'. He warns his men that the Allied air challenge must be accepted. 'If, at the end, our Luftwaffe be smashed to pieces to gain our victory our sacrifices will have been worthwhile', he says.

Saturday morning 17.6.44

My Own Vic, xxx xxx xx x

I have missed you today, and oh, how I missed you tonight. I have been trying to imagine what you will be doing and where you will be, but you have now passed beyond the things that I can share in, into another world in which I have no part. This is one of the last of our unshared interests, and I am hoping that even this will have vanished by the next time you write. Poor darling, it is not going to be very nice for you, I know that. I hate 'rows' and any sort of unpleasantness too. That is why I wouldn't let you do it until it was really necessary, and now, Vic, it is absolutely essential. Bear up, Vic, and don't mind too much what they say, because they can't hurt us whatever happens, nor can they touch any of the lovely things that lie buried deep in our hearts for all time. Pull our love around you, and wear it with confidence. It won't fail you, my Vic, it is indestructible.

'Wanting you, every day I am wanting you.' A voice has just broken into my thoughts with the words of this song. Dear heart, I don't think I really kissed you last night. Did you realise that? – except for those we stole upstairs in the Hotel Lounge. I know I wanted you then, almost as much as I want you now. I know that your thoughts are with me, I know that your heart belongs to me, but these are not enough for my poor human needs. I am hungering for your touch and your nearness. I want to feast my eyes upon you, with our faces nearly touching and your breath merging into mine and your eyes ablaze, as we did last night. I can remember nothing of that bus-ride back to Camp after I left you – nothing, except that I had been drained of all feeling, all sense, all emotion. My body was an empty shell, out of which my eyes looked unseeingly. Something had left it; the part that made it work had gone. Now all I have is the ache, a dull gnawing ache. I can't do this very often, Vic darling, not voluntarily. I love you, and the roots of my love go deep, and to pluck you from my side every six weeks, or so is like a major amputation without an anaesthetic.

Sunday afternoon

You will see from the above that I have been reading your book. I haven't got very far with it yet, but it is very absorbing. I will send you 'The Loving Spirit' tomorrow, as the Post Office does not open today. Parcels take two days, don't they?

Your voice has just reached me from London. I knew it was you, darling, even before you spoke, and the note of triumph didn't escape me. You are now a free man, free to pursue the dictates of your heart, free to 'navigate' your own 'course' to the desired 'target'. I wonder did you have no feelings of regret? How long will it be before I can say: 'Vic, I too am a free woman now, but please ask me to wear your chain'? I hope that I shall have as much good luck as you, in that the whole transaction ran smoothly. It seems amazing to me; there must be a snag somewhere. How about your aunt? Your father? Her mother? Have they all been told, I wonder, or just Pauline? Oh, I shall know the answers to all my questions when the time comes, and I am dying for your letter to come. Please tell me that Pauline didn't mind too much. It would make me feel so much better. Yet I can't understand why she couldn't mind a lot. I should, gosh, yes.

Monday pm

Vic Darling,

Just one more thing I remembered during last night – those socks of yours that require darning! Do please send them. There was no letter from you this morning, so I must possess myself in patience till another day has dawned.

You will be on your way back to Foulsham now I suppose, and your glorious long-awaited seven days' Leave is behind you. I hope it was all you wanted it to be – and more, if possible. There is another seven days' Leave in front of us, don't forget, Vic, dearest, and that is going to be even more wonderful than the last. It will be like that with our life together too; each successive tomorrow will surpass even the breathtaking glory of each yesterday, and so we'll go on, from strength to strength.

Here's something that will make you laugh, Vic. The MO fell off his bicycle yesterday and broke his wrist!!!! ...... !!!

I hear today that it is very unlikely that Leave will commence before next 4th Sept. as everyone has so much Leave due to them that a quarter of the Air Force would have to be on Leave in the next three months to get it in this Leave year.

Lots of love, darling.

And lots of these xxxxxxxxxxxxxxxxxxxxxxxxxxxxxx till I can give them to you personally.

Always, Your Nina.

PS I love you, Vic.

Wings Club, 11 Grosvenor Place SW1
Saturday evening

My own darling,

London has greeted me, welcoming me home with about five alerts in less than seven hours. There seems to be a war on at this end of England.

I made one mistake in the above paragraph. Substitute 'back' for 'home'. London is no more my home now than the North Pole and I'm glad of the fact. After lunch I took a bus ride to see Dad. I thought that he would at least be glad to see me for after all I am his only son and heir. But I thought he was more put out by the fact that I had walked in just as he was going out to witness a local bowling match. Rather different from the welcome I received from mother, wasn't it? He made no enquiries about my ear or reference to the fact that I had been in hospital for a week. There was no attempt to enquire if I liked my new posting or what I was doing now. Perhaps I am wrong in expecting him to be so interested in me but I didn't reckon on such a cool reception. Nina, my home now is Pensby when you are there, in fact, my home is right in your heart. I live in and for the things we do together depending entirely on you for all my future happiness. I am not going to waste time or energy on sorrowing about what was my home. Suffice it to say that my home is with you and wherever we choose to build it I know it will be complete and happy.

I am meeting Pauline tomorrow morning to break the glad tidings of great joy to her. I hope to be able to write on Monday and tell you I am a free man again. Free in as much as that old mistake has been rectified, but I have belonged to you for a long time now and have been possessed by you completely.

Such a happy feeling to be loved by the one you love! I know that I am a better man now than when I first walked with you. No, I don't mean that I was ever bad, Nina, what I mean is that I am improved. We have indeed delved deeply into life and the great extremes of sheer happiness and dark despair all help to mould your character in the way that it should go.

London has brought with it loneliness, Nina. I promised you I wouldn't worry and I'm not, for I have your pledge and I know now that your faith in me is complete. But oh darling, I can't help being lonely. Last night as I sat beside you, drinking in every light and shadow on your face, I found it difficult to hold back the tears that came into my eyes. I don't think I've ever seen you looking more beautiful, Nina, your eyes and lips were soft and full of your love for me, and the suspicion of a tear in each eye made them glisten like stars. I'll carry that picture with me 'til we meet again, dear, and it will bring me comfort in my great loneliness. I always knew you were very lovely but in this last week I have seen your true beauty revealed in all its glory. You are indeed the most beautiful thing on earth, ma cherie, so beautiful that I could cry at my own poor efforts to express my appreciation. Who am I to love someone so lovely as yourself? But love you I do and with every ounce of strength and life that I have in me.

On Thursday, when I saw you dressed and ready to go out, I felt suddenly shabby and conscious of my own shortcomings. Here indeed was a goddess! But after a moment I realised that your love for me was as great as my love for you. What right had I, then, to make myself out as shabby? No, indeed, it could not be so. Rather was I a god to walk beside you for had I not been caressed by those fair hands? Those tender lips had clung to mine in life-giving kisses and that fair body had mingled its life-giving warmth with mine. Because of you, dear Nina, I am immortal.

I hope that this letter will reach you on Monday and on Tuesday I am hoping to hear your voice. Your voice and your letters will be like guiding beacons in the lonely darkness of these next few weeks. Keep the beacons burning, my darling.

Your lover for ever and a day,

Vic xxx xxx xxx

Wings Club, 11 Grosvenor Place SW1
Sunday afternoon

My beloved,

Now I am free. The offending article of jewellery is safely tucked away in my pocket right now and I am yours for the taking. I am not trying to make it sound easy, darling, for it was not. No, I had no signs of weakness for I love you far too much for that. But the words didn't seem to come out in the right sequence and I was not helped by a sudden burst of heavy gunfire which interrupted my story at the crucial point and caused us to make a hasty dash for shelter. I finally managed to tell the story coherently and Pauline agreed that there was nothing for it but the return of the ring. She was not happy about it, Nina, but rather a little heartache now than repercussions all through life. We have decided to tell everyone that it was broken by mutual consent. I didn't wish her to be pitied, although I am willing to take full blame if necessary. God! I sweated blood this morning but all the time I had the support of your love for me, Nina. How I wish I was back with you again. I wanted to be safe inside that cosy love nest that you build about me with your love. Right now a smile from those lips would bring warmth and sunshine into my heart. I am lonely without you, Nina, very lonely indeed. I am glad that I'm free at last, free to ask you just once again to marry me when the time is ripe. Now you know I belong to you alone, and soon you will be free too so that we can both tread the common path – our destiny, our life together.

The day is hot and stifling in London and I am yearning for Pensby with the fields and the river, with the mountains as a background. And most important of all I am yearning for you, my beloved, you who makes all the beauty so easy to see. Will you snuggle under my arm, Nina? Shall we walk across the fields together and wander slowly back home for tea with Mum? We have seven whole days together and the world seems a very good place in spite of all its shortcomings. Our nine o'clock will be spent in each other's arms, and we shall be at the top of the cloud-capped mountains. We have seven whole days in which to love and forget the heartaches of parting.

And then I hear that orchestra thunder forth a base chord. I shake my head, blink my eyes and find I am in London – alone. My heart sinks to the depths with those low, trembling notes and I realise that I am still lonely, as I am doomed to be for the next six weeks. All my instincts tell me to go to you to find balm for a tormented heart and soul, to find once again safety, contentment and understanding that your love for me has brought. But I must resist. Instead, I am going to Church tonight to ask His blessing for us both and to ask that we may soon find the only complete way of expressing our love for each other – marriage.

You know, Nina, I was thinking this afternoon of cases where men have been badly injured and maimed and they have sacrificed the company of the one thing they love most because they would feel an unnecessary burden. Morbid thoughts, perhaps, but the more I thought of it the more certain I became that if anything ever happened to me I could never leave you. I don't think I would have the strength to be that noble. As I want you now so I shall always want you – come rain, come shine.

Nina, you said I could alter your relationship from 'friend' to 'fiancee' on my next of kin form. Please write that once again so that I may be certain my poor ears did not deceive me and I'll go straight away and do it.

I have your toothpaste still with me; in the mixed emotions of Friday evening I forgot to give it to you. I will send it on with some 'Imperial Leather' and some – socks!! Almost blackmail, isn't it, Nina?

Au revoir until Tuesday at nine, darling, when if Fate is kind, I shall hear your voice.

Entirely your own,

Vic xxx xxx xxx

Tuesday night 20.6.'44

My Own Vic,

Tonight I have spoken to you, but you won't have heard one half of what I said – just the same, I suppose, as I have heard but a fraction of what you were trying to tell me! I have been thinking so much today of what I wanted to say to you, but it was useless to attempt anything more ambitious than a few simple sentences. I doubt even if you heard me say 'I love you, darling', followed by some kisses, just before I rang off. Did you hear that, Vic? Oh Vic, Vic, isn't it disappointing? Somewhere on the end of that line were your lips framing the words I was dying to hear, and all I could do was stand there helplessly, whilst the barest whisper of your voice came through, like the echo of a half-remembered dream. Instead of feeling elated, happy, I am only left with a feeling of frustration. It takes so much effort to hear but one word of what the other is saying that it only serves to accentuate the terrific gulf that now stretches between us. Lover, come back to me. Was it only a few short days ago that we were so happy? Oh, I remember the keen pleasure I felt at seeing you again after an absence of four weeks. It was like a river, that has been dammed up for so long, running swiftly again on its course and overflowing its banks, the cool feel of it, the playful rippling edges, the hot turgid torrents and the strong pull of the tide. Oh darling, I feel so lost without you. You have taken away everything but the shell of mere existence. Vic, give me Life in all its entirety. There is only you can do it. Xxx

Wednesday

I am not sure even now whether you said there would be a parcel for me tomorrow or whether you said you were sending it tomorrow. However, I have been to the Post Office and there doesn't seem to be one so you must be just sending it. At long last, darling, I was able to make out that word 'shampoo' which you say the parcel will contain. I am so sorry, Vic, to appear so stupid, but honestly it was a tremendous effort to hear just an odd word here and there. I could have sobbed with the excitement of hearing your voice, the voice of the man I love, and then for the words to become just an unintelligible blur across the mists of space.

There wasn't time last night for me to finish this letter, Vic, after speaking to you, and I hoped to be able to finish this in time for this afternoon to post, but the opportunity didn't present itself. So here I am in bed again writing to you, and loving you and longing for you.

A great lump came into my throat, my dearest, when I read the first of the two letters from you written on Saturday last. I could have cried for you. How could your father treat you so? I feel I have so much to make up for you, Vic, all those years of love of which you have been deprived, yet I know I have so much love to give you – more than enough to cover even your capacious requirements. Oh, the years are stretching ahead of us both, lovely golden years of happiness and love and laughter and life – together! That magic word! Meaning only Vic and me, for always. Make me your home, Vic; you'd do me an honour. I'll be your mother, your father, brother and sister, friend, sweetheart, companion – and wife. Yes, oh yes, I have sufficient love in my heart for you, to cover all this – aye, and more. I love to hear you say you find me not displeasing to look at, because such beauty as I possess is all for you. I think you put it there, because I know I wasn't beautiful before. Perhaps you caught a glimpse of the spirit inside me, the loving spirit that can never die and which will go on living when this body is dust. Your spirit and mine, Vic. We have started something, you and I, that will have repercussions a thousand years hence. We can never lose each other now because we love truly, as God meant us, and so we are immortal.

Are you quite sure, Vic, that you want to lose that freedom so lately acquired? Don't you want to enjoy it a little first? – before it is taken away from you again? But perhaps you think of it as I do – that it is only when we are apart, that we wear chains, that our lives are aimless and unimportant – free? – yes, I suppose so, but with no meaning or purpose. Together, we find a true expression of ourselves, and surely that is freedom in its widest fullest sense.

Vic, I have an idea. I promised you, didn't I, that in every letter I wrote to you I'd reassure you of my love. And I think that if our 'nine o'clock' trysts could take a definite form so that we'd each know for one short minute during each day exactly what the other was doing, it would help us to feel more one during this separation. I am going to say 'I love you, Vic darling' and I'll keep on repeating it as long as I can, in the hope that the wind will be blowing from the north west to pick up my message and whisper it in your ear. And every time the wind caresses my cheeks and lifts my hair, I'll think you have answered the call of Your Goddess.

Nina xxxxxxxxxxxxxxxxxxxxxxxxxxxxxx

Officers' Mess, RAF Station Foulsham, Norfolk
20th June, 1944

Nina, my own xxx,

Life can be very unkind at times, can't it? There were so many things I wanted to say to you this evening on the phone and we finish up with a duff line. Even when it was changed the results were not much better. When I had rung off the steward showed me a coin phone tucked away in a dark passage in the Mess completely enclosed in a box. There is no need for me in future to put my calls through PBX. If fortune is kind on Friday I'll phone from that box with, I hope, better results.

First and foremost, Nina, I want to say, I love you, love you with all my heart. But above all I want to give you all the tenderness that goes with my love for you. I want to hold you close to my heart and kiss you to our cloud-capped mountain peak, to that dizzy height that sets our spirits free and gives us untold happiness.

My stay in London, short though it was, was too long for me. But I achieved what I set out to do. Namely, to gain my legal freedom. I have always belonged to you, my darling, with my heart, soul and body and of that fact there has never been any doubt. But one has to show the world that or it will never be accepted. Now I have cut my last bond with Pauline, not a difficult thing really for it was but a material one, a piece of jewellery with none of the fine backing that our love could give and will give to that plain gold band that you will wear, and I hope we have mentioned the name Pauline for the last time. Believe me, dear Nina, that I am happy in my freedom and my new power to be able to make you my wife when you say – 'Yes, Vic'. With your pledge safely tucked away in my heart and the knowledge that your faith in me is now unshakeable I will keep my promise not to worry. I have complete confidence that you will to quote my photo, 'take care of my happiness'. But I cannot help feeling lonely, Nina. When every fibre of my body calls for you how can I help but feel lonely. Only the touch of your hand can restore my complete happiness and your whispered 'I love you, Vic' take me out of the valley to soar up, up to those heights.

London was lonely and stifling. I wandered through St. James Park, down the Mall to the Palace. I walked my lonely way into Hyde Park, through Piccadilly, down Oxford Street. It hurt, Nina, hurt like hell, but I would accept no man's company. I walked with a spirit. I walked with Nina pace again. Why oh why must we ever be parted! My lips have often said: 'Don't ever leave me, Nina', but really the cry is from my heart. Don't ever leave me, please, please never leave me, Nina. Don't ever say to yourself 'will he always love me like this', believe and trust as you have always done and know that deep down in my heart is a yearning for you that words can never express. No matter what the world may say or do, remember that to me you are like the very essence of life, my life-blood, my all.

On Monday morning I walked into Peter R's and bought some 'Imperial Leather' and on looking round saw some shampoos so I thought that my lady's eyes would indeed sparkle on receiving them and forthwith bought two packets (four shampoos). I think 'Camomile' is the correct shade. I had a letter from Peter's wife waiting for me on return. She says thank you for the Polyfoto and also for my offer to be of any assistance during Peter's absence.

Tomorrow I am going to write to Mum. I know you won't mind me sharing her with you, will you darling? I can still hear her 'God bless you' as we pulled away from the platform and I remember thinking as we sat side by side in the train, 'God has indeed blessed me'. I will cherish you always, Nina, the richest gift a man could receive.

When my promotion came through I knew it wouldn't be long before some crafty little job came my way. It has. I'm squadron censor. You know, the bloke who sits with another person's letter in one hand, a huge pair of scissors in the other, and a sadistic gleam in his eye. A nice boy like me, too. No, actually it's not as bad as that. I have a choice of sixteen 'bods' to do the job for me and I only see that it is carried out and handled properly.

And now, darling, I'll weave my way to my lonely bed. My feet are cold but for the present I'll just have to grin and bear it, one day, Nina, you can provide the remedy.

God bless you, dearest, and keep you for me.

All my love,

Vic xxx xxx xxx

Officers' Mess, RAF Station Foulsham, Norfolk
22nd June, 1944 Thursday evening

My own darling,

Your parcel arrived yesterday and now I am well on my way through 'The Loving Spirit'. I like it, Nina. Janet could easily be you with her love of natural beauty but Thomas is never me. Perhaps Joseph is Vic but thank goodness Vic will be you husband, it saves complications, doesn't it?

I was at Stafford this afternoon, Nina, but I could not catch the bus out to Wheaton, not without splattering myself all over the roadway. So in spite of my urge to come to you I decided you would rather have me in one piece in a few week's time.

Darling, you say I passed into a world in which you have no interests when I left you, that I had something in which you cannot share. No Nina, because I have no interests in that world either and now I have put that behind me. Whatever other people's opinions may be I care nothing. I have been faithful to you and I have to mine own self been true. I love you with all my heart and I honour and cherish you above all else in this world. When I fell in love with you I was determined that nothing should stand in our way, that no obstacles should hold up our journey together. Well, Nina, I've cleared them. I'm free and I'm happy. I believe that my faith in our future will be an inspiration to you when the time comes. I'm hearing you say 'I WILL marry you, Vic'. I can hear you saying it now, Nina, and it brings joy to my heart. That a woman so beautiful as yourself should belong to me makes me feel very humble indeed and very thankful too. You are right, Nina, they cannot touch us, our love is a shield against the cruellest tongue.

Poor darling, that you should suffer such agonies of loneliness. Yes, I have suffered too, Nina, and I will do so until we can be together again but it hurts to think that you must feel the pain too. But you must feel this way about me, Nina. I feel that no matter where I go or what I do I can never be completely happy unless I am with you. That is a simple fact which will not be denied. You are my compliment, you make me one hundred per cent and I know that I serve you in the same way.

You hope that my Leave was all I wanted it to be. Nina, what I wanted was you all to myself for the whole seven days. You and the fields and the sky. You and mum and Pensby and – and – oh darling you know the thousand and one things that my heart clamours for. Nina; that one name, that one person with her love for me fills all my requirements. Darling, I was thankful that I was granted those few precious hours with you. You must have seen how much I needed you, how much I longed for you. I was ill, Nina, sick of spirit and it was affecting my body. But like a soothing hand came your pledge. Your reassurances and your kisses quietened my fears. I daren't think of losing you and yet I feared it. Now I am confident. I am free and waiting for you, my Nina, my life. I feel at rest with the world because I have done what I know to be the right thing, in being true to our love I have been true to myself. A clear conscience is one of the greatest assets a man can have.

Well, Nina, worldly news is scarce. At least, I'm doing lots but it must remain forever a dark secret. I am looking forward to tomorrow night at nine and I'm praying that I won't be flying. I have a feeling we shall be luckier this time. Goodnight, beloved, and God bless you.

Your lover,

Vic xxx xxx xxx

'For thy sweet love remembered, such wealth brings,

That then I would not change my State with Kings.'

I love you, my Nina   Xxx

Sunday lunch-time

Sweetheart o'Mine,

I am terribly sorry that I didn't speak to you on Friday evening as we had arranged in our previous phone conversation, and I do hope that you received my telegram in time to save further worry and disappointment.

As you know, I wanted to make arrangements with my friend, Pauline, to go with her to visit a friend of hers just back from France and in a Hospital at Tean. She didn't know the way and didn't want to go alone, so I asked for my day off to coincide with hers – unfortunately clashing with the time of our talk. Please don't begin to worry or wonder; believe in me, darling, and I am looking forward to speaking to you tonight so much.

There was quite a good film on in Stafford on Friday night called 'The Sullivans', which is supposed to be the true story of a family who lost five sons at once, because they refused to be parted, and served together on the same ship which was sunk. It is very sad, yet full of ordinary everyday occurrences which make one laugh in spite of the tears. I liked the way the father and mother handled the more difficult of children's problems; what they didn't know about child psychology wouldn't be worth knowing. If ever little Victor is discovered smoking cigarettes in secret, I know a fine way of putting a stop to it so that he'll never smoke again!

From there, Pauline and I proceeded to the Toc.H. to spend the night in a most novel way (for me) on double-decker beds. The place wasn't quite what I thought it would be, although I don't know what I expected for 1/3d per night. It reminded me vividly of the old doss-houses, as portrayed by Dickens, for tramps and vagabonds of the road. There was only one room reserved for the female of the species, a very small one at that, in which were four two-tiered beds. I was lucky in that I was consigned to a bed on the ground floor, but the intermittent rocking motion of the WAAF suspended above my head made it very difficult for me to gain a firm grip on Sleep. In the grey light of dawn, I opened my eyes and gazed about me in terror. It seemed that I was the only soul alive – all about me were hard flat slabs on which reposed a motionless body covered by a sheet, layers of hard flat slabs reaching almost to the ceiling. Then while I gazed, into my bewildered vision came a pair of dangling pink legs that dropped lower and lower until they reached the floor, the WAAF who lived on the next floor descending in the life for - . Well, I don't have to explain that, do I? ADVENTURE, Vic, ADVENTURE – I love it!

The next morning, we visited the market and I bought a fruit-set from you and me – 'With Love to Dodo and Rea on their 1st Wedding Anniversary'. I shall be taking that with me tonight when I go visiting them for the party to be held at their old place in Church Eaton (now occupied by Don and his wife since Reg's posting to Perton). They want me to go there as soon as I can get this afternoon, probably 'sixish', but I shall leave them in good time for our nine o'clock date, never fear. Besides, it will be a good excuse to get away if there is too much beer flowing.

After a coffee at Jenkinson's (very good coffee, Vic), we got the 11am bus to Uttoxeter where we had lunch; then we got the 1.30 bus to Tean, and, after a long but very lovely walk through tree-shaded lanes and past rose-covered cottages, finally reached Health House only to find the object of our visit was out till 7.30. However, the Sister showed us round the wards and grounds, etc. and we talked to some of the injured men (mostly Airborne, Commandos and French Marines), nearly all with leg wounds. We returned in a very roundabout fashion via London to Stoke for tea (more trifle) and saw another good film there: 'His Butler's Sister' with Deanna Durbin, which I can thoroughly recommend for those with a sensitive ear and a well-developed sense of humour. That means you, darling. Now, don't you think that was a very busy day? And it was a very pleasant and interesting one too.

There were four letters waiting for me on my return to Camp, one of them being yours, which bucked me up no end as I haven't heard from you for ages it seems – but on reference, the last time I heard from you was last Tuesday, when I had two. Yes, darling, I know I am greedy where your letters are concerned; they are a great weakness and I could make a real pig of myself with them. I hope we shall be able to use that coin-box in the dark passage for our meeting tonight; it may make a lot of difference not having to go through a Branch Exchange.

In this letter, you answer my question regarding your new-found freedom and your feelings about relinquishing it so soon; you answer it as so often happens without ever hearing or receiving my question. You say, you are 'happy in your freedom and your new power' – that is what I wanted to know – and now I take care of your happiness AND your freedom and everything that is for your good. Don't I, Vic? I won't leave you, my Vic, I won't leave you. How can I separate from part of myself? I hope I shall be able to take the place of that spirit the next time you walk the streets of London. How exquisite a feeling to walk at your side, with head held high, and to know that we are two complimentary units of a complete whole. I'll find out soon what it is like, although I know in some measure already. I have had a glimpse of what awaits us in the Land of Heart's Desire through the half-open door, and the vision I beheld was blinding in its beauty and caught at my breath and enveloped me. I know that what lies before me on the other side of that door will be so all-embracing, all-consuming, that I shall lose myself, and the new Man-Woman will be born, and our spirits shall be woven and interlocked for all time.

One of the other letters was from Mum, the first since our visit. I have been waiting for this. You know, Vic, that is another funny thing. I have thought all week that I'd like you to write to Mum; I know she would appreciate it, especially such letters as you would write (although I would not for the life of me have suggested it to you) and then in your next letter to me you say you HAVE written – what is this? – the age of miracles seems far from dead. And then in Mum's letter she write: 'I should have liked just a few lines from my adopted son, Vic, but I suppose he was too busy'. Amazing! – the same thought seems to go round in circles. She goes on to say: ''Vic seemed quite at home with us and I like him very much, but act wisely, Nina, and don't spoil his life'. ...'I hope Bill will take the disappointment like a man .... Marriage should never be contemplated lightly, only DEEP PURE LOVE will avail and carry us through the stress and store of life with a ONENESS in everything, then it IS 'Heaven on Earth'. I promised I'd let you know the verdict, didn't I? She's a grand person, and I admire and respect her, quite apart from the fact that she is my mother, but as she is, then of course it makes all that much difference. Believe me, Vic, she really meant that 'God bless you', just as I meant that unqualified 'Yes'.

I love you dearly, Vic, and I'll tell you so tonight, if the telephone line is kind.

Ever yours, Nina xxx xxx xx X

PS Would you like to know the sequel to the Dando-Bell 'affaire'? Edna has been posted? – up to York, not an ordinary posting at that. She is attached there, while someone from York is attached here. There are two other Accounts girls who live at York and who volunteered their names in her place, but no one other than Edna would do. Is that a glaring example of an 'arranged' posting, or not? I begin to feel we were lucky, but I wouldn't be if it weren't for you. Your good luck must cover me too now.

Officers' Mess, RAF Station Foulsham, Norfolk
24th June, 1944

Nina, my darling,

A letter from you today and I was really thankful for it. I like to receive one on Saturday for it makes the weekend seem less lonely. I am wondering how long it is taking my mail to reach you now it is going through official channels. They do say it has been speeded up. I hope so because as you told me, it is not much fun reading week old mail.

Last night I went into Norwich for the first time since I've been here. Every Friday a bus takes a party to a theatre in town where we have a couple of rows reserved. At a restaurant just a few yards from the theatre we book a room for a meal after the show and it makes a very pleasant evening. It was quite a good show last night with Leonard Henry and Charles Heslop in a musical revue. Quite funny and anyway a break from camp routine.

On Friday our 'Salute the Soldier' week started on the camp. We aim to raise £2,000. I am in a darts competition, and tomorrow evening I'm going to try my hand on the miniature rifle range. Last night there was an all-ranks dance but I chose the theatre in preference to the dance. I can't face a dance without you, Nina, and I don't intend to try.

Darling, was my voice like the echo of a half-remembered dream? No, Nina, I shall never be a half-remembered dream. My love and my body exist even though we are parted, and as I feel and as I love when I am with you, so it remains when we are parted. Except that I cannot express my love as I would and I feel frustrated.

Nina, I will give you life, life that is so full and gloriously happy that you will think the day we met was holy and that all through life we have been guided by the gods. I think we have been guided by the gods, Nina, and they have taken us to all the beautiful places in the land. After all, have they not shown us Olympus?

Nina, I long for you with a desire so strong that it will not be dismissed. I remember, as if it were but last night, our days off in Chester. Catching the train the evening before, the worry and last minute fears, the dash to the station, and the sigh of relief when we realised that it had worked out again. For the next twenty four hours we were Vic and Nina. From midnight 'til six we left this world, not knowing whether we were sleeping or waking, secure within each other's arms. It's all fresh in my memory, dear Nina, never to die. And now I say, Roll on happy wedding day, that my love for you need no longer be pent up but that I may be free to give and receive – all.

Nina, I have seen your eyes close to mine so many times since we parted. That suggestion of tears is still there making them more lovely than the stars above. I will kiss away all tears when I can hold you in my arms once again, and soothe away all the aches of a lonely heart. That shell will be filled, Nina, filled with love and life and laughter, and one day (soon I pray) you will have me back for all time and by God! It will take wild horses or more to part us. You are the only one I have in the world, Nina, the only person in whom I trust and to whom I can give my heart and know that is secure. I love you more than I have ever been able to show you as yet. When we are married and on our own then will you see what is in my heart, what I have been trying to express ever since I met you. Yours will be a love that has accumulated over the years. Some should have gone to mother, she went away. Some to my father, but he didn't seem willing to accept. Some to brothers and sisters, but there were none. And now, Nina, it's yours and no half measures. It's a big heart that I have, darling, and it's generous with its love.

I said I was going to be on the top line when I saw you next and I mean it. I have cut smoking down to four cigarettes a day and I hope to stop altogether soon. My appetite has improved and my tunic is starting to fit again. I'm getting in some cycling and tennis so you had better watch your step when we get on the court, young lady. But seriously, Nina, I got pretty run down before Leave and I'm pulling out of it now. And so I must for our altar of love will accept 'no maimed or worthless sacrifice'.

It's nearly 1am, Nina, so I'll bid you goodnight. Shall I put out the light, dear, or shall we read some more? OK then, lights out. A click; darkness. A kiss, a sigh of happiness as your arms enfold me and I pull you even closer to me, just as we planned at Wheaton, when we were in the Air Force and times seemed very troubled and hard. Goodnight, my Nina. I have battled and won you. You are my Nina forever. And I? Well, I am

Your

Vic xxx xxx xxx

Officers' Mess, RAF Station Foulsham, Norfolk
25th June, 1944

My Nina,

Sunday is dragging it's weary way towards conclusion and today I have had plenty of time on my hands to watch that second hand ticking its way towards our next leave. Plenty of time to feel lonely, Nina. Do you ever wonder that anybody could miss another person as much as I miss you? Perhaps I am right in saying that not many people attach so much importance to one person for they spread their love out over a family. But to me, Nina, you are all. I have always been a very intense person emotionally. Either I have no feelings or I place my all. You have all my love, darling, and I feel confident that is safe from all harm. With you I wear no armour-plating and for the first time in my life I feel no fear of a mortal wound, for the first time I know complete happiness and freedom. You were right, Nina, when you said that real freedom is when we are together, for it is then that our spirits find completion and are free to climb to those silvery heights. The only chains now are the chains of separation and loneliness which it seems, we shall be compelled to wear for a little while yet. But we shall throw them off one day, my dear, throw them off with a prayer of thankfulness.

8.15 Since writing the last line I have been putting in some darts practice with Bill Parker. Judging by my form I don't fancy my chances in the Station darts competition. But perhaps fortune will smile on me when the time comes. In a few minutes time I am going to put in my call to Wheaton Aston 24. Please, oh please let us have better luck this time. I live on your letters and my phone calls to you these days. A poor substitute for my Nina in the flesh but they are more than welcome during our enforced parting.

The enclosed bill I found in my old tunic as I was clearing the pockets out. I looked at it dumbfounded for a minute and then everything came back with a rush. I stared out of the window with unseeing eyes while my spirit was riding through the lanes once again – with you. You stop to pick some forget-me-nots and before we ride on again – we kiss. A gentle brush of my lips on yours and my heart skips a beat and then races like a steam hammer. I look at you and wonder at your beauty, and beside you the flowers seem confused as if suffering from an inferiority complex. We ride on. Over Cuttlestone bridge until we come to the lane through the wood. Another stop, for nature will have its way. On to the 'SpreadEagle'. A drink, a long, long talk and once again we forget the world around us as, hand in hand, we plan our future. The meal. Egg with lashings of hot chips, bread and butter. The ride home with bags of time to spare and yet we always arrived at camp in a hot, breathless state. I think we must have been held up on the way, don't you?

26th – My heart is light today, Nina. Last night I spoke to you and the line was clear, and today I have a letter from you.

Of course I understand about last Friday, my dear. I was looking forward to speaking to you but I knew when I received the telegram that there was a good reason for it. I trust you implicitly.

No Nina, I will never think things out for myself any more for now I have you to share my burdens and halve the load. I'm sorry that my thoughts should have been so morbid when I wrote that letter but they were inspired by the sight of ambulances delivering their grim loads at a hospital door. You know that things have been a bit hectic down that way. Believe me, I shall never try to be noble.

Yes, there is a vacancy on my staff for a fiancee. At least, there was, Nina. It is now filled most ably by yourself, and your recommendations – the happy times we have spent together and the prospect of a life that is complete in all respects. That magic word, Nina – together.

I went to St Paul's Cathedral on that Sunday evening and my footsteps were guided there by a memory. The memory of you and I standing beneath that massive dome and the feeling that the moment was indeed one of majesty. But the majesty of St. Paul's is not apparent when you are not there. I know we must do things together always if we are going to find real happiness, and so I sit here, waiting, knowing that I must just do my work and leave my search for real pleasure until we are TOGETHER once again. I must close now, Nina, to catch the afternoon's post, but I will write again tonight. All my love goes to you with this letter, my dear, and my hopes are high for the late summer and – Devon. I love you, my darling.

Your own,

Vic xxx xxx xxx

Officers' Mess, RAF Station Foulsham, Norfolk

27th June, 1944

Nina, my darling,

Having completed the rather dreary business of reading other people's letters, I can now turn to the other extreme and be happy in writing to you. When we said 'au revoir' in May we said we would write when we felt like it and not on certain days. A sound scheme, Nina, and yet I write a few lines to you nearly every day. You see, darling, I feel closer to you when I am writing and I find comfort in 'talking' to you. I do talk to you, in my imagination, as I write. Here you are standing beside me and I can see that smile that won its way so easily into my heart and caused me to bring you all sorts of unnecessary odds and ends to be typed, just for a smile, a cheery word, a cup of tea in 'the warmest spot on the camp'. With a smile that is brighter than the sun, and eyes more lovely than the stars above can you wonder that our friendship grew and ripened into a love that is indestructable.

I am trying hard not to worry, Nina, and in the main I am succeeding. I cannot help but feel lonely without you, and the days seem very long and the evenings seem aimless, the nights cold. Where once I used to cycle beside you through sunny lanes to Blymhill or the 'Spread Eagle' there is now just a void. The sun doesn't shine so often now and the evenings are nearly always cold and dull. Life is not the same, Nina. There is something inside me that keeps straining upwards, perhaps towards our star. I'm restless and too often unhappy. Nina, I do worry a little. I mustn't lose you or for me all is lost. Darling, do you see why I worry just a little? If a person is so terribly important, if they represent your whole life, your present and future happiness, the be all and end all of living, then surely you must feel a twinge of anxiety. Nina, I must keep you and to that end I am always on my toes.

It would be hard indeed to find words that would do justice to the hope and happiness that you have brought to me these past months. I don't remember anything before last Christmas. If I was ever happy before then, it has been completely overshadowed by the months that followed. I have been happier with you, Nina, than at any other time in my life. I have lived life to the full with you and climbed to higher peaks of happiness than I ever knew existed before I met you. Do you see why I worry just a little, Nina? I dare not lose you now, my darling, for then all would be lost.

Oh how I wish I could see you again, Nina. I wish we had never left Pensby a fortnight ago. I have a wild spirit that wanders where it will and too often it brings me unhappiness that is hard to bear. I am with you so often but my arms cannot hold you and I do need that physical contact very much.

After lunch: My darling, your letter which I have just received came like balm to a troubled, lonely heart. The confirmation of your vows was as if you knew I was worrying a little, and the news that mother has adopted me made my heart lighter. Nothing can stop us now, my darling wife. I am going to send mother the gardening book that I spoke about. I hope she will find it useful and it will always be available for us in the not-so-distant future.

I'm glad you enjoyed your day off at Tean and I am a little envious of those rose-covered cottages that received an approving glance from your eyes. Do you remember I saw half of 'His Butler's Sister' in Stafford on the Monday but in my anxiety to see you again could not sit the whole film through. I will do my best to satisfy that insatiable appetite of yours for my letters. I love writing to you, Nina, so it will not be hard.

In her letter to you mother has voiced the sentiments that we have felt for months past. 'A ONENESS in everything'. That is our complete Man-Woman, Nina. The 'Heaven on Earth' is our own cloud-topped mountain peak and she need never fear about 'spoiling my life'. You have made my life, dearest, and I thank God for it.

We cannot fail to be the happiest man and wife in the whole world, Nina, and I am looking towards our life together with eagerness and an impatience to start. I won't worry about after the war, darling, for you have given me great confidence. With you at my side the whole wide world is mine.

I love you, my Nina, and tonight at nine I am going to tell you as much even if that whole world is listening.

For all time,

Your Vic xxx xxx xxx

29 Thursday Informed that I am an LACW from 1ˢᵗ July – Hobby tells me, just like that!!! Why can't I have a Test like anyone else? But no, he wouldn't give me the satisfaction. Write letter to Vic:

479352 LACW Chessall N.
SHQ, RAF Wheaton Aston,
Little Onn, Staffs
Thursday night 29.6.'44

Vic Darling,

You are right on time lately, no waiting at all – I just walk straight into the NAAFI, and ting-a-ling, the telephone bell. A fellow beat me to it, but the call was all mine. Vic, I get terribly excited about long-distance phone calls, don't you? I get all keyed up inside, waiting for it, and look at the clock two or three times a minute, then gaze at the telephone as if willing it to ring. But last night you arranged it beautifully. Do you book your calls these days, Vic? I think you must do.

Did you say that you had received the parcel of cigarettes, Vic? Well, I find I only posted them to you on Monday night. It must have taken less than two days to reach you, which, living as you do in that far-flung corner of Britain, is mighty quick, I think. I don't really know whether I ought to encourage you to smoke, darling, especially as you are making such a valiant effort to cut it down. What do you think? I'd like to help you keep that resolve if possible, but don't be too drastic at the beginning so that it makes you miserable. After all, I suppose smoking is the lesser of all the vices. But I think that anything is a vice when done to excess. What is that quotation about 'moderation in all things'? I supposed if it could only be done in moderation so that it doesn't get out of its proper perspective. But let me know, darling, as soon as you reach the stage of 'No smoking at all', won't you? Then I shall have to find another market for my wares.

Tell me, Sweetheart, do you have much experience of these terrible flying bombs where you are stationed? It made me think of this, when I read in your letter about what prompted you to think of such grim possibilities as would make you feel 'noble' enough to leave me. And again I thought of this when you mentioned having an accident last night. I felt relieved to hear it was only on your bicycle – sorry, Vic. I shouldn't have put 'only', because you can do some pretty heavy damage in this way. I think of you such a lot, my darling. I put your face opposite to me in the mornings at breakfast and I imagine myself asking 'More coffee, darling?' or 'More bread – white or brown?' I put your face a top a cycle sometimes when I am riding my lonely way between the perfumed hedgerows, and I smile involuntarily at the tender glances we would exchange, if we could. I put my two hands around your photograph sometimes, when I am alone, and try to infuse some colour in those cheeks. I love you, my sweetheart, and I would that your likeness could come alive for me. I lay in bed at night and put your face alongside mine on the pillow and I feel the warmth of your form and the thrill of close contact. I admit it, my dear one, I am hopelessly in love with you. You stir my heart, my intellect and my sense, all these. I think that has been the trouble previously with me. I have been fond of someone, but my senses have not been touched; I have been attracted intellectually; but never before has any man ever touched my emotions, that part of me that I began to think was made of ice, and yet which so often since knowing you has been white hot with the flames of desire, least of all has any man ever combined all these attractions for me – except You. I love you, Vic, with all my heart, with all my soul and with all my strength. Now you have a three-fold pledge, and I want that to cover every department of my life and yours. Oh, my Vic, it is going to be so wonderful.

I bought some linen last night coupon-free, which has been supplied to the WAAF for dress-making classes, and I think I will endeavour to regain some of my lost art. I must get some clothes together somehow, so that I may delight the eye in some measure as well as your heart. Did you say you had a new issue of coupons, darling? Would you mind saving some, I wonder, for our next shopping orgy? I'd like to please you in every way, and how the gift is presented does matter a little bit – maybe not at all to you, darling, but only for me to satisfy the instincts of 'the eternal woman'.

I shall never cease to wonder at the complete unity we have attained of body and spirit. Do you know, Vic, you expressed in your letter an identical idea in almost identical language that I included in my letter home? I was telling mother how much I loved you, and that she need never have any fear of your love for me. I said that on me you had lavished all the love that most fellows would have expended through the years on their brothers and sisters, father and mother, and so to you I was all that – I couldn't let you go. The next morning, you express exactly the same thought and I was struck with amazement. Forgive me, Vic, but this experience is still so new to me and it is so wonderful and it has such tremendous possibilities, that it will take a time for me just to accept it. This gift is not given to everyone. Why should we have been favoured by the gods? I sometimes wonder, Vic, whether your life hasn't been marked out for something special, to be one of the chosen, to lead others? From what you have told me, you have been guided almost uncannily towards some special destiny. What it is I cannot say, but the future will reveal its secret. It won't be an easy path – I don't think it ever has been – but it will be a life of fulfilment, of self-expression, of complete obedience to that inner self without which there can be no peace, and of a sublime joy in living. Who would ask for more?

That bill from the 'Spread Eagle' Hotel and your words describing a particular beautiful episode in both our lives were the means of spilling another drop of fragrant perfume for me. I didn't think, I just closed my eyes and allowed the sweetness and the magnificence of the aroma to flow over my senses, until I was drowned in it and lost in another world. You may judge its potency, its strength, when my knees felt weak and I groped for your support, which was not forthcoming. Then my eyes flew open, another mirage. There were no arms around me, no smiling mouth, no eyes the colour of the sky. Yet I felt richer for that momentary glimpse.

Ever Yours
And All of me.
Nina

JULY

2 Sunday BOMBS HIT TWO MORE HOSPITALS Two more hospitals in southern England were among buildings hit or damaged by flying bomb blasts during Friday night and early yesterday. Seven out of 30 patients were killed when the wing of one hospital received a direct hit in the darkness. Search was still going on last night for others. Two wards were wrecked.

3 Monday Letter from Vic.

Officers' Mess, RAF Station Foulsham, Norfolk
30th June 1944

Nina, my sweet,

This is about the first time in two days that I've had the time to sit down and write a letter of any length or measure or coherence. Yes, I've actually been busy for the first time since I arrived here.

Yesterday I had lunch somewhere on the south coast and for an hour or so was able to view the briny ocean. The Mess was an old house complete with genuine oak beams and stone-flagged floor, most peaceful I thought but it could be very cold when the snow is on the ground. Today I have been away for the best part of the day on duty and so these past two days have literally and metaphorically flown.

When I got back yesterday your letter was waiting for me and if I felt a little tired when I walked into the Mess you can be sure I was soon full of the 'fail devivre' once more when I read it.

Tell me, darling, where do you find the patience to untie the knots on the parcels you receive? I usually set out to do so but I must admit that if my efforts do not meet with an early success I soon resort to a knife or a pair of scissors. I'm glad the parcel arrived intact; the only thing I am disappointed about is that, for the time being, I am unable to collect the kisses in person. Since there are forty six in all and the answer to your question, have I had enough yet, is decidedly 'No'. But the days are passing my dearest, and I'll soon be with you to show you once again that the more kisses I have the more I want.

When I post this letter in the morning I shall post another parcel to you with the socks inside. Oh yes, and some chocolate too. I thought I had better get the chocolate on its way quickly as I have a weakness for 'Fry's Chocolate Sandwich'.

I am keeping the smoking down very well, setting myself a maximum of three per day of which I smoke one after breakfast, one after lunch and one after the evening meal. I find it surprisingly easy not to smoke in between meals and as a result of cutting it out my appetite has reached almost frightening proportions. I certainly feel better and I believe I have started to put on weight, you know that feeling that your collar feels tighter today than it did yesterday. Purely imagination probably.

Nina, can I pay my share of the present you, sorry, I mean we bought for Reg and Ronnie? You always insist on forking out your share of any expenses incurred on our many happy occasions together, so won't you please tell me fifty per cent of the cost and make me happy. If only I could be with you to use my powers of persuasion. Nina, I don't think you could refuse me anything when I have my arms around you and my lips close to yours. I can say that in full confidence because I know that in those circumstances I could never say no to anything you asked.

On the table in front of me, as I write, is a vase with some flowers, the names of which I do not know. They are pink and white and the blooms are about the size of your fist. But I don't have to know the name that Man gave to them to enjoy their exquisite beauty and be thrilled by their perfume. What a pity we are not together now for I feel sure we could talk about them for hours, and if we were married we could talk ourselves up the stairs, between the sheets and so to sleep … safe in each other's arms. Oh happy wedding day! If it's possible to love you any more than I do, Nina, then I am doing so day by day. From waking in the morning until my prayers at night I see your smile (such beauty), your lips (so very tender) and your eyes (well, the stars never seem to be able to shine so brightly even when they are doing their utmost). Don't wonder if, for a minute every now and then, you are certain I am with you. I think of you so often that I believe I succeed in bridging the miles that part us and for a short while am able to slip my hand inside yours and bury my face in your hair. Xxxxxx

I love you, my Nina, love you more than life, because without you there is no life. When we are apart I just exist, flitting from the past to the future but mainly to the future because there lies all our happiness. When these mad days are behind us, when our plans are fulfilled and we can shut our front door behind us and leave this world on the other side, when we have our garden, our bicycles, our Sunday morning breakfasts on the biggest plates in the world and the picnic afterwards, then my beloved, I shall feel that at last I have started to repay you for all the joy, love, companionship and confidence that you have brought into my life by walking with me. God bless you, my sweetheart, God bless you for being … My Nina xxx

Ever yours

Vic xxxxx

Monday night 3/7/44

Vic dear,

I am just cooling down after a very hot and breathless game of rounders. Yes, you did hear right, darling, although I expected you to raise your eyebrows. The game does rather savour of the Upper Third. However, apparently Group are taking a keen interest in it so we must perchance display some sort of zeal. We must humour them a little in these things just to keep them amused. I was detailed for it, by the way. I shouldn't have minded if it had been a proper game – like tennis, for instance; but all the people I know who play tennis have been posted – Vic H, Jim Hoyland, (and Lilian has been in Sick Bay with gastric stomach), so that one-and-only game of tennis this year has never been repeated.

I do want to give you a game on your next Leave, especially since you threw out that challenge. It is going to be fun, Vic, and I think it is going to work out all right for us, don't you? in spite of our fears? How far away is it now? – only three weeks. We have got halfway already. I could hug you, in anticipation.

This just goes to prove that 'Don't worry – it may never happen' is a very good maxim to follow, and I suppose the most difficult, when one's whole future life is at stake. I know it too, my Vic. It is the mentality of everything that makes one cleave like a drowning man to a straw to those things that last. One false step, one single catastrophe, one stroke of misfortune and all one's fine dreams and hopes and ambitions could turn to dust at one's feet. If one could only be certain -! and yet, Vic, life would lose its savour, its zest, if every step were reduced to a cut-and-dried standard method of procedure. You would never be holding your breath for what was round the next corner; you would never greet the day with that wonderful 'what-have-you-got-for-me' feeling; your powers of resources could never be tested; your gift of initiative and courage and faith in the teeth of adversity would be unknown. And what would happen to your fine character? And there wouldn't be any heroes. No, it is really only a small price to pay, Vic. Let's keep it as it is, shall we?

My courage was tested quite a lot last night, oh damned elusive one. What happened, Vic? I was waiting. I was terribly disappointed and very near to tears when nothing happened. The NAAFI is such a depressing place, and I can't sit down and make conversation with stray people when you may be struggling through the ether to contact me. You might, of course, have been flying, or otherwise engaged, a (since reading your letter written on 30th June and received this morning – is that a record?) or you may even have been away from Camp. In either of these circumstances should I have been so worried as the other more likely one, that you were doing your damndest to get hold of me all the time on the other end of a telephone cable, and I couldn't do a thing to help except wait. I felt more certain than ever that things had gone wrong from this end, not yours, when I tried at 9.30 to contact the WA operator, and after a quarter of an hour I was still unsuccessful, although the line was by no means 'dead'.

Vic, what has happened to your fountain pen? I notice that this last letter is written with a finer pen, and it doesn't suit your dashing handwriting half so well. Has it gone for a Burton? This pen of mine is on the way there too, at least the nib is, but I manage with it in a fashion. Is it terribly bad to read, Vic? If it is, I'll have to resort to the typewriter, but I more often that not write to you in bed. Perhaps you have noticed already, but every time I use the blue notepaper I am writing to you from the billet, and the white notepaper I use from the office. I keep a set of stationery in each place, so as to be within easy reach of it when the spirit moves me, or the opportunity presents itself.

After such good luck with your letter this morning, I crossed my fingers in the hope that maybe your parcel of socks had also arrived.

Dodo seemed pleased too with the present, and honestly Vic, the cost was negligible. I'd tell you, really I would, if it were expensive, but I was surprised myself at the bargain. Oh, by the way, you won't leave me to buy presents always on my own, will you? Have you ever thought of the fun we could have at Xmastime going shopping for presents, and buying holly and mistletoe? Well, we wouldn't have to buy holly and mistletoe; it grows wild in the hedgerows. We'd buy all our presents together, except my present for you, and I'd keep that a big secret until the very last moment, when you found it on your very large plate at breakfast time.

Another thing I meant to report on – our roll of films. I took them to that chemists at Stafford but they were still unable to accept them. I suppose I must wait until you can attend to them personally and 'flannel' the girl behind the counter.

I am glad you are putting on a little more weight, Vic, because then it won't make my curves more noticeable by contrast. No, I have never had that feeling of being tight around the collar, but I have sometimes lately felt tight around the skirt, especially in civilian clothes.

Oh darling, o'mine, what heavenly pictures you paint – of our garden, and our home, and our bicycles, and our Sunday morning breakfasts on our enormous plates. I too am dying to start.

Nearly 'Lights Out', Vic. In the darkness I'll say 'Please God, take care of Vic and bring him safely back soon to –

His Nina

4 Tuesday Telegram from Vic. Letter from Mum. Parcel from Vic containing socks and chocolate:

My darling,

I commend the socks to your tender care. Will you send them back as soon as poss. because they are about all I have. A reward for your labours is enclosed and more letters are on the way.

I love you dearly, Nina.

Your sweetheart

Vic xxx xxx xxx X

Tuesday Night 4.7.44

Vic Darling,

This morning I received your telegram. Did they have to keep you in Sick Quarters because you had no more socks to wear? It couldn't possibly have been that you were sick again – could it? It couldn't have been, because you promised me, remember? Perhaps you have had another mishap on your cycle, which of course can't be helped. But I know that you haven't been worrying again, not so much that you have become ill through it, surely, my darling? I wish I could prevent this. I suppose you would still worry even if I said 'Yes', so long as we were parted?

Anyway, Vic, here are the socks completed and I will post them to you tomorrow. I have darned solidly for the past two hours, and now I think I'll sample a little of the reward. Mmm! – delicious. You are a real saint, Vic, to send it to me – although I had to laugh when I saw one of the corners missing. I don't want to deprive you of all your pleasures, though, my dearest – smoking and now chocolate-munching. You know, I'd much rather share it with you. It is so nice to think that we've got the same food inside each other, as we used to do, on that one day in the week when we threw the Air Force and the War to the four winds.

'Now I'll sew on my first pair of props'.

(They always put this in books to denote the passing of time, but the next paragraph usually begins with – 'Next morning they woke … etc'. Not so in this case.) For the first time since your body bade 'au revoir' to mine, I left the confines of this camp and traversed the lanes that were once the scene of so much happiness for us. Pat borrowed a cycle and we passed through Blymhill. I hardly dared look at the Church as I caught a glimpse of it through the trees. It seemed so sad and yet it was smiling at me. The rain had stopped only a short while previously and the leaves were still shedding tears. Why should sweetness and sadness seem so akin? Perhaps some moments are sadly sweet, because one must live the present to the full – God only knows what sorrow may be in store for us – so we taste and drink of the cup of happiness now, yet always conscious of that lurking shadow.

Perhaps other moments are sweetly sad, because the day of sonar has dawned, the thing we feared has come to pass, and now the ghost of Memory haunts us – the same scenes, the same visible objects, the same beauty – yet how different. Their very similarity is like a knife in an old wound.

You remember that very steep hill just after the village of Blymhill, where we sat in that sort of watchman's hut at the top opposite the farm, and looked down on the panorama of the countryside spread like a patch-work quilt beneath us? We went past there for about two miles, a totally undiscovered part of the world for me – there was no incentive to stop awhile, you see – and eventually found our way to Marston by 'The (famous) Fox'. I thoroughly enjoyed the ride, but oh! how heavy is the weight of my heart. Somewhere my Vic is calling me, and I am answering 'Here am I,

Yours, Vic, Yours – Always.

Nina

Officers' Mess,
RAF Station Foulsham, Norfolk
2nd July 1944

My own Nina,

I am in Sick Quarters once again. Just when I should be speaking to you on the phone I am laying in the same bed that I was in four weeks ago, but it's not my ear that is troubling me now. All last night I was troubled by a stomach ache, severe headache and I felt hot and feverish. I decided to report sick this morning and the Doc told me I should have come into Sick Quarters. I was greeted by a dirty big dose of castor oil which did its work so well that the pains in my stomach made me violently sick. And so this evening finds me about as strong as a new-born kitten and feeling depressed and lonely.

Oh Nina, I wish I could be with you now. I feel so hungry for your kisses and the touch of your gentle hand. Always, always it is loneliness and an aching heart when we are apart. The loneliness seems to tear me apart inside, Nina, I cannot be happy without you.

I love you with every ounce of strength in my body and I feel desperate because I cannot give you what is rightfully yours and take what is mine. The memory of nights spent in your loving arms haunts me and I am proud of having loved you so passionately. The sheer beauty of it will for ever be fresh in my memory, darling, and I am happy to think that forever I have a part of you which no one can take from me and that I belong to you for all time, body and soul.

If only I could find the words, Nina, to express the love and devotion for you that is in my heart. I always feel that words fail miserably. Only when I am holding you close to my heart, our lips blending in those all consuming kisses, do I feel that you can hope to know the emotions in this wild heat of mine. I pray that we shall not be parted much longer, my love. I pray that soon all these weeks of loneliness will be behind, the war finished, and the prospect of years of love and peace and happiness be before us.

There is a programme of community hymn singing on the radio as I write to you and they are singing :

Praise My Soul, the King of Heaven,
Well our feeble frame He knows,

In His Hands He gently bears us
Rescues us from all our foes.

We are parted, Nina, but God is with both of us and in our prayers to Him we can be together. In the quiet of Blymhill Church He was with us and He heard us say 'I will'. You are my wife already, Nina, why do we have to put on a show for the whole world?

And now I will try and make up some lost sleep, dear. With my thoughts very much with you I'll say goodnight, God bless you, Nina, and – I love you with all my heart.

Your very own,

Vic xxxxxxxxxxxxxxxxxxxxxxxx

XXX

Officers' Mess,
RAF Station Foulsham, Norfolk
3rd July, 1944 (Mon evening)

Nina, my sweetheart,

Please forgive me if the letter I wrote last night carries a depressing note with it, but I felt pretty groggy then and it was hard to find the words to describe how lonely I felt and how much I needed you. Words are definitely not the best medium for love-making, Nina, the sense of touch and an exchange of glances carry far more meaning for us, don't they my sweet. About an hour ago Himmy, our Gunnery Leader, popped in to see me and brought your letter with him, an act which makes me for ever in his debt.

Congratulations, on the LACW, Nina, but you understand my powers of observation, my love. I noticed it long before I reached the end of the letter. I know for certain that you deserve far more than your LACW. There's not a person more capable and hardworking than yourself and the Stn. knows that. But then your present occupation is very temporary, and by the time you've changed your name and your occupation you won't know yourself. Every time I write your name on an envelope I cheer myself up by thinking that is one time nearer the end of Chessall and one time nearer the beginning of Vinnell. Mrs Nina Vinnell! I like the sound of it, darling.

Yes, Nina, I too get that queer, excited sensation inside when I am waiting for my call to you. A sort of nervous, tense feeling. So much seems to hang on those few minutes. So much to say and so little time to say it in:

'F/Lt Vinnell?' 'Yes.' 'Your call to Wheaton Aston, sir. Go ahead.' 'Hello, Nina.' 'Hello, Vic.' ... and then all is blank.

I had so many things to say a few minutes ago but now all I can think of is: 'I love you, Nina, love you more dearly than life; more dearly than the sunlight and moonlight, for you are my sun and moon, my day and night, my be all and end all of living.' I hear your voice; surely now I can touch your hand and kiss your tender lips. I am bewildered and before I know where I am a voice, a cold, impersonal voice says: 'Your time is up'.

A few seconds to arrange our next call, a hasty goodbye and ... Click! I'm left staring dazedly at a black object which I am holding. It seems so hard to connect you with this very worldly thing in my hand. As I put the telephone back on its rest I stick my chin out a little more and vow that when the days of peace come round again we shall be parted for only a bare minimum of time each day, for a very few hours only. In fact I think I'll become an author and then I can work at home and we can be together the whole day through.

Please keep sending me the cigarettes, Nina. I have not quite stopped smoking altogether. Yesterday I smoked one and today the same but then I have not been 'on the top line' the past two days. As a rule I smoke about three or four a day now which is quite a cut from fifteen or so, and in time I may cut it out altogether. But I see no harm in three a day, do you Nina?

In answer to your question about the flying missiles I can say that you needn't worry about me while I am here. But just after I left you on Friday and journeyed South I was soon one of the initiated. They're a queer do altogether.

Darling, I shall be glad when the days come when we can cycle through the lanes together once again. They were very happy evenings, weren't they, full of sunshine, love and happiness. They can never die but until we can relive them again (and be very sure we will) we must each cycle with a spirit. Nina, if no man has ever stirred your heart or your desires before then you have never been in love before. That's true isn't it? But how very different it is now, darling. The whole future hundred per cent complete, and secure in that knowledge we can face life without fear of whatever it may hold for us.

Nina, I have always believed that distance could never really part us and it is being proved true. That at almost the same time we should both write identically the same words shows that there is a bond between us which is stronger than flesh. It has happened several times already. Our love is so strong that it recognises no barriers, Nina.

Listen!! Oh Nina, music. Music so strong and soul stirring. You are here now with me. I know it. Hold my hand and listen with me, darling. It is Tchaikovsky's Pianoforte Concerto in B flat minor and I wish that I had been the composer that I could have dedicated it to you. But I can dedicate it to you, Nina, it is yours because it is mine and it ours because it is beautiful. Just like the daffodils by the river and the lambs in the fields and the fields and the sky at Pensby. They all belong to us, dearest one, because we love one another and God is so pleased that He has given us the whole world.

Today I sent you a telegram explaining why I could not phone on Sunday. I thought I had better say Friday as our next nine o'clock date as I believe you are going home on Thursday. I am feeling much better today and my temperature is more or less normal but I feel so darned weak. In my efforts to pour my inside out of two ends at once I've lost a few pounds in weight but I'll soon pick up again.

Before I go to sleep, Nina, can I tell you a story? Yes? OK, here goes:

There are three Storks. Father, Mother and Baby Stork and they all went out on business one day. When they came home in the evening they started talking 'shop'. Mother said: 'Where have you been today, Father?' and Father Stork said, 'I dropped in at Mrs Brown's in Wheaton Aston village with a baby boy.' 'Did you, well, I've dropped in at Mrs Green's at Gnosall with a bouncing baby girl.' They turned to Junior. 'And where have you been today, son?' 'Oh, said the young Stork, 'I've been to Wheaton Aston RAF Camp scaring the daylights out of a couple of NAAFI girls' ... Which only goes to show that this gooseberry bush stuff is all hooey!

Goodnight, darling. Sweet dreams.

All my love, Vic xxx xxx xxx XX (in deep red).

Thursday night 6/7/44

Dear Heart,

Put your arms tight round me and hold me close. Let me lay my head on your shoulder, and feel the soothing balm of your touch on jaded nerves and tired body. Kiss me, Vic, in your own special way, which is more 'a caress with the lips' – a life-saver! I need all that, darling. Today I should have been at home, but late yesterday afternoon Hobby cancelled my pass, because of 'pressure of work' – a phrase beloved of HQ. It was too late to send Mum a telegram to let her know in time, so I expect she would spend a disturbed night watching out for me. And yet, Vic – and yet, I can waste all afternoon at Clothing Parade yesterday and nothing is said. From five past two until twenty to five I stood in a queue outside Stores, and at the end of it I could change nothing but a tie – there was nothing else left. And to crown everything, we were told to come back and work late. I was here until ten o'clock last night, doing work that I could have finished but for that wretched Clothing Parade.

I have had my moan, and I feel much better now. Mmm, I know just what it would be like to snoozle down within the shelter of your arms. That is where I should be. I wish I was there. I wonder if you are still in Sick Quarters. Somehow, I think you are, and somehow I think you are going to have a bit of a job persuading the doc to let you up for tomorrow's date at nine. If you can't manage it, darling, don't pretend to be better just so that you can keep our appointment. The main thing is to get properly better, Vic – please do that for me. Don't you see that you have in your care a sacred trust? – you promised to look after something for me; I can't be there to look after it myself. Vic, please don't let anything happen to you, at least, not anything you can help. Your body is the home and shelter of my heart, darling; keep it safe.

How strange that you should be listening to the same hymn that we were singing on Church Parade last Sunday! – 'Praise, my soul, the King of Heaven'. It was the WAAF 5th Anniversary on 28th June and Dominions Day on 1st July, so the full-blown Church Parade, led by the visiting ATC Band, was to celebrate both occasions. Most of the WAAF had been allowed to celebrate in the nicest way possible earlier the same day, by having an extra 'lie-in', and a special late breakfast of bacon and egg was served from 09.00 hours until 09.30. Wasn't that thoughtful of someone? WA is looking up.

The service was conducted by an RCAF Padre, a very much more alive edition of the clergy than old Calver, and his text was 'This one thing I do – ' His Address was definitely not meant for you, Vic. Singleness of purpose is your forte. A press photograph was taken of the March Past, and a group photograph was taken of the entire WAAF Section in all their glory led by the Queen Bee. I saw a print of one of them today, and they are collecting orders for them. I thought I might as well have one, for the sake of the grandchildren. Do you think that, in that case, one print will be enough, Vic?

Oh, Vic, your coloured miniature has arrived, not here – it is at home. I'll try again to have a day off on Monday next, going home on Sunday night, so I'll collect it then. I do want it very much. On Saturday I am detailed for another of these 'Salute the Soldier' efforts, so that rules the weekend out for going home.

That is a jolly good idea of yours, my love. No, really, Vic, I mean it. Why don't you become an author? Why don't you write a book? – lots of books? You could, you know. I have been trying to think of something that would entail your being near me for the whole of twenty-four hours, and I'd love to help you. Oh yes, that would be fine – the Vinnellski's at home. Don't let's be parted ever, Vic.

That music you heard, Vic. I have been trying to recall how it goes. Could you write it down for me? I'd know then. … 'It is yours because it is mine and it is ours because it is beautiful'. How very simple it is and yet how truly exquisite! I love you, Vic. I love you with all my heart. Let's always be like that, Vic. Let's always have time to appreciate the truly beautiful things. Everywhere the grim and the sordid and the coarse press heavily upon one's spirit, but over it all shines our star, and somehow we must struggle towards it always. As WH Davies puts it:

'A poor world this, if full of care
We have no time to stand and stare.'

As you will have guessed, I am typing this in the office and I am duty clerk once again. It is after one o'clock and it is almost time I was asleep – but first – x x x x x x Goodnight, my dearest one. Be there in the morning, and let me hear your voice tomorrow night if at all possible.

xxx Bless you xxx

Nina

Officers' Mess,
RAF Station Foulsham, Norfolk
5th July 1944

Nina, my own, xxx

If I say that today has been trying that would be a gross understatement. I have felt quite well all day but the Doc said I must stay in bed and so here I am at 8.30pm on a glorious evening sitting amidst a mountain of assorted material (they were orderly bedclothes this morning) and wishing I was a little over a hundred miles from here on a bearing of about 267 degrees true. That should put me about Wheaton Aston or at least near enough to reach you in half an hour.

It is such a glorious evening, darling, bright sunshine and a breeze that stops it from being too hot. Where shall we go? 'Spread Eagle', Blymhill, 'The Bradford', Ivetsey Bank. Top or bottom triangle? Oh Nina, it will never never fade. I have vowed that not a single second of any of the beautiful time we have known shall be forgotten.

Do you remember the first time I said 'I love you, Nina'. St Val's night at the dance. I just couldn't keep it back, darling, my heart couldn't hold any more love without letting some of it out. I felt so utterly miserable whilst you danced with someone else, I wanted you for myself and hated sharing you. Now I can truly say that you are mine and the happiness that then I could only hope for is mine in reality. I always wanted someone to whom I could give all my love and affection with no restrictions and in return receive the same from the other person. I must have been able to see into your heart from the beginning, Nina, for I gave you all, never doubting that I should be rewarded in full.

I love you, Nina, and because of the past I believe that my love is greater than and stronger than anyone else's could be. In my heart there are a thousand and one reasons why I will always treasure you. I try to tell them to you, Nina, but oh, there seems to be such a shortage of words in the English language. Strange, I never noticed it until I met you, darling.

In spite of being confined to bed suffering from robust health it turned out to be a very happy day after all. I received your letter written on Saturday, Nina, and with the confirmation of your love for me and with your vows for our future came the necessary power to boost up my morale, ease the pain of loneliness and give me once more a glimpse of those fairy peaks.

Oh Nina, why did you think you would not miss me when I went away? I knew that I would be lonely nigh unto death, I knew that there would be a void in my life that could only be filled when we met again. I dared not think how desperately unhappy I would be when we parted --and now it has happened and I have been more miserable than I could have believed possible. I have pined until my health has left me, leaving me easy prey to any disease that comes my way. That's how much I love you and want you, Nina. And you didn't think you would miss me!

I wish we were together now never to part again. I'd hold you so close to me that we would become one person, one life, the bloodstream from one heart. Of course I was referring to YOUR smile and YOUR eyes, darling, and the only thing I regret is that I haven't something more radiant than the sun and the star to compare them with. To me, Nina, you are beauty personified and your lovely face is forever before my eyes. In its beauty I find peace when I am troubled and inspiration when I am listless. I have always praised you for your charms, I have held you close and, with my lips to your ear, told you that I adored you for your hair, your eyes, your lips. They inspire my love-making, Nina, and the memory of them will keep my love for you as strong as ever whilst we are apart. God bless you for your sweet charms and the joy they will always bring me.

This is the last sheet of paper I have, Nina, and I have pages more to write. Did you get my fourteen pages OK? I had to stop that because I ran out of paper. But in the remaining few inches I have enough space to say I love you with all my heart, soul, and strength and to remind you that it is only about three weeks to go now.

God bless you, dear mistress. Vic xxx

PS I have written to Mum tonight.

Officers' Mess, RAF Station Foulsham, Norfolk

9th July 1944

Nina, my Sweetheart,

I am writing this from the Mess having just been discharged from Sick Quarters. I guess I'm more or less OK but so wretchedly tired and feeble. I looked for a letter from you yesterday, Saturday, to tide me over the weekend but I was doomed to disappointment. Somehow I feel so very alone when I don't hear from you, Nina. Last night as I lay in bed I felt for a while that the whole world had deserted me. I longed for you to come along and touch my soul into life, to lay your cheek against mine and tell me not to worry. I wanted your kisses, and the pressure of your body against mine to make my heart beat faster and show me that I am young and full of life. I need you, Nina, my companion, my mistress, wife. I know you could sweep away this tiredness with one touch of your hand; a smile and my heart would be right again. It's not usual for me to sit back and let my life flow over me, not caring which way the stream carries me, too tired to resist. But last night the chin was not quite so square as usual, Nina, and I guess for a few hours life had me against the ropes and pounded the daylights out of me.

But I'll shake it off, darling, believe me I will. I write and tell you about it because I want to share everything with you and it is to you, Nina, that I can open my heart and find understanding. I'll come back fighting in the next round and you must admit that it's very seldom I concede a round of the fight to Life. I know that you will understand how I felt, dear, and not be mad with me. I miss you terribly day by day and very often life without you doesn't seem to be worth living now that I have found someone to share life with, someone to whom I can give all and fear no injury, it seems very cruel that we should be parted in this way.

15.00 hours: Nina, darling, I left this letter for a few hours and decided to write some more after lunch when I had been down to the Flight and found out what the score was. And now here I am back in the Mess in a happier frame of mind. I have met my pilot, Jack Fisher, a Canadian w/o. He is a very pleasant lad about my own age and I think we shall get on very well together. My first impressions of him are good and I think that goes a long way. He knows some of the boys from my old squadron so we had something in common straight away.

Some more cheerful news is that my Leave is on the board for AUGUST 2nd. Now that may be a little fluid, dear, one day or so either way, but Mike my Flt/Comm. has said he will fix it for certain in a day or so. Only three weeks now, Nina! It's a lovely thought, and to add to that I may be able to see you for an hour or so before my Leave. But I won't say any more about that as it may not come off.

I am glad I am out of sick bay and about again. Nina, did you understand how I felt when I wrote the first part of this letter? When you are keen and anxious to be flying, when all you ask for is to be in the spot where the 'flak' is heaviest and the danger greatest, then you feel hopeless when you are weak and confined to a room. I want to get in there and take my share of the risk, my conscience is easy when I have done that. I am no slacker or coward and not afraid of dying, but inaction gets inside me and hurts, especially when there is so much good, clean fun going these days.

This afternoon I began to see where I stood and now I have got some prospects. Do you see what I mean, Nina? I think you do because you know that I am happiest when I am doing my level best. I want to work hard, as hard as I love when I am with you, my darling.

I do love you very deeply and sincerely, Nina, and you must remember that always. Don't give me up as a hopeless worry-head. Just think of me as you have always known me, a man with very deep, passionate feelings. I pray that soon I may give you all the love that is growing and nearly bursting my poor heart.

11th July, 1944

Nina, my darling,

Thank God I have been able to speak to you at last and to tell you with my own lips that I love you. Oh Nina, I'm so lonely without you! To hear your voice brought me pleasure which defies description. And yet when those six precious minutes had elapsed and you were once again beyond recall, the old overwhelming loneliness came over me once more and the cold, chilly fingers of fear clutched my heart. That voice within cried out that I mustn't love you. If only I could cure that dread, Nina.

The news that Bill is home and that you will be seeing him came like a kick in the stomach to me at first. Of course I knew it must come sooner or later but somehow I have been so happy in the thought of having you all to myself that it took me off my guard.

Well, Nina, it seems that words are out of place at a time like this, doesn't it? If there is any big burden to shoulder I like to shoulder it myself and fight my way out, or at least let you share it with me. But this time I cannot shoulder any part of it and you must now be strong, Nina. You had implicit faith in me and now I must have the same in you, my darling. Oh God how I wish it was all over. Now that I have found my love all that I ask for is peace and quiet.

How straightforward it would have been if I had met you in peace time. We have had to fight so many difficulties already. We could not even meet as man and woman, as two equal people. Yet in spite of difficulties which may seem insurmountable at first sight our love grew and flourished until now its roots are so deep that it is indestructable. I love you more and more as the days go by, Nina, and I live only for our next meeting. I read in the paper today a passage which said that a strong wind will blow out a candle but fan to fury a raging fire. So with parting will a weak emotion die, but a strong love grow ever deeper with each day of parting. It's true, dear, and if ever our love needed a test (God knows it has withstood enough already) then it has shown itself worthy in these past weeks.

I can only pray now, my Nina, pray that soon all our worries and trials will be over. That soon I may be able to lay my head on the pillow along side yours and let my heart rest, and let my heart rest ......rest ...... rest, please my darling. XXXXX

Tomorrow morning I hope to be able to fly over and see you and so I am saving this letter in hopes that I can deliver it personally – with a big kiss. But I am addressing the envelope in case my luck and the weather does not hold good.

Nina, what was the news about Mother? It sounded as if you said something about a weak 'ticker'. Did you mean heart trouble? Is she all right and is she getting the proper attention? Nina, nothing must happen to her. But then fancy saying that to you, darling, she hardly means less to you than she does to me. In case I can't deliver this personally just write back and say that I am once again worrying unnecessarily. I guess I'll be grey long before my time, Nina, but if it is so then no-one will ever be able to say that I didn't care for anyone. My whole world has clustered itself around you and mum. If mum went it would be a terrible loss, if you went away I should never recover, Nina.

12th July

No Nina, 'til not to be today. Perhaps tomorrow I shall be able to get over. I'm not giving up hope. I love you with all my heart. God keep you, sweetheart, and give you strength! Please love me for ever and make my dreams come true is the prayer of the man you married in a quiet country church one night as the clock struck – nine!! His name was

Vic xxx xxx xxx

13 Thursday Marvellous presents that Bill has brought back for me, but I refuse them all. Bill helps me quite a lot. Day off. Stay the night at Saughall and Bill and I talk cheek to cheek in my bedroom till 5.30am, yet neither of us show any desire for love-making! Bill calmly discusses the question of our engagement ring and even things it a huge joke. I have no idea of his real feelings at all. Wake up at 10.30. Look through album. Go a walk in the afternoon with Bill and decide finally to break it off. Awkward moment during tea. Give Bill the ring on way to Liverpool, for 7.5 train to Stafford. Feel rather dazed and numb, he's been a trusted friend – always will be. Send telegram to Mum.

14 Friday Unexpected surprise visit from Vic – just when I need to see him most. Comes in an Anson and stays for an hour or so. Swap cigarettes and chocolate. It's Vic I want; I'm sure now. He has been so worried. Wave him off into the air. Phone call from Vic at 9pm. Write letter to Vic:

Friday evening

Vic, My Vic xxx xxx xxx

This is the first letter I will have written to you since I became outwardly, as well as inwardly, in every way, truly undividedly yours. Oh darling, when your voice sounded over my shoulder and your dear face xxx appeared at the window, my heart became a living thing that leapt to meet you. I am not cold and sexless and lukewarm, as Bill would have me believe, but it needs the touch of the master hand to make me come to life – your hand, your lips, and all the warm nearness of you. Now, I too can join with you without reserve, and match the tenderness and warmth and consuming fires of your love with my own. Yours, Vic, through ever verdant spring that is yet to be; yours, in the heat of the noonday sunshine; yours, in the freshness of woods after rain; yours, in the cool peace of evening; yours, to kiss under the canopy of sun, moon and stars; yours, in the all enveloping hours of night time, when the star winking in at us through the parted curtain will beckon, and we will follow, through time and space, to become forever a part of every flower and tree and rain-cloud and dawn – and again in the morning, all yours, to await the glory of another new day, to make of each one a golden age of happiness and love. Oh Vic, darling, we can't die you and I; we belong to the eternal. Wherever you go, you must take me with you. I love you, my Vic, for life itself, through life and into the beyond. And I don't have to tell you, do I? that there are no more stumbling blocks? I think you know you need only ask just that once more.

My love, life is too wonderful to allow even one moment to pass without the one person in the world who makes it all possible. In every sphere of our activities; in every phase and circumstance of life. I vow here and now that our love and our marriage is going to be dual-controlled. If we do everything together, what have we to fear? I remember when I was a child, it was only when I was alone in the darkness of a room that I was afraid. I hated to sleep by myself, and I slept with my little brother until I was quite old. And that is how Mum would find me in the morning, little Fred and me with our arms round each other. After that, I slept with my mother, who soon discovered that she needed less bedclothes. Yet I never felt afraid out in the woods and quiet lanes, or in the garden, where the shrubs became people I knew and the trees were my friends. I shall never be afraid of anything again, so long as we are together. Even if your body has of necessity to be elsewhere, please leave me your heart and your spirit. I am sure I should know instantly if you ever took them away from me. It would be like a chill dark shadow passing over the sun.

I remember the first time you said: 'I love you, Nina' so well. It was as though we both saw a vision, and even then my heart yearned to answer your call, but my lips remained sealed. That look of dejection when I danced with someone else, how I hated being responsible for it and how I wanted to change it. Vic, dearest, it has changed now, hasn't it?

You looked a lot happier the last time I saw you. There was just one thing that worried me – your nerves. Was it really just shock, just relief, after days of worrying? Even so, darling, they shouldn't be that bad. I do wish I could get you really better. Then I'd really know I was good for you. As it is, I do begin to wonder sometimes. You see, my darling, from now on, you and all that you are will be a reflection of me and my effect on you. I shall feel as proud of myself as well as of you, if we achieve all that we want to achieve, because I'll know that I helped in a small measure by being right there beside you all the way. And Vic, we'll never know the meaning of defeat – never, what did that Indian woman tell you? – just a little luck, and the fruits of happiness and indeed all life will be ours.

I am so glad you have heard from Mum. Did she really say all that? Believe me, it seems quite amazing! Up to now, she has always taken the traditional attitude for mothers to adopt towards possible suitors, that they weren't anywhere near good enough for me. And yet, here she is, after only one meeting, actually encouraging you and adopting you as her son! Old ladies and young alike – all fall for it! And yet I have the audacity to feel so blandly confident that I can 'hold my man'. What is the secret of her success? – Ah, she uses 'Imperial Leather' nightly, so who could resist her subtle charm? De dah, de dah… Oh, and talking of chemists (indirectly), reminds me that I cheated rather about that roll of film. I tried to be a good Vinnellski and, rather than admit a second failure, I took them to a shop in Pensby to be developed. Mum will collect. And now I come to the NAAFI telephone to tell you of my undivided love. A kiss first xxxx YOURS always.

Nina

Officers' Mess, RAF Station Foulsham, Norfolk

14th July 1944

Nina, my very own,

You must pardon me if I am still a little dazed but the truth is only just sinking in. Darling, I wonder if you realise my capacity for worrying. I can be anxious over the smallest thing if it is not going well and here I have been for the past seven months desperately, passionately head-over-heels in love with you and all the time the happenings of the past week have been hanging over my head. Nina, I have been worrying more than you will ever know. From our very first hours together you became necessary to me. It was such a great luxury to relax from everyday life and for the first time that I can remember I showed someone the real Vic. When I had said, 'Goodnight' and was walking back to my room, I was conscious of an empty feeling inside. I had left part of myself with you, Nina.

That was in the very early days. As time went by I found myself re-acting to you more and more. With a word you could condemn me to utter misery or lift me so high that my head spun with happiness. In the hours that we were apart I missed you more and more and I found myself living for the evenings that I may walk or cycle by your side and place myself once again at your mercy. I longed for your kisses, and I wanted you in my arms all the time. I felt my body respond to your touch and, Nina, I wanted YOUR body. Yes, my darling, I was in love with you completely. I tried to stop myself telling you but it was too strong an emotion to be held back and it was on St. Valentine's night that I knew it had to be. I knew then that if we went through life together, I should find my future happiness and that if I lost you I should lose a vital part of myself, there would be no more day and night, I would exist and not live. That is why I said I would reach for a star at your command, our star, dear Nina. And then came our nights together. It seemed that nothing could ever part us after those sacred hours – and it couldn't, Nina! I can never imagine moments like those with anyone else and I know you feel the same.

I came home with you at long last and when I walked through the door of 396 I walked straight into heaven. In these past weeks I have kept telling myself over and over again that all this beauty can never end. You have become not a part of my life, but my whole life. Can you wonder, Nina, that I have been worried? Can you see what would have happened to me if I had lost you? And now you are completely mine. This thing that has been hanging like the only dark cloud in the brightest of skys, this cloud has gone. Forgive me, Nina, if I am a trifle dazed.

Saturday morning

When I saw you yesterday, Nina, I felt alive for the first time since we said 'Goodbye' three weeks ago. The warmth of your greeting brought untold joy and when my lips touched yours my heart said, 'This is life, Vic'. When you said that you were free to be mine, I wanted to take you in my arms and be free to kiss you as I have always done when we are alone. A long, warm, lifegiving kiss. I pray that you may be able to get some Leave in three weeks time, darling. I will make it the happiest week of your life because it will be the happiest week of mine. Not that a week could be long enough for us, Nina. We have lots of plans to lay down now, real live plans that will be the basis of the realisation of your dreams. Now that we belong completely to each other there is nothing to hold us up. Can you imagine any obstacle standing in our way after the past seven months? No, neither can I. The whole future is ours until the dark angel spreads his wings over both of us, not leave one of us to suffer the agonies of spirit that the parting would bring.

Believe me, my darling, I will love you all my life as I love you today. There is only one person to whom my heart belongs and that is you, all of it, Nina, and you share it with no-one. I will always treasure you and protect you, do all in my power to make you happy, and I know no sacrifice that I will not make for you. Place your trust in me, love me always and take care of our love while we are apart. We are toes on the line, Nina, and we can fire our own starting pistol. Let's fire it soon, my darling, for now there is nothing to stop us.

When I arrived back yesterday I found a letter from you and a book and a letter from Mum. The book was 'Wings in the Morning' by Patience Strong, a peaceful book – could Mum have written it? She's a great lady, Nina, a great lady.

I am writing this paragraph from just outside London. No, I'm not here on pleasure, but duty. As you can probably guess I have been pushing the old 'Annie' round again. I seem to find myself in many old corners of England these days. But in three weeks from now I hope that we shall be in our favourite corner – together, walking across the fields by the river, my arm around you and your cheek just handy for my lips. I'll post this letter here and it will reach you Monday morning.

Keep your chin up, my darling, remember that you are always in my thoughts and that I am

Your lover for all time, soon to be your husband,

Vic XXX

Monday evening 17/7/44

Vic, My Darling,

Once again I come to you in the quiet of the evening, when the day's work is through and we may reasonably expect a little of the luxury of relaxation and happiness and sweet content. My happiness is with you, my Vic, and so are all my thoughts, but you need some tangible expression of this. Besides, I get some queer sort of satisfaction in my puny efforts to express the extent of my love for you on paper. I often read over the results of my labours and wish that you could have been present when some particular portion of my letter were being born, that you could have felt the tremendous surge of feeling within me before I translated it in a very poor way to writing. You wouldn't worry or doubt me then. Believe me, I am no facile letter-writer; I wrestle with myself and struggle for hours. So that I do in very truth spend the whole evening with you.

This is the fourth night I have spent in this way and I desire no other way when you're away. I didn't want to promise to write to you at certain stated intervals, or we should both have looked upon it as a duty, just another 'bind', whereas now you know I write because I want to – and vice versa. I wouldn't want letters any other way. I write often, because I love you, and I want you to know it.

There were no letters from anyone this morning. Perhaps it was a good thing in a way – I have to think of some advantage – because I still have two letters of yours to answer and it now gives me an opportunity of getting even with you. This one was written last Tuesday, just after our phone interlude that gave me strength for the morrow, when my dark hour of decision was at hand. I needed you then, Vic, and I was fortifying myself as you spoke with me. When I emerged at last from the telephone box, I know I was ready. I felt very calm as I made my announcement (to Bill) and it all seemed to happen from a great way off. Nothing anyone said could really touch me and I felt nothing very acutely, There was a strong invisible wall all around me, and I knew it was the shield of our love. I was with them, but not of them; I was safe with you and your arms were around me and your eyes gazed into mine.

It was just after I returned to Camp and on the train from Liverpool when I felt most miserable. I felt stranded and alone, with one door closed behind me and the other door not yet open, and I felt tremulous and shivering in the dark passage, alone – a great desolate patch, sandwiched between all that had been and all that was to be.

A stray black and white dog has just come up to me and snoozled its wet nose against my legs. Everyone wants to be loved, and it looked as grateful when I pulled it closer and stroked its fur. It has now found a comfortable spot between my knees, so I must be careful not to disturb.

I think you WILL go grey, Vic, if you worry like this. You can always find something to worry about, you know. All one can do is to savour each precious moment as it comes, and take care that our actions now bring no regrets in the moments to come. I could worry myself sick over you, as I told you, but 99 per cent of the things we worry about never happen, so isn't it better to leave our worrying till that 1 per cent is needed?

Mum has suffered terribly with her nerves ever since those raid experiences when she was far from well to begin with. She has greatly improved in every way since living in Heswall and Pensby, but the smallest thing knocks her off her balance again. I think she worries about Fred too. This time it is the nerves of her heart that make it jerk and beat unevenly. The doctor says there is nothing organically wrong, just rest and no worry and plenty of fresh air. I noticed when I was home that one can see the rise and fall of her heart beating beneath her frock in great uneven bumps. It is just weakness generally, Vic, and it will improve again. If we could only end this wretched separation and parting! This it is that tears a woman asunder. We have been so much a part of each other –

'Each the others' joys possessing
Each the others' burdens bear,'

and that to me is the real meaning of a family – a union of hearts and minds and spirits. If one has a trouble, then we all share it; it is brought to the family conference table and a plan of action is evolved. If only there could be no more vacant chairs! It is harder for the one left at home, because she is surrounded by remnants of the old life. Old books and old playthings remind her so vividly of those absent faces, the old guitar now silent in its case, the well-thumbed sheets of music bring the echo of a boy's voice, the set of tools, the chess-board, the racket in its press – oh God, I implore, please bring those days back again and with them my mother's health, and the dawn of a grand new world with my own Vic, to make all our dreams come true.

Vic, I think I'll marry you the second time, when the clock strikes nine. But shall we make it nine in the morning? with the whole lovely day before us? with the whole of our lives? never to part, darling, never again to say 'Goodbye'. You'll never lose me now, Vic. Be very sure of that. We have come through troubled waters, you and I, Vic, but now we have reached the calm of the other side. Our love will always be beautiful. It will always remain, a fragrant towering monument to the power and the glory and the permanence of two hearts welded by love.

Your Ever – Missing-You,

Your Ever – Longing-for,

Your Ever – Hoping-to-be

Yours in very truth

Nina

Domestic evening 19/7/44

Vic xxx My Very Dear Owner,

My floor-space is polished and gleaming, my lampshade has been dusted, my shelves tidied, and now here I sit on the grass outside my billet enjoying a quiet parley with you in the evening sunshine. The weather has been more worthy of the month of July these past few days, and I do hope the sun will shine for us too on your next Leave. If only I could get some Leave! There has been no word about it here. I wonder if it could be possible?

Which reminds me, that I must get my bike mended somehow. There is a puncture in the front wheel and the left pedal has broken – the outside bit of iron that holds the three things together has come off (So a certain Cpl reported to me after I had lent my bike to her for an evening). My bike has never been in order, I am afraid, since you were posted.

Vic, I haven't quite made up my mind regarding these Italian 'co-operators' (they call them) that have arrived on Camp, about 25 of them. Apparently they are ex-P, of W., (and in that respect alone I supposed we ought to hate them) who have consented to do GD work for the Allies. They are a mixture of Army, Navy and Air men, and are billeted quite separately way down on the banks of the canal. (I suppose if life becomes too difficult they can always end it all, and the murky waters may act as a constant temptation). Indeed, they do everything separately. They are marched up to meals which they eat in a curtained-off portion of the Airmen's Mess and are allowed at no Camp Concerts or Shows.

This is where the difficulty comes in. Up to now, I have found it perfectly easy to say I disliked the Italians and hated the Germans WHEN THEY WERE IN THE ABSTRACT, but when one is suddenly confronted by a bunch of weary travel-stained dusty-looking men, with the mark of suffering on their faces, unloved, hopeless, representing some far off mothers' sons, some distant wives' husbands, then I can feel nothing towards them but a vast yearning pity. There is so much misery and tragedy and death in this world. It doesn't cost very much just to be kind and it may make all the difference to a man down-and-out. What do you think, Vic? They are all men after all, be they Italians, Germans, Negroes, English. And if my brother were to be a P. of W. in Italy I should like to think someone was being kind to him. Is my brother in Italy responsible in any way for the sins in the past of this country? No more and no less than are these Italians. I think it is stupid and unworthy to want to spit at them, etc. which view so many people have expressed. I certainly think I'd do what I could to help if the occasion arose. I can't forget the look of gratitude almost dog-like, that one of them gave to me when I saw he was lost and I unwittingly smiled when I spoke to him. Just a small thing in a way and yet I felt glad that my scale of values had been sufficiently pliable.

Yesterday was Divisions, a complete day of it. And the famous Vinnellski's pupil was excused!! Are you proud of me, Vic? You see, I am carrying on the old traditions where you left off, keeping the old flag flying. By the way, have we Vinnells got a family motto? Don't you think we ought to hurry up and think of one, in case the family arrives before the motto?

I guessed you had been going places, Vic, when I saw the postmark of your letter. 'The Hyde, NW9'. I didn't really notice until I came to the end of your letter. I was in too much of a hurry to hear from you and to see those worthwhile words, 'I love you, Nina'. Ever since Friday I have been continually hoping that once again your shadow would pass across my window (I have left it unlatched purposely) and that your voice would cut across my thoughts of you, and my arms slide round your neck again and my lips return to where they belong. Now, of course, I know from your letter received this morning, that you won't be doing that again. Well, my sweetheart, wherever you are I am with you also, suffering with you, enduring – and winning through. Remember that, my Vic. You hold my whole future in your hands and I am entirely yours to have and to hold -. Oh darling, you remember the beautiful old words we repeated together, with all our forefathers gathered together as witnesses through those special moments at Blymhill Church? I meant them then. I felt you must see my love shining out of my eyes. And soon there will be another audience, but they will matter even less, and perhaps I'll even love you more. Sounds impossible now, but it seems I am only just discovering another self whose depths are as yet unplumbed. It is waiting for you, Vic.

Till you come

Always

Your Nina

---

21 Friday BOMB PLANTED ON HITLER Thirteen Men who opposed sacked Generals are blown up. Within hours of dismissing the latest of the Generals whom he suspects of trying to throw him over, Hitler last night announced an attempt on his life. He himself, said the announcement from his headquarters, received slight burns and concussion, but no serious injury. Thirteen others were hurt – three seriously, ten less seriously. All were members of his personal staff, the men who provide the material for his military 'intuition' in opposition to the regular military leaders.

GESTAPO START HUNT A Gestapo hunt of suspects is on, and revelations were promised in a few days on the German radio last night.

MORE CHILDREN URGED TO GO A new campaign to persuade parents to evacuate children from flying-bomb areas is to be launched this weekend by the Government. Posters will be put up in certain districts stating that the Government wish all schoolchildren in the area to be evacuated. There has been a big falling off recently in the number of evacuees. Since the peak of 41,000 reached on July 8, the daily average has fallen to a few thousand. On Wednesday the total was 3,802. More flying-bombs were over Southern England, including London yesterday, after a night in which the attack was not quite so heavy. The night robots met the biggest AA barrage yet. During a prolonged burst of fire three bombs blew up in a minute or so.

22 Saturday Make application for Leave (???) And it is granted (!!!) for August 5th!!! Write letter to Vic:

Saturday night 22/7/44

My Beloved,

It is my turn this week to have a gloomy Saturday and the prospect of an even gloomier Sunday. There was no mail from you this morning, so I shall have to depend entirely on that phone call we are going to have tomorrow at nine. Nevertheless, Vic, I must add that although today began in a very unpromising fashion, it certainly progressed into a very successful day indeed.

There was first of all the matter of my cycle and its broken pedal. One or two of the fellows offered to mend the puncture, but they didn't know quite what they could do about the pedal. And then I thought of F/Lt Stringer – within an hour the cycle was ready for the road, puncture mended, pedal repaired, cleaned and oiled – and I finished up by having to go round apologising to the other fellows who were falling over themselves to mend the puncture!! However, I've got them all lined up in turn now for mending each puncture as it occurs! Go one better than that, if you can, O Vinnellski. I can see I'll have to teach you how to flannel!

And now for my piece de resistance. Just wait till you have heard this. I'll deserve your 'Well Done', and anything else you have to offer. It is a pity really that I am speaking to you tomorrow night; I know I'll not be able to keep it to myself. So that when you read this letter you will already know what the tremendous news is, which will spoil the effect somewhat. You see, Vic, when you read the next sentence, you ought to look completely thunderstruck, dumbfounded, and now you won't – still, I am looking forward to the thrill of saying it tomorrow night over the phone and listening to the dead silence which follows. Ready? – It is about Leaves, and if this isn't an act of Providence nothing is, or was, or ever will be. I happened to type a letter regarding 'compassionate leave for a Waaf Officer', and I noticed the latest addition to the file was a Signal which made me think furiously – after which I typed furiously – a letter to the CO, putting forward a very pathetic case – (I'll show it to you when I see you!) – and threw it in the 'Out' tray, never really giving it much hope. The outcome of it was that directly I returned to SHQ after tea, to do some typing for the SMO, there was my application sitting pretty on my typewriter with '7 days approved' scrawled across the top of it. It had been recommended by Miss Jenny and Mrs Meggs and the Adj., all in the matter of a couple of hours! I could have hugged old Stuart, and when I told him so he looked most abashed.

So now, Vic, all I have to do is make out the form. Shall I make it out AD 5th? – and to Liverpool? I cannot expect an early chit, of course. And anyway, I'll have to cycle to Stafford or Gnosall, if I want my bike at home.

Xxxxxxxxxxxxxxxxxx Oh darling o'mine. I'll never be able to sleep tonight. I have so many plans chasing through my heart. I must answer your wonderful letter tomorrow. Tomorrow is my day off and I may cycle to Wolvs with another girlfriend. I'll be back for nine, never fear.

Yours

Always Yours,

Nina

PS I've just realised it, Vic. I am not four years older than you – I am only three and a half years ahead, that's all, not much compared to eternity.

Officers' Mess, RAF Station Foulsham, Norfolk
21st July, 1944

Nina, my beloved, xxx

Thank God for a few minutes breathing space! For three days now I have wanted to sit down and write to you, to get a little closer to you for an hour or so but I have not had sufficient time to write a coherent letter.

I am eternally grateful for your letters this week, Nina. Thank goodness I have not been greeted by an empty rack any day. I want to write to you every day, Nina, because I feel so very much with you, I try to talk to you in my letters, and I usually do find time for a few lines. But these last few days have had me well and truly foxed. You have been as ever to the forefront of my thoughts perhaps even more than ever if that is possible. I am clinging very closely to you now, Nina, cherishing every beautiful word of your letters, longing to hear your voice and praying that I may be able to keep my next nine o'clock date on the telephone, and praying that above all letters and phones may soon be a thing of the past for us. I want Nina and Vic in the flesh, one life, one love and not this everlasting striving to overcome the distance that parts us. I don't want you to be sitting in the evening sunshine by yourself, darling, it's my right to be with you, my arm around you, your smile making my heart light and your lips ever ready for my kisses.

Nina, I knew that the complete turnabout had to come. We have belonged to each other for a long time now, how could we hope to let anyone else share our lives and find complete happiness. I have wanted to belong to you and you only ever since the night I told you that I loved you. The force of that love was so overwhelming that I knew it just had to be you and I, and that is why I always had such faith in the ultimate outcome. Do you remember, darling, that I always used to say that I was certain things would work out our way? If you asked me why, I guess I could never give a logical answer, but then my faith was not based on cold logic. It was based on a warm, true love of the heart.

I am sorry, Nina, that I nearly asked that vital question over the telephone but can you imagine the way I feel now that a terrible weight has been lifted from my shoulders? As I have loved you, so I will always love you, but up 'til just recently there has always been a dark cloud on the most beautiful of blue skies. I belonged solely to you and I know that in your heart you belonged to me. And yet I knew you were holding back just a little bit. Not very much, Nina, for you loved me too much, but oh how that little bit has worried me. I always seemed terribly conscious of it and in moments of depression, terribly afraid of it. Sometimes that small cloud could be magnified in my imagination until it completely blotted out the sunshine and the tears in my heart were the raindrops the cloud could shed.

And then one day, when that cloud seemed more ominous than ever before, I flew over the see you and learnt that the sky was indeed completely blue, that the sun of life was shining in all its glory, that at last we were completely one. It seemed that all I could do at that moment was to take your hand. I have never hated my surroundings so much as I did then. The leash that you had unwillingly put on my emotions was off. Can you wonder they started off with a rush, Nina? Forgive me, darling, I didn't want to ask you over the telephone. But when August 5th comes around you can bet that the delay will be negligible. Those 'straggly ends' will be cleared up for all time, sweetheart, and we will take our first steps along the road of life TOGETHER.

I want the day to come very soon when our photographs will be just – photographs, not a cold substitute to kiss goodnight. The cold print doesn't appreciate the emotions behind a tender kiss or the unsatisfied desires that lie behind a pressure of the hand. I want the deep, red kisses on my letters to become live kisses, so much alive that the only possible outcome of them is the pouring out of my life into your dear, precious body. Yes, my darling, the grandest, sweetest, most intimate kiss of them all X. There is a whole lifetime of them for you, Nina.

Yes, darling, I have quite a wrestle too when I write to you. With a love in my heart that is so deep and sincere it is with disappointment that I read over my letters to you. The words never do justice to my emotions, Nina, and you must wait until I am with you again so that I may express with my lips (no, not words) all the thousand and one desires that it has pleased mankind to sum up very briefly in that word 'Love'. Poor, puny mortals we are.

You know, darling, when I read your letter telling me about mother and the real reason for her previous poor health, I mentally raised a glass in toast to the unsung heroes of this war – the Mothers. God bless 'em. They are left behind amongst a thousand and one memories of their loved ones, they are left to be lonely, to pray, to hope, to long for the end of all this madness. They receive grim, heartbreaking news and they have to carry on. They are not young and have earned peace and quiet in their later years. Instead they are given bombs, loss of loved ones, empty chairs some never to be filled again. Gallant women are these, Nina, and most gallant of them all, our Mum. May she find happiness in the reunion of her family very soon now.

And so, my beloved, I will away to bed. To put it in the vernacular 'I am on my knees'. But I never really go to bed alone any more, Nina. You always go with me in spirit and very soon now you will be there in the flesh, my arms around you all night. Just think, darling. When we are married we need never be parted for a single minute. A comforting thought that will bring the most pleasant of dreams to

Your lover for all time

Very, very soon your husband

Vic xxx xxx xxx

My Dear Understanding Vic,

Today I was overjoyed to receive three letters from you – actually three! Do you find it very easy to write to me? I think you must do, because as I read them, it is just as if I heard you speaking the words.

You didn't enjoy your visit to Jimmy's home very much, it seems from what you were saying on the phone. It does make me feel sad, when one sees the good things of life treated carelessly as of no importance, or even ignored altogether. And everywhere, men and boys are suffering and dying for just those things. What a dreadful heinous crime to waste such bountiful God-given gifts! We mortals must be made of very poor stuff. God has given us everything to make us happy, a beautiful world in which to live (and we try to destroy it!), home and friends, husband and children – everything. There is nothing else He could give us. Then what is it that is wrong? The fault must lie with the individual, perhaps a wrong sense of values, putting the emphasis on inessentials, chasing shadows only to discover too late that the real thing lay within one's grasp all the time. Until we learn to see things as they really are, to appreciate the good and true and lasting things of life, and to return to the simple natural way of living, I don't think we should ever know true happiness.

Vic, whenever I see into the home of a couple, I try to see it as a kind of object lesson for our future guidance. I try to discover just where and how they have gone wrong, and then I say, 'Nina, take heed. Go thou and do not likewise'. I wonder if they have ever tried prayer.

Something else you said on the telephone the other night had me thinking. Have you really, darling? Have you really thought such a lot about OUR baby? Now that you have confessed, Vic, I admit I have often seen pictures of him in my mind's eye. (I notice, by the way, that as yet to you the poor child is sexless. Tell me, Vic, you can't just have an 'it'; will it be a 'he' or a 'she'?) I know exactly how you will play with him in his cot, and take him walks in the pram, and help him in his first hesitant steps, and spend hours teaching him to say 'castle' the proper way. Oh Vic, my darling, why did you start me off on this? I have wanted to be the mother of your child, ever since you stopped very suddenly in the middle of the road once, during one of our cycling expeditions, and said: 'Nina, are you fond of children? How many do you want?' That started me, I admit, because I had never wanted any before, but something inside me awoke. But please, Vic, please let me first have only You. That is all I ask for at the moment, as I know that everything else in life will follow. I know you want a child, our child, badly, and I want to give it to you. That is part of the eternity of our love, a living tangible evidence of it. But not yet, Vic. Let me bask in the satisfying completeness of our love – and then –

But, Vic, Vic, we are years ahead of schedule, talking about babies and we have only just got engaged! Foresighted, darling. I should say you are! Let's be married first, shall we? We have had so little opportunity to be 'selfish' with each other so far, that I think we could be forgiven if we wanted to be so, at least till we are really ready for the next step.

Are you keeping Peter posted about us? Does he know that we are both disengaged, and engaged again to the one love of our life? I think he would be pleased. It is a pity he won't be here, because Peter did really mean something to you. I am terribly sorry for his wife – India, the tour for married men is 3 years, isn't it? Oh Vic, Oh Vic, if that ever happened to us, these partings we ensure every six weeks, these terrible agonising partings, would seem in comparison like a preliminary rehearsal. Just to think of it as a vague possibility makes me wince and shudder.

I think so hard about you while you are away, Vic, and especially at nine o'clock when I do everything in my power to reach you and to let you know I am with you. I close my eyes tight beneath my shading hand and whisper, really whisper, all my love for you and longing for you. It is like a prayer, to someone present but unseen and invisible, it is a prayer to you from my heart. My other prayer I say at 11 o'clock to Our Father to keep you safe through the night, so that when the dawn breaks at last over all the earth, we may greet it together. God bless our love always, and keep it fresh and pure and glowing. So keep that chin up and out, darling. I love you so very much, and here's my hand on it as a pledge. Lead it to the place you'd like it to be; it's waiting for me I know. I'd love to be giving you a 'facial' right now, to kiss your eyes till they drop in sleep, deep satisfied sleep.

Goodnight, darling.

Till the morning, Nina xxx xxx xxx

25 Tuesday Telegram from Vic to book room at Station Hotel. Stafford with Edna and Alwyn – too wet. See film: 'Submarine Base' and 'Melody Parade'. Hopeless to find Hotel accommodation!

Officers' Mess, RAF Station Foulsham, Norfolk
22nd July 1944

My sweetheart, xxx

How I hate the fact that you have to waste these beautiful summer evenings writing to me. Yes, they are wasted when you think of all the happy things we could be doing together, when you think of all the winding lanes yet to be discovered by us, all those furry little throats pouring out their music on the desert air, of all the picturesque little bridges waiting for us to lean on them, of the great big moon inviting us to kiss and assuring us he will not tell.

The night and day are filled with a very special beauty when we are together, dear Nina, and I miss it very much in these weary days of parting.

My darling, I try very hard to tell you in my letters how lonely I am, how much our love means to me, how much I feel the pain as I desire you and cannot have you. Last night I was very tired indeed and for my rest and peace of spirit I wrote you a long letter and when I read it through I almost wept at my own weakness and inability to find the words to describe this overwhelming passion that I feel in side me. There is only one way, Nina, that I can come anywhere near to making you realise how much I really do love you and then words are not needed. There are many moments during the day, just fleeting seconds which, if I had time to jot them down, would probably help me to tell you more fully in my letters just when and how I think of you. A passing moment when I see your smile so very vividly, a sudden longing for your lips on mine, a long drawn out, passionate kiss that would set my lonely heart beating oh so fast. At bedtime when I can recall as clearly as if 'twere last night the feel of your arms around me and the beauty of your caresses on my body, the surge of warm life as our bodies meet. There are a thousand moments like these in one day, Nina, but words can never do justice to their beauty because they defy description. The spoken words are hard to find but God, I feel helpless when I read my letters through. I pray that you may glean from them just a little of the love that I bear for you, and when I remember that you love me in the same deep, passionate way then I hope that your emotions will fill in and make up for my shortcomings and stunted vocabulary.

Nina, you do hear me calling to you, don't you? Now that the final obstacle has been cleared away and I know that you belong truly to me, I feel more lonely than ever. Lonely because I know how happy we could be. I don't want this everlasting parting, I don't want to lose you ever. Please, Nina, say that I will never lose you. No, I'm sorry, darling. I shouldn't have said that. I know I won't lose you now, but I get a little depressed sometimes, Nina, and the more I long for you the more minutes there seem to be in the days before our next meeting.

With a touch of your hand you can make my heart light again. Nina, I'm waiting anxiously for your hand to slip into mine. I'll squeeze it oh so hard, my darling wife-to-be, that you'll never be able to take it away again.

Nina, whatever my opinion of Italians may be I know you won't make a controversy of it. It is too small, far too small a matter to ever cause a difference of opinion between us so I don't hesitate to give you my frank opinion.

I lost one of the best pals I ever had in this war, F/o Ian Thomson, while he was flying over Italy. Maybe he was shot down by Italian guns. But this I do know. That he was a clever, talented Scotsman and true blue. He had a full, useful life in front of him, Nina, it wasn't really necessary for him to die over there so far from his native Highlands. I've still got his last letter in my trunk, it means something to me. I'm afraid that I could not look at Italians without remembering Jack. But I think it's only fair to say that I would never judge an individual by the whole.

Do you think I'm blessed, Nina? Don't take it to heart if you do. Perhaps we could make it a subject for one of our many discussions. We're pretty versatile, you know, and anyway we shall finish up by talking about elephants. There's always an excitement, the thrill of adventure in our discussions. We never know on what subject we shall finish up, do we darling?

Oh Nina, Nina, I heave such a big sigh when I think of all the happiness that is denied me at this moment. My heart is open to someone at last, to you, my very own beloved Nina and I am the happiest man in the world because you love me. And at the same time I am the loneliest because we are parted. I pray, oh I DO pray, my darling, that we shall be reunited soon for all time. I devour, yes devour, your letters when they come. Over and over again I read them and when I come to the words, 'I love you, Vic', I pause long and savour the beauty behind those words. I imagine your hand writing them, I can see the light in your eyes, Nina, a tender light. No wonder the stars grow dim beside such beautiful eyes. You are beautiful, my love, very, very beautiful and desirable.

Your presence is like the scent of a fragrant garden and when I am with you the world is a good place to be in. Do you remember one morning as we walked out of the gate at Pensby. I said that I felt shabby beside you? It is my way of bowing before a very lovely lady, Nina. Just as I stand before a garden of roses and see in it a beauty and grandeur that is beyond my reach, something which I can acknowledge but to which I must ever be subordinate. So, my darling, it is with you. The radiant beauty of your whole body is ever apparent to me. I try to acknowledge it with my love but feel that my best is still short of the deep appreciation that you deserve. Because you love me, Nina, I feel that I have seen deep down into your soul, and what I have seen there is so grand that I feel very humble. When we are married, darling, and I am free to worship you in the way I desire most I am going to change the whole world for you. Change it into one glorious continual sunset, one long, peaceful evensong. I am going to atone for these letters which, to me, seem feeble attempts at expressing the great love I bear for you. Please, my Nina, be patient just a little longer. Believe me, I have untold wealth waiting for you, a complete loving heart that will find its expression through the nearness of our bodies at night and happy, staunch companionship by day. A whole hundred per cent, Nina, not one thing lacking.

Do you want the family motto in Latin or English, darling? Just say the word, we have a fine line in Latin tags today, lady, and at a reasonable price. The only place in town with such a bargain. Walk up, walk up!!

Nina, just one more thing before I push up the switch and say, 'Goodnight'. Nina, stick close to me these days, please darling. A strange request? No, not really. I'm not afraid of losing you, dear, but there are moments when I really desperately need you. Just a moment when I get a queer, empty feeling inside and life becomes suddenly very sweet. Think of me at those times, Nina, very hard. I don't have to say when they are, do I? They are the moments when I remember your prayers, when I think of a note you put in my tunic when you sewed my wing on for me one memorable duty clerk night. It says, 'May this Wing and my Prayer bring you home – always'. That means to wherever you are, my darling, where I can find my complement.

God bless you, my darling wife, and keep you for me.

I love you with all my heart, my soul and my body for all time to come.

I'm kissing you goodnight, Nina. If only you could step out of this photo and return the pressure of my lips.

Sleep well, dear.

Your own, Vic x x x

Wednesday night

My Dear Sun, Moon and Stars,

At long last I have some word from you. From yesterday afternoon I have been inundated with telegrams and messages, and it is becoming difficult to keep up with you, Vic. Once you move – you move – faaast!

I have been trying to sort out just what I should be doing about them all. The first one you sent asking me to book accommodation for you in Stafford. Well, I went to Stafford last night with a couple of other girls and everywhere is booked up, at least, the Station Hotel could manage ONE single room for the night of August 5th, but The Swan and The Vine are both booked up to the end of next month. Besides, I could tell that you didn't yet know about my Leave, so I knew it was no good booking only one single room. By the way, I think Mr Smyth must be giving up the management.

Then this morning I heard of the message for me at the Waaf Picket Post. Whether this was a telegram or a telephone message I could not discover. This said that you had heard the news and would see me in Stafford on the 5th August. This afternoon I was told of another telegram with almost the same wording, to confirm the phone message I think.

It has been difficult working all this out, Vic, because I have no idea when you will be arriving in Stafford on the 5th. I should like to leave on the 5.10 bus from Camp, but there is the question of my cycle. I could, of course, go into Stafford the previous evening and leave my bike there, then I should only have my case to cope with. We must try to get the 6.38 train to Liverpool, which arrives at something past eight. I had thought of getting the 9pm train to Chester and staying there the first night. It was a good idea, but The Queen's (which I rang up this lunch-time) are booked up to 9th August. I am just beginning to realise, Vic, that it is a jolly good thing I have got Leave – otherwise I shouldn't see very much of you if you were unable to get accommodation in Stafford, which looks very possible.

It seems that you will be too busy to phone me from now till I see you a week on Saturday – otherwise, you would have given me a possible date in one of your telegrams. Darling, I want more than anything to speak to you. It has been awful these last four days keeping such stupendous news to myself, and knowing how happy it would make you if you knew.

Vic, I too long to be in your arms and to know that all I have ever longed for has come to pass. Oh Vic, what unspeakable joy! Darling, I've got an idea. You realise that this will be impossible at home? But The Queen's are booked up only to the 9th. Shall we spend our last night there in the one and only Chester, instead of our first as we planned? That would mean leaving home on Friday night, and spending Saturday in Chester. I'll try to ring them tomorrow.

Yes, darling, you always knew that things would work out right for us in the end, and I am grateful always for your blind sublimely illogical faith in the triumph of our love over any and every obstacle. God bless you for it, Vic, and soon I'll say my evening prayer in your arms. Our blended lips will breathe the words together and will soar skywards till they reach His Throne – One Prayer.

Till then,

Our prayer will arrive there together – at 9 o'clock.

Yours Always and All of me,

Nina

PS Queens Hotel is booked for our last night, so I'm stumped!

Wednesday, 26/7/44

Just after hearing your voice

My One and Only Adam –

I am eating an apple. Could I tempt you? It really seems a waste that I should be eating it like this. I am crunching it very slowly once, twice, three times and not swallowing, all ready to transfer it should I suddenly see your parted lips. Since I left you I am undressed and in bed. Everything went beautifully tonight, didn't it, Vic? I had just left the counter with a large glass of lemonade, hoping it would last me for an hour or so, when yoiks and tally-ho! – my call! The wireless had either been turned off or else it wasn't working, and there was hardly anyone in the Naafi, so I could hear you fine and it was just dandy to talk to you. But always at the end of it all, I get a moment of panic. I hear the operator's voice intervening and I think of all the things still lying in my heart unsaid and I know that you are going soon, soon, and I haven't told you. I hear myself calling you back, 'Vic, Vic, Vic, don't go yet, listen to me darling, oh I love you xxx xxxx – '. With a sigh of unsatisfied longing I realise you have gone and I must turn away from the dead thing in my hand that I had once clutched so eagerly. Oh well – (another sigh there, Vic) it won't always be like this. Will it?

And now I must get down to answering these letters of yours. Regarding Leave, yes, it means I am entitled to another seven days plus a 48 this quarter. I was never so lucky in all my life before. But I forgot – that's the Vinnell in me. Vic, I have not quite reached a decision as to whether I should have all the 48 at the beginning or the end of your Leave. You suggest having it at the beginning, but I do so love arriving home with you and feeling that there is a whole seven days before us. Besides, Vic, you would still have to leave before me on the day you return, so I should still have to travel back alone. No, let's have at least one journey together. Or would you really rather I met you in Liverpool? You would never need to see me in uniform then, and you might be able to forget that I am a Waaf. Would you like that better?

Which reminds me about something I must remember to tell my mother to 'laugh-off'. As I told you, Marjorie called to see Mum a few days ago, and it seems she (Marj) has been very worried about me, as the story she had heard was very alarming. 'I have been going around with Yanks, etc. so that no decent fellow would look at me, and not at all the sort of person for an officer'. I was quite interested to hear of all my activities; it sounds very exciting. Heavens above – Yanks! I don't believe I have ever spoken to one, except in a railway carriage once. The bit about being 'only a Waaf' tickled me. I can't think why Mum is getting all het up about it. What's it matter? I am glad she was able to relieve Marjorie's mind somewhat. It is my fault for not writing, I s'pose?

Oh well, Vic, I thought I'd better tell you what sort of a girl you are going to marry at the very beginning. I can't understand what sort of kick Bill and his family get out of spreading these kind of rumours, unless it is that making me look small acts like a salve to their own damaged pride. Funny how, in wanting to blacken my name, they bring in the 'Yanks'.

I didn't know that you prayed for me too, Vic? I always thought you would be too busy with pressing affairs of the moment. But I am glad you do, because already our combined prayers must reach His Ears together, and soon I hope we shall be able to be together as we say them. Yes, Vic, I think that too. I think our love will always be safe, always remain, because it is built on a solid foundation of truth and prayer and faith, and because God Himself has blessed it, and He is at the helm. Our love is in the hands of the great Creator, and He would not destroy His own handiwork.

Sure you won't have the last bit of my apple? Then I'll have to eat it myself. They are good, aren't they, Vic? I suppose yours are all finished? I must remember to send you some more when I am home.

Oh – I am thinking of when I was sitting in the train from Liverpool the last time I was home, and as usual, thoroughly immersed in thoughts of you and mouthfuls of apple, (mostly the latter you'll say!). When I had finished and become once more conscious of my surroundings, the man opposite, who must have been watching me, said: 'You enjoyed that, didn't you? I could tell it tasted good. Little bit tart though, wasn't it? A bit acidy? Yes, just a little, I could tell by your face.' Well, to say the least, I was startled. It would be useless, it seems, for me to go in for crime. Mothers are usually clairvoyant, but complete strangers!

Vic, I like the sound of my new name – the whole four of them, I mean. Oh, and now I'm puzzled. Will I be Mrs Henry Victor Alexander Vinnell? or will I be Mrs Nina Vinnell? Do I just take my choice? – Well, when I am really terribly proud and want to sound really important, I'll be Mrs Henry Victor Alexander Vinnell. The other one is shorter and will do for signatures. I'll be wanting to sound really important and I'll be feeling terribly proud very soon now I think. Poor old Nina, nearly on the top shelf, and 26 if she's a day, will arrive at the church supported by Nunk. And Mrs Henry Victor Alexander Vinnell, Vic's proud and happy bride, not a day more than 22, will pause for a moment on the steps of the Church for all to see, before starting life anew at your side.

Vic, I have been meaning to ask you – what would you like the organist to play? Which 'Wedding March'? There is a piece I like from 'Samson and Delilah' and there's Handel's Largo', but we ought to have something different from these, something that is the essence of sweetness, emerging from a deep low rumble of discord and disappointment and War, something that proclaims the triumph of our love. What shall it be? Has such music ever been written? Shall we have to go to the rushes and the heather to hear it again? I often hear your voice singing to me, Vic, and I wish I were drowning again in the blue depths of your eyes.

C C

G B I G B B

E A I E A A

C

'When I hear that re - frain,   oh my heart ach – es again'

For you, Vic, xxxxxxxxxxxxxxxxxxxxxxx

For you and your love, And your kisses

X X X (in all shades of red!)

You hold the missing pieces of my life to make me complete. Keep them for me please, darling. Goodnight, my love.

Yours, All Yours,

Nina

My Darling 'Gen Man' xxxxxxxxxxxxxx X xxxxxxxxxxxxxx

I still have two letters of yours to answer, although none arrived from you today, but at least it gives me a chance to catch up. It is just as well to keep one letter in hand for a rainy day, and anyway, I like to pay your letters the compliment of answering them pretty thoroughly. There is nothing more annoying that putting something one considers to be 'bang-on' in a letter, only for the other person to ignore it completely in her reply. I hope I don't do that very often – do I, Vic?

Now darling, you say you are 'simply bursting with gen' – what sort of 'gen'? I don't want you to be getting ahead of me, Vic, as I haven't yet found an efficient briefing instructor. How wonderfully thrilled your friend's bride must have been to be able to give him the glad news, right at the eleventh hour, that his posting overseas was cancelled! It occurs to me, however, Vic, that it would be a very good way of bringing matters finally to a head, especially if the bride was the 'put-off-till-tomorrow' sort. I wish I could find a Mrs Newly-Wed who would give me a few helpful hints, but those that I have met here would only be willing to talk about those things I should much prefer to discover for myself. I know you don't argue with this idea altogether, do you, Vic? But apart from the broad outlines, which could be acquired from a book on the subject or a reliable authority like one's mother, I want it all to belong to just we two – no technical terms or scientific explanations, but all new feelings, all delicious sensations, all a golden sixth sense.

I am afraid, Vic, that things are not moving very fast at all my end, except that I can see my way clear, and I have listed various items, such as the names of prospective guests (which come to 19, by the way, counting your father, aunt and uncle and cousin). Perhaps we could buy the Invitation Cards and Cake boxes (how many of those do you think we need? – quite a few, I should think, as we shall have to send some cake to all those friends we would have invited had we planned our wedding on a more lavish scale) where was I? – oh yes, we could buy those when we are again on Leave. You see, Vic, I am rather stumped because of Mumsie being in bed. However, I hope to see Marjorie on my next day off, and she already knows the position. Thank Heavens she isn't in the Forces or I'd be crossing my fingers for fear she couldn't get Leave at the same time – she is in the Land Army and lives at home.

Vic, whereabouts is the address in N. Wales? There are some very pretty spots there – but, you know, I have still got a longing to see those violets in Devon. Perhaps because I have never been to Devon, or indeed any place South (except London, but I meant souther than that).

We can always go to Devon some other time perhaps, and every one of your Leaves afterwards will be another honeymoon. We have discovered that it doesn't really matter very much where we go, so long as it is not among crowds, and so long as we are together, to worship each other how we will. We have our own special way of doing that, haven't we, my sweet?

Vic, I am sorry, but I have no more writing paper. I have left the rest of it at the office, but am afraid my stock is getting very low. Will soon be writing on our official paper. Will continue tomorrow. Sweet dreams, Vic.

Nina

Officers' Mess, RAF Station Foulsham, Norfolk
25th July, 1944 (Tues evening)

My very own Nina xxxxx

And there's strings of them for you, darling. If you intended your letter today to dumbfound me then you certainly succeeded. When I read it I was speechless with sheer delight, but only for a few seconds. Then I let out a yell that startled everyone in the room. A yell that was the pent up hopes, longings of the past few weeks. Oh how I wanted you to get Leave, Nina. It means that now we shall not have to talk with the whole world listening in. I will be able to kiss you when I want to, long, lasting kisses, the sort that I used to lose myself in when we stopped at a gate on the ride back to Wheaton in the evenings. When I kiss you, darling, everything that is Vic goes into the kiss and there meets his Nina, the complete, loveable, adorable Nina. I want these things, my love, I want to be alone with you more often. Oh yes, I can worship you with my eyes and I feel that my eyes tell you all that my heart is saying. But the smallest physical contact with you brings me such delight, a quickening of the heart, a spontaneous response inside me and I am so weak, so human that I need these physical contact, and they are so sweet, my darling, because I feel you respond to them. We are indeed on the same wavelength'.

Yesterday I had begun to despair of you getting Leave and so I sent you a telegram asking you to book rooms for me (Gosh, I am so excited, Nina, I can't write straight.) Today, I sent another one and this said that I will meet you in Stafford on the 5th and we shall go STRAIGHT HOME. Glorious words, Nina, and they mean a hell of a lot to me just now.

This evening I am sitting here looking very resplendent in No.1 Blue. I am shaved. I have enjoyed the luxury of a long soak in a hot bath, my hair is cut (not too short!) and one might say that I am 'all dressed up to kill'. Just ask me where I am going, Nina? Go on, please be curious. You are? Good, because I am going nowhere. I am keeping an imaginary date with you, my beloved sweetheart. I dressed myself up especially to write this letter. You see, these last few days I have been forced to write to you in odd moments. I don't like doing it that way, Nina, because I think of you so much and always have such a lot to tell you that the sequence becomes broken. You are for ever in my thoughts from waking to sleeping and if I am a lucky man then you are in my dreams too. If a day goes by when I don't write a few lines to you then I feel miserable. But it is a strange day for me sometimes, darling. And I am sleeping when I should be wide awake when I should have been in bed hours ago, and so I know you will understand and be patient if my few lines don't always reach the letter box as early as they should. But this I want you to know, Nina. That I love you with all my heart, soul and body, that I am missing you terribly every moment of every day, that I am praying earnestly that you will always love me as you do now. You are the only person I have in the world, Nina, and if you ever went away I should never really live again, never laugh again, never know the meaning of true happiness. I am looking to our great love, darling, and the protection I find behind its impenetrable shield perhaps more than you know these days. It gives me confidence in the knowledge that I have my feet fair and square on firm ground. I look to you, Nina, as the personification of all that is good and true, of all that stands for peace and happiness, and for all that is love and companionship in the fullest meaning of those words. You have my life completely in your hands; yours to build up or cast down, to take and cherish and care for or to cast away and leave it's owner hopeless and lost.

I have belonged to you ever since our first ride on the 'liberty' bus to Stafford, Nina. My heart so readily opened to you and I felt I was free for the first time in my memory. Oh Nina, the past years have seemed so dreary to me. Full of weary hours and unhappy memories. You have banished all that, and now I can remember nothing before last Christmas. All I can think of now is a pair of very beautiful smiling lips, of happy thrilling hours, of bridges, daffodils and winding leafy country lanes. It would indeed be a sad day for me, Nina, if you ever went away.

You certainly have a useful lot of boy friends lined up, darling. Bicycle repairs while you wait, eh! My goodness, you can never accuse me of misusing my charms any more. You are indeed an apt pupil of the great, colossal stupendous, the only show of its kind in the world, THE Vinnellski. (Pardon me, Nina, while I take a bow.)

And now, my lovely one, I am going to remove this glorious No.1 Blue complete with crease in trousers (God bless all batwomen) and crawl into my little cot. I am not going alone, Nina. Your spirit is going to snuggle up close to me, slip a knee between mine, put its arms up my back, its lips within easy kissing distance and lull me into a contented sleep.

God bless you, my Nina, happy dreams of seven glorious days of love and freedom and – I love you very, very dearly, my sweetheart.

Tired, but very much yours,

Vic xxx

X (Happy wedding day and very soon now)

---

7 days approved   RAF Station Wheaton Aston, Little Onn, Staffs
                                                                22nd July, 1944

Sir,

I have the honour to make application for leave from 5th August 1944 on the following grounds:

(i) that I have been unable to take leave since the beginning of January 1944.

(ii) that I have had only five days ordinary privileged leave since 3rd September 1943. (I was granted fourteen days' leave for compassionate reasons' on 4th September 1943 – my mother, who is a widow and lives alone, was confined to bed with varicose ulcer of the leg and I applied for leave to take care of her until some other arrangements could be made.)

(iii) that I am very worried about the health of my mother, as she is still under the care of the doctor and is far from well. (I have no sisters, and both my brothers are in the Forces.)

I have the honour to be,

Sir,

Your obedient servant,

Nina Chessall, LACW

479352 – Clk/G.D

The Officer Commanding,

RAF Station,

Wheaton Aston,

Little Onn, Staffs

AUGUST

3 Thursday GERMAN FRONT COLLAPSES Allies win greatest victory since Invasion Day. The German Front west of Caen has collapsed. Allied tanks rolling into the interior of France are meeting virtually no opposition. America armour, fanning out in strength from the north-east corner of Britanny, is well on the way to Rennes, key to all communications to the British Peninsular, and St Malo. British troops have broken through the German positions 15 miles south of Caumount, and an official spokesman describes the British attack as 'a major success'.

6 Sunday BIG NEWS! Russian are fighting on German soil – Montgomery busts through. This morning we bring you news of two events that will rank among the most important in the history of the whole war. They mark the final turning of the tide after nearly five years of war. In the West Montgomery's two-fisted blows have struck home. American tanks have not only reached the outskirts of Brest, at the tip of the Brittany Peninsula, but have smashed across the frontier of East Prussia – and for the first time the Allies are fighting on German soil. Montgomery has burst through the German defences. Our whole line is on the move, and the road into France becomes clear. And in Italy, Florence has fallen. The beachhead fight in Normandy has become the Battle of France. Reeling under Montgomery's attack, the Germans, while attempting to hold a hinge in the Caen area, are swinging back their whole Front.'

Seven days leave – first with Vic. Church with Mum and Vic, another Dream come true. Walk through Churchyard to the shore, which we were very loathe to leave, to return to dinner. But Vic was glad to get back to change his hot uniform. Lie in next to nothing in garden, take snaps, and have tea 'al fresco'. Make an effort to reach Liverpool to bring back bike, but give up and go a short walk instead. Today I said 'Yes – yes please'. Breach subject of 'When?' to Mum.

7 Monday Begin day in only way possible. Miss a lot of buses, but finally get 10.50 bus to Birkenhead and collect bike from Central Station, returning by boat. Meet Vic at ferry and cycle to Parkgate via Barnston. Have lunch en route at Devon Doorway. Lie in rushes and learn delicious way to eat apples. Buy lovely little plaice and some shrimps and fry them for tea. Sing songs round piano till very late. Serenade in the night.

8 Tuesday In bus queue for Liverpool when a visitor arrives – Mrs Burrows (Bill's mum) come to investigate. Introduce Vic and leave her to Mum's tender care. Cycle to Birkenhead, leave cycles at ferry. Shop in Liverpool for shoes for Vic and have lunch at The State. Cycle home and glad to get away from town. Water garden and inscribe names 'Vic and Nina' on largest marrow.

9 Wednesday Letter from Fred, a bitter pill to swallow. Maybe if he were here he'd think differently about Vic (I'd like his OK). Cycle to Parkgate again and answer the call of the rushes. Leave this world for over four hours and find, on descending to 'lower regions' that I am wearing Vic's engagement ring (solitaire – one Life, one Love).

10 Thursday Letter from Mrs Burrows, returning photo which Vic said he'd like. Rain this morning for the first time, but clears up into a lovely day. We take Mum out to West Kirby. Tour shops for yellow wool without success. Have very nice lunch at Blenheim Cafe, but no ventilation. Sit on Prom, go to sleep in sun and get well and truly burned. Tea of crab salad at café on Prom. Branston bus home. Disturbed night – Mum's independence at stake. Decide to leave Wedding for a bit.

11 Friday A real domestic sort of morning, a taste of what life could be like if there wasn't a war on. Vic cleans and oils my bike thoroughly, getting very dirty in the process. I mend his shirts and sew tabs on one for wear in warm weather. His 'Well Done!' all the reward I want. Cycle to Dales and lie hidden among ferns and heather. I believe it rained but rain can't reach our mountain top. Live on apples until supper.

12 Saturday Vic wakes me, nice way to wake. Cycle with him to Heswall village for shoe repairs. Take snaps in garden. 10.30am bus to Liverpool, have coffee at Forum Café and Au Revoir to my Heart. ('Lover, come back to me – xx soon). Walk dazed and numb to Coopers for coffee. Buy Imperial Talc, Vosene Shampoo and Setting Lotion, some savouries from Reece's, and some braid from tailor's as a gift. Sleep in the garden after lunch. Nunk sees me off on 7.5 train to Stafford.

13 Sunday Dreadful nightmare of a day. My head somewhere in the rushes at Parkgate, looking up at wheeling seagulls and fleecy clouds, my feet somewhere among the ferns and heather, and always the eternal taste of an apple – that food of the gods. So different from the unpalatable platesful I try to eat today. Sew braid on Vic's shirt, eat an apple, write a letter to Vic and sleep, dreaming of a soft shoulder.

Sunday evening

Dear Heart,

What did I feel, I wonder, as the train drew away from the Station, carrying you with it, and as you waved to the solitary figure on the platform? I felt as is someone were plucking at my heart, and slowly unravelling its strings as you pulled away from me, stretching it almost to breaking point. Oh Vic, dearest in all the world to me, didn't you see it lying bleeding between us? and I wanted to clasp you to me again to ease the pain of it.

(Vic, - Vic, - Vic, - I love you dearly. I belong to you and only await the day when you will claim your own. Beside you I count everything as nought. Just for this moment when our thoughts are united, don't be lonely, my darling. This is nine o'clock and a solemn sacred reminder to us both of that hour we spent in Blymhill Church. How often that chime has rung out for me in memory, and what comfort and peace it brings to me still! I love you, Vic.)

I have just finished eating an apple and I hoped I might be sharing it with you. Every good and lovely thing is a symbol of you, so how can I forget you ever? Today has been a nightmare. Don't ask me what I have done – I can't remember. I only know that my head was somewhere in the rushes, with the blue sky above and the wheeling seagulls. It might have been raining, but the rain was outside our world.

Your shirt is now all set for the post and I shall send it to you as soon as the post office opens tomorrow. I hope it will be all right, but there is just one point of doubt. Should the braid be the thicker variety for a Flt/Lieut? I went to Burton's the tailors opposite Central Station, and he had only a small amount of braid left, just sufficient for what we wanted, which he gave to me – yes GAVE to me!

I also bought some Imperial Leather talc, like we saw in West Kirby, some coffee and cakes, etc – and all the time I could have cried with the hole that grew larger inside me. Something outside myself controlled my movements, as I walked away from where you had been but a few moments before, but the real me was shedding great heavy drops of blood, just as scarlet Vic as our kisses – the bitter as well as the sweet. I didn't stay in Liverpool long, and after dinner I lay in the sun beneath the apple tree and followed you in your journey to where I may not follow except in thought, and after a while I slept. In my dreams you came to me and pillowed my head in your arms and this brought me a great measure of comfort

The 7.5 train back to Camp was very crowded and I had to stand all the way. I was glad I didn't take my bike. I think that now I want to keep it clean, after all your work. I feel terribly tired tonight, darling, and a little bit 'cheesed' too. Your photograph is now on the ledge above my bed and with 'our ring' on my finger in your favourite spot, I think I'll go to sleep. I can hardly keep my eyes open. I wonder how you feel. Tomorrow perhaps I shall know.

God keep you, my dearest one, always, for your devoted, Nina.

Monday

I think there is a possibility of my being able to have a 48 hours as everyone else has been granted a 48 hrs. tacked on to their seven days. Should I save it until your next leave, as from all accounts, it seems unlikely that normal leave will start in September as we thought? We could spend it in Chester. I believe Lillian and John got their ring there. She was telling me that at one o'clock in the afternoon Joyn hadn't got a ring and the wedding was at 3. She was very thrilled about us, and looked for a ring when she saw me in the bus queue.

Must get this post. Till we meet. Keep on remembering, Vic,
your Nina xxxxxxXXX

Officers' Mess, RAF Station Foulsham, Norfolk

Sunday Afternoon 13th August

My sweetheart of the rushes; xxxxxxxxx

This isn't true. I am sitting in the Flight Office in battle dress – waiting; but isn't it all a bad dream? A dream that you want to wake up from but can't? Oh Nina, I'm sure my heart is breaking. As the train drew out of the station yesterday and I signaled to you to keep your chin up, it was as much to encourage myself as you. I could still see you standing on the platform waving, long after the train had turned the bend. My eyes refused to lose your image until it was washed into my heart with tears. I could not bear to sit down and anyway I dared not do so until I had gained control over that lump in my throat.

The train slowly drew out of the city as if it too was reluctant to part us. I looked across the city but I did not see the dirt and squalor below me. Instead I saw the river as we had known it but a day before, calm and gray, the hills behind with summits vague in lowering clouds. I felt the gentle rain on my face, the warmth of your soft, sweet body as we drew closer together under the sheltering ferns. And there we were eating OUR apple once more. I heard the crisp snap as part of it came away between your lips. You parted it once, twice, three times, four times, and then – oh my Nina, the gods never made nectar so sweet as the apple that came to me from your lips! I never dreamed that such ecstacies were of this world. I never knew that life could be so full. Then we were in the rushes. Tall, waving, whispering rushes that made the softest, most sweet-smelling bed that lovers could desire. The most peaceful sleep in the world safe within your arms. Peaceful because I knew that when I eventually awoke it would not be to that soul-destroying loneliness. I knew that I would wake to your lips, your caresses 'neath my unbuttoned shirt, to the protection of your arms. I felt you holding me once again, holding me during a very intimate moment and I felt it was the most natural thing in all the world that you should do so. I lived those heavenly moments in the heather and ferns when we sheltered beneath your coat, our bed under the sky. We shall always sleep like that, my Nina, we can never go wrong if we do.

This past week has been the happiest of my life. I have never lived so fully before, never loved anyone so passionately, never laughed with such complete abandon. It has confirmed my opinion of what I have always thought life would be with you, my darling. No-one can ever take me away from you, Nina, not even the Dark Angel. I would live on in those whispering rushes, in the full moon. You would hear my voice in the gentle rain on the heath and find the full passions of my love for you in the strong winds and the blazing sunshine, even until the far corners of the earth. There is no death to our love – ever.

You are my whole world, the only possessor of my heart's love. There is no father, mother, brother or sister for me. Every emotion that I am capable of feeling, every ounce of strength that I can pour into loving is in my love for you, Nina.

Yesterday's journey took me precisely 13 and a half hours from door to door. I arrived in my Billet at a quarter to midnight. The trains were crowded to suffocation point with giggling women and hot, impatient men and all the trains were a good hour late. But it didn't seem to matter somehow. I felt impervious to all these irritations. I felt that my senses were blunted. I didn't even feel sick at the odour of crowded, sweating humanity. I travelled all day on the four sandwiches and one cup of tea. I did not feel hungry. The room was empty when I arrived back last night. Mechanically I undressed, took my pyjamas from the case and put them on. I think I washed and cleaned my teeth, I'm not very sure about that. I switched off the light, climbed into bed, pulled the sheets over me and – slowly put my hands between my legs. It was then that I had to take a firm grip of myself. Like a flash the tiredness was gone, no longer did I feel blunted and confused. I was vital and alive and I wanted you, Nina, my body cried out for you, for your caresses and your kisses, those passionate deep scarlet kisses and it was something akin to panic that I felt inside me because I knew that you could not take that which is rightfully yours. I went to sleep with a prayer 'Plesae God, bring us together soon, please God bring us together soon ... please God ... xxxxxxxxx

Today has brought confusion with it. Try as I might, I cannot grasp facts yet. I look at people, friends of mine, as if they were complete strangers. I asked the WAAF coach driver if she was taking the bus up to the Mess. I called her Nina. I called a F/Sgt 'Sir' over the phone. But out of this chaos I have managed to retain enough sense of order to start a very important deal. Nina, I want you to convey to me somehow the diameter of the third finger of your left hand. THE finger, the one with our ring on it. You see, darling, I am already negotiating for a wedding ring, a pukka one, and once I have the measurements it's just a matter of a short time before I get it. I think that's a really smart piece of work on my part (trumpets and banging of drums!) and I intended it to be so just in case our most precious dream is realized in six weeks time. Which reminds me to impress on you NOT to worry my beloved Nina. Promise me you won't worry. I know that you want us to be married just as soon as possible and you know that I will marry you tomorrow if you ask me to do so, I am living for the moment. But we cannot do so if it means hurting Mums. Remember Nina, she's my mother too. You must trust in my love for you and realize that it will never change under any conditions. We shall not have to wait long, my darling. I can feel inside me that we shall not have long to wait. Get your dress ready, get the cake made, the invitations ready, we'll buy the bridesmaid's present. I've already got the ring in view, that's the correct spirit to tackle the thing. And above all, trust in my love and my understanding. Oh my sweetheart, if only you could see inside my heart you would never worry again.

Nina, how artificial this life seems here! There is nothing here for us. Looking round me I feel certain everyone is parted from someone who is very dear to them. In the next room some fantastic swing tune is grinding its cacophony out of the radiogram. In front of me a bowl of Madonna lilies bow their white heads to the tobacco smoke. Dearest, kindest, passionate Nina, I want our rushes, the clean pure sincere rushes and heather. We will always find our greatest happiness in those surroundings and I am thankful for it. The lonely little boy who used to find his chief delights in the rain, the wild wind, who found his music in the disturbed tree-tops is no longer. His delights are still the same, but Vic has found his Nina and he is the happiest man on earth because he married his Nina on the stroke of nine in a little country church at Blymhill in the presence of He who is all-seeing and all-powerful. God bless our love and keep it forever as strong as it is today.

Your lover until the end of Time,

Vic X X X

Xxx

X X X   .

Wednesday evening 16/8/44

Vic my Dearest,

At least I can WRITE your name so that you may READ it, even if I can't SAY your name so that you may HEAR it. I had so looked forward to speaking to you tonight, especially when I waited in vain for the phone to ring on Monday. Vic, you are all right I hope? You're not sick again? You're not hurt? I feel so helpless, just sitting and hoping and praying and waiting, my mind a prey to all sorts of wild possibilities. If only I could do something to help tear down the veil that separates us from my end, instead of leaving it all to you! But there's nothing I can do – is there? I must just wait, and carry on writing.

Your shirt ought to have arrived by now. What is your verdict, Vic? Your 'Well Done' is the best reward I could have, but don't say it just to please me – tell me the truth, the truth, Vic, even if you don't like it. Oh, I hope to be sending you something else at the end of the week, something I have just acquired, but which I haven't yet got the cash to pay for. No darling, it is no use guessing; it's a surprise and I am not even going to give you any clues, except – except – (don't hold your breath for too long, darling xxxxxxxxx) except that it is something you have been wanting.

Mums wrote me a lovely letter on Sunday afternoon, sitting under the old apple tree, and missing us both very much. She says the marrow looks fine, but that she will be puzzled to know what to do with it, as it look like a memorial to two happy lovers. It would be a shame to just eat it. I do hope the snaps of it come out well.

Vic, just once or twice, I thought that you were feeling swamped out of the picture, there was too much pressure of other interests on my side. But Vic, dear Vic, don't feel hurt. I remember on St Valentine's Night you told me how you felt it was a disadvantage to have no background, no family, no place to invite a girl. Vic, don't think that, don't look back in vain regrets. Rather do I want you to share all my good fortune with me, yes, even the love and prayers and blessings of my incomparable family. You must share everything, Vic, all my friends as well, and if you find something you can't share, then that something must go. Let me share all your life too, my Vic, won't you please? You see, none of my family seek to take me from you or be a rival to you in any way, but rather if my family could be your family too, then your life too would be more complete. Sometimes I feel terribly selfish when I think of our wedding and all (or most) of our guests belonging to the Chessalls. Don't mind that too much, Vic, my darling. I shall soon be adding one more to the Vinnells, and maybe even adding more than that, in due course. But know that I love you with a single-mindedness of purpose that cannot be turned aside. I love you completely, undividedly and no-one and no thing can take me from you. No-one has ever counted so much in my life before. I am yours, Vic – just that – all yours.

Last night I went to Stafford with Jean at her request. She was feeling 'cheesed' and wanted to tell someone her troubles. We saw a horrible thriller at the Odeon called 'Soldier Woman', featuring the immortal Sherlock Holmes, gruesome and horrible. You haven't seen it by any chance, have you? It is about a subtle form of murder designed by the female of the species, who uses deadly horrible spiders to kill her victims. Definitely not a film calculated to amuse.

In my last letter, Vic, I told you about a proposed 48, that is all different now, as leave has started again as from 15th Aug. So I shall be entitled to another 7 days and a 48 this quarter when you have yours in Sept. My day off this week I think will be Saturday, as I shall not be having a day off next week when Pat is on leave. I think I'll go home. If only you could fly over and see me this week! I watch for you every day. But don't, please don't, come over on Saturday when I am not here. That would be too disappointing. You know the worlds heard on the radio: *'I'll never smile again until I smile at you.'*

Make me smile again, darling, and soften the stiffness around my heart. Oh what an artificial unnatural life this is! Won't I be happy when we can spend our days as we did on Friday morning last, serving each other solely for the pleasure of the other's smiles. Oh Vic, I love you, and I want you to fill all my needs. You can do it, that I know, but what we lack is the opportunity, companion, playmate, lover, the missing piece of myself – all these you are to me, and now I want to combine them all in the one heading – my husband. I have never called you that yet, have I, Vic? But I too feel that I will soon.

Nearly time for 'shut-eye'. But first, a last long kiss, a caress inside your shirt, a squeeze and a 'Goodnight Darling'. See you in the morning.

Your Nina X xxx X xxx X xxx X

Officers' Mess, RAF Station Foulsham, Norfolk
Wednesday even 16th August

My beloved Sweetheart,

Your first 'after-leave' letter arrived today and believe me, it was received with open hands if not open arms. I did not want to come back last Saturday. God knows I didn't. It was the most painful parting I have ever experienced but what hurt me most of all was the pain that I knew must be in your heart. Dearest Nina, I pray that these lonely heartbreaking days may soon belong to a past era, not a forgotten era for so many things have happened that I shall never forget. We shall be able to keep the sweet memories and try to forget these dark, lonely weeks.

On Sunday we must have gone to the rushes together, my darling. Did you not see me? Did you not lay on that soft, sweet bed with me and caress me As you did but a few days precious? Did we eat an apple together? Of course we did, my heart's love. I am going to try and contact you tonight and I am hoping with all my fingers crossed that I shall have time to do so. It promises to be a very long and busy evening. Think of me, my sweet, think hard about nine o'clock of everything we have been to each other, of our marriage at that sacred hour. Never forget to say your prayers, Nina, and before you sleep please slip your gentle hand into mine. I feel in need of the peace and confidence it inspires in me. And our ring, darling, put it in my favourite spot each night. When I have my ring I shall do the same for you.

Now, my Nina, I would like some 'gen'. Great changes have happened here as follows.

The leave year starts on August 15th now. Also everyone can go on leave once very three months. Now, presuming the first three months starts from August 15th does that mean you are entitled to another seven days plus a 48? If it does then Sept 25th is the date. If you cannot get leave, then save your 48 until my next leave and we shall go to Chester together as you say. I should love to go there again. We have left part of our love in many places, darling. One day we shall go back to them all once more. To Stratford in Spring with the daffodils. To Cuttlestone Bridge when the hedges are waking to the first warm sunshine of the year. The world belongs to us, Nina. It breaks my heart to let these lovely sunny days go by without you. This afternoon I took my shirt off (no singlet, Nina) and lay down on the grass to acquire some more suntan. Unfortunately I was not there for very long. I had to attend the call of 'N for Nina'. I am going to have your name painted on the nose then you will truly be with me.

My darling, I have just received the shirt. A beautiful job of work, but I'm afraid you have boobed, dear. You have sewn on two thin rings and it should be two THICK ones. Don't worry, Nina, I'll buy some thick braid and send it back to you. Or would you rather I had it altered here? You won't have a sewing machine to hand, will you?

There's just one more thing before I close, Nina. You are not worrying are you, darling? Please say you are not. I don't want you ever to worry about me, dear. My love for you will never change no matter how many difficulties face us. There is nothing left for me in life if you ever went away. My love for you is more lasting than the hills that are so dear to us as we look at them together across the Dee. Tomorrow the earth may quake and swallow the hills, but my love would not case with my death. You would always know where to find me, Nina, when you needed me. Go ahead with our plans and have faith in US.

God bless you, dear Sweetheart.

Keep close to me. I love you so very much.

For all time

Vic

Xxx X xxx

Officers' Mess, RAF Station Foulsham, Norfolk
Thurs even 17th August

Nina, my very own, XXX

My luck held good tonight and with the kind of co-operation of Lilian I managed to contact you. I'm sorry I could not make it last night, dear, but I didn't have a dog's chance. I know you will understand. I'll try hard for Sunday night. It does make me feel hopeless trying to squeeze a whole week into something under six minutes and condensing a heart running over with deep, lasting emotions into three words, 'I love you'. Being parted from you is one of the hardest things I have had to bear in life. No-one but yourself can possibly know how keenly I feel it, how it sometimes makes me feel sick and ill. All the time I am longing, hoping for the happiness that is ours when we are together. As I write my letters to you my spirit strains to reach you. I see your eyes, your smile, the lock of hair that falls over your forehead. A sweet, comforting, and yet a heartrending vision, a vision of my Nina, who is to me the embodiment of all that is good and pure, of all that spells complete happiness and contentment, of all that is splendid passion. You are never out of my thoughts, darling, and at nine o'clock each evening I never forget our date no matter how pressing the business of the moment.

When it was just about 'lights out' for you last night I said my prayer for you, Nina. I asked God to keep you safe through the night. I thanked Him for our love and asked Him that you may always love me 'til the end of time. I asked Him to take care of Mums, Nunk, Fred and Joe because I know that so much of your happiness in life depends upon them. Finally, into His Hands I commended my life. I have never considered prayer so much as I have during these past months. You have taught me to believe in it, Nina, and its power has been proved to me. I know that I will always be safe because I firmly believe that God has built our love, tested it, and found it very strong indeed. He would not knock it down now by taking either one of us away from the other. I believe that we were brought together by some guiding power outside of our control. That power said 'Love. Go on, love and see if it is not the sweetest thing on earth'. We said that it was, indeed it was, and so the power said 'But life is not easy, not straightforward and you must learn to love each other under dire difficulties, and so I will put you both on the testing ground'. And so it has been, my darling. We fought for days off, when plans fell down we pushed the ruins aside and built new ones. Many obstacles, some very formidable, stood in our path and we surmounted them – TOGETHER, as they came along, all the time going from happiness to even greater happiness. We have never looked back, my Nina, nor shall we ever look back. We overcame parting, one of the biggest obstacles so far, and the reward last week was the happiest week of our lives. And now, Mrs Henry Victor Alexander Vinnell, the PRIZE, that for which we have always headed, our 'target' is very clearly in view. In a matter of weeks we shall be ONE in everybody's eyes. One name, one life, one love. We shall sleep in each other's arms and say our prayers together. We shall read our chapter, have our breakfasts as planned, and – Nina – come closer. Closer still, I want to whisper … between the chapter and the breakfast we shall visit those heights as often as you wish. Could anything be sweeter, dear heart o'mine?

And now I must write to Mums. God bless you, my sweetheart and keep you safe for me – this night and always.

Your own

Your devoted

Vic

Nina, I wonder if you can get a ring from Woolworths that fits your finger. Or any ring if it comes to that, so long as it gives some good idea of the fit. I will send you an address to send it to, or if I have not done so by the time you obtain it, then send it on to me.

Find out about leave as soon as you can because I want to book in Chester soon if you cannot get seven days.

Goodnight, beloved.

XXXXX

---

22 Tuesday Court of Inquiry re: Sgt Abbotts, killed at rear of girlfriend's house, low-flying for her benefit.

---

22 Saturday: FRENCH GO WILD AS GERMANS SURRENDER PARIS
Paris is clear of Germans – except dead ones. The German Commander surrendered unconditionally yesterday. Last night General de Gaulle, Fighting French Leader, re-entered his capital, which went wild with joy. A commentary by liberated Paris radio was made against a roaring background of shrieking crowds, the thumpings of a military band and bursts of gunfire.'

RUMANIA DECLARES WAR ON GERMANY Rumania's declaration of war against Germany yesterday has thrown the whole of the enemy forces in the country into a state of chaos. Twelve German divisions are surrounded in a new Russian encirclement trap south-west of Kishinev. More than 13,000 Germans have already surrendered, and the Moscow communiqué said that fighting was going on for the liquidation of the forces.'

Saturday 16/8/44

My Dear All,

Tonight I may not speak to you, but I can write to you, so – here I am darling. I bought my usual large glass of lemonade in the NAAFI, and drunk it all. All my friends had gone out tonight, so I sat at my table alone, drumming my fingers on it, waiting, waiting, looking at my watch, reading your last letter, gazing at the little black instrument in there hoping it would come to life – truly a nerve-racking experience! At twenty to nine I collected my rations (not Senior Service this week, darling. Sorry.) and a skien of black darning wool, and returned to the billet to mend your socks, which arrived this morning, by the way. Your shirt now belongs to a Flight/Lient Vic, and your socks are all shadow-proof. I haven't seen these black socks before. Are they new ones? You must have a wayward big toe, Vic, whose fighting instincts you will have to control – a fighting Vinnell every inch of you, from your unruly hair and obstinate chin to the tip of a determined big toe. I know your name is Victor, but you don't have to win all the time – you or your toe. Roll on the day when I shall be the ONLY ONE to darn your socks, my sweet. Hm, yes, that does almost sound as if your fiancée is a jealous woman, Vic. I must remember in future to pretend I am not.

I know I didn't have my much-longed-for talk with you tonight, my darling, but I must not grumble as it will not be a lonely weekend for me now. This morning I had a typically 'Vickish' letter from you, unparalleled delight, and at lunchtime I collected your parcel containing shirt and socks and 'sweeties' for which Very x Very x Very x Very x Many x Thanks. I just thought – did you know you sent me an odd sock? I notice you are withholding your 'Well Done' until the job is quite correct and finished – very right and proper too – but I am eager to hear it, so will post everything to you as soon as I can which will be Monday.

Another thing I must remember to thank you for, my Vic, is the registered letter containing your clothing coupons. This arrived yesterday. You are such a darling, that if you were here in bed with me I'd smother you with kisses – yes, all over, Vic, right down to that wayward big toe and right up to your crisp curls, depending on where I started, and covering the whole area between. I love you so very much, and your love and thought for me seem to give you almost as much pleasure as they give me. Love is a greater pleasure to be got out of giving and the knowledge that in doing so you are making your loved one divinely happy.

I promise you, darling, that I won't spend any of your coupons needlessly and will probably tell you first what I want to buy. Most likely I'll take so long over spending any that you will be in possession of your next year's coupons before these are used. I read an old Chinese proverb this week: 'If you want a thing long enough, you find you don't'. Somehow I don't like it. It is true in a way about small things, I suppose, but there is a typical twist to it, a grim sort of humour, that makes me shudder. Most Eastern philosophy affects me like this. To revert to the coupons – don't I travel a long way from the subject? – I may even have been issued with my own civilian book by then. I wonder, Vic, if when this European War is over, they will start demobilising some of us. There will not be the need for such total warfare then, surely. Already they are closing down stations in this Command every week, and some of their personnel have been posted here. Possibly this will be the last to be closed. Don't you think that a lot of the WAAF will be demobbed at the close of hostilities in the West? And also some of the men who would hold key positions for post-war reconstruction? It is a safe bet that married women would be one of the first to be released AT THE SAME TIME as their husbands, if their husbands are in the Services, and also Govt. employees, Civil Servants, and the like, which would only be like a transfer from one Dept. to another. So, you see, Vic, that in either circumstance, I ought to be one of the first out of uniform and able to get cracking on plans for OUR LIFE. The only 'fly in the ointment' is if it also means your transportation to the other side of the globe.

God help me, if that happens, because no-one else can. You said you were having horrible nightmares. Vic, did you dream that I COULDN'T answer your love, or that I WOULDN'T? Both would produce the same results, I suppose; but My Dearest One on all the Earth, don't you know yet that, you being you and me being me, the latter circumstances is a physical, mental and spiritual impossibility? The former circumstance happens often as we well know, but give me the opportunity, Vic darling, and I'll pay it all back what I have been saving, with a generous interest. Six weeks is too long to be frustrated, and I dare not contemplate what a longer period would do to us, so I don't contemplate more than I can help. If your happiness in life depends on me, Vic, you will always be a Very Happy Man. My love for you is undying, my faith in you unshakeable. It will not be in vain.

Your Life, Your Love,

Your Nina

xxx xxx xxx

Officers' Mess, RAF Station Foulsham, Norfolk

Monday even 21st Aug

My Beloved,

Although it has rained here again today and the skies have been grey yet there has been sunshine in my heart, the sunshine of your love for me so beautifully expressed in your letter.

The weather has been squally with a gusty wind driving a thin misty rain, just the sort of day for a walk over some wild moor or down by the sea. The sort of day when we could pit our strength against Nature. If only we could have gone to the Dales. I know we should have been alone there. Just you and I, darling, with the mad wind and rain, the sweet smell of the ferns and heather all to ourselves. We shall always find our happiness 'neath the skies be they winter o summer skies. The azure skies of spring and summer are beautiful, the breeze is warm and caressing, almost sensuous. There is a soft, verdant beauty all around. But the autumn and winter too are grand, when Nature becomes wild. There is something attractive, something invigorating about a mad wind. The keen excitement of danger, of mystery; the ragged clouds have an air 'of dirty work' about them especially when a watery moon tries vainly too shed a soft glow on the earth beneath. Winter with you, my Nina, has a special beauty of its own. Every season of the year and all the years that are to be, will all be beautiful so long as I can live them with you – one life, one love X xxx X xxx X xxx X.

I was looking through a magazine called 'Flight' a few days ago and I saw an offer of some very attractive portraits of aircraft. One in particular caught my eye. It is entitled 'Mosquitoes Sting at Night'. It shows a mossie in silhouette against the night sky with a moon obscured by clouds. It looks very attractive and you can almost feel the loneliness of the pilot and navigator. I hope you like it, Nina, as I thought it would be the first picture for our new home. Don't be afraid to say if it does not appeal to you. We can always use it as a present to someone. But somehow I know you'll like it. You see, Nina, in years to come if we ever strike a hard patch, the picture would serve to remind us of the difficulties that we overcame in these years of war. Of the courage that we have both needed and also of how lucky we were to find one another. It will represent 'N for Nina' who always brought me back because my Nina's prayers – your prayers, my darling – always went with me. And just a wee, small thought aside – think of what a horrible line I will be able to shoot to our children and grandchildren. I do hope you like it, dear. I have sent instructions for it to be sent home. The actual picture is 17x12 inches on a 25x20 inch plate-sunk sheet. Just a nice size.

The ring will probably reach me tomorrow, Nina, and Geoff Evans (my representative) will bring the real stuff back with him from leave on Sept 10th.

And now, my dear, the old eyes are beginning to droop a little so I will bid you 'Goodnight' and 'God Bless'. I'll say my prayers as always, darling, and in them I'll ask that soon our prayers may go to Him at the exact same moment from the same bed. Happy, happy day.

Sweet dreams, beloved.

Always your Vic

PS I'll write to Mums tomorrow and tell her that a picture is coming. Enclosed is a photographic representation.

Officers' Mess, RAF Station Foulsham, Norfolk
Wednesday even 23rd August

Dearly beloved,

I spend as happy a day as possible. I say that because none of the days that we are apart are happy ones. There is always that gnawing pain of loneliness inside. But it has been eased for me today in many ways. First of all there was your letter waiting for me at lunch-time. It was a long one, twelve pages, so I tucked myself away in a corner, slipped my hands into yours and read it, and one of the lines that I was happiest to read was 'No, I am not worrying now'. Oh Nina, you need never worry about my love for you. You know that I have never been in love before, don't you? No-one has ever possessed my heart before, and most certainly not my body, in the way that you have. I shiver to think of the terrible catastrophe that would have occurred had I met you a few months later. It would have been a living hell for me, Nina, a hell upon earth. Ugh!

But to return to the happy present and future. (I always think of the present as being from last Christmas onwards. That was when I started to live, Nina) After lunch I looked at the parcel list. F/Lt Vinnell had a registered parcel. I made a bee-line for the Post Office and I was greeted by a small, very mysterious parcel addressed in your very dear hand. Back to the mess – no time for ceremony so I borrowed a penknife – a few seconds later the package was opened and I was greeted by – twenty 'Senior Service' xxxxx. Just a moment, though, what's this tucked away at the bottom – it's a – no, it can't be. I pulled it out and – yes it is, oh my darling, it's a real live, working lighter! xxx (very scarlet, but only on a/c).

Nina, I am very thankful to you. It's a beautiful job. This evening I worked on it for about half an hour cleaning the case and trimming the wick and now it's working perfectly. Indeed a most pleasant surprise and 'Well Done, my Nina.

This evening I got through to you in ten minutes and I could hear you perfectly and it was the same your end. Almost incredible isn't it, darling? I don't know if I said all I wanted to, but I know I said 'I love you, Nina' and that was the most important thing. I have that on the tip of my heart all day, every day.

And to round off a happy day here I am with you once more as I am writing, putting my arm around you with your cheek just about lip-height ready for my kisses. I like walking with my arm about you, darling. You fit very snugly underneath and I steal a kiss even in the busiest thoroughfare. Sweet, disturbing physical contact. I miss it very much, my Nina, it means a great deal to me. Twenty per cent but a very important twenty per cent. I never dreamed that such passionate moments, such strong desires for only one person existed before I met you. I felt this new emotion stirring inside me last February, the first time I told you that I loved you. Since then it has grown with the passing months, grown with your love for me because I felt you respond so readily. It has been added to companionship, sympathy, complete understanding to complete one hundred per cent true love. I was blind before I met you, Nina and blindly was I walking up the wrong road, without a true friend.

I am glad the wedding plans are going ahead. Why, we have covered more than fifty per cent of the ground already. Ring almost in our hands, bridesmaid briefed and material almost made up, gosh, the vicar had better look alive, we're coming in on the beam.

Goodnight now, my precious, can you feel my lips on yours? They are there, Nina, in a long, passionate kiss x I love you with all my heart, soul and body

Your devoted

Vic

'friendship is forged in the flame of adversity'

It is, Nina, and when it ripens into love then it's a love that is strong and true. A love that knows no ending and death cannot part the lovers.

God bless you, my beloved. My prayers are watching over you – always

I love you very dearly

Officers' Mess, RAF Station Foulsham, Norfolk
Friday morn 25th August

Dearest Nina of the heather,

I have been wanting to start this letter for the past two hours but could not do so as I was waiting to do a spot of work. As is usual in the RAF, I waited for nearly two hours and then it didn't materialise, so I came back to the Mess and – oh joy! – a letter from you, my darling.

Oh yes, my sweet, it is so very easy to write my letters to you for the reason that in my imagination we are together, you and I am talking with our heads close together just as we always do. I find the words flow so easily from my pen and so they should with an incentive like my love for you. One day, dear Nina, I shall write a book about the most beautiful love story that ever was. The story of Nina and Victor.

I asked one of the ground crew yesterday to get cracking with the paint brush. I hope this afternoon I shall find 'Nina' on the side of my kite. Some of them have some weird and wonderful contraptions on the side but 'Nina' is all I ask for. I know she will see me through.

Yes, darling, I have thought about our baby many times, but as you say - not for some time yet. I want years of just you. The child will be a natural outcome of those years. I don't mind how HE says 'castle', in fact I'll teach him to say it as you do. But I plan to keep him just an idea in our heads for a long time after we are married. I'm not selfish darling, but I don't want to share you with anyone for a very long time. I have waited long for a love like this, Nina, I'm just not willing to share it.

Yes, dear, I'm keeping Peter thoroughly up to date with our great progress. I think I told you, he still wants to be our best man, but I'm afraid he will be a bit late. Please, darling, I don't want you to worry about me going the same way as he has gone. That would be crossing a bridge before we came to it. Let's just live for all the time we can get together, being very happy and enjoying life to the full. But if it did so happen that I went overseas I would wish you to marry me before I went, dear. I would want to come back to you as my wife. Every time I addressed a letter to you as 'Mrs Vinnell' it would not make you seem so far away.

I've got a new battle dress. Did you say about time? If you did I quite agree. The old one was assuming a delicate green hue through old age and the left elbow was through. But I was sorry to part with the '1941' label inside. Are you sporting our observer's brevet, dear? The one I gave you on leave. I would like you to sew it on a very prominent place for all the world to see that you have joined the noble (?) union of navigators.

And now I'm afraid I'll have to conclude, darling. My lunch hour is nearly over. God bless you dear and keep you safe – and I'll be with you at nine.

Until we lay in the rushes again, Nina

Your very own Vic

I love you my darling xxx

Officers' Mess, RAF Station Foulsham, Norfolk
29th August 1944

Dear girl of my dreams,

Of all my dreams, Nina. Since coming back from our leave not many nights have passed without you coming to me in the wee small hours of the morning. I think we must be fast overcoming the distance that parts us I these long, dark weeks. We may get it down to such a fine art that we could go cycling together again to Blymhill xxx, who knows.

Today I read your letter at tea time for the first time instead of at lunch time. The reason being that I have been away for most of the day and, agony of agonies, I passed right over Stafford. Yes, right over it, Nina. I saw the Odeon, the 'Station', the High Street, all in one sweep of the eye but here was nothing I could do about it. I consoled myself by remembering that in just over three weeks I would be with you on that very railway station and waiting impatiently for the 5.27pm for Liverpool.

I also saw x Chester x darling, but I won't dwell on that. I can leave it to you to imagine the thousand and one visions that flashed before my eyes.

Nina, dear, I think you have wrong idea of the 'gen' that I am bursting with, or rather, with which I am bursting. The 'gen' I referred to concerned the etiquette of the ceremony. Which side of the church I sit on, when I rise to meet you, which of my arms you take, where the best man stands, and lots of little things like that which are important to the nervous groom. That was the 'gen' I was gleaning from Geoffrey, who no doubt still has it freshly imprinted on his mind. After the ceremony is over, darling, I am leaving all the rest to our glorious love. Believe me, dear Nina, I know no more than you do about the 'technical' terms. I don't believe that there can be anything technical and I hate the thought of it. The instinct of our love for one another is enough to guide, Nina, and I would ask no-one for advice. I'm longing for our honeymoon, my love, and I know that we have both lived it in our imagination a thousand times. I know I have.

Yes, Nina, we'll buy the cake boxes on our next leave. I'll make a list of those I think should have a piece and we can add it to yours. (I shan't want very many) It's a relief to know that Marjorie will be free and at our disposal. Jack, of course, will be on leave with me so that takes a big weight off our mind. Its very bad luck that mums should be confined to bed as she is our main stay but of course she must stay there until Doc gives her the OK.

The address in N Wales is; 'The Cecil Court Hotel, Morfa Nevin, Nr Pwllheli, Carmarthen'. Do you know it, dear? I have also got a couple of addresses in Windermere, Lake District. You will have your violets in Devon, my darling, believe me you will, another honeymoon for us. All our leave will be honeymoons, and we will have one in our beloved Chester for certain.

Nina, I'm living for our wedding day and all the glories that will come with it. Companionship and happiness twenty four hours a day, no more lonely nights, your arms always ready to enfold me, your lips ever ready for my kisses. When I dream of you at nights I shall no longer have to wake up to bleak loneliness. There will be no line between sleeping and waking. Remember Chester, Nina? Remember how we 'lost' two hours one night? That's how it will always be, my angel. A golden, continuous stream of love whose source is in silvery cloud-capped heights.

I am enclosing the letter which I received from the firm, who are selling the picture. I know you will want to see it as it is OUR business transaction. I imagine that Mums received it today and is highly puzzled by it, but I know you will soon satisfy her curiosity. Leave it at home, dear, because I don't want it damaged.

When I get a day off I will try to borrow the Tiger Moth and, weather permitting, come to Wheaton and stay the night. Perhaps I could borrow a cycle there and we could visit Blymhill, the place where we were REALLY married.

Goodnight, my sweet. Happy dreams, dreams of you and I together. God bless you, my Nina, and keep you for me always

For ever your lover

Vic

Xxx

SAMSON CLARKS
Incorporated Practioners in Advertising
57-61 MORTIMER STREET, LONDON, W.1

F/Lt H. V. A. Vinnell

Officers' Mess

RAF Foulsham

Norfolk

Twenty-fifth
August
Nineteen
Forty-four

Dear Sir,

We write gratefully to acknowledge your order for one print of Frank Wootton's oil painting, together with your remittance for which we enclose a receipt. The print will be dispatched as indicated by you within the next day or so.

We feel sure you will be interested to know that these prints have already raised over £3,500 for the Royal Air Force Benevolent Fund. Half of all remittances is immediately handed over to the Fund and, when the bare cost of production and distribution has been recovered from the balance of subscriptions, the remaining payments will also be given to this most deserving cause.

.Yours faithfully,

SAMSON CLARK & Co. Ltd.

Officers' Mess, RAF Station Foulsham, Norfolk
Wednesday even 30th August

Dear Heart,

It's almost nine o'clock, darling. In a few minutes time the clock in the church tower at Blymhill will send its chimes across the sleepy village. The wooden gate of the churchyard creaks as a boy in Air Force blazer opens it for a girl. She is in the uniform of the WAAF. Together they walk up the path towards the church door, stopping on the way to admire some fresh daffodils on a silent grave. They whisper something and pass on to the Church.

Inside it is almost dark. The last rays of daylight slant across the deserted pews, the shining cross on the altar is still visible through the gathering gloom as they kneel together in the back pew, hand in hand, heads bowed in prayer, prayers some of which have since been answered, the rest will all be answered in God's good time.

Solemnly they open a prayer book and together read over the wedding service. Together, in God's Eyes,, they say 'I will'. They promise to love, honour and obey, to cherish each other in sickness and health until the Dark Angel spreads his wings. The clock chimes the hour of nine, and as the echoes die away Nina and Vic leave the church as man and wife in their own hearts and in God's Eyes. They are inseparable, two people living, thinking, acting and loving as one.

I am with you every night at the magic hour of nine, my darling, no matter how busy I am or where I am. I say my prayers for you before I go to sleep, and if I am not going to bed for a little while then I say them about half past ten. I think of you continuously throughout the day and it takes the form of a yearning – a longing to hold you in my arms and kiss you passionately yet tenderly – a longing to walk and talk with you, to sleep by your side at nights, my arms about you, my lips close to yours. I long to prove my love for you in the most convincing way I know. I'm striving to give you my love right now as I write this letter but the words just stare back coldly at me from the paper. Touch them with your warm heart, dear Nina, make them live again for it is a real, living, vital love that I bear for you, my darling, a love that knows the dizzy, silvery heights of passion and happiness when I am with you – a love that knows the deepest despair when we are parted. Soon, my Nina, there will be no more despair.

A queer thing happened to me today, Nina, talking of demobilisation. The Adjt presented me with a form to fill in (not in triplicate this time). It required details of civilian employment, name and full address of employer, type of business and a couple of more questions on similar lines. It was for all Officers commissioned before a certain date in 1942. I don't know the exact date. Perhaps I shall be getting the proverbial bowler hat pretty soon. Gosh! Then we would really be getting somewhere. I should think that your days in the WAAF are drawing to a close, Nina. I'm certain that as a married woman you would stand pretty high on the list, and also as a Civil Servant. As you say, it would only be like a transfer. A happy thought indeed, Nina. Mr and Mrs Vinnell, civilians.

In the bad dreams that I had, Nina, you COULDN'T answer me. I don't know why I had those dreams but I refuse to believe that they are premonitions. Rather would I say they were caused by eating Canadian cheese and chocolate before going to sleep. We'll laugh the bad dreams off, shall we darling, and just remember the good ones. There's enough unhappiness in the waking day caused by loneliness without going to bed and dreaming of it. The good dreams are by far in the majority, dear, the drams in which I come to you and love you as I want to do.

Darling, you must realize that 'N for Nina' is not your rival by any stretch of the imagination. Rather is she an embodiment of you, taking care of me in the dark hours, a fast and nimble creature who has your interests at heart. You have no rival, my darling, in all the world – most certainly not in the world of machinery. Won't you be friends with her, please – just to make me happy? Yes, I knew you would. I might have known better than to try and 'flannel' the woman who loves me. I surrender, Nina. The picture will make a wizard line-shoot in the years to come but it will carry a meaning of its own for we two, a meaning of obstacles surmounted because we love one another.

I love you dearly, my Nina, and I'm longing for you. Tell me as soon as you've fixed your leave up. I must admit that I will worry about it until it's 'in the bag', and when I start worrying you know what happens. I'm living for those seven happy days, Nina, to know the thrill of being with you again, to go down to the rushes and the river, to see the hills and the heather. All these things spell HOME to me now, dear, and they are very precious indeed. Please come home with me that I may see again the true glory of them.

God bless you, my sweetheart, my wife.

For ever and ever

Your Vic X xxx X xxx X

SEPTEMBER

4 Monday The War – 1829th Day

BRITISH OCCUPY BRUSSELS AND ANTWERP Germans say Boulogne and Calais evacuated. Brussels has been liberated. Allied troops which crossed the Belgian frontier early yesterday morning rapidly freed Tournai and pushed on to the north and east to enter the capital in the late evening, says Shaef communiqué. An Associated press report today datelined 'The French Frontier' said it was reliably reported that the Allies had entered Antwerp. British troops have thus advanced 180 miles since they crossed the Seine at Verdun on August 26th, only eight days ago. Boulogne and Calais have been evacuated, according to German reports in Switzerland.'

FINNS QUIT AFTER FOUR YEARS OF FIGHTING After over four years of fighting the war between Finland and the Soviet Union came to an end today. The cease-fire – the first of this war – on the Finnish held sectors of the Eastern front was ordered by Field Marshal Mannerheim, the Finnish President, at 8am today (10am London time), it was officially announced at Helsinki. The German forces, estimated to number 160,000 men, have until September 15th to get out of the country, failing which they will be disarmed and handed over to the Russians by the terms of the preliminary armistice conditions.'

NAZI AIR FORCE RETIRING The Luftwaffe is now drawing back into Germany for the defence of the Reich, says Major W MacLauschan. The Star's Air Correspondent. During extensive operations yesterday only a few enemy planes were encountered over Holland and Belgium, and two out of three were shot down in the neighbourhood of Louvain.'

Glorious radiant Monday 4/9/44

Dearest in All the World,

I was nearly in despair – (the hands of the clock were moving towards nine). I was nearly in tears – (I have been longing to hear your voice with an ever-growing intensity, and I love you so). I was nearly overwrought (with the ceaseless chatter and raucous laughter all around me and the blaring notes of the wireless) – and then, the telephone rang so loudly it started me, and I knew before hearing my name that it would be for me.

The weather is terrible here lately, darling. It has rained almost continuously for the past week. Perhaps it is saving all the sunshine for 25th Sept and the week following. It teemed all day while I was home, but I managed to buy some wool from the Village (coupons supplied by Nunk) for jumpers for myself. Mum has nearly completed your pullover and it really looks swell, so she was agitating for 'more knitting please'. I hope to have a jumper in almost the same shade as your pullover, a little darker and richer, like the colour of tawny yellow chrysanthemums. You won't mind my copying you, will you, Vic?

I travelled with S/Ldr Grovenor on Friday night as far as Crewe. He had his Court Martial the previous day and was found Guilty, of being Absent Without Leave for (guess how long?) – three quarters of an hour!!! He wasn't in the least perturbed about it, and seemed delighted at the opportunity of telling some of the 'diehards' just what his opinion of them was. The Waaf Officers, he says, have shown up pretty badly, and since his arrest have cut him dead. Obviously, I suppose they thought that was the correct thing to do to keep in with the rest.

Your picture of a Mosquito is very lovely, Vic. I like it even better than I thought I would. It is all coloured in various shades of blue, ranging from deep midnight to a pale turquoise where the moon shines through.

The war news is terrific, isn't it, Vic? We have been more successful than we ever imagined we could be. This is the end I am sure. Every time I hear a News Bulletin, I feel I want to dance a polka with you. There was a United Service on Camp last Sunday to commemorate the 5th Anniversary of the Declaration of War. We committed to His Care all those we loved, all those in places of danger. I prayed then on my own for you and Fred. The whole service was very enjoyable (old Calver is posted, by the way, and we now have a new Padre, a S/Ldr Vincent, very decent type), all except the singing. We had to 'la-la' all the hymns, except the first which I knew, there were only enough hymn books for the officers.

It was a very nice Sunday altogether, even though I spent it away from you, yet never once did I feel you were very far away. In the evening, I went to RAF Cosford, where the BBC Symphony Orchestra had volunteered to give a repeat performance, the entire proceeds of which were to be given to RAF Funds. I loved it, Vic, and so would you. At nine o'clock they were playing a fantasy 'Romeo and Juliet' by Tchaikovsky and it was then, as in lots of our moments together, I 'lost' twenty minutes with you. I wasn't sleeping, I wasn't awake, but I know I was hand in hand with you, your face so near my own that it was a blur and we were earthbound no longer. Oh you know what it feels like, Vic. I know you do. You often try to describe it, but it is impossible, isn't it?

Other pieces they played were – 'RAF March' by Sir Walford Davies, Overture 'William Tell', 'Valse Triste', Overture 'Tannhauser', and selections from 'Carmen' – not too highbrow, and I found I recognized lots of tunes. Sidonie Goossens played the solo harp, a beautifully toned instrument, and Paul Beard was the solo violin.

On our return the Educ Officer arranged a late supper. I had purchased a ticket for this second concert when I sent you that telegram on Friday. That is why I did not suggest Sunday. And tomorrow, I am advertised as taking the floor at the Station Discussion Group – subject 'Women in the Post War World'. I must prepare some sort of introductory talk for that. I hope you didn't mind, Vic, but I thought you might possibly try to get hold of me those days, if I didn't warn you. Tell me you didn't mind.

Today I exchanged your old moth-eaten tie at Clothing Parade, so there's a new one waiting for you as soon as that one BEGINS TO SHOW signs of wear. Don't, Vic, don't let it get so bad again. It is awful bad for the morale. I have heard my mother say so often: 'What if you were run over and they took you to hospital – what would people think?' Usually, if this had happened when I was a little girl, they'd think I had holes in my pants, and they'd be right. So now I always make sure that what goes underneath wouldn't 'make people think', if they saw. That applies also to your tie, darling. xxx xxx xxx

Tuesday

I have been thinking about this remustering all weekend, Vic, but I didn't want to do anything about it until I had seen you – I mean spoken to you. Today I filled in the application form, got signatures from the MO, CO and Educ Officer, and saw it dispatched to Records. It would mean first of all an interview, then an NCO's Course, and then a Cypher Course. Perhaps that would take me to the end of the war. There's just one thing I am thinking of, and that is – suppose I am sent on a Course before our next leave. Oh well, it is no use supposing. I do want to get away from this Camp, and remustering seems to be the only way of doing it.

Vic, next Saturday is a very special occasion. The date is the 9th Sept and it marks the occasion of one month's engagement. 'Ring' and I send you our best wishes and we hope to see you soon. No darling, that's far too mild. 'Ring' and I are always talking and thinking about you, but 'Ring' wants you to know it's a very cosy spot she sleeps in at night. We love you so terribly. It doesn't seem possible that we have only been engaged for one month, only four weeks! I have always been engaged to you (as far as everyone else is concerned) and only we know that we are really married. I'll put in my application for leave at the end of this week – that will be heaps of time.

Your Loving Adoring Wife to be,

Nina X xxx X xxx X xxx X

Officers' Mess, RAF Station Foulsham, Norfolk
Saturday even 2nd September

My Nina,

I have just come back from a cinema show on the camp, 'The Great Waltz'. It was a film of the life of Johann Strauss and the waltzes he composed. Oh Nina, it was grand! For an hour and a half I was in dreamland with you. Together we danced gaily to the strains of the 'Blue Danube', 'Artists Life', 'Tales from the Vienna Woods'. In each other's arms we waltzed madly to our silvery heights, stepping lightly on singing violin strings, evading flashing bows, humming gaily to the flirting notes of the wood-winds until the last resounding crashes of the timpani we reached our cloud, way up high – together. With the strains of the lilting waltz in our ears we sunk slowly into our rosy valley in each other's arms. Music, gloriously sweet, pulsating music! Oh Nina, isn't it a wonderful gift? So often music brings me close to you, waltzes, concertos, marches, overtures. Music sad or music gay, its all good and because it is good and so very beautiful it helps me to be near you – you my beloved Nina, are the essence of all that is good and beautiful. And I – well, I love you, Nina, with all my strength but don't pretend to be worthy of you.

I received your telegram this morning, dear, and I will try and get through to you on Wednesday, Wednesday or Thursday. Here's hoping it's Monday. I'm longing to hear your voice again, Nina, you will never know the comfort it brings me and the confidence it instills. It's not easy to tell you when we are together because then I am so very happy and these dark, lonely days seem far behind. Believe me, darling, it will not take me so long to forget them when we are together for all time. The sunshine of our love is a cure for all ills whether of the heart or the body. This parting is like an insidious disease that saps the very strength from you, a feeling of emptiness inside, and well may it feel so for I have left all this is Vic with you. All my heart's love is with you, my Nina, safe in your keeping. The living, vital man that holds you so close is the result of the empty shell of a body finding it's completion. You hold the key to my life, dear heart, you can make me an unqualified success.

I have had another airgraph from Peter in the last few days. He is now on 110 Squadron and I'm afraid he's not taking too kindly to India. Don't blame him, really. It's too far from England's green and pleasant land. I intend to drop a short line to his wife when I close, Nina, just to let her know I have made contact with him and that I am still at Foulsham.

Isn't the news grand these days? In places our blokes are right on the borders of the Third Reich or whatever Adolf calls it. I hope that it is the third and last Reich. When our son grows up I don't mind shooting a line every night to him about this war if he wants me to do so, but there's one thing that I want to avoid at all costs – another war in his time. I want his life to be full of happiness. I want him to be devoted to his parents and his home and to find in both an example to guide him through live. Believe me, Nina, no sacrifice will be too great if, by that sacrifice, it means his betterment. These are concrete plans, my darling, and together we will carry them out.

Sept 25th – not long now, Nina. Seven glorious, happy days of love, laughter and happiness. I love you darling x.

Goodnight, beloved mine. God keep you safe for me
    Your life-long love
    Vic Xxx

5 Tuesday Discussion Group 'Women in Post War World'. Give Introductory talk. Decide that women who are married should put their homes first, but that they should be free to choose what they do. For all others, equal pay for equal work.

7 Thursday 'LONDON'S 80 DAYS: 8000 Fly-Bombs came over: only 9 p.c. Reached London in last days: Fighters got 1900; Defences had 2000 balloons, 2800 Guns. 'The Battle is over', says Duncan Sandys. The first full story of Britain's battle with the Flying Bombs in which 92 per cent of the fatal casualties were in London, is revealed today. Mr Duncan Sandys, MP, Chairman of the Flying Bomb Counter-measures Committee, revealed that during 80 day's bombardment 8000 flying bombs were launched, of which 2300 reached the London area. The story tells of a gun belt which stretched from Maidstone to East Grinstead so as to screen London, and how it was decided later to move the entire AA belt down to the coast so that the guns should have an uninterrupted field of view...'Except possibly for a few parting shorts, what has come to be known as the Battle for London is over', said Mr Sandys.

GERMANS PUT UP STIFFER FIGHT German resistance is stiffening, and they are putting up a determined fight around Nancy, Metz, Calais, Boulogne and Le Havre. Elsewhere the German withdrawal is continuing .. but there are increasing signs that a considerable force of German troops has still to be engaged and defeated on or before the Seigfried Line. A new threat to Germany is developing from a drive by the American First Army, who have pushed a column across the Meuse and through the Ardennes Forest beyond Auchamps .. Other columns of the First Army, who crossed the Meuse at Namur, are operating south-east of Namur and north-east of Givet. This drive across the Meuse is developing well.'

Letter from dressmaker – yes, she'll do it. Sit in NAAFI – will be wearing a permanently anxious look on my face soon. Spend another anxious unsuccessful evening – meaning no Vic. Write letter to Vic:

Thursday 7/9/44

Dear Heart of me,

Oh how I want to hear you say, 'Nina, I love you'. Oh, Vic, I am dying for want of you. The time seems to drag on leaden wings waiting for the date of our next reunion – that moment when I see you and am immediately united with all that is myself. The melting into your arms, and the sudden urge of exultation through my veins. I can find no satisfaction in anything that doesn't begin and end with you. The time is 9.30 on quite a passable evening, and here I sit in the billet, dull and listless, and completely unaware of all else except my own acute disappointment. Vic, this is a fast becoming my natural expression – this anxious look on my face, and this twitching of my ears at any sound that resembles a bell. You are probably feeling very disappointed too. Perhaps you really need me again tonight, as you did one night last week. If you need me, Vic, I should be with you, at your side, in your arms, giving you comfort, sympathy, courage, love, or whatever it is that you lack – not here, at the other end of a great wide gulf. It is so cruel to keep us apart, my darling. We know that our thoughts and our spirits can never be separated, but our bodies are very important too, because during our sojourn here on earth they are the temples of our spirits. Your body is the temple of my spirit and my body is the temple of yours. All the time we are apart, my darling, our spirits and bodies are torn in twain. That is why we feel so 'lost'. We will never be of any use as citizens until we are made complete. When Nina and Vic are untied into one great Vinnell, then there is nothing we cannot do and no heights we cannot climb. We'll probably amaze ourselves. 'Faith, Hope, Love – (we have these three) – 'but the greatest of these is Love' – (and this we have in an unbounding measure) xxxxxxxxxxxx

I think, Vic, that when the 'day of our liberation' is at hand and we stand once more at the altar together saying the sacred words 'I will', I think that I shall be back again in fancy at the little church in Blymhill, and I shall be conscious of nothing except our two selves and our overpowering, blinding love. When the clock strikes nine slowly and sonorously, I shall know that our names have been written in letters of fire and for all time in the Book of Life, under the letter V. Do you know, darling, I still have that rusty old nail from the wooden gate of the churchyard? I came across it again yesterday and I wouldn't part with it for anything. Incurable sentimentalists, aren't we? I meet you at the gate every night at nine, and I live again through those dear precious moments we spent there together. You described them so vividly in your letter, Vic, that I had two 'nine o'clock' the day I received it. You have got your letters to such a pitch of perfection, Vic, that every one of them lifts me up to heaven. No, no, no, Vic, believe me, I know. There are not words, mere words that you write to me. I think you dip your pen in the essence of all that is you, a mixture of your love and your life's blood, and in so doing touch the nerve center of your whole being. You suffer often when you write to me, I know you do, Vic. You tear yourself apart in an agony of expression, and that is why for no obvious reason when I am reading your letters, I suddenly find the tears welling up in my eyes and my heart nearly bursting. I find I cannot read your letters in public, my face is so often too revealing. I see the light and shade of your face as you talk to me. I see the passion in your eyes, and so often my lip trembles with the kisses you have implanted there and I find myself thrilling to your caresses.

No Vic, I can't do it. I feel your nearness too much. It is like making love in public. In these days of enforced separation, that is our way of making love. And for the life of me, I cannot write to you in public, say in the middle of the Naafi, and sometimes, whenever everyone is 'at home', it is very difficult indeed in the billet. It seems to me just as bad as – undressing in public –

worse, in fact. It is like my spirit climbing out of my body. Nothing pleases me better than when everyone is out and I can be completely alone with you.

I am completely reconciled with 'N for Nina', sweetheart. I never seriously considered her a rival, you know. And when I saw her smile at me from the picture you send home, I knew then that she didn't want to take you from me but was on my side – a guardian angel complete with wings and far more well-equipped. We seemed to have a lot in common.

I love you, I am always with you
Nina

Sunday 10th Sept 44

Dear Love of my Life,

The day is ending as it began – very cold, with the first nip of autumn, myself in bed again, and the rooks in the treetops a couple of fields away making a great ado about – what? One can almost tell the exact time of black-out by those rooks. Every night at twilight they start settling in for the night, and every morning at the first faint flush of dawn they begin to stir in preparation for a busy day.

Yesterday, I was home again. I managed to sneak out of SHQ at 5pm on Friday evening, and so organized a lift into Stafford in time for the 5.27 train to Liverpool. I was home just after eight. Mum is still in bed and the leg is progressing slowly. Everyone else is much the same. Oh, and Joe came home during the afternoon en route for a Battle Course at Newcastle. I am afraid he has started on a career of crime, because although he has finished his fourteen days CC, he still awaits the Hearing of another charge. He was hoping there was a train the following day (that's today) to get him to Newcastle at the same time. If there isn't, he'll probably collect another black mark. Joe came with me to Liverpool to see me off, after which he was going to wend his way to the Enquiry Office. I do hope he got there OK and at the required time.

I have more developments to report with regard to our arrangements. You know, two dressmakers that I tried were all booked up for months ahead, and I began to think that even if we were contemplating marriage next summer, it was none to soon to make preparations. Yesterday, however, I took the material to a dressmaker I heard of by chance and to whom I wrote during last week making an appointment. I was measured and fitted, and now the dress is in her hands. Marjorie has still to buy the material for her dress yet, but this dressmaker will do everything required. So that's a load off my mind. I was so afraid of your coming home in three weeks time and I should have no progress to report. You might think I had not been trying. Would you have thought that, Vic?

You will be pleased to know that the snaps are at last developed and I enclose them herewith for your comments. I know you will laugh, probably heartily that you won't be able to say or write anything. The funniest of them all, of course, is the one of yourself showing the bullet wound. That is where the Nazis got you, isn't it Vic! Oooh yes, you can tell it is sore even yet. And look at Mum in the background – foaming at the mouth? Looks as if she is ready for a shave! That is what I call carrying 'camouflage' to extremes though – daubing your body with warpaint. Nice torso, nevertheless – xxx all over.

Next one, 'Can me and my muvver come in?' or 'Love me, Love my Muvver'. Poor Mum doesn't look very well, does she? Funny we are both wearing the same expressions. I never knew we were so alike till I say that snap. In your determination to avoid Mum's feet, you just about managed to include our heads. Was that how you wanted it, Vic? I like the one of Mum and Nunk, don't you? ('How does that suit you? – a little strong perhaps?') Of course, I have a private joke of my own, with that other invisible person not shown on the snap. Know who I mean?

4. That marrow must be terribly heavy. I can hardly hold it high enough to be included in the picture. You can just see the inscription on it – 'Nina and Vic' – see it? I am glad of that. I have a feeling you just made the marrow an excuse.

5. It is a pity that one of us on the Lilo is a little blurred. But it's a good snap all the same. What are you cuddling down there, Vic? Just look at our waving legs. Notice a shapely calf just visible between your trouser bottom and the stocking top. The bit of white in the top left hand corner is your shirt, by the way.

6. This is a good one, Vic – 'Neath the shade of the old apple tree'. Mr and Mrs Vinnell, but still sweethearts. It never struck me before that you wear my initial over your heart. Don't tell anyone else what the 'N' stands for, will you, Vic? That hand clasp means a lot to me too.

7. And now we come to the best of them all. Isn't it a lovely snap, Vic? – tasting the first fruits of our love all among the leaves. This is the modern Adam and Eve. Do look at our ring, darling – see it? It is the only photograph we have of it.

I love you Vic XxXxX. You are the epitome of all I want from life, of all I have ever wanted; even before I met you, you were just the sort of person I was looking for, but I had been foxed so often that I thought I should never find you. And then, you found me. I am very grateful to you for being so determined, for seeing further than I could.

Oh Vic, would you try to get the eighth snap developed? It is of our beloved Blymhill Church. I suppose it is rather faint, but I WOULD like a picture of it to keep. Do you think it would come out all right with a bit of care? Can't get much more on this page, but know that I am with you always, soon to be with you in flesh.

Nina

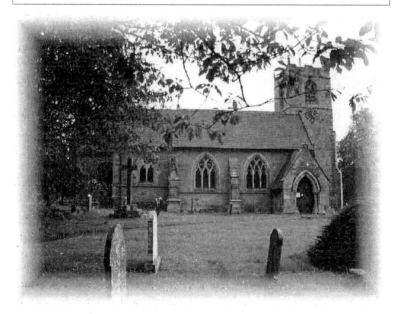

Blymhill Church

11 Monday Beautiful letter from Vic, in SSQ, assailed by the old bitter thoughts, and oh, my heart aches for him.

BRITISH INVADE HOLLAND

Officers' Mess, RAF Station Foulsham, Norfolk
Thursday evening 7th September

Oh Nina, my Nina,

What a crazy world this is !!! All today I have been cooped up in bed in this room, cut off from the world, unable to do anything for myself. Not a soul has been near me – not even my skipper. Why oh why can't you come to me, Nina? I knew that I didn't have many friends but I never realized that the number was quite so small. You are all I have in this world, Nina, the one and only possessor of all my heart's love and friendship – and I was even denied a letter from you, darling. It's three days since I last heard from you. Are you well, dear? Please don't ever let anything happen to you, my one and all. I put in a call to you as I said I would at 7.30 and there was no delay – but here it is 8.25 and still the phone hasn't rung.

This morning I woke up full of life, Nina, there's nothing wrong with me physically. All day I waited for your letter but no-one made a move to collect my mail. So this evening I phoned the Mess and they told me there was nothing in the 'V' rack. I couldn't believe it, but they assured me it was so.

I feel like an empty shell, Nina. It's hard to tell you how heavy my heart feels and how very lonely I feel. I love you with a passion so deep and strong that inside I am a seething cauldron. Oh if only I could be with you! If only I could give you this love instead of bottling it up. All day I have been wondering and worrying in case there should be anything wrong with you; it would break my heart, Nina, if anything ever happened to you.

Probably you are wondering why this outburst. I guess that really everything is OK and I am putting in too many 'worrying hours'. I've a great capacity for that! But when it's a matter of life and death (and by you, Nina, I either live or die) then there are grounds for worrying. Please bear with me, darling. Please let me unburden my heart to you for I cannot nor want to turn to anyone else. To you I can tell all, even the silliest of little worries, without receiving a hard or cynical word in return. With you all is sympathy and kindness and my feelings blend in with yours and I am comforted. Oh how stupid it is to keep a strong, healthy body coddled between sheets. In here the world just passes you by. Where are the fellows who call themselves friends? They say 'Cheers' easily enough when you buy them a drink at the bar, ready to slap your back and call you 'Pal'. But I guess it's just too much of an effort to branch off to Sick Quarters for a minute or so during the day. There's no bar here!

I'm sorry, Nina. I left off writing for a few minutes. I mustn't carry on in that bitter mood. It's too much like Vic before last Xmas. I won't tear it up, darling, as I was strongly tempted to do, it wouldn't be very honest, would it? Believe me, dear Nina, it's a long time ago since I used that vicious sting in my tongue. To all intents and purposes it is dead – killed, thank goodness, by the soothing beauty of your love. My nerves have been a bit jagged today. It's bad enough being cooped up in here when you don't feel well – it's ten times worse when you feel as fit as a full blooded stallion.

Try and understand, my Nina? I know I'm far from perfect and in so many ways I fall short of the perfect human being. But if you are so full of spirits as I am then you've got to do everything with a passion that demands your last drop of strength. I love you, Nina, with every drop of blood and life that is in my body, with a single-mindedness of purpose that will smash all obstacles. If I lash anyone with my tongue it seems twice as bitter because I throw all my passions into it. At least, that's how it WAS, Nina. I used to throw all my strength into being bitter because it seemed that the world was always against me. It seemed that people were always condescendingly offering me charity – and the hardest blow of all was that we had to accept it – or starve. That 'Christmas hamper for the Poor' we used to receive each year! – oh, the utter humiliation of it! Luxuries! Why Nina, they were truly the everyday things that every man has a right to keep him alive. No wonder Christmas had no meaning for me. Instead of giving gifts to others and seeing the joy in their faces it just meant more charity than usual – a larger, more bitter pill to swallow than for the rest of the year. I shall never forget so long as I live the visits paid to our three poor little rooms by an agent from the Public Assistance Committee. A man whose job it was to dig right into the soul of your family life (thank goodness we hadn't much anyway) to root out every little thing of value, to tell you how much coal you need to burn to keep warm, how little you can eat and still stand on your feet. Why, Nina, I've seen men collapse outside Labour Exchange in the winter time through malnutrition – men who go seeking for jobs that are not to be had and they have not enough strength to carry them to the Exchange yet alone to do a full day's work. Many a cold morning have I done a paper round with my shoes full of water because there was not enough money to get them repaired. Not enough money! Why Nina, there's more than enough of everything in this world for everyone.

To my Aunt Rose at Stretham I am for ever indebted. Without her kindness to my father and I we should have indeed been in a sorry plight. She clothed me while I was at school – she gave me my first holiday, a whole fortnight by the seaside. She gave me courage when Mum went away and Dad ceased to almost care about anything. She gave me the courage to carry on at school and keep on studying when my heart was almost broken. But the battle was hard, my Nina, and when you are fighting Life instead of living it you haven't must time to love. You build a shell around your heart and guard it with all your strength.

When I joined the Air Force and made my way upwards, the shell remained. I did not need money then. I had enough to get by. My next meal was assured and it was invariably good. My shoes were whole and my feet dry. Life was not so hard now.

But the bitterness remained with one difference. It was joined with cold contempt. Cold contempt for all I came into contact with. Contempt for the well fed people who grumbled at the food, for those who worried about the 'car that was decaying in the garage', for those who moaned through lack of batman service. I felt a strong admiration for my fellow aircrew and kept as an example the Battle of Britain fliers whose tireless courage was so often evident over London's rooftops in the war's early days. Always I had admiration for the strong – and contempt for the weak.

That's how you found me last Christmas, Nina.

And now – the bitterness gone, that imprisoning shell broken, do you realize how much I love you? Why Nina, I even had contempt for Pauline and her childish petulant ways. Oh God! To think I nearly …

I have told you many times that life started a new for me last Christmas. Do you see why, darling? That was my FIRST CHRISTMAS. Yes, Nina, my very first.

Oh darling, I don't want to bore you with the past, but it is the terrific contrast between the past and present – between before last Christmas and after it – that has made my life. The terrific change over from lonely bitterness to real, live, pulsing love for someone, the change over from contempt to sympathy and mutual understanding. It's very hard for me to express in words how grateful I am to you – and to Mums – for the warm loving kindness you have given me. The words when expressed, although well meant, always sound shallow and inadequate compared with the gratitude I really feel.

Many times I have written 'Please never leave me, Nina', and so many more times has my heart said those words because you are indeed my saviour. Somehow I feel less helpless because I can never hope to repay you in full. But this I can and will always give you, Nina, my whole, undivided love for all time. To make you happy, darling, is not an ambition – it's an obsession, something to which I can devote my whole life, a purpose for living.

I feel tired now, Nina, and I shall be 'torn off a strip' if I keep the light on longer. There's a goodnight kiss on my lips for you, sweetheart, and a heart full of love for you in my breast. Don't ever be angry with me, will you, Nina?

Always yours,

Vic Xxx

---

12 Tuesday ALLIED TROOPS FIGHTING IN GERMANY Allied troops are fighting on German soil. General Hodges' US Third Army, after a fierce artillery bombardment, yesterday smashed their way five miles into the Reich north of Trier. The border was crossed from Luxembourg in 'reasonable strength', Supreme Headquarters announced early today. Trier is in the heart of the Siegfried Line defences.'

BRITISH SLAUGHTER THEIR WAY INTO HOLLAND British armour and infantry have entered the 'inner porch' of the Dutch frontier, and, in the words of a fighting officer, 'have got stuck into the Germans and fairly slaughtered them', says Doon Campbell, Reuter war correspondent with the British Second Army. In a fight for a vital road junction the British attacked with everything on hand, won the junction and moved on through 200 German corpses. They took 500 prisoners in this operation.'

13 Wednesday CODE AND CYPHER INTERVIEW at 09.00 hours, (supposed to be). Sit about waiting all morning and afternoon till 4pm. 'Boobed' in subtraction, didn't remember where Trinidad was, but RECOMMENDED for course. All my cronies successful.

Wed. 13th Sept '44

Vic Darling,

As I predicted last night I did not sleep very much. I was even glad to get up. Still, it was somewhere to sleep and the YMCA only charged us 2/-, including breakfast. This, by the way, was a very frugal meal (served specially early for us at 8am) consisting of a cold slab of sausage meat, some bread and butter, and very watery tea with no sugar. Oh, we were very definitely only there on sufferance! Even the toilets bore a mark of distinction – on the door of ours was the word 'Women', the door of the Officers had the word 'Ladies'. Vic, I think I'd rather be a woman.

From nine this morning till half past four this afternoon, we have been cooped up in one little room over the Recruiting Depot (excluding an hour's break for lunch, of course). As is usual in the A.F we haven't been doing anything, just waiting – waiting for a Squadron Leader to come in, and then waiting our turn for interview. This can be quite a nerve-racking business, listening to all the lurid tales of those who have just come from the ordeal, and realizing with a painful shock what a pitifully small number of these questions we would be able to answer satisfactorily. I managed to spend my time quite profitably, listening to the various questions, working out my answers, and dashing upstairs to 'gen up' from an atlas. So that when my turn came, I was able to tell them where the Alentians were (the existence of which I had never heard of before this morning), and Telaviv and Aden. But I needed my Navigator when it came to Trinidad. I believe it is an island in the Pacific somewhere, but whether it is in East Indies or West, I just don't know. Oh, and I boobed when it came to a tricky subtraction, but I managed to rectify it before it was too late. Vic listen, there's one thing I am worried about. They asked me if I would object to going overseas and for what reason. I told them because my fiancé was in England, to which no comment. They can't make me go overseas if I don't volunteer, can they? Anyway, I have been selected for the course.

And that brings me to another little problem, Vic. The Waaf Officer advised me to put in for Leave as soon as I returned to my Unit, as I should be going on the CYC? Course lasting six weeks very soon. You don't think you could bring your Leave forward to next week, do you, Vic? I am so afraid now that I may not get it in, and please darling we must spend it together somehow. I will be three weeks at Wilmslow in our Admin Course and four weeks at Oxford Radio School. Do you think I could see you if I were in Oxford?

I am writing this on the 6pm train bound for Birmingham, so please forgive if my writing is not too legible. Hoping with all my heart to hear from you tomorrow.

15 Friday SIEGFRIED LINE BREACHED 8 miles into Reich, first forts fall. American attacks are tearing apart the Siegfried Line. As reports came in hour by hour last night telling of the success of General Hodges' newly launched assaults, it became obvious that the Germans are merely attempting a fierce and protracted delaying action. Their plan is to cover a general withdrawal of their whole remaining strength in Western Europe behind the Rhine. There, with as many men and as great a concentration of armour as he can muster, Model will make his all-out stand in the great battle for Germany. But his plan may be upset. The rapidly developing American thrusts may carry the Allied troops to the Rhine before the German forces can mass.' 'Prepare for the worst, says Berlin.'

'Battle for Britain' Parade. Pay Parade = £2.4-0d. Sit in Naafi and again draw a blank. No phone call. Oh, what can be the matter? Then, out of the blue – a Telegram from Vic:

> 'MAKE LEAVE AFTER DUTY HOURS MONDAY 18TH
> PLEASE CONFIRM   ALL MY LOVE = VIC'

'Make Leave after duty 18th. Yip peeeh!! I want to shout and dance. Everything comes to those who wait – everything (if they wait long enough!).

18 Monday SKY ARMY IN HOLLAND OVER RHINE Airborne army captures dutch towns near Reich border. Thousands of Paratroops landed before AA guns opened fire. Men of the First Allied Airborne Army, who landed behind the German front line in Holland today from a great sky-train of more than a thousand gliders, troop-carrying planes and towing planes, had cleared the enemy from several Dutch towns before nightfall. Strong units swooped down near the German border, and by night English and American troops were established. The strong fighter and bomber support made the move a success. Losses from flak were small.'

20,000 NAZIS SURRENDER WITHOUT FIGHT Twenty thousand German troops with their commander, General Elster, surrendered to a 24-year-old American Officer on Saturday without firing a single shot. They had been cut off at Beaujency, near Orleans, by the junction of the Third and Seventh Armies.'

Early chit from 2pm. Travel to Stafford in transport with Jean and S/Ldr Grovenor. Forget poor Jean when I see Vic. Travel on 3.8 train to Liverpool. Home for tea. Glad to see Mum up and about again. Vic had no sleep last night (on Ops.) so bed early. Read to Vic.

19 Tuesday LEAVE COMMENCES. Rather late start. Real eggs for everybody. Take Vic's suit to the Cleaners. Make appointment for hair. See film at the local: Ginger Rogers in 'Tender Comrade'. Unbeatable for sickly sentimentality. Walk home, see lighted windows for first time since 1939.'
Mum very ill. Vic and Florrie go for Doctor, who gives Mum an injection. Glad of Vic. Spend night with him at Mum's bedside.

20 Wednesday **BRITISH REACH THE RHINE AFTER 50-MILE RACE** Dempsey deep in Holland: the trapped Germans hit back. General Dempsey's Second Army was last night engaged in heavy fighting on the southern bank of the Rhine close to the Dutch town of Nijmegen, three miles from the German border. Nijmegen, where Dempsey's tanks have linked up with the second of the three Air Army groups dropped in Holland on Sunday, was reached before midday yesterday – an advance of more than 50 miles in less than 48 hours. Thirty-seven miles were covered yesterday. The Airborne Army is also fiercely engaged. Some of the 70,000 Germans trapped between the Dutch coast and the border by the Allied air swoop have joined up and are attempting to break through the Allied corridor. They have brought up heavy artillery to help them to smash through.'

> **WAR OVER BY NOVEMBER 15** Delegates to the U.N.R.R.A Conference were told by military observers recently back from overseas that all indications were that the war in Europe would be over by November 15, according to today's Montreal Star.'

> **'IT WILL BE ALL OVER THIS YEAR'** says Monty. 'Before we started this business I gave it as my opinion that if we did our stuff we could have the war against Germany over this year. It is now the middle of September, and I will go so far as to say that that statement is absolutely right. There is no doubt about it.''

> **WINTER MILK RATION IS THREATENED** Anxiety is growing over whether the winter milk supply will be sufficient to maintain the consumer's ration. The ration from November 7 to April 10 last year was two pints a week for each person. Drought in the South and excessive rain in the North have seriously diminished the crops grown for cows and spoiled their quality, and the National Farmers' Union have placed the facts of a 'grave outlook' before Mr Hudson, Minister of Agriculture. It is felt that only by an official grant of emergency supplies of feeding-stuffs in the areas chiefly affected can a serious decline in the winter output be prevented.
>
> Footnote. Although the milk ration may reach its lowest level yet, the weekly cheese ration will be increased from two to three ounces from Sunday, October 15.'

Too sleepy to remember much of this morning. Dr Carlisle calls about lunchtime to say we all imagined it – only a bad dream! Dr (?) Carlisle! Cycle to Heswall for prescription with Vic and discuss doctors. Send birthday card to Vic. Exile Vic in Mum's bedroom while I ice his birthday cake. Allow him to pass through kitchen blindfolded for a drink and …

21 Thursday VIC'S BIRTHDAY – the first we have ever shared. Wake Vic today like I'll always wake him. Present of yellow pullover from Mum, cigarettes from Florrie, wallet from Nunk. Shampoo and set while Vic goes to the Bank. Stuff marrow for dinner. Cycle to Parkgate and vow that 'shyness is out for all time'. Talk till dark and walk part way home through Barnston. Stop at Wishing Well and 'help' Vic. Birthday party. Vic cuts cake and makes speech. Mum comes downstairs.

---

22 Friday **DEMOBBING – FULL PLANS**

Pay rises for long service. New call-up of deferred men. Here is the news for which this country has been waiting ... how the men and women will be demobbed, what will happen to the men now deferred, the new rates of pay for the Services. Main points are:

> After the ending of the war with Germany and while that with Japan continues, young men now deferred will be called up and also men reaching military age, while at the same time demobilization will begin.

> Men and women from the Forces will replace those called up so that there will be no loss of output.

> Demobilisation priority will be based on age and length of service. Neither overseas service, marriage, size of family, nor having a job waiting will count.

> Certain skilled men will be released out of their turn to assist in restarting industry and building houses. They will not be allowed to go back to their old jobs but will work where directed.

> No man will be forced to leave the Forces out of his turn and all will be able to volunteer for further Army service. Those leaving out of their turn will lose certain benefits.

> Service pay rates are increased as from September 3rd by one shilling for the first three years of service for Privates, with 6d for each succeeding year up to five. NCOs and Officers receive proportionate increases.

> Japanese campaign pay will range from one shilling a day increase for a Private to 11 shillings for senior officers. This also applies to troops in India and naval men serving ashore.

> The cost of these increases will be £100,000,000 a year.

9.30 bus to Chester from Heswall Village. Read about demobilization plans from a borrowed newspaper. Coffee at Brewster's. Loads of shopping. First and foremost, buy Vic a signet ring for his birthday. Buy kippers, (fish that looks like herring) calling graylings, sausage, pork pies. H. Rub, Soap and

Shampoo. Vic buys me a super leather shopping bag. Lunch at Bollands (mushrooms). See Film at Odeon: 'It Happened Tomorrow' and 'In Old Chicago'. Cook fish for supper.

23 Saturday Florrie attending to new house so I am in charge. Vic does shopping. Prepare (with Vic's help) the vegetables and part-cooked dinner for tomorrow. Stroll down Gills Lane (with my arm around Vic, not his jacket) and learn a whole lot more about him. Rain stops play.

24 Sunday Harvest Festival. Church with Vic. Bit of a panic to do it, especially as I suddenly decide to have a bath when Vic wants to shave. Vic says it is a 'wizard' lunch. Talk with Mums and keep Vic's feet warm. Shampoo Vic's hair before tea, the cause of Mum's petulance, and have a long session with her upstairs. Poor Vic goes a lonely walk with moon, but united again and walk to Dales. Vow on an Undivided Front always!

25 Monday Our last day together soon comes around. Mum doesn't wake till late, good job. Vic has a bath and a rub down (wonder how I know?). Iron Vic's underwear. Cut a variety of sandwiches for Vic to eat on his long lonely journey. 4pm bus to Liverpool for 5.25 train, which will carry Vic back to Norwich. Heartbreaks of parting, last kisses on platform. Oh, how it hurts – more and more each time. Life itself stops.

---

396 Pensby Road, Pensby, Wirral, Cheshire
Tuesday, 26th Sept 1944

Dear Joy of my Life,

This has been a very lonely day without you, Vic. I woke up this morning early, anxious to get up and give you my morning salutating and then remembered – and lay back again. What use in getting up early when the day had nothing to offer me?

The house seems strangely quiet and silent and empty, and all I can hear is the hiss of the gas, the occasional movement from the fire as the coals drop lower in the grate, and the rain against the window. It is a wild blustery night and I am in a queer restless mood. I want to go out and do battle with the wind and be cooled by the rain. Perhaps the taste of it against my lips will recapture some of the glory of our last evening together. Was that only twenty four hours ago? I feel I have been parted from you now for at least a week.

Every mealtime today there has been one place less to set, one cup missing and no-one to sugar my tea. Oh Vic, my darling, I can't tell you how I miss you. It made me weep to see your bedroom this morning – empty. Your clothes were there, everything except what goes inside them. I completed the darning of your socks this morning while waiting for the spuds to cook. (We had to have dinner early today because of Nunk going to the hospital. He had nothing to report, however, as the doctor was apparently too busy to see him and he has to go again next Tuesday.) Your shirts I patched this afternoon and I also remembered a pair of underpants needing elastic. All these are in the oven now airing and will be sent to you tomorrow along with your suit, that is, if it is ready. If not, I'll send these things on, and leave the counterfoil for the cleaners with Nunk, for him to collect.

Mum is a lot better today and has even ventured downstairs for a while. She came down for her coffee after lunch and stayed till after tea. This was by her own special request, by the way. I wouldn't have dreamed of it. She wants me to go back to Wheaton Aston tomorrow and then if Nunk has to go into hospital next week or she finds she can't cope, she says she will send a telegram. Nunk will definitely be at home till then.

You see, Vic, there's another snag. If I ask for an extension of Leave on the grounds of sickness at home, I shall need a supporting certificate. How can I go and ask Dr Carlisle for that when he tells me there is nothing wrong with Mum? Needless to say, he hasn't bothered to pay a second visit to the house. If the doctor doesn't back you up, you're sunk. I have wondered since why he should suggest her removal to hospital, in view of the shortage of hospital beds and medical attention, when these things are entirely unnecessary. Surely he wouldn't take up the valuable time of trained doctors and nurses, in attendance on someone whose illness was only imaginary! He's not that sort.

Your ring was posted today, Vic. I remembered it as your train was drawing out of the station, and I remembered too that I had only sixpence. Freda posted it for me. Which reminds me – I was allotted the distasteful task of 'having it out' with Freda (Florrie's youngest daughter). She has beaten me, Vic. She has beaten me completely. I didn't SEE her take the chocolate, and if she maintains she didn't, there is nothing else I can do about it. I told her that she was suspected of stealing, and she looked at me straight in the eye and said 'Oh no, Miss Chessall, it wasn't me. I didn't take it.' I said again, 'If it is the last thing you do, do you still maintain you didn't take that chocolate, those packets of chewing gum, those sweets – on your word of honour, Freda?' And she said emphatically, 'I do'. Well, what can you do in the face of that? – except apologise! All we can do now, I suppose, is to see it doesn't happen a second time. Whew, I didn't know how she can! I really don't.

Did you have enough to eat, darling? And how did you fare on your journey back to the lonely grind? Is there a clamp tonight? I woke up at quarter past three this morning (Mum's back needed rubbing at exactly the right time) so I ate your chocolate then as I said I would. I too had fish for tea and beetroot, and for breakfast I too had pork sausage. It was some compensation to know that we were eating a part of the same fish and that I was eating the other half of your sausage.

I am now going to warm some milk for supper, to have in bed. There is heaps of milk now, Vic – four pints every day, a thing unheard of before you came. The only way we can keep up with supplies is to drink it.

Vic darling, Goodnight, and I hope there's a clamp tonight so you too will be in bed, perhaps with

Your

Ever Loving

Nina

Xxxxxxxxx

Officer's Mess, RAF Station Foulsham, Norflolk
Wednesday morn 27th September

Oh Nina, my Nina, xxx

All the old heartaches and loneliness are back again. This seems like a dream to me, a dream out of which you must surely wake me soon with your gentle kisses. All yesterday I sat and waited, waited for you to take me in your arms, to kiss me and say, 'Wake up, my Vic, it's morning and we have another whole day in front of us – a day together.' And when I awoke I could tell you how I dreamed that we were parted and how I felt terribly lonely and lost and you would soothe away this bad dream with the comforting warmth of your 'nearness'.

When bedtime came 'round I realized that this was no dream but cold, stark reality. We were parted; I am lonely and desolate and I am condemned to this fate for six long weeks unless God is kind and brings us together sooner. I never accept six weeks of parting. I never accept any parting from you, my darling, but am constantly watching and scheming to bring you into my arms as soon as possible. Living as I do, through you and for you, these long weeks are like a living death for me, the death of all happiness and peace. Gone is the warmth of your kisses, the heaven-sent thrill of your caresses, the inspiring touch of your hand in mine. I am very much alone and lost. I am dependent on you for all that makes life worth living, Nina I am not efficient, not happy, not contented when we are apart.

Oh darling, there were tears in your eyes when we said goodbye on Monday. Your tears were my tears, your eyes were crying for my own poor heart. I felt torn apart inside as the train moved off, my spirit stretching out to you as the distance between us grew. Nina, know that I never left you on Monday. My body gave up its spirit and left all my love and my strength with you. Whatever you do, wherever you go, my darling, I am by your side. I am absorbed inside you with all the love that I bear for you. We are one being and no distance can part our spirits, no chains bind the happy freedom of our love

I won't say much about my journey back, dear, except that I did get some sleep and I was in good time yesterday morning for the nine o'clock parade. I was fast asleep when I arrived in Euston and luckily someone woke me or I would probably have spent the night in a siding.

Goodnight, my beloved. May sweet dreams be yours, and God keep you for me.

Xxx/xxx/xxx (all scarlet, my Nina from ME to YOU)

OCTOBER

3 Tuesday BIG US THRUST FOR THE RHINE Shock-troops two miles through pillboxes. Troops of the American First Army today crashed two miles through the Siegfried Line north of Aachen in their new offensive towards Cologne, on the Rhine 40 miles away. Shock units swept over the little River Wurm and cross the Aachen-Dusseldorf railway. By noon they had advanced about one and a quarter miles through the Siegfried Line pill-boxes, but this afternoon opposition was more stubborn and the advance was slower'.

THE PEOPLE WHO DO NOT SMILE Their need – Orders. Nine thousand Germans living in this occupied corner of the Reich have now been under Allied rule for two weeks – and their behaviour has been 'exemplary' but utterly negative and blank. That was the answer given by officials of the First Allied Military Government when asked: 'How are the Herronvolk responding to live as a conquered people?'

BRITAIN'S POLICE TO BE REORGANISED Regional police forces, run on the lines of the National Fire Service and involving the extinction as separate units of many of the 180 independent forces now operating in England and Wales, are proposed in a report which has been drawn up by Home Office experts. The report suggests that when the war ends, the wartime amalgamation into six county police forces of 26 county and borough forces in Southern England, carried through by Mr Morrison at the end of 1942, should not only be continued but extended to other parts of the country.'

Tuesday
3rd October, 1944

My Beloved xxx xxx xxx

Thank you for a very lovely evening. We actually had nine whole minutes together, which was even more than I had wished for. When I rang you that second time, it was after half past eight and I realized it was a bit late to get hold of you, but I was determined to speak to you somehow last night. I don't know why specially last night, but I was desperately in need of you. I longed to lay my head on your shoulder and snuggle up against you, to put my arm beneath your coat and feel warm, and to raise my lips for your kisses. So I gripped the telephone, gritted my teeth and wished – hard. Oh Vic, my dearest, with all my puny strength I willed you to be there, to answer my calls. So much so, Vic, that when your voice did answer me – I couldn't believe it. I thought it must be something I had conjured up myself out of my own sheer necessity. Forgive me, darling, if I sounded inarticulate. You were so much an answer to a maiden's prayer that I nearly choked at the wonder of it, and I suddenly found that my cheeks were wet – for no reason at all – 'cept that I was happy. I am so glad sometimes for the darkness of that kiosk. To me, during the weeks of our separation, it represents a sort of sanctuary, where I can shut myself in with you away from the rest of the world, and we can be alone TOGETHER – that magic word again. That is very true what you say, Vic – 'the surroundings don't make our live, our love glorifies our surroundings'. Perhaps none of the places we have been to are really so very wonderful. Perhaps even Blymhill is only a very ordinary village church. Perhaps that is why I am afraid to go there again without you, even though I want to see it again very much. Perhaps it is our love, not a cloud, that puts a halo round its spire, and mellows its old brick and ancient timbers, Perhaps it is our love that enhances the charm of the old wooden gate, and makes the trees look greener. Perhaps it is our love, Vic, that tints the sunset with such radiant hues and makes a symphony of a bird's song. I believe it is, Vic. Then how can we live without it? Why should we? I know beyond all doubt that my happiness lies with you.

Have you seen the latest AMO on the subject of post war training? And the Appendix that will be required to be filled in by every individual, officers, airmen, airwomen? I feel sure that no-one will be left high and dry after this was to fend for themselves without training or aid of any kind. From the questions on the pro forma, practically every individual is catered for, and his most urgent needs will be met. We'll be okay. Darling, you have no cause to worry about a job.

Yes, my beloved one, when I close my eyes, I can feel your arms around me holding me tight – tighter, tighter, and I can feel the warmth of your lips on mine and your breath fanning my cheek. I hear you whisper in my ear of your love for me and your great loneliness. Yes, Vic, I do hear you, I wonder why I close my eyes. I even close my eyes when I speak to you on the phone. Perhaps because you are really inside.

All my love, Vic, from the other Vinnellski - Nina

Officers mess, RAF Station Foulsham, Norfolk

Wednesday morn 4th October 1944

Nina, my own,

. You are right, when you say that our loneliness shared is our loneliness halved. Yesterday I received you letter and my heart reached out to you. My own loneliness forgotten, all I wanted was to take you in my arms, hold you oh so close and kiss away the cold desolation that must have been in your heart. The knowledge of your unhappiness hurts even more than my own, and times without number I vow silently that I will make up for these dark weeks with a life full of love and complete happiness. I am devoted to you, my Nina. My whole life is at your service, at the service of our all-powerful love. Our love is the making of my life, everything I ever do is influenced by it. It will always be my inspiration, Nina. It will see me through when I am down, and in my successes I can attribute them all to that love. My darling, you have made me live, not only have you aroused my body to life but my spirit too. I know now that the spirit of my love for you is immortal. I must express my love through my body because we are but mortals and must worship each other in the flesh. But should my body be smashed into a thousand pieces it would never tell my love for you, the spirit of that live is free, Nina, and will live for eternity. You would never lose your Vic. But while I am here on earth and parted from you in this cruel manner I shall forever be the slave of a smile like sunshine, of a lock of hair, that falls over a sparkling eye, of a pair of warm red lips whose kisses take me into paradise, of a beautiful body, the thought of which goes to my head like deep red wine. If love can make you rich, my Nina, you will be the richest woman in all the world. That I can promise.

We will return to Blymhill again. We must remove those ghosts. The ghosts of dread, uncertainty, of the crushing fear of losing you for ever. Oh no Nina, It could never have been that, could it? If I had lost you my heart would have been broken beyond repair. Nothing nor no-one could have ever taken your place. Life would have been one long drift, purposeless, until thankfully I gave up this life. Believe me, Nina, I would never have ceased to love you – never.

This afternoon I went into Norwich with the 'Wingco' to see two chaps from our flight who are in hospital there. One of them is Dick and the other his pilot. They crashed whist I was on leave and Dick has lost part of one of his legs. I was quite shaken when I heard the news on my arrival back here. Dick and his pilot are on 'Mozzies' and the unfortunate incident was the result of technical failure. Since I saw them I have heard that Dick is rather worse. He lost quite a bit of blood and I think his disability is depressing him. His spirit, on the other hand, is quite perky and wondering whether he will be able to play rugger this season (in spite of two broken legs) I think he's a trifle optimistic.

Yesterday, I passed the afternoon by paying a very brief visit to York. So brief, in fact, that I never went outside the airfield. But it was a nice afternoon and a pity to stay on the deck. One day, darling, I want to go inside York Minster. Perhaps one weekend. Yes?

Your typewriter can talk without doubt! Oh please, please come quickly, our Wedding Day. Take care of our love, dear, while we are apart. Guard it and treasure it and fight tooth and nail any evil that threatens it. You won't be lonely much longer now, my Nina. Our Day is coming fast and with it the realization of my greatest dream – to make you completely happy by never leaving your side again.

I love you, dear heart,	...xx
For all time	xxxxx
Vic	x x
	x x
	x

7 Saturday Phone call from Vic. He always seems to know when I need him. Feel depressed over things I can't put into words. Do tapestry. Ring Vic. Not very satisfactory time. Practically the only world I can hear is 'Nina' and it seems like a call I can't answer. Write letter to Vic, then back to embroidering firescreen.

Hullo Vic, Vic Hullo, Hullo Darling, And way back through the mists of Time, comes a faint reply .. Nina .. Nina .. Nina .. Nina. My heart sinks within me. It is you, you're there, and you are speaking to me, and yet practically the only word I can hear is 'Nina', and it only seems to my ears like a call. Perhaps a call for help, from the depths of some bottomless pit. You need me, Vic, and here I stand yearning and longing and ready to help you, to comfort you, to drive away your fears, with my arms waiting to enfold you, and a heart so full of love for you that it is spilling over the sides. Oh Vic, it hurts so much to be so helpless and incapable. My whole body is put on the rack. Not a very satisfactory line, was it, Vic? Apparently all the Kings Lynn circuits were fully engaged, and the only way to get through to you at all was via Wisbech, which must be a branch line. (I have seen this postmark on some of your letters.)

I was very grateful indeed for your phone call this afternoon. I felt very worried about you somehow, perhaps because of there being no letters from you for a couple of days, neither from you or home. I felt depressed over – well, things I dare not put into words. You know those awful terrifying nameless fears, that sometimes creep into one's mind unbidden, and which it would be a sin to acknowledge. I am sure they are the work of the devil himself. You haven't had any more 'near escapes' have you Vic? Well, thank you, my darling, for putting my mind at rest. You always seem to know when I need you most. And somehow you manage to come to my aid. I wish I could do the same for you, Vic.

The firescreen is looking at me very pleadingly, darling, and no letters of ours to answer makes my pen strangely dumb. So I'll away to my dreams. I can do that xx and sew.

But first I must say that
I love you, my Vic,
I am yours Alone Xxxxxxxxx
I am For Ever Your Nina, Soon to be your Wife

Friday morn
LONDON

Nina, this is the craziest thing. I was given a day off yesterday – the usual midday to midday – and was all set to spend most of it storing up sleep when someone grabbed me, said an aircraft was going to London and so here I am on Friday morning sitting in a railway carriage in Liverpool St. Station waiting to go back to Norwich with Ted. Actually, the whole thing was an utter waste of time. The one thing I really wanted to do – buy something for you – I didn't have time to do.

Ted and I arrived at the Wings Club about six last night, found them full up, managed to get in a small hotel near Victoria, went back to the Club for a drink and some dinner, a few more drinks and so to bed. This morning we had enough time to grab some breakfast and tear across London for the 10am. Fantastic rush from beginning to end and I am saying 'never again'. Besides, my Nina, there are ghosts in London. Won't you come back with me one day soon and shoo them away?

The train's moving now, darling, so I think I'll close.

Yours for always Vic X

Officer's Mess, RAF Station Foulsham, Norfolk
Friday evening 6th October, 1944

Nina, my love

This evening finds me back at Foulsham and believe me I'm not sorry to be here. What the heck I went to London for I don't know. It was one mad rush from beginning to end and even then we were about four hours late back. I sighed for the days off we used to spend together, darling.

But to compensate for the past miserable twenty four hours I came back to some good news. In fact, some very good news indeed. Tantalising isn't it, the way I keep you waiting for it? In fact, the news was so good that I executed a little dance of joy! Are you ready for it, Nina? You are. You're sure you are? You're certain. Good!

We-e-e-ll ….. in my pocket, my jacket pocket, the left hand pocket of my jacket, the jacket that has just been cleaned … is … the x x x x x x x x x THE RING !!! Yes, my Nina, our Wedding Ring is in my pocket right now. Oh darling, how it sets me yearning. It seems useless for me to try and translate into words the rich emotions that are in my heart. Words can never take the place of kisses, words can never describe the whole world of meaning that is behind the meeting of our eyes. Do you remember when we were in the cinema in London, Nina?

And so it is now, my darling. With your ring in my pocket I feel too full of love and longing to write it down. You would know and understand if you were here. Nina, I think you will understand even though we are parted. I love you very much; my dear. Perhaps those few words come nearest to expressing my emotions.

We will be married just as soon as possible, Nina, just as soon as we can do so without causing anyone any hardship with next April as a deadline. A quiet wedding and a honeymoon in some quiet village or farm if possible, somewhere that we shall have just each other without the rest of the world.

You'll find me a very quiet man in the years to come, Nina. I'm a home-lover and, although I have not had the spirit of home for a good many years now, I have not forgotten what it used to be like when my own mother was at home with us. I have always longed for a home of our own somewhere that I can walk about without a collar and tie and wear any old pair of grey flannels, a place that is not part of the everyday world. I want a sanctuary, Nina, a place that is ours alone, a home that will be rich in love and kindness. You can give all this to me, darling, and only you can give it to me.

Nina, I don't wish to appear morbid, and I'll cut this paragraph short, but I want to ask one thing of you. I shall put a written statement or similar with the Adj to the effect that the ring is yours. Should anything happen to me in this last stage of the war I want you to see that you get the ring. If it is not forwarded to you then write to the Adj and see that it is. I won't dwell any longer on that, darling. It's a remote possibility anyway and, in any case, the ring will soon be safely on your finger.

What a lot this plain golden band means, Nina. It is the whole key to our future, to our complete happiness; a symbol to the world of our 'oneness' although we have known this in our hearts for a long time past. I wish you could see it, dear. Believe you me, it's a thrilling sight. But of course it is not for your eyes until the great day. There's only one thing that worries me a little, Nina. Suppose it didn't fit !! But surely it will if it is the same size as the ring gauge. It doesn't quite go on my third finger and neither does your engagement ring so that should be all right.

All the time I have been writing this letter I have been waiting for the phone to ring. It has rung many times in the past two hours but not for me, Nina. You were going to phone me, weren't you? I had a horrible feeling that you might be waiting for me all the time. Tomorrow night if I am not on duty I am going to ring you, darling, then if you are doing the same we can have twelve whole minutes together.

Goodnight now, Nina. Sweetest of dreams and God keep you for me – always. You have my heart, dear. Take care of it for me.

Vic XXX

Officer's Mess, RAF Station Foulsham, Norfolk
Sunday morning 8th October

Nina, dear heart,

I feel hopelessly depressed and lonely. My whole heart and body is crying out for you; I need you so very much, my Nina. Oh how hopeless I feel during these six dark weeks that seem like a decade to me. How tightly I cling to my memories and to any little thing that reminds me of you. At nights I look longingly at your photo and it is so very hard to force down a lump in my throat. I suppose tears are unmanly, Nina, but the anguish I feel inside me, the pain of 'nothingness' caused by an aching void can easily bring tears that no physical pain could arouse. Sometimes, darling, the chin doesn't stick out quite so far and the loneliness overwhelms me, it's hard to stop it doing so when I am missing you so much. I need your love as the flowers need the sunlight. They won't grow if they are starved of light; I cannot flourish and live life to the full without you.

Last night I felt heartbroken about our call. There are so many intimate things I want to tell you in those few minutes. I want to open my heart and pour out my love to you, to try and tell you what I feel so deep down inside me. I love you so madly, so desperately that I feel that I could cry with sheer frustration when you cannot hear me. I could sense the pain in your voice, Nina. I could hear the longing to say 'I love you, my Vic' and every fibre in my body reached out to you, yearning – yearning to make love to you in the only possible way. Oh to taste the sweetness of those strong passionate moments with you, to blend my body with yours taking everything that you can offer me and giving my all in return. I've wanted you for a long time, Nina, and soon now I shall have you as I desire, no longer to wait and yearn but to have and hold – our Acacea, my darling, our Shangri-la.

I try to put my love into my letters to you, but how can words hope to take the place of physical contact. Only in your heart, Nina, can these words be transcribed back into the warm lasting love that inspires them. You will do that for me, won't you, darling? You do understand how very much I love you and need you? If you can find my true heart in these garbled letters of mine then their mission is fulfilled and there is a light spot in these dark weeks.

Oh the irony of that day off, Nina! But the Anson had to go down to London and I don't think it could have been diverted to Wheaton or even via there. In the midst of London's roar I sought out Blymhill and wished with all my heart that we could have been there together. My spirit is never in anything I do if I cannot share it with you, darling. I am waiting, waiting until we can be together once more that I may live again and be happy. You are right when you say it is our love that garnishes the beauty around us. The sunsets are not the same when we're apart, the birds don't sing or I don't hear them, there are no hills and no river for me, no rushes or heather, and I see the world through dull, listless eyes, a world that is as cold and grey as my body. Please, my Nina, come back and change all this. Please come back to me and give me life.

The mail situation has helped to add to my bleak loneliness, more so because you have not heard from me either. I can't understand it, darling. I knew that you may not have a letter on Saturday but not so on Friday and Thursday. There's never a day passes but that I write a few lines to you and, puny and inadequate renderings of my love for you though they are, my letters are my only way of slipping my hand into yours and seeking the comfort that only can give me, Nina. I just can't understand why you have not received them.

But we stand on the threshold of a new week, darling, a week that will bring us nearer together and so I will wish it quickly away. Monday will bring us both letters, Wednesday will bring us together on the phone. Don't forget, dear. I will phone you about five first and then later in the evening. And if anything goes amiss on Wednesday we will try Thursday and so on until we are successful.

Our ring for me should be back next week, complete with Nina and Vic well and truly intertwined. The Wedding Ring is safe in my trunk and each evening I take it out, slip it on my little finger and say softly to you 'Soon, my Nina, soon now, dear heart'.

With all my heart, Nina, I love you, with a single-mindedness of purpose I resolve to make you happy. My love is not divided, Nina, there are no brothers, sisters, or near relations who take any part of my heart. My love is all for you, darling, for my wife and her future happiness.

May God unite us again soon.

Your husband

Vic

Tuesday 10th October

My Dear Missing Part of Me,

There is just you and me and the firescreen in tonight, Vic. Most of the girls have gone to the show on camp, the original 'Happidrome', but I like this much better than Enoch.

I had a letter from Mum this morning, which I was very glad indeed to receive, although (as she says) I ought to know that no news is good news. I don't know though, it isn't always so. She says she is feeling better, but finds that her slogan must be 'Go easy'. She had her first walk out of doors last Friday.

You know, Vic, although we have a Naafi and a YM on the camp, we still cannot procure even the most ordinary necessities. For a week now I have tried to buy some darning silk for my stockings. I have three pairs that need darning. As a last resource, I cycled at lunchtime to Church Eaton, hoping to buy some from the only shop there. The lady, however, closed the shop at lunchtime and refused to serve me, with the parting injunction that 'she was entitled to a lunch hour (12 to 2 by the way) same as everyone else'. So that was that! If you could get hold of a card of A.F stranded mercurised thread, Vic, I would be most grateful if you would enclose it with one of your letters. I am looking out for 'The Times' book of crosswords for you, darling, as you asked.

I yearn in these lonely weeks to live a normal life, Vic, to have you at my side in the morning and to look forward to being with you again in the evening. That would change the whole day for me, if I could have that to look forward to. I long for our own home too, Vic, really our own, I mean – where we can close the door and shut out the rest of the world completely, where we can do all sorts of silly exciting things without fear of criticism and of what other people may think. You are tired of always being done up in a collar and tie, and tired of your life being run to a schedule, of always being 'on parade'. I know, darling. In our own little home, there will only be our two selves and we can plan our days as we want them, 'Nina and Vic' days for a whole lifetime. Oh, the mere thought of them makes me sigh deeply in anticipation.

Is that a fact, Vic? Is that another superstition connected with weddings? – that the bride must not see the wedding ring before the ceremony, nor even try it on to see that it fits? Oh, but that's just stupid, just utterly ridiculous. There's no sense at all in that. Now, what point is there in waiting till the final moment before discovering whether it is OK? – Er, Vic, I haven't succeeded in making you change your mind, have I? I – er – I couldn't persuade you to let me have just a small peep at our ring, could I? No, I thought not – impervious to all my appeals! I can just see you wearing that 'Donald Duck' expression when the ring remains the wrong side on my knuckle, and you have to place it on the little finger instead.

May we soon be together for good is the wish and the prayer

Your bride (in blue)

Nina

Officers' Mess, RAF Station Foulsham, Norfolk
Tuesday evening 10th October

Nina, my love,

Not for me tonight is the cold darkness and the lonely stars, but rather the warmth of a log fire and a friendly cigarette, an evening that I can spend with you as I want to spend all my evenings. I know that writing is a poor substitute for the touch of a gentle hand, that ink marks on paper are a mockery of warm passionate kisses, but, Nina, you know what is in my heart, don't you? You know I am longing for our love expressed in the flesh, the sound of your voice, the thrill of your eyes looking into mine, the happiness that your comradeship brings to me. You are the only person in the world that I have ever been at one with, into whom I can sink my individuality and remain perfectly happy. I am very lonely without, my Nina, and so the present is not for me but the future for eternity and the past as far back as last Christmas. I never ceased to be thrilled at the fact that in reality our toes are on the starting line. It is said that only the young are disappointed, but darling, when hearts are young and very much in love they will recognize no set-backs. Lonely I am, Nina, and lonely I will be until we are together. So long as there are partings I shall always feel that my heart is breaking when I leave you. But young hearts will always look to a golden future, and so it is with mine. Our future, Nina, with its home, its love and happiness and the expression of that love in our child (boy or girl, darling, it's up to you). As I stare into the fire I see pictures that one day soon will leap from the flames and be a reality for you and me.

Do you remember our star, Nina? Do you remember that I told you I would reach for it if you commanded? That night I laid my heart at your feet. The Star has never ceased to shine for me. No clouds can obscure its light and nothing can weaken my efforts to reach it. To me it is as if our love is a divine inspiration, the brightness in a dark world to which I can turn and say, 'This is good', 'this is the right thing'. I always think of our love as being born on earth and fostered in Heaven.

To be successful in life and to find any peace on this earth at all, a man must have an ideal in life, something that he can hold sacred above all else. He is a poor man who holds nothing sacred, poor in spirit and weak if tested. Some men choose religion as their ideal, some choose politics, some aspire to build the biggest bridge ever, or the fastest aircraft. I have an ideal, Nina. That which I hold most sacred above all else is – you, you and the love I bear for you. To this end I turn all my strength that you may never want for happiness. My ideal in life is your well-being and after all, Nina, I think personal happiness is a very good ideal for that is what I receive from making you happy. My childhood ambition or ideal (an ideal is really an ambition, isn't it?) was wealth. Because I had always lacked it I thought that was the reason I was not happy. I thought that money and the power to buy almost anything I wanted would bring me paradise on earth. How foolish that was!!

I still desire riches, darling, but of a very different sort. I want the riches of a happiness born through a lifetime of serving you, a lifetime in which to give you sincere love and devotion of the heart.

And just as the haze of cigarette smoke clears from in front of me, so will the cold mists of loneliness clear from our hearts in the warm sunshine of a perfect love. Perfect it is, my Nina, and perfect I will keep it even though it cost my life.

These few pages have taken longer than I thought, darling. I've spent too much time staring into the glowing logs. Oh how I wish you were here. It would be so easy to tell you my thoughts, Nina, much easier than writing them down into a letter which may sound garbled. They are clear and concise even if they don't read that way.

You see, Nina, I have always lacked happiness until I met you. When you came along you brought with you my ideals, that to which I could turn all my energy. It was obvious to me that you would be the happiness I have been so long without and that I would always love you all my life. That is why I have always been so certain about us, darling, that is why I fought for your love and why I nearly broke my heart some nights at Wheaton when you unknowingly dealt some hard blows. The tears were not shed in vain, my Nina.

Try to understand me, Nina. When those twenty obstinate little toes are together in front of a fire you will remember this letter and think 'Poor dear, he DID try hard to tell me then, but he's far more successful in the flesh'.

I'll be with you soon, Nina,

Sweet dreams,

Vic

X xxx X xxx X

Had sight of new CO G/Capt Caswell Pay Parade = £2.4.0d. Film Show: 'The Hard Way' with Ida Lupino and Joan Leslie, the story of a possessive woman who wanted to rule the life of the sister she loved. Ended in hatred and suicide. Type letter to Mum.

> Officers Mess, RAF Station Foulsham, Norfolk
> Wednesday evening 11th October

My darling xxx

Another fireside evening. I shall become quite a philosopher if I stare into the embers much longer. It is a good time to dream my dreams and lay my plans for our future, to get them cut and dried in my mind before placing them before you for approval. It helps to ease the loneliness, Nina, and believe me, I am terribly lonely without you. It does hurt, doesn't it, darling? Always this cold ache inside. We are very much dependent on each other and I believe that our spirits leave us when we are parted and meet – who knows where? Perhaps amongst the daffodils at Stratford or the rushes by our river, caressing each other in their mystic way and waiting for our bodies to be united again.

I could hear you very plainly tonight, dear. I'm sorry there was such a rude wind blowing at your end. I needed your comfort tonight, Nina, and a peace swept over me when you told me that you love xxx me. Those words are all important, the crux of all our brief meetings on the telephone. You have such a terrific influence over me that a word from you, a touch of the hand, a glance into my eyes can all ease a fearful heart or a furrowed brow. The touch of your hand is denied me, so is one glance into the paradise that exists in your sparkling eyes, but I can have your voice and you may never know how many times and in how many different ways you have been my saviour. I am deeply grateful to you, my Nina. Xxxx.

Can you manage to get the safety razor and the tooth-POWDER dear? I emphasise powder because that is what I really want. I can get tube but they are not satisfactory. When you have a day off will do nicely.

Soon I may ask you to get a couple of shirts for me. I'm afraid that my present ones tear more quickly than you could ever hope to mend them. They are really finished but the have not lasted too badly. The sports shirts I bought in Canada two and a half years ago.

Outside it is a very dark night and the first gusts of the gale have just reached Foulsham. We were expecting it as we had a gale warning this afternoon. I don't mind the mad winds if we are sharing them, Nina, and tonight we are.

Gosh! But the crackle of the fire sounds good. Fetch my slippers, darling, and come and sit on the settee beside me. – Comfortable? – That's good. I feel that I could talk to you for ever, Nina.

Darling, don't worry about me too much. I know you must worry about me sometimes and humbly I thank you for it. But if anything happened to me, Nina, you would be the first to know and within a matter of hours. Have faith in the prayers you send up to God and trust me when I say that things are a bit safer now. They are really, my darling, and I am not trying to be kind when I say that. If I was injured in this country I would send for you straight away even before my father, because you are the first person I am responsible to before anyone else. I know how you feel, Nina, when you don't hear for a couple of days because I have a great capacity for worrying myself, perhaps even more than you have. That is why I long for the day of our permanent re-union and the unbounded joy it will bring. The peace may not be all smooth sailing, darling, and I'm sure that neither of us expects too easy a passage. BUT WE WILL HAVE EACH OTHER and, Nina, I firmly believe that there can be no troubles ahead of us that will hurt us a fraction as much as the heartaches of parting. Our love takes the sting out of all difficulties and they are easily overcome.

Oh Nina, what COULD hurt us when we are together in each other's arms at night?

You know, darling, I am longing to see my rival, this thing that can enjoy the touch of your hand when I cannot, that can sit on your lap and demand your whole attention and attract your eyes for hours – the firescreen. It sounds lovely from your description, Nina, a real work of art. I am going to be proud of our home with so much of your handiwork about it. Oh yes, I shall show it off to all my friends with the artist standing by my side. You are going to give me the home I have always wanted, Nina, you, God bless you, are going to realize one of my greatest ambitions.

(The Padre, who is sitting the other side of the fire from me, has just emitted a very dirty chuckle. I notice he is reading an American magazine. Could it be that some pin-up girl has dazzled him with her charms? You can never tell with these Padres. That collar covers a multitude of sins.)

Will you walk to bed with me through the wild wind, darling? It's the sort of night when banshees howl and witches ride their brooms. (Did you hear about the air-gunner who shot one down in mistake for an enemy night-fighter?)

The fire is very attractive and is doing its warm best to keep me from bed. But nights off are precious and I'm determined to get nine hours sleep.

Goodnight, my love

Fireside husband, toes-toasting Vic xxxxxx

14 Saturday Day off. Letter from Uncle John in Belgium. Do washing. Cycle to Stafford quite early, and do lots of shopping. Buy Vic's tooth powder and Times Xword book, apples and pears, tarts, mags for Fred. Lunch at Co-op. Tea at YM. See film: 'Tawny Pipits' and 'Her Jungle Love'. Cycle back before dark. Headache and bed.

15 Sunday Harvest Festival Service. All work commences after Service. Have new job, putting whole of personnel into demobilization groups.

479352 LACW N. CHESSALL
S.H.Q
Sunday Lunchtime

Vic Darling,

I haven't written to you or spoken to you since the night of the storm, and that seems an age ago. There hasn't been time during the daytime. Right up to the last moment I was expecting you to accompany me to see the Halle Orchestra at Cosford. I had your ticket and seat booked (in the name of ACW Smith) and kept your substitute waiting until the very last moment before definitely saying she could go instead. Oh darling, perhaps that was why I didn't enjoy it half as much as I did the previous performance, of the BBC Symphony Orchestra. For one thing, the pieces chosen were rather above my head, long meaty symphonies, with no bits that I recognized and for another thing, the Wheaton Aston crowd arrived late and had to wait for nearly half an hour till the end of the second piece. Then, when we did file in, the whole audience and orchestra was held up while we found our seats. If you have ever seen John Barborolli, the conductor, you will imagine the look he gave us. I thought he would have jumped off the platform in a towering rage at any moment. They call him dynamic, but he is a madman if ever there was one. He rolled and shook all over his little platform in an absolute ecstasy of passion, and his thick black hair flopped about his face. He reminded me rather of the smallest of the three Stooges, with his staccato movements and the way his hair was cut, which if anyone could know what I was thinking would have been considered utter blasphemy. The programme I have forwarded on to Mums, hoping she might understand it better than I could.

My day off yesterday proved to be far more enjoyable than it promised to be the previous evening. I should have known that plans never do go smoothly on a Friday, the 13th. For the second time in succession I planned to go home, and for the second time my plans failed. This time the bus was full and there were no seats either for the last bus on Saturday night, oh, and my bill is u/s. So that settled that. I had to find an alternative.

Friday night I went to the Film Show on Camp – quite a good one for a change – 'The Hard Way' with Ida Lupino and Joan Leslie.

Yesterday I got up quite early and did my week's washing and then slowly and leisurely cycled to Stafford. It was a glorious day, Vic, and the trees and hedgerows looked marvelous in the early morning sunlight. I felt refreshed and exhilarated. The clean cool air that exists outside the confines of Wheaton Aston has blown through my hair and somehow, darling, it was like your breath on my cheeks and you were not very far away. You would have loved to be with me, I know, but if you were not there, then there was no-one else. I spent the day entirely alone, I like it that way. There was a very nice film at the Odeon that was in exact keeping with my mood, called 'Tawny Pipits'. Go and see it, Vic, if you can. It all centers around a very rare bird of that name found nesting in a quiet little English village by a wounded pilot and his nurse on sick leave. It portrays the ordinary everyday life of the village folk and you will find this very refreshing after the slick gay routine of musical comedy so popular with American film Coys. The film ends, of course, with the pilot and his nurse being wed in the old village church.

I love you, Vic, always.

I love you, I love you

Your Nina   X xxx X xxx X

Hockey Match – win: 6-4 at my expense. The ball smashes nail off index finger and I have to be treated at SSQ. Ring Fakenham, but no Vic (telephone ban).

Officer's Mess, RAF Station Foulsham, Norfolk
Thursday evening 12th October

My beloved Nina,

I don't know what you're going to do with your husband in the winter. You'll never be able to drag him from the fireside to go visiting. If you want to take me somewhere one evening, darling, I think your best plan would be not to light a fire.

From which you may gather that I am in an armchair once again, packet of cigarettes and matches balanced on the arm, my toes near the logs and my heart very full of my love for you.

Nina, how else did you expect me to spend all my evenings except at home with you. Only God and ourselves know how terribly lonely we have been in these long weeks. Dark weeks full of heartaches and longing to fulfill our glorious love. My darling, I swear that I'll never spend a moment away from you if it can possibly be avoided. To hell with my 'boys' and your 'henparties'! It's YOU I want, Mrs H.V.A Vinnell, you my wife, my all xxxxxxxxx

I'm sorry I could not be with you at the concert tonight, Nina. The weather has clamped good and hard today and the Anson has not been airborne. I love good music, Nina, and I know that when I share it with you it will be enhanced beyond the composer's wildest dreams. Think of me tonight, my darling, think hard and often that I may share the beauty of the music with you and it can be my evening with the Halle too.

This morning I managed to get airborne (not for too long) and had the roughest ride I've had for some time. It was a foul morning and I was more shaken up than that bottle of Mum's medicine. One moment I was sitting on the seat, the next I was suspended in midair and a second or so later I would be ruefully rubbing my head where it had come smartly against the top of the cockpit. We soon decided that enough was even better than a fest of this kind of treatment and sought the solidarity of Mother Earth, God bless her.

Flying's a queer business, Nina. One day you can look down on a sunny patchwork of fields and skittishly chase fleecy cumulus clouds across the sky. The next day you can't see more than a couple of miles ahead and have to work like a nigger to keep the kite the right way up. On the one hand a 'fole de viore', a happy 'at one' with Nature, and on the other the tang of danger, the tingling excitement of engaging in battle with the elements. Both sides have their charm.

I started this letter at nine o'clock, Nina, our trysting hour, and thus I have been able to stretch out the chimes of Blymhill Church so that I can hear them for two hours. I have kept my nine o'clock date with you in some strange places, darling, sometimes hundreds of miles from England's shores with only the twinkling stars as company. But I have always kept it and I feel that you slip your hand in mine at that magic hour and whisper, 'I am with you, my Vic, never fear or fret'. And I am comforted, Nina, the world is not so bleak or the task so tiring. Thank you for being my Guide, my Comforter, Sweetheart, mistress, my wife – MY Nina.

Goodnight, dear. God bless, and – sweet dreams xxxx Always take care of me, Nina, and always love me. Undividedly yours, Vic   Xxx

---

Transport to Cosford for Xray of finger (with very charming officer). Ascertained no bone injury. Domestic evening for special inspection tomorrow. Polish floor, etc. Additional parcel of handicrafts from Education Officer, 2 cushion covers for me. Phone call from Vic in Naafi. Have supper with Audrey. Tapestry.

17 Tuesday Sick Parade, final. Excused typing for four days. Engage instead on demobilization group numbers. Letter from Mum. Letter from Vic.

Officers' Mess, RAF Station Foulsham, Norfolk
Friday evening 13th October

Nina, my life-blood, xxx

A fireside evening but I just cannot settle down. The logs are just as bright and warm, the haze of cigarette smoke is there (I've been smoking far too many during the last hours) but, Nina, I'm so terribly lonely and unhappy. During these evenings when my mind wanders into the not-so-distant future to our own fireside I try to capture the charms of those evenings-to-come – and only succeed in nearly breaking my heart. It's only too easy to live them in advance. I know what we both want, I know the almost delirious happiness of 'Nina and Vic' evenings and in knowing that I realize only too well what a hollow mockery these present evenings are in the Mess with a writing pad on my knee, reaching, striving to be with you and to taste the sweet nectar from your lips and the warm glow of your vital body, to hear the music of your voice and back again in the sunshine of your smile.

My Nina, I'm so very lonely and unhappy. The days are passing so slowly, long interminable days of heartaches and longing, weeks in which my cold, unfeeling body calls for your touch to wake it into life. No wonder my resistance has been so low, no wonder that the smallest ill can develop unchecked when I feel so sick at heart as I do this evening. This is no life for us, my darling. There is only one possible way for us to live and that is as close together as possible – ALWAYS.

In bed at night I find it hard to check the tears of frustration when my body responds to our love and you are not there to accept it.

Am I writing a depressing letter, darling? Forgive me if you can, but I feel so low and miserable tonight that I must pour it out to you. I know you will understand me, Nina, you know how much you mean to me, how full of love for you my heart is, and because you love me too I know you will understand the misery of reaching out for your completion until something inside you must surely snap. Oh Nina, I love you so dearly. Xxxxx

I'll do my best to get your darning thread, dear. I'll pester the coach drivers again, they are good types and will do anything for the aircrew (unlike the majority of people who seem only too willing to get in a crack at anyone wearing a wing when chance so offers).

Darling, I WILL bring our Ring on Leave with me. I think it would be a good idea to see that it fits perfectly and avoid any 'Donald Duck' expressions at THE vital moment.

And, Nina, when have I ever been impervious to your appeals? Oh Nina, you know you have only to ask ANYTHING AT ALL and it shall be done if it is humanly possible. My whole life is devoted to you and your happiness, your smallest wish is my command, my darling, a command to be executed with the utmost speed and efficiency by your husband who is also your very willing slave. I WILL make you happy, Nina, so help me God I'll make the happiest woman in the whole world. I have always dreamed of giving all my heart and love to one person, and now that she is here, now that you are in my life to stay, darling, I can find my true happiness in loving and serving you 'til my dying day.

It's a bit noisy around this corner of the world of late. The odd buzz bomb travels this way and rattles all the windows of the Mess. This evening one zipped over the 'drome smartly but continued on its way out of hearing distance. It's all right while you can hear them but when the jolly old motor packs up you have to start seeking the most convenient table to crouch under.

Goodnight now, my Nina. Don't forget – Sunday at 7.30pm. I shall be waiting for you and I'll ring you in the afternoon if I can.

I will bring the Ring on Leave with me on Nov 7th. No, it will be Nov 6th, won't it? After duty the day before.

Goodnight, darling. God bless.

Your lonely lover

Very much in love with you

XX

X Vic   XX

Send parcel of cigarettes and tooth powder to Vic, also Book of Xwords. Post magazines to Fred. Send birthday card with diary to Joe.

Wednesday evening 10/10/44

My Darling,

I have just put down the telephone from my ear that brought your voice to me across the distance that divides. We didn't even say Goodnight. I didn't know that you had gone until, when I paused, I heard no comment and a frantic 'Hullo, Hullo – Hullo, Vic' brought back no answering echo.

You sounded very sad and lonely tonight, my sweetheart. I have never heard you sound like this before. Always before when we have spoken you have been so happy and excited, eager to make the most of the brief time at our disposal. Tonight, Vic, the load of unhappiness and loneliness that you have carried all these weeks must have become so heavy that it didn't life an inch even when we spoke. That worries me, darling, because I can do nothing – nothing.

It would not be so bad if we could see each other on our day off, would it? At the moment, that idea seems a remote dream, something I am always wanting to happen but which never does. I was thinking, Vic, that perhaps when I am posted after this Course, it is more than likely that I shall be sent somewhere on the east coast to an op. Unit, when we may be more accessible to each other for spending our days off together. That would lighten our darkness considerably in these intervening weeks, wouldn't it?

Oh Vic, I forgot to ask you – how did the jewellers finally arrange the intertwining of the letters 'V' and 'N'? Does it look good? And are you sure the ring fits OK now?

My group number for demobilization is 45. Is that lower than yours? Wouldn't it be awful if you got your release before I got mine? – then I would desert. But whatever happens, you must not go overseas, Vic – you must not. We would both curl up and die. What number did we work yours out to be? – remember how we poured over that lady's newspaper on the way to Chester? But whatever number you were would make no difference at all if you went overseas, because they could always argue that your duties in the Air Force were far more important. And you would be in no position to argue, miles away from anywhere and far from home.

Nine o'clock, Vic, by my watch – it may be a little fast – and I am saying 'I am with you, my Vic, never fear, never doubt me. I'll always love you.'

Undeniably and completely, Your Nina xxx

Thursday 10/10/44

My Own Vic, xxx xxx XXX

Once again I have spent another lonely day off in Stafford. These are becoming far too usual for my liking, but somehow unavoidable.

I began the day by taking a long lazy bath and carefully dressing, and pretended to myself that I was preparing to spend the day with you. Actually, Vic, I did spend the day with you, in though, as there were no other distractions connected with work and other people to take my attention from you and my love and longing for you. As I cycled leisurely along the country lanes, first to Wheaton Aston for some apples you asked for (and which are now neatly parceled ready for posting tomorrow), and then to Stafford after lunch. I talked to you inside myself practically the whole time, and sometimes I think I must have spoken out loud. Often and often when I am alone I do that. Vic. You never received one quarter of the letters that I address to you, because they never get written down – and then, when the paper is before me and the pen is in my hand, I cannot recapture the glory of the lovely things I should have liked to tell you. On the way to Stafford I told you how lovely the trees looked, how the gentle wind stirred the leaves and sent them parachuting down to earth in cascades, how I'd like to capture some of this glorious array of colour and translate it into a woodland suit, or a tawny copper-beech coat, or a frock the colour of ripe berries. It would be impossible to improve on Nature for colour schemes. I told you how a flock of sheep sheltered together 'neath the spreading boughs of a huge oak tree – they weren't lonely, and how I found myself in the middle of a herd of cows on their way to be milked and was rudely stared at in passing. I even saw a squirrel, Vic, a pretty russet brown little creature. This is a rich and bountiful countryside, and a great peace stole over me as the lines of that childhood hymn came into mind:

'God, who made the Earth
The air, the sky, the sea
Who gave my Life its birth,
Careth for me'

Do you like Harvo loaf, Vic? – rich, dark brown and tacky? I haven't seen any of it for years, until I discovered a shop in Stafford that sells it. It tastes delicious, spread with 'duty clerk' margarine. I also bought some Xmas Cards.

Are you sending any this year, darling? they are very expensive, 8d and 10d at least, but just now there is a very wide and choice selection.

In the afternoon I saw that widely advertised, much talked of film: 'For Whom the Bell Tolls', and – well, I don't know yet whether I liked it or not. It was an unusual film, but the whole emphasis seemed to be laid on the least important things. For instance, the theme of it was supposed to be The Spanish Civil War, yet Ingrid Bergman's hair style stole most of the limelight. Gary Cooper was given an absurdly wooden part to play. For the most part, he looked as though he had forgotten his lines. You have seen it, haven't you, Vic? I though the most colourful character of them all was Pilard, Pablo's wife – don't you agree? And I found her philosophy of life most interesting, if not exactly attractive.

It is such a pity this snap of Blymhill is so faint. I had hoped it might have been a little clearer than it actually is. But at least I am thankful we have some likeness of it, to prove that it wasn't just a dream. Looking at this print now though, Vic, faint and misty, it might be a ghost church, dimly seen, faintly remembered. But in my heart, the memory of it is strong and undying. It is the birthplace of our life together, and I thank you most humbly for making that birth possible. It is only a baby yet, our love, and already we have accomplished miracles. When it grows stronger still, and stronger, it will be the greatest living force ever known. I love you, my Vic. I can't tell you how much.

I love you,
Please believe
I am always Your Nina xxx X xxx

Officer's Mess, RAF Station Foulsham
Thursday morn 19th October, 1944

My beloved Nina, xxx

A successful evening don't you think? I could hear you very plainly, darling, and please forgive me if I used most of the six precious minutes to pour out my unhappiness. This six weeks has been the worst so far, the loneliest ever and that makes it pretty lonely, Nina. There's only one thing I want to do when we can't be together and that is fly, fly, fly until I'm too tired to do any more. Unfortunately, that has been denied me so far and so I have had plenty of time to think of all the unhappiness that could be ours if we were together.

After I had spoken to you last night I wandered into the bar and there met a new 'bod' just arrived about ten minutes ago. He has come from Calveley where he was Signals Leader and so over the odd pint we got to nattering and comparing notes. We nattered until the bar closed, quenching our thirsts every now and then which might, of course, explain this thick head I have this morning. He knows Jock Williamson and Sgt Jones at Wheaton. Are they posted yet, Nina?

This morning I received the 'Times' Crossword book. Thank you, darling, thank you with all my heart. There's enough work there to keep me occupied for the next ten years. I love wracking my brain over the trick, ambiguous clause the composer provides, and I'll be a bit happier now, Nina. We have a sort of crossword syndicate here, three of us, Ted, Bill and myself who grab the 'Times' when we walk into the Mess and go into session, thoughtfully chewing pencils the while. Yesterday, we completed it – gala day!

I joined the RAF in December 1940 and my demob number is 36, Nina. It's been POR'd here and I'm afraid I could not make it any lower. It's too high to be comfortable, Nina, if something cropped up suddenly you would marry me before I go? God knows how I should survive such a long parting, but I know I could draw comfort from the fact that you are my wife and I could write to Mrs V. Vinnell.

Don't worry about Marjorie's frock, darling. I shall not have eyes for anyone but you on The Day and I don't care if she wears slacks. All I shall care about is the fact that you and I are being bound together under one name for all time. To be quite honest, Nina, I wouldn't care if the church was empty. I'm a quiet sort of guy and a quiet wedding will suit me fine.

Friday Morning

Things have happened since I stopped writing yesterday. I'm terrible sorry I was unable to get this letter in the post, Nina, but I think you understand by now and you will forgive me when I say I was a little happier last night because I was busy. If I can get a good period I shall have my tour finished in no time but it will need an improvement on the past few weeks.

Your parcel arrived safely this yesterday and I kissed your photo this morning because your packet of cigarettes saved me from a smokeless morning. The tooth-powder is wizard too. It's just what I wanted, Nina, and will last me for a long time. You have received my parcel OK, darling?

Nina, did you purchase the dinner service you saw in Stafford. It sounds quite attractive and I fully believe that coloured china has not gone for good, only for the duration. Do you need the money for it, darling? Surely you would ask me for it if you did because it IS for our home. Please don't let anything slip by if you believe it is worth having because we shall need everything we can lay our hands on. Don't forget that, will you, Nina

We can buy 'Ovaltine' in the bar so I have a tin which I'm going to forward to Mums. I wonder how she is keeping. I've had no word from her since my return from Leave.

You have gone far too long without a letter already, darling, so I'll catch the morning post with this one. All my heart's love comes to you with this envelope, Nina. Don't forget your prayers every night, will you? I shall be needing them more and more.

I love you, my Nina, and always will

Always your Vic X xxx xxx xxx X (Blymhill's chimes)

---

23 Monday Decide on Hut 76 Reunion. Sept 3rd 1950. 12 noon. Station Hotel.

Monday evening 23/10/44

My Darling Vic,

I was so glad to hear your voice yesterday, after the spot of bad luck I encountered the previous evening when trying to contact you. Did you find out what happened?

Your letters to me do not seem to have suffered as yet, because of time otherwise spent on the Xword Book. I have still had one from you regularly.

Jock Williamson and Sgt. Jones are both here at W.A still. Oh no, I think Jock Williamson is at Perton. Talking of Joneses, Vic, reminds me of a 'prang' at Calveley three or four days ago, when F/O Jones bought it. Remember? He was in the lounge of the Victoria Hotel, Wolvs. when we were waiting for lunch there. Arthur, I think his name was. And someone else I think you knew was F/Sgt. Smith, a Rhodesian, who had the same ending. P/O Le May (he was Sgt. W/Op Air here in your time I think) has been recommended for a medal.

Vic, as soon as I get to Wilmslow I'll call at the Railway Hotel there to confirm your booking – that is, if you haven't written to me before then to let me know it is OK. I think it ought to work out all right in the circumstances, don't you? I am not looking forward to this NCO's Course at all though, and I am scared to death at the prospect of taking a squad on the parade ground. However, I suppose I shall square my shoulders, take a deep breath, and bellow forth like the rest hoping no-one will notice how scared I really am. And all day long there will be the thought of you waiting for me and the time we shall spend together in the evenings and weekends. With that as a spur I ought to do well. You don't think you will be too bored and lonesome during the day, do you, darling? I am so sorry, but we'll have to make the best of it for a while. Just a little time together will be better than none at all. I close with a prayer, and a wish, and a kiss, and a memory (soon to be realized).

Ever yours,

Nina

25 Wednesday Bags of panic to get my pass signal in time for 5.10 bus to Stafford. 5.27 train to Liverpool, and home by 8.15. Joe also home on Leave. Glad to see Mum looking much better.

PACIFIC: <u>BIG SEA-AIR BATTLE STARTS NEAR PHILIPPINES</u>

HOLLAND: <u>GERMANS 'CAVE IN' UNDER BLOW ON 12-MILE FRONT</u>

EAST FRONT: <u>RUSSIANS DEEPER INTO EAST PRUSSIA</u>

<u>**POWERFUL JAP FLEET HAS COME OUT**</u> In a 42-word communiqué issued by Admiral Nimitz at Pearl Harbour tonight, it is announced that powerful enemy forces moving towards the Philippines invasion area have been attacked by US planes. It may be the beginning of a Pacific show-down.

MILK – The weekly milk allowance is to be cut from two and a half pints to two pints on Sunday week, November 5th. Supplies to catering establishments will be reduced from seven and a half to six pints per hundred hot drinks served. Recent stormy weather with three months' rain in six weeks has reduced output …

26 Thursday Day Off. Mum goes to see Dr and arranges a visit to the Specialist next Tuesday. Do tapestry while Mum first snoozes and then plays piano. Change from slacks only half an hour before time for leaving. 7.5 train for Stafford. Write letter to Vic on train:

Thursday 7.15pm
26/10/44

Dear Part of me, xxx xxx

I am just returning on the 7.5 train from Liverpool after a day off at home. It has indeed been very enjoyable and you will be glad to know that Mum was looking very much better. She went this morning to visit her apology of a doctor, and also arranged an appointment to see the Specialist next Tuesday. I was glad indeed to know this. In fact, I may be able to go with her, as I shall be travelling to Wilmslow on Tuesday, and I thought I might be able to break my journey at Crewe and travel to Liverpool in time to meet Mum before her 12 noon appointment, returning to Crewe afterwards, to pick up my kit and resume my journey. Anyway, I'll see if I can do it.

Joe too arrived home last night on Leave. So today I lit a big fire in the lounge (the chimney of the living room smokes too badly that I was unable to light a fire there) and we had breakfast, dinner and tea grouped round it. I love such lazy 'round-the-fire' days, and I am afraid I didn't change from jumper and slacks into uniform until half an hour before I was due to leave – at half past five precisely.

The Ovaltine you so kindly sent had arrived, by the way, and was very much appreciated. The only snag is the milk question, which we are waiting for you to come home and put right. You see, the priority concession was only available for four weeks and is now expired. This morning the doctor refused to grant another one – no qualifying statements, just a plain, 'No. No'.

It is nearly nine o'clock, my loved one, and I am thinking only of you and of how much I love you, and of how soon now we shall be together again. Tonight (as always) I shall offer up my prayers to God for your safety and guidance, and I shall know that I may rest in peace and that all will be well with my world this night.

Officers' Mess, RAF Station Foulsham, Norfolk
Monday morn 23rd October, 1944

My darling,

Well, it had to come and I am glad really that your posting is through. I know you will be glad to leave Wheaton and now you will be settled somewhere for my next Leave. I have written off to the 'Railway Hotel' and I'm crossing my fingers very hard indeed for success. I may wire them yet as it would bring a much earlier reply. If by any chance I can't get accommodation in Wilmslow I may try Manchester, although I can see complications about getting back at night. Oh how I wish the confounded war was over and we could live our life in our own Nina and Vic way. Nobody will appreciate the peace more than you and I my darling.

Today is THE most wretched day. Dull, misty, with a fine cold rain falling – typically East Anglia. The fire in the Flight office refused to burn this morning causing frayed tempers and finally considerable damage to the stove. It's nice to vent your temper now and then.

I was really burned up about the message you received on Saturday when you rang. Why, they didn't even call me on the Mess Tannoy and I was there from about 6.45 'til 10.15, and then to tell you I hadn't been in all day was adding insult to injury. I went to the telephone desk, tore off a colossal strip from the WAAF on duty, and had to end up with apologies to save an outburst of tears. Tears seem to be the woman's most effective line of defence, Nina, and I just couldn't cope with them. But I don't think you will receive any more false messages.

I shall have to hurry away in a minute, darling, although heaven knows why. I think someone in high places must be as nutty as a fruit cake (pre-war). Before I go, Nina, just slip your hand in mine. Squeeze gently, my love, and say that everything will work out OK. We're planning this Leave from a very long distance at a place neither of us know much about but we've always coped and we must this time. I need you now more than ever, Nina. Help me all you can when you get there and I know it will work out.

God bless, Nina
Your sweetheart,
Vic
Xxxx X xxx X xxx

Officers' Mess, RAF Station Foulsham, Dereham, Norfolk
Tuesday afternoon 24th October, 1944

My Nina,

I have just returned from a lecture in the Gym on 'The Far East' given by F/Lt Healey who is MP for Brighton. Apparently, he has spent a good deal of time in Japan in the past and possesses a sound knowledge of their national life and their individual character. He believes that the Japanese will sue for peace very soon after the end of the European war if not before, and after he had finished talking I could quite see that the grounds for that belief were very sound.

It then depends on whether or not the Japanese Army obey the orders from Tokyo or decide to ignore them and carry on fighting as to the amount of men and the material we have to send out to that part of the world.

I'll tell you more about it when I see you, Nina, but I attended the lecture because I felt that the whole thing affected us both very closely. I gained new heart from it but I think it would be unwise to dismiss the possibility of a short visit to that part of the world from my mind entirely.

This morning, my Nina, I received two letters from you. The first told me of your lonely day off in Stafford. My heart aches for you, Nina, for I know only too well the longings and unsatisfied desires that the word 'lonely' covers. I think that perhaps my letters are not so impotent after all because when I say I am lonely you can extract the full meaning which it conveys. I will give you happiness soon, my darling, and I only hope I can give you enough to neutralize these weeks of suffering.

I had to smile at a line which you crossed out which started: 'I'd like to wear some new clothes'. Are you afraid of expressing a feminine desire to me, Nina? Surely you didn't think it was too human or material for my consumption? Because I spend part of my life above the clouds you mustn't think I'm beyond earthly contacts. Nina, why don't you use my coupon book? That's what you have it for and the happiness that a new dress, new shoes or whatever you want will bring to you will be my happiness too. You will be helping me to express my love for you in a very small way. Just save enough coupons for a couple of shirts which I shall need very soon.

Nina, I don't know if you meant it this way; if you sent me the lines of the hymn for my own personal comfort. If you did then know that you succeeded and gave me a greater peace of mind that I have known since I left you nearly five weeks ago. The tears in your eyes that day hurt me terribly and perhaps it was then that I lost faith a little, for if God could bring you that grief, you whom I believe could do no wrong; then surely I could not have much chance of comfort. But now I know that 'God, who made the Earth … Careth for me!'

The picture of Blymhill Church is dim, Nina, just as though seen through the mist of time. But, darling, don't ever let it grow dim in your heart if only for my sake. To me it is the scene of one of the most important happenings in my life, and the words I spoke in that church the sincerest and most heartfelt that have ever passed my lips. I can't hope to tell you in words how much I want you as my wife, when I try I fail miserably because I am not a sufficient master of words to justify my heart's love. But when The Day comes, my darling – our Wedding Day – I will start right in from the beginning to show you exactly what Blymhill and all the past year have meant to me. I will show you that my ideal of surrounding you with a complete love and undying happiness is not a fair-weather dream of the comfortable fireside. Circumstances force it to be that way now, but have faith in me, Nina. Whatever happens to us never lose faith in me and the fact that I love you beyond all else in this world. I kick against these wasted, barren, unhappy weeks that we have to spend apart and soon, my Nina, I shall kick so darned hard that you, Mrs H.V.A Vinnell, will be in your husband's arms for keeps before you quite realize how it has all come about. The Vinnellskis are not only good at cycling tricks. Remember darling?

Yesterday I wired the 'Railway' in Wilmslow for a reservation. I don't suppose they will wire back so I shall have to wait for the postman to bring me a reply. Phew! A nerve-racking business! My hand will probably be unsteady when you see me.

Ted (of the Syndicate) is waiting for me to go to the first house of the cinema so for today I'll close.

Not long now, my love, 'til our meeting. Don't blame me too much if I break a couple of your ribs when I hug you. I've really been lonely this time.

All my fondest love is yours, Nina.

For ever and ever

Your Vic X

PS 28 done. 22 to go. I'll soon be finished, darling.

NOVEMBER

1 Wednesday Code/Cypher Course. Posted to Wilmslow via Stafford and Crewe (so foggy could not see other side of platform).

2 Thursday Day begins at 6am, breakfast at 7. Kit Inspection. CO's Opening Address on 'Why We Are Here'. Lecture on Passes, etc. FF1 and Chest Xray. Lecture on RAF Organisation by S/O Veales. Cpl. Parker's instructions for Hut. Domestic Evening. Polish and spit and clean. Word from Vic at last. He phones at 7.30 (staying at Queen's Hotel, Alderley Edge, from Monday).

3 Friday Hear Tannoy this morning. Lecture on Etiquette and Customs by Cpl. Parker. PE. 'Waaf Organisation' Lecture. See collection of irrelevant films. Address by Padre. Letter from Mum (has to go to hospital). Another phone call from Vic (after waiting half an hour in vain).

4 Saturday Drill. Called off Parade Ground to see S/O Veales for Weekend Pass. Lecture on AMO. 209/43 (Waaf substitu.) Practical problem (write letter to a civilian asking for a job). Drill theory. 36 HOUR PASS. Pinch Cpl. Parker's taxi while I book out. Bus to Manchester. 1.30 train to Liverpool. Home at 3.15. Aunt at home with Mum, who is back in bed and lost her voice. Seems better for seeing me, and for more of our talks together. Take her some books.

5 Sunday Day goes too quickly. 8.10 train to Manchester, 10.35 to Wilmslow.

6 Monday Lectures all morning in Office Organisation, broken up by PT. Letter from Vic:

Officers' Mess, RAF Station Foulsham, Norfolk
Saturday evening 28th October

My Nina,

It's almost three days ago since I last wrote, three confusing fearful days which I am thoroughly glad to have survived. When I say survived I don't mean it in the sense that my physical well-being has been threatened, but what I do mean is that there has been a very real threat to our immediate future happiness.

To tell the story briefly, two 'bods' were needed for a Far East posting and about nine of us, of which I was one, were asked if we would care to volunteer. Well no two 'bods' stepped forward and of course someone had to go so it was decided this afternoon that our names should go into a hat and two be drawn out. You can imagine the state of my nervous system, and I think you can imagine too my relief when at the zero-hour two volunteers were found. That was what you might call a close shave, darling. Believe you me, Nina, I shall be happy just to be with you and hold your hand on the night of Nov 6. That's all I ask for.

I'm glad you were able to get home and see Mums on your third attempt. The news about the visit to a specialist is very good indeed. If he is able to tell her that there is nothing really to worry about it will do more good than all the medicines. I hope he can. I thought the 'Ovaltine' would be the thing but I'm sorry the milk is so short. The milkman must be taking advantage of my absence. Mum did not write to say she had received the parcel and it is many weeks now since I had a letter from her. Isn't she going to write to me any more, Nina? I used to look forward to her letters very much. Ask her to drop me a line when you write next.

I cannot very well post this letter to Wheaton, dear, as you will be left long before the GPO condescends to deliver it. I will add to it each day until I receive your address.

I hope to God I am free to phone tomorrow evening or I fear you will start worrying your head off about me. Don't panic about that Far East scare, Nina, it's not likely to happen again before I finish my tour.

My pass went into the Wingco yesterday and is probably signed and sealed by now. I was at a loss to know what address to leave in the book for that week so I put my own home address.

This past week seems to have been a very confusing one all the way round. Do you remember, darling, just before our last leave your interview cropped up and we wondered how things would work out? It's much the same this time but there is the added difficulty of seeking outside accommodation. I feel that I shall have to rely completely on you, Nina, to solve that problem and I know you'll do your very best for me – for us. I'm longing to see you again and find my happiness because there has certainly been none for me since we parted. Perhaps too, when we know the result of Mums' visit to the specialist we may be able to make some concrete arrangements for Our Day. There is nothing that is really holding us up apart from Mum's health, is there darling? and our Leaves together will be longer because the nights will be ours as well as the days. But we'll talk it over between the 6th and the 12th. I'll bring the Ring with me for your approval and fitting xxxxxxX

Thursday evening

Oh Nina, my darling, what a week it has been! Every night when I have come back I have been told of your phone call and I have felt so helpless. There have been so many things to tell you and the most important of all that I love you with all my heart and soul.

Tonight I was able to speak to you, Nina, and some of the load that I have been carrying on my mind for the past week lifted. As I spoke to you I knew once again the happiness of being at one with you, but out of all the emotions in my heart all I could say was: 'I'll make it up to you, Nina'. And I will, my darling, indeed I will.

Just one more thing, Nina. I shall be arriving in Wilmslow somewhere about 5pm. As arranged I'll meet you at the station at 6 and we'll proceed to the Queens. I hope you can manage some late passes and the 36. I'll see the Sq/O if your request fails.

At last I can put this letter in the post box. All my fondest love to you, Nina.

Soon your husband,
       Always your lover,
          For ever
            Your Vic X xxx X xxx X xxx

PS 30 ops done – only 20 to go.

'Moral Welfare' Lecture by W/Off Camella. Accounts (Pay Parties) (B'ham JP). Scootle off Camp to Railway Stn. and meet Vic. 6.5 train to Alderley Edge and Queens Hotel. Have dinner there and talk in lounge. Bus back to Camp for 10pm with Vic.

7 Tuesday Lectures on Gas and Station Defence. Pay Parade = £2.4.0d. Lecture on Current Affairs. Lecture on Messing (S/O Veale informs me of phone confab with Vic). Drill. Meet Vic rather late and have dinner at Queens. Pork again. Vic accompanies me back to Camp.

8 Wednesday Lectures 'Responsibilities of NCO's (F/Off Noble). Lecture 'Messing' (S/O Veale). Drill and Flight Inspection by F/Off Noble). Gas Caps drill, a real farcial effort. Dinner at Queen's. discuss 'dead-beat' as The Appropriate Time', 'No Loitering' SP, and Vic's help (bless him). Find gloves for Vic on bus.

---

10 Friday <u>CHURCHILL SPEAKS ON V2</u> A number have landed in widely-scattered points: casualties and damage are not heavy: German stories highly coloured. Mr Churchill made a statement in Parliament today about V2. H said: 'Last February I told Parliament the Germans were preparing to attack this country by means of long-range rockets, and I referred again to the possibility of this form of attack in my statement in this House on July 6. For the last few weeks the enemy has been using his new weapon, the long-range rocket, and a number have landed at widely scattered points in this country.

In all, the casualties and damage have so far not been heavy, though I am sure the House will wish me to express our sympathy with the victims of these attacks.

No official statement about the attack has hitherto been issued. The reason for this silence was that any announcement might have given information useful to the enemy and we were confirmed in this course by the fact that until two days ago the enemy had made no mention of this weapon I his communiqué. Last Wednesday an official announcement followed by a number of highly coloured accounts of attacks on this country, was issued by the German High Command. I do not propose to comment upon it, except to say the statements I this announcement are a good reflection of what the German Government would wish their people to believe, and of their desperate need to afford them some encouragement'.

<u>BOMBERS GO OUT FOR 3 HOURS</u> A three-hour procession of heavy bombers flew out over the East Coast today while Londoners saw part of a force which went out over the Channel across the South Coast. German radio at various times reported bombers approaching North-West Germany, bombers over Western Germany and bombers heading for Thuringia and Franconia. Later the 'Achtung' radio issued a continuous series of coded air-rai warning, says Reuter's radion station. Bomber command Mosqitoes attacked objectives in Westen Germany last night.

---

11 Saturday 36 HOUR PASS. Vic meets me at Waafery with taxi at 12.30. Take bus to Manchester. 'Wizard' lunch at Kardomah, mixed grill. Go shopping. Buy scarf and razor for Vic. Buy torch and batteries for me. Consider furniture. 4.30 train to Liverpool. Train and bus to Aunty Lucy, stay for tea. Bus to Pensby.

12 Sunday Such relief to be home. No inclination for bed till 3.30am and rise at 9am. Dress in slacks and prepare breakfasts with Vic's X able help. Eat it in Mum's bedroom, only room with fire. I have bath, also Vic, with combined help. Mum keeps better but due to us. 'Nina and Vic' way of preparing dinner, rice pudding (lots of skin) and coffee. Sit round fire, relaxed and happy, right up to last moment. 7.30 bus to Liverpool, 8.10 to Manchester, 10.30 to Wilmslow. Here we part, a painful experience. Sweets from Vic.

13 Monday Lecture 'Waaf Law' (S/O Veale) Drill, take Squad for first time. Mock Discussion Group. Tremendous tea and eat it all. Tidy belongings. Write 2 minute speech.

Hut 23. 'B' Flight, NCO's School, RAF Wilmslow, Cheshire
Monday 13th Nov

My Vic,

Is there any need to tell you of my lonely heart? and my yearning for you? and my love? Is there any need to tell you of the painful poignancy of our last kiss, on that dark, murky platform of Wilmslow railway station? I walked away into the fog, with my lips still clinging to yours, with my head still resting on your shoulder, with your arms still holding me tight, and long after the train had borne you away into the darkness I could hear your voice still whispering in my ear: 'Nina, my Nina, my Nina'. I think that perhaps you WERE still whispering those words and that you could also hear my reply: 'Yours Vic, I am yours and you are mine. My Vic, my Vic'. I like to think that you did. No, my dearest one, I don't think there is really any need to tell you. You know, you understand, because you too are suffering. But don't dwell on it too much, darling, think more of the bright light that is already shining so unmistakably at the end of this long dark tunnel just ahead of us. Think of that, plan for it, and perhaps the tunnel will seem less long – at least, I am sure it will seem less dark.

I reached Camp all right last night. It was raining very heavily, wasn't it? But I didn't know until I took off my coat how wet it was. Your torch was very useful.

Today the old routine began all over again. There was also an interview with the CO of the Course, a Sq/Off. Bilney. I am afraid that whereas before I tried to maintain an impartial opinion about her wretched Course, this time I really told the truth. 'No, I hated drill as performed in the Services, and NCOs and airwomen were both women to me.' Now I feel a whole lot better, even though I have probably shot my bolt.

I shall be speaking to you tomorrow, with a little co-operation from the GPO operator. Now I must get on with a subject for this cursed talk. I am really quite surprised how much I can say in two minutes.

Vic, I am not going to thank you for all your help this last week, and all your love, and all your many ways of expressing it. I suppose you wouldn't like me to do that. But I know how much you have helped, I know that I hold you very dear, and I'd like you to know too.

Goodnight, my husband – soon to be.

It's just after nine and I am saying 'Deadbeat soon, Vic – next Leave?

X Nina X

---

14 Tuesday RAF QUAKE BOMBS SINK TIRPITZ Hit 10.30, Ablaze 10.45, Capsized 11am. The Tirpitz, Hitler's last big naval unit, has been sunk. The Royal Air Force did it. Launched on All Fools' Day, 1939, the 45,000-ton battleship had been able to make only one operational sortie – the 1943 raid on Spitzbergen. Now the crews of two RAF squadrons have put the finishing touch to the Allied plans for incapacitating the German surface Navy. British Navy spokesmen said last night that there was no longer any German surface naval menace.'

HITLER HAS SHUT HIMSELF AWAY ... in the last weeks of October Hitler was still alive, but was causing his immediate entourage the greatest anxiety. Living in his armoured train he was so restless and apprehensive of Allied bombing that he hardly ever spent more than two days in one place. At night his train was run into the deepest convenient tunnel. Deitrich, his Press Chief, whose duty it is to give the Feuhrer a word-of-mouth report on world opinion each morning was gain and again sent away without seeing him. During October, Hitler paid only two brief visits to Berchtesgaden. Heinrich

Hoffmann, his personal photographer, has not been able to send out any photographs of him since the second week of September, when one showed Hitler receiving the Japanese Ambassador at his headquarters. New indications of the uneasiness in Germany over Hitler's failure to make a public appearance were given in official statements today.'

15 Wednesday Hear of some mystery person's efforts to phone me yesterday. Think it's Gerry. CO's Inspection followed by Drill. Two-minute Talks: I am No. 39 (last). Subject: 'Love from a Stranger'. Drill. Station Cinema: 'The Beautiful Cheat'.

> Officers' Mess, RAF Station Foulsham, Norfolk
> 15th November, 1944
>
> Dearly beloved Nina, xxx
>
> Last night I hugged your voice close to me. Long after I had put down the phone I could hear you saying: 'I love you, Vic', and your kisses came so clearly to me I could almost taste the sweetness of your lips. I had been very depressed and lonely all day but you soon put me on my feet and I was walking on air when I left the phone box. You are a great inspiration, Nina, lifting me out of the darkest valley with the sunshine of your love for me. I am dependent solely on you for all my happiness and you never fail me, darling. God bless you xxxxx
>
> Although I only had to walk from the Mess to the hut last night I got pretty well soaked again. It was a mad night. Outside the hut is a deep pool of water so you can be sure of starting off each day with a very wet pair of shoes and cold feet. Even if the shoes dry the cold feet remain until well past bedtime. Oh Nina, what will you say if I plant a pair of cold feet on you every winter night? I shall have to make sure they are well and truly toasted before quarter to nine each night.
>
> When Mums goes into hospital will you let me have her address? I don't like to write home in case she has already gone and the letter will lay on the mat until Florrie goes there. I can keep her supplied in 'Ovaltine' for months to come.
>
> When I arrived back on Monday I found a letter from my cousin in the rack. Can't think what's come over him these days – at least two letters inside a month. There was also a statement from the bank and I am happy to say that I saved £5 last month making it £130 all told. It's very much on the

ascendant, Nina, and since I've been at Foulsham I've saved about fifty quid. This isolation definitely has its advantages, not that it would have been different anywhere else. I'd like to make it at least two hundred before the war closes and with a bonus on top it would give us a fair start.

Love and happiness will be ours in abundance, my darling, and I just want to make sure that we have a nest-egg behind so that we can be really independent and live our glorious Nina and Vic life without outside interference of any sort. Yes?

The portrait I told you about is safely at my Aunt's place and Terry (my cousin) assures me the situation was kept strictly under control during the handing over ceremony. Thank goodness I've got it back; that's definitely the last thing. Another picture for our home, Nina darling. I wonder if you will think it a good likeness of me. Did you see it at Wheaton? The fellow Hunter drew it, he did several for the boys there.

I heard from Bond, that 'Jock' Williamson and Sgt. Perry had both gone to India from Wheaton. Phew! I'm glad that I was nominated for Signals Leader even if it was done without my consent. Indeed a blessing for both of us.

The news that you may leave Wilmslow next week is excellent news, Nina. I know you're not happy there and that alone hurts me. I am very thankful that my leave happened while you were there because I feel that I have helped to take the worst edge of it off. An early finish to your courses will make it all the easier for the great DAY darling, and it's very close now you know!

Oh Nina, how I long to have you as my wife. Our Star, my love, is within reach. I shall have pulled it down for you as I promised you at Gnosall on St Valentine's Night and with it has come all the happiness I ever dreamed of and a lot that I dare not think existed. I always knew you would realize that I was sincere in my love for you, I knew that in spite of the war and almost every situation being against me I could make you see that an ideal love still existed in this world of shattered morals. Thank you for your faith, my Nina, it will be repaid with the deepest devotion that ever a man had for his wife, with the warmest adoration that ever a lover had for his mistress.

I am yours, Nina xxx (deepest of scarlet)

Till the end of time

Vic

Xxx X   xxx X   xxx

17 Friday Prepare essays on National's Health and Self-Reliance of Airwomen. Mum goes to hospital (Birkenhead General).

18 Saturday Two hours written examination. And what a rush to get it in in time! Six questions in all. Passing Out Parade.

Officers' Mess, RAF Station Foulsham, Norfolk
16th November

Nina, dear heart xxx

Forgive this serious breach of etiquette but the fellow who has loaned me his pen for the last two days is not available this morning. But ink or pencil, darling, I love you with all my heart and I'll try and give you that love in my letter. My letters are not a very true picture of my heart, Nina, for its wealth of emotions defy words. There is only one adequate expression of my love for you and this is complete surrender. Soon now, my darling, very soon now ….

Is the pen working OK? I know it has a nasty trick of 'flooding' sometimes, caused I suppose by flying with it in my pocket. Hang on to it, dear, until I can get yours fixed up.

The events of last night nearly drove me frantic. 'Never have so many been mucked about by so few for such a long time' (apologies to Mr Churchill). Finger trouble seemed to be the order of the day and I finally reached bed feeling disgusted. Still, I'm paid for it.

Nina, are you worrying very much about taking the flight for drill? I had a feeling that it was troubling you more than you said. Look, darling, it's not very long is it and really it is only a means to an end. You'll probably never have to do it again when you've left Wilmslow. Just make up your mind that for those few minutes you'll step outside of the sweet, gentle Nina and raise your voice as you've never done before. Don't forget to address that tree-top or the cloud on the horizon, don't forget to stand to attention – and don't forget that Vic is always at your side. Keep your chin up, darling, but don't forget to return to Nina at the end of it, will you?

One of the coach drivers came up to me yesterday and said that she had something for me. She produced two little balls of the darning silk you needed so badly a few weeks ago. It's in my pocket right now but I shan't send it to you until I know where you are going to be for at least a week ahead. I think it would be too risky to send it on to Wilmslow.

It will be Saturday when you read this letter, darling, at least I hope it will be. The start of a lonely weekend for you. How I wish we could spend it together, Nina, starting off with a lay-in on Sunday in the same bed, one of those big breakfasts we've planned (don't forget the mushrooms) and a picnic later on in the day. It will come true, Nina, I promise you. You are not alone this weekend, my darling, you are never without your Vic for he belongs to you, heart, body and soul. If Fate is kind I'll be speaking to you on Saturday at 7.30 and if I'm free on Sunday I'll phone you.

Surround yourself with our love, my Nina, hold my hand, feel my kisses on your lips and body, deep, passionate, scarlet kisses from your lover. My spirit and my heart are with you night and day, dear, you are constantly in my thoughts. Soon my body will join my spirit at your side, soon our weeks of parting will be a thing of the past.

Look forward, my darling Nina, look to the very near future and feel comforted.

God bless you, sweetheart xxx

Your Love , Your husband, Your Vic xXxXxXx

Saturday night
18th November, 1944

My dear Lover,

Tonight I am completely alone with my thoughts, which are all of you, having just returned from the telephone box. I was almost giving up hope, darling, so that when the bell rang it startled me. The whole station seems deserted, and there was no queue for the kiosk, so I stood inside the darkness and prayed for you to come to me. There was three minutes to go before nine o'clock when you rang. Bless you for saving my life.

This morning we had a two hours' written examinations, and I don't feel too badly about that, as it is more in my own line. Actually, darling, I don't mind very much one way or the other, whether I pass or not, except that it will hurt my pride quite a lot if I don't.

I went to Wilmslow this afternoon, principally on an errand for the remainder of 'B' Flight, who desire to make a presentation of flowers to the officer and the Sgt. i/c. Now isn't that just like women? They pretend to be so tough and masculine and regimented, and then suddenly the pretence cracks, and they stand revealed as weak and sentimental and human – just women after all!

While I was there I saw a most stupid film called 'On Approval', a sort of mid-Victorian burlesque. By the way, sweetheart, I didn't choose a double seat this time – far too much room. I was practically forced into the cinema on account of the rain, but I returned to Camp in time for tea.

Oh, another little story connected with finding things is one concerning my towel, which I have not yet been able to explain myself. To begin with, I left Wheaton Aston with one towel (my own, marked in my own handwriting) and another raggy thing that the laundry presented me with, and which I was obliged to retain. After a week at Wilmslow, I sent my own towel to the laundry here, and so carried on with the raggy one. Until one morning when I was hut orderly, I noticed a spare towel lying on the table in the middle of the hut, and on looking at the name, discovered it was my own! (marked in my own handwriting). Now that I have collected my laundry I find I have two towels, both of them my own original ones, AND the raggy one. Have YOU any explanation, Vic? I haven't.

Thanks for your very useful tips on taking a flight for drill. I shall try to remember them on Monday morning when we have the Drill Exam. I'll pretend that I am trying to address you all the way from here to Foulsham.

My pen has run out, Vic, and no ink seems to be available. But my love for you will never give out. There is an inexhaustible supply available when the most loved man in the world claims

His bride,

His Nina.

X from Me to You

X from You to Me

Officers' Mess, RAF Station Foulsham, Norfolk
Friday morning 17th November

Darling mine xxx

I wish that I had arranged to ring you last night, Nina. I was free all the evening and I was very tempted to take a chance on whether you were there or no. It was very cold in the Mess and after listening to a thriller on the radio and nattering for a while I went to bed perchance to dream of you. When nine o'clock came round I told you of my love for you, Nina, not forgetting to say the password 'Deadbeat'. Things are not moving very fast just now and although it's rather early to say yet it looks as if I shall have another week's leave before the great Day. The date of my next leave is 21st – 27th December which means I shall be free on the morning of the 20th. It includes Christmas, darling, and I want to be with you wherever you are. Christmas is our anniversary, the day when a new, happy life started for both of us and if we can both get home for it then our cup of joy will indeed be full. Perhaps I can fix some poultry for the occasion but won't make any promises yet.

It will indeed be a time of despair for me, darling, if we cannot be together. The festivity of the season will only be a sharper knife of loneliness in my heart. Wherever I am forced to spend Christmas my heart and all my love and desires will be with you, Nina, leaving my body a lifeless shell. Oh please, my precious one, fight with all your might to bring us together over the holiday. I cannot, I dare not think of us apart at such a time when our love for each will be all-powerful. Oh Nina, I feel so helpless when I have to leave it all to you but I know you'll cope if it's humanly possible.

I feel desperately in need of you, darling, I need your kisses, your arms about me, your caresses on my body that responds to the very thought of you. I want some Nina to take right down inside me, I want your scarlet kisses and want to give you mine in return. I want you to help me at those moments when your help makes me feel so very close to you, as if you were part of my body. In my thoughts I worship you a thousand times a day. My adoration kisses are always on your body, Nina, and I yearn to fill that aching void that you have to bear.

Nina, my Nina, I love you passionately and only my complete surrender to your caresses, only your complete surrender to my worship of your soul at its beautiful shrine can bring me happiness. I'm lonely, my darling, horribly lonely without you. There is no deliverance for us, Nina, until we sleep secure in each other's arms, until Nina and Vic cease to exist as two separate bodies but unite in worship to that supreme love which has bound us so closely together.

Claim me with your kisses, Nina,

Make me

Your own Vic X xxxxxxxxxX

19 Sunday First in for Breakfast. Leave Camp just after 8am for 8.50 bus to Manchester. YMCA for tea and a chat to two M. Navy blokes, who find half a crown and give it to me. 11.5 train to Liverpool and on to Birkenhead.
Proceed to hospital to see Mum, joined by Nunk and Aunt. Tea at Aunt's. U/G to Liverpool for 8.10 train. Taxi back.

20 Monday Drill exam at 9.30. Manage it without making a boob somehow. Given 'breaking into mark time'. Our squad congratulated by Flt/Off. Oral exam. Mostly common-sense questions.

Wilmslow
20th November, 1944

My dearest Vic,

This is Monday afternoon and for a sort time there is break in the proceedings. The exams are over now, thank heaven. We had the drill and oral this morning. I tried to remember all you told me about taking a squad for drill and somehow I managed to do it without making a boob. That is because I think I was telling YOU what to do, not the quad – gosh, I hope I didn't say 'Squad, darling…Atten..tion!' The most I can tell you is that, at least, I have passed in drill, all the rest is still hanging in the balance, governed by the very vague but all-powerful 'suitability mark'.

Honestly, though, Vic I am not worrying in the least about the result now. It is no use worrying about something that has past, and I only feel profoundly relieved that it is all over. Still, I'd like to tell you I had passed, even if I had 'only just'.

I left Camp very early yesterday morning, immediately after breakfast at 7.30, yet even so I did not arrive at B'head General Hospital till quarter to two. Visiting hours are not until 2.30, but the Sister allowed me to go in. Mum seems quite comfortable there and the hospital staff are very pleasant and cheerful. She had nothing to report about a diagnosis, as the doctor told her to get settle in first. Aunt and Nunk joined me during the afternoon and I went to Aunts for tea. There wasn't time to do much else, I am afraid. Incidentally, darling, during the journey I found half a crown. It is incredible, isn't it? I just put my cup down on a table in the YMCA and there was half a crown! A Merchant Navy bloke saw it at the same time as me, and nobody claimed it, so he gave it to me. I never found anything before.

I am glad we have your portrait back, Vic. I never liked the idea of some other girl gazing every day at a life-size portrait of you, because she hasn't an right to, has she? No, I have not seen it. I couldn't have known you well enough when you were having it painted. Is it a good one, Vic?

I ought to be able to have seven days leave at Xmas, as a new quarter began on 15th of this month. It all depends on whether I have completed the course at Oxford, (if I get that far) and if I am posted anywhere else as a Clerk. I'll apply for Xmas leave on arrival there. Right now, it is impossible to plan anything except with the prefix 'if'. Tomorrow morning I shall know the worst, and I hope to be giving you the news at 7.30 tomorrow night. If difficulties arise, I'll send you a telegram.

I too am waiting to be introduced to the Vinnell's fireside, and don't worry about being a suffered from cold feet – I feel confident I shall be able to cure that. Soon you will know, soon you will be a 'deadbeat'. Our Star is beckoning for us to follow. Till we answer its call, I am just as surely

Your Nina

For keeps xxx X xxx

---

21 Tuesday Five names called out for interview with Fl/O ... two C and C, mine amongst them. I am last to be told sad news that I have failed the Course. Pricked my pride more than anything. Consoled Zeita. Interview with S/O Veale. Gain nothing except official jargon. Long walk around Camp clearing. Try to ring Vic unsuccessfully. Stay night at Zeita's home

---

Tuesday 21/11/44

Vic Dearest

This has been a queer unreal sort of day. Even now I feel dazed and bewildered with the sudden unexpected turn of events. I must admit I was very surprised when five names were called out this morning for interviews with the Flt/Off, mine amongst them, as failures. As in all such interviews, I was given no reason, beyond the fact that I had 'insufficient Service experience', which information (as pointed out) could be obtained and should not take three weeks of a Course to find out. Another unreconciled fact is that I was actually complimented on my written paper and was told I did quite well on the oral part, as regards the drill, the whole of our flight was told on the parade ground we had passed for that. The criticism then is not on account of service knowledge, but that other indefinable something called 'suitability', which I am inclined to think is so elastic as to be nothing more or less then 'personal like or dislike'. You either impress or you don't. Maybe you don't agree, Vic? Maybe I am only saying that because I feel sore? I am disappointed naturally because it has struck at my pride. She said I had no air of authority, that I lacked guts and 'go'.

I was last to be told the sad news, the only other COC .. LACW having burst into tears as soon as she was told. Determined not to allow the Flt/Off this satisfaction, I greeted her with a bland smile that took her off her guard. She asked if I knew why I had been called, and I replied that judging from reactions of previous candidates, I ought to. When she asked (like the judge to a prisoner at the dock) if I had anything to say, I said that 'I had tried and failed', and that 'I hoped I was sufficient of a sportswoman to know how to lose as well as win. I would try to lose gracefully.' She didn't expect this either, and she jumped up from behind her desk exclaiming: 'And a very praiseworthy sentiment, Chessall!' whereupon I saluted and withdrew. It was from S/o Veal that I got the rest of the details, and she I think would have most of the say. Honestly, Vic, everyone was surprised when I failed because they could find no reason for it. Are you very surprised? Don't I look the typical Seargeant type? I have been wondering – you don't think the duchess at WA had any hand in the matter? I remember with a sudden clarity what she said when she signed my remustering pro-forma. She said: 'Oh, this is one of those cases that require a separate letter of recommendation, in addition to the pro-forma'.

I am writing this letter on the train bound for Liverpool. This is one of the consolations of failing, as the two COC 'throw-outs' were given an SOP till tomorrow night and, of course, were not allowed to take part in the passing-out parade – another piece of good luck! You know, Vic, this is the very first time I have ever failed in anything I have ever attempted, and the experience is a new one to me.

There is one thing I am sorry about, darling, and that is that you will be ringing Wilmslow tonight and I shall not be there to take the call. I debated as to whether I should stay on Camp tonight in spite of the SOP, but honestly I can't tell you how glad I am to get away from the atmosphere of this place, which would be made even more uncomfortable for us tonight. I couldn't abide it if I were offered condolences, which is perhaps another reason for the smile on my face and the lift to my chin.

We had a long wait in Manchester (this train was over an hour late) and I filled in the time by trying to ring you, but all the circuits were engaged between 7 and 8. It will be a nearly 10.30 before we reach Liverpool, too late to get to my Aunt's or Marjorie's. Zeita has asked me to spend the night with her.

God bless, my Vic. And don't please be too disappointed with

Your Wife (soon) to be X Nina X

---

22 Wednesday Day Off. Rise very late. Go shopping with Zeita and buy some cakes to take to Mum. Visit Mum in hospital who is asleep when I greet her. Stay all afternoon. Try again to ring Vic. Send telegram.

23 Tuesday Eat breakfast in Permanent Staff Mess and share special privileges in Naafi. Report to Orderly Room to do typing. Interview with Adjutant about 'those clearance certificates'. Feel not least bit sorry. Domestic evening: darn. Film on VD. Phone call from Vic. Collect letter from Vic and feel heaps better:

Officers' Mess, RAF Station Foulsham, Norfolk
Sunday evening 19th November, 1944

My beloved Nina,

I may not be able to post this letter yet, but there's nothing in the world that can stop me writing to you, just as there is no parting that can stop me saying: 'Nina, my Nina, I love you, darling' a thousand times a day. It's a lonely Sunday evening as I sit in the hut, deserted except for one fellow who is also doing a spot of writing. The rain is beating against the windows aided by a stiff, gusty wind making Foulsham seem even more isolated and forgotten than usual. Last Sunday we were together by a friendly fireside. Last Sunday was a Nina and Vic day, but under the happy feeling of having you by my side was the dark haunting fear of the impending parting. Inside myself I felt like a doomed man to whom life has suddenly become very dear. I had to touch you, Nina, I had to hold your hand, to put my arm round your shoulders and pull you close to me because I knew that in a few hours I would know again the dark valley, a desolate life without your smile, a terribly lonely life without your kisses and caresses; the start of another vigil of waiting and longing to be with you again that I may live in peace and happiness.

This Sunday finds me watching and waiting, watching for the first chance to have you in my arms again, to claim your lips with kisses, to whisper that you are my own darling Nina and no matter what life may hold in store for us together we shall see it through and find happiness in our supreme love.

Nina, I am waiting with a fearful heart to know if this Christmas will be a Nina and Vic Christmas. What am I to do, darling, if you cannot get leave? The burden of a lonely heart will be doubled if that is possible, and I feel sure I shall be ill with loneliness and longing. Oh Nina, please fight tooth and nail for that leave. But I don't have to ask that, do I? I know the pain will be as much yours if we are apart, darling.

You made me very happy last night, Nina. The sound of your voice thrills me and sets me tingling with pleasure and anticipation. My body lives again in those few minutes, my love, and I know that I am indeed your Vic.

Nina, I don't know what the result of your sudden outburst of honesty will be, but I do know that you were never cut out to be the sort of person they are trying to make of you at Wilmslow. From what you have told me of some of the stupid things they try to make you believe I would have told them exactly the same as you did, only a little more forcibly expressed. If they fail you, Nina, don't reproach yourself. Believe me when I say you will have lost nothing of real value. Your home (which is ours) our love and your Vic are things that matter, the WAAF being purely incidental. I don't want you to go back to Clerk GD if you are not happy in that capacity but I do think it's a hard road to your new trade and if I were in your place, Nina, I'm afraid I should have shot my bolt in the first couple of days. Luckily you possess more patience than I do.

Monday morning

My darling, because of your letter I have decided to post this and take a chance. Nina, you must keep your chin up. I haven't got much time but I want to impress on you that pass or fail your course you must not tell yourself you are no good.

What does it mean to you when I tell you that you are the world and all to me? You must know now that my whole life lies in your hands and knowing this how can you think yourself a failure just because you don't meet the requirements of some piddling old loggerheads at Wilmslow?

Nina, my darling, I love you with all that is Vic, with my whole heart, soul and body. Look forward, Nina, for my sake, look forward and remember that you are responsible for my life's happiness. That is something in which I know you will not fail.

Your lover for eternity,

YOUR Vic X xxxxxxxxx X

PS I will write to Mums as soon as possible. All my love, Nina.

24 Friday Learning to type quite well. The Adjutant even makes use of my shorthand. Must not make myself too useful here though.

> **Officers' Mess**, RAF Station Foulsham, Dereham, Norfolk
> Thursday morning 23rd November 1944
>
> Nina, my beloved,
>
> Last night your telegram came so I think I am safe in posting this letter to you at Wilmslow. I am wondering whether you are through the course or not, Nina. It doesn't make any difference to us, of course, but I do want you to be where you are happiest. I guess I shall know when I speak to you this evening (I'm almost certain I shall be free). The other day I pushed the score up two, so now I have seventeen (missions) to do but I can say for certain I shall not be finished before my next leave, which is, incidentally, only just over three weeks away. I have gained a few days this time.
>
> The parcel arrived safely yesterday, darling, and thank you very much for the cigarettes. Don't worry about the note, Nina, I know the lunch-hour is very short and I know too that all your love comes with the parcel. I see you managed to iron the shorts after all. I hope they were not a source of embarrassment to you.
>
> Nina, I had to smile at your story of the flowers. It is typically a feminine move and I like it. May our women always stay like that for it would indeed be a dull world if the only outlook on life was a masculine one. It would be a terrible blow to me if I came home and found you regimented up to the eyes. But there's no fear of that, is there, my darling?
>
> I hope I'm not too cautious, Nina, but where would one manage to find three pairs of silk panties? I've got to hand it to you, you certainly have a flare

for it. If you can find the old piano or radiogram lying around somewhere it would certainly come in useful for our home. Or is that too ambitious, darling.

Surprisingly enough I still have two pairs of gloves!!

There is only one way I can account for the towel, Nina, and it is that somehow it must have been returned in some laundry to Wilmslow, although how it got from Wheaton I can't think. Anyway, it's a good thing to get it back again.

They seem to be very lax about collecting mail at Wilmslow, Nina. Your letter written on Saturday was not collected until 5pm on Monday and reached me on Wednesday. That's a fair time considering there's a big city so close, isn't it? But never mind, you will soon be away from that bind of a place and I will admit I shall feel easier. It hurts me to know you are unhappy and Wilmslow is alien to all that is Nina. Our full happiness lays ahead of us, my darling, in the days when we are Mr and Mrs Vinnell and uniforms laid away and forgotten. Please God it may be soon now. My whole heart years for that happiness and until it is ours I shall always be a very lonely, miserable, discontented Vic. My love for you is supreme, Nina, coming before all other considerations. I WILL realise my ideal, I WILL give you complete happiness and no matter how long the road may be, with you at my side, with your love and companionship to guide me, together we'll reach our Acacea xxx.

All my heart's love is yours, my Nina, and I am lonely because I long to lay that love at your shrine.

X x x These are yours, darling, in the deepest scarlet hue. With closed eyes I stretch my imagination to breaking point. Please be with me soon is the desire of

Your lover

Vic

Xxxxxxxxx (always mine)

X from you to me

---

27 Monday POSTED! To 14 Base, Ludford Magna. Find it is in Lincs – not at all what I wanted, except that it is a Bomber Command. Pack bags. Spend most of today cleaning. Lots of washing. Iron and press uniforms.

28 Tuesday Leave Wilmslow at 8am having arranged for removal of kit to Station myself. Make it in two journeys. Manchester for an hour, which I spend shop gazing with Sgt. Major. Very slow stopping train to Lincoln via Retford. YM for tea. 5.7 train to Market Rasen and transport to Ludford 6 miles away. Wait a long way outside Camp to find telephone to phone Vic. Supper in WAAF Naafi.

29 Wednesday Terribly cold all night. Report to Picket Post at 8.45 then go on my rounds with arrival chit. Write letter to Vic. Working as P3 Clerk in O. Room (inbetween doing Xwords). Have not yet made up my mind about them. Naafi phone out of order, so there are no telephones at all here. Write letter to Mum.

DECEMBER

1 Friday New huts look very crowded with 26 beds in them. There's hardly room to walk between beds. Told today Xmas leave not granted. May have from 28 Dec. At last unpack belongings, and able to sort myself out. Walk to N Whittingham, two miles away, to phone Vic – 'Not in Mess!' Get lift back to Camp. Have bath.

2 Saturday At last, a LETTER from someone – from Mum containing two telegrams

---

396 PENSBY RD. PENSBY WIRRAL CHES.

DULY REGRET TO INFORM YOU THAT YOUR FIANCÉ F/LT HENRY VICTOR ALEXANDER VINNELL IS MISSING AS THE RESULT OF AIR OPERATIONS ON THE NIGHT OF 27/28 NOVEMBER 1944.

ANY FURTHER NEWS WILL BE CONVEYED TO YOU IMMEDIATELY STOP. LETTER FOLLOWING STOP. PENDING RECEIPT OF FURTHER NOTIFICATION FROM AIR MINISTRY NO INFORMATION SHOULD BE GIVEN TO THE PRESS.

192 SQUADRON

---

27 NOVEMBER STOP. ENQUIRIES ARE BEING MADE THROUGH THE INTERNATIONAL RED CROSS COMMITTEE AND ANY FURTHER INFORMATION RECEIVED WILL BE COMMUNICATED TO YOU IMMEDIATELY STOP. SHOULD NEWS OF HIM REACH YOU FROM ANY OTHER SOURCE PLEASE ADVISE THE DEPARTMENT STOP. HIS FATHER HAS BEEN INFORMED.

VIC REPORTED MISSING on 27/28 Nov. And with this news, the bottom drops out of my world. Interview with WAAF Officer, who grants me the afternoon off and advises me to go out and get stinking drunk!?! Write letter to Mumsie, then get into bed, draw sheet over my head, close my eyes and try to bring Vic near. Find it easier in Great Outdoors where Vic and I belong. Walk miles in bright moonlight between hedge-lined lanes and have cup of tea at farmhouse where I knock on door and pour out my sad heart.

Saturday, 2nd Dec '44

My Own Darling Vic,

This morning I heard the news that something terrible happened to you last Monday night. Vic, why didn't I know about it? All this time I have been writing to you, trying to phone you, and somehow that was the last thing I thought of. As I mentioned in my last letter, I walked last night a distance of two miles to the only telephone that works around here. I was informed, as I was informed last Monday night, that you were 'not in the Mess!', but I left a message for you to ring me on Sunday night at 7.30pm on that number – Tealby 236. I shall be there on Sunday just the same in spite of the telegrams, because you may have come back to me by then.

Vic, my dearest one, please come to me soon. This horrible agony of suspense, of not knowing where you are or what has happened to you, is more than I can bear. Remember Vic, we promised that we would always be together? – the undivided front? – and it is my business to find out the place where you have gone so that I can follow you there.

Today when I received the two telegrams, which have only just been forwarded on to me from home, I thought the bottom had fallen out of my whole world. It had – until I realised that the worst has not yet happened and I will not give up hope. I will pretend that you have been posted to some station in Western Europe unknown to me as yet, but I know that you will get in touch with me somehow. You told me once, I remember, not to worry too much if you were ever reported missing, because you would always reach me and find your way back to me again. And I am banking on that, my darling. I was told I could have some leave if I wanted it, but there is nothing for me at home without you or a mother, and besides, I don't want to upset her just as she is getting better. I shall want my leave anyway to have at the same time as you over Xmas, or for when you are a 'deadbeat'. Oh Vic, don't forget that, when you are a 'deadbeat' – you must be back in time for that.

I did agree, however, to having the afternoon off. I wanted to be some place where I could be quite alone, so that I could close my eyes and concentrate on bringing you close to me. It was so cold in this hut that I got into bed for a while and drew the sheets over my head. Somewhere in that darkness I found you, and warmed your cold fingers and caressed your bruised body. We talked together of Chester and Blymhill and Stratford and we both felt comforted. Nothing can ever spoil those glorious memories. If we had them all over again, we could not squeeze another ounce more of happiness out of all the times we have spent together. Life for us both has been very full since last Xmas, and it is good to know that there could not be any regrets. It is nearly a year ago, Vic, since we first met and it seems I have known you a lifetime. It has been a year of unparalleled happiness for me, a year of unbounded promise of a greater life that is yet to be. That is why, my dearest, you cannot leave me now. Oh Vic, you just cannot. If you go out of this life, then I must go too. I am afraid to go on living without you. You do understand that, Vic, don't you? – you, who felt alone if I left you for half an hour in the next room? You would want me to follow you, wouldn't you? I dare not think how you are feeling tonight. Here am I in a warm comfortable bed, and you are still wandering about outside there, cold and hungry and friendless, and maybe hurt and in need of help.

Oh darling of mine, the place where my heart belongs has been experiencing strange things today. Something is happening to my heart, for where you are, there dwells also in my heart. If you are suffering, my heart is suffering with you. If you are cold or in pain, my heart too is enduring these things with you, and it gives me a strange thrill of pride to be able to suffer with you.

I have walked a long long way tonight, further than I thought, until I came to turn back. I wanted to walk and walk and walk, and tire myself out so completely that I should find some respite in sweet oblivion from the fears that torment me. There was a moon tonight, pale and clear and just past the full. It looked painfully beautiful. I watched it rise. And as it climbed slowly and painfully into the sky, it seemed to tear something from out of myself. Our Star was there too, Vic darling. I'll always remember your promise to reach for it for me, if I asked you. I am asking you. My heart has been crying out for that Star for a long long time, and I really want it, Vic. If you cannot reach it, please let me reach for it for you.

I wonder if you can see this same Moon, this same Star. From what strange inhospitable country are you looking at it? My fears, this agonising torment, would be considerably diminished if only I knew you could still look at it. It is the horrible nameless dread that haunts me, of your dear face cruelly battered, and those lovely blue eyes gazing up sightlessly at an alien sky.

Vic, my Vic, if only you would come to me soon and make me laugh at my fears and tell me funny stories about the adventures you have had. Vic, couldn't you make me laugh again?

3 Sunday Put on my face this morning and wear it all day perfectly. 'Strength sufficient unto the task!', and today I am granted superhuman powers. Keep my date at telephone box, Tealby 236, and wait inside box for three quarters of an hour. I pray for a miracle to happen, but still just a stony silence. Mad to expect it, but I clutch at the chance like drowning man to a straw.

Write to Vic:

Sunday 3rd Dec. '44

Tonight I kept my date at Tealby 236. I remember I walked there with a spring in my step and my head held high. I thought I was going to meet my lover. It was like old times. There was a gale blowing and it was very cold, but I fancied that I could hear you whispering my name borne to me on the wind, and who cared about anything so long as there was just a chance that the telephone may yield up your voice. To have heard your 'Hullo, my Nina. This is your Vic', would have been sweet music in my ear. I waited inside the telephone box for a very long time, but the instrument maintained strong silence. What I said inside that telephone kiosk I cannot recall, but I know I called upon God to answer my prayers in an agony of spirit such as I never knew existed. When I looked at my watch it was 8.15. I had been there for three quarters of an hour, and when I came out I felt spent and limp and lifeless. How I got back to Camp I do not know. I felt too tired to cry any more, as though my grief had gone beyond tears.

I was mad, I suppose, to expect it. I was mad to go there tonight. But then isn't the whole world mad? I thought that miracles do sometimes happen, and it seemed worthwhile to take a chance on the odd freak of fortune or a strange caprice of Providence, call it what you will. I clutched at it as a drowning man would clutch at a straw – and now, God help me, I am still in danger of drowning.

How many more days like today have I still to face?

I put on my mask this morning and wore it perfectly all day, until darkness fell and there was no-one to see and no-one to watch when I slipped it off. What I have gone through today, I should have thought once was impossible without something inside cracking. Yet here I am, crushed and spent, but still a survivor. It must be a truth that we are given strength sufficient until the task, and today I was granted superhuman powers.

Every day I will write to you, my darling. If I stopped writing now, it would seem that you had really gone beyond my reach, and I will not admit defeat easily. It will be such a relief to see you read this letter.

I must leave you now, Vic. Wherever you are, I know that I leave you within the pale of God's love and care.

God bless you, my sweetheart. I will remember your name Victor, and you were not called that for nothing. You MUST be victorious.

I love you,

Nina

4 Monday No letter for me as I had hoped. No respite for me from this quagmire of doubt. Nothing but this weary routine of living, hollow mockery of life as it should be, as Vic and I know it. Still there is hope - ? Feel more hopeful and in better spirits tonight than ever before since The News. Good sign? Read Vic's poetry book. Write to Vic:

Monday, 4 Dec

There seemed nothing for me to go out for tonight and nothing for me to stay in for either. I was in a queer restless mood. There are things I should be doing, but how I am to set about the task is more than I can think. I wish I had asked you more about what I should do in just such circumstances as these. The main thing to remember is that you said I was not to worry if you were reported missing, that it was a million to one chance that you would be safe, and that you would find your way back to me somehow. I cannot write to the Adjutant of your Squadron for news, as I have not yet received his letter confirming the telegram. This I am awaiting with some impatience.

Another thing I have thought of, Vic, is that you do not know my new address. All the letters I have written to you during this last week will probably have been dispatched to Colubrook (Central Depository) for safe custody, pending further news of you. So you may not know where to find me, especially as there is no-one at home to direct you. Oh Vic, my darling, what is there I can do to help? I have all sorts of wild ideas at odd times during the day, only to discard them in a saner moment. However, I have now decided to await the Sqdn. Adjutant's letter with as much patience as I can muster. Having come to this decision, my eye happened to alight on the book of poems you gave to me at WA, and I opened it at your favourite poem, one that you often used to quote:

'For thy sweet love remembered such wealth brings
That then I scorn to change my state with Kings.'

I pondered over those lines for a long time, Vic, and I fell to musing.

Darling of mine, it was you who showed me what love really was. I didn't know before you came into my life – we were both on the verge of making an irrevocable mistake – I didn't know that love was like this, so all-consuming, so all-embracing, demanding everything. I had thought it lukewarm and unimportant, almost a pastime for one's leisure hours, a thing to be taken up and put down at will. I have learned a lot since then. This sweeping tide of deep scarlet emotions that caught me in its grip almost a year ago has grown and developed and taken possession of me so completely that it is greater than myself. I am myself no longer, neither are you just you; we are a combination of all that is best in both of us, welded together for all time by the power of this same love. We have known a lot of its glories; we have glimpsed its silvery heights for a few brief moments. Yes, my Vic, because of you life has been very sweet. We have given freely without counting the cost, each for the other, and so in return we have received – everything. And now, dear heart, I am tasting some of the bitterness. I am experiencing a grief so great and a torment of spirit so overwhelming that I dare not admit it to the full. I keep on telling myself that tomorrow relief will come, that soon I shall have word from you, that the next delivery of mail, the next ring of the telephone, the next opening of the door, will lift me soaring to the heights, all doubts and fears forgotten in the glad knowledge that my beloved is here, alive and in the flesh.

Oh darling xxxx darling Vic, such a wealth of loneliness has engulfed me in this last week that I shall want a whole lifetime of you to make up for it. I want to feel the warm shelter of your arms around me and your heart beating against my own. I want to press my face close against yours, and look deep into your eyes so that soul brushes soul. Remember those moments when we felt that happen? – it happened first in London in a cinema, when for no reason at all you turned and looked me, and it was then.

And yet, Vic – and I write this fully realising the grave issues at stake and while this tremendous burden of agony and heartache is still upon me – and yet, Vic, if I had no more than this year I would not choose a longer period of time as a shoddy substitute with any other. Also quoting from your book:

'One crowded hour of glorious life (without you)
Is worth an age without a name.'

But Vic, dearest in all the world to me, you will not let me put this to the test? Our lives are only just beginning, our happiness has yet to be completed. Oh come to me, Vic. (Dear God in Heaven, be merciful. You gave him to me for such a short while; You cannot take him away so soon.)

Goodnight, my dear x x x

5 Tuesday Still no more news. No letter. 1/c P3 today, Mary on day off. Helped by someone called Arthur. Do washing. Write letter to Vic:

Tuesday, 5th December

Once again there was no letter, no word from you, still no more news – nothing but this awful nagging silence that eats right into my bones. And still this weary routine of mere existence goes on. I walk to and fro from the places I am supposed to go like an automaton, I chew food but I do not taste it, I look at people and things unseeingly. I rise each morning as I went to bed the previous night, unrefreshed and with that same dull ache. If this day-by-day set of actions that I am obliged to perform is all that life is to hold for me, then without you, Vic, my life is already over, this war is already lost. The foundations of my faith are tottering, all hope for the future is hanging in the balance. It rests with you, Vic, whether we live together or die together.

An odd thought struck me today, my darling, not of any consequence, but I happened to remember it now. Do you remember the story of Tony and Kathe, and how they lost each other for twelve whole years? I remember being frightened by that prospect at the time, as I somehow always associated you with the character of Tony. I could not think then how I could possible lose you, even for a short time. Now I know, but it won't be for twelve years, Vic – unless it be that I have lived all the anguish of twelve years in these last few days. We will find each other soon, I know it, because of the old undivided front. That always holds good. And somehow, Vic, I can't possibly believe that you are very far away from me, that you are separated from me by death. It just doesn't seem possible. I wouldn't feel so near to you if you were. And surely, when we have been so much a part of the other, surely I would know! Somewhere I feel that you are breathing this same air that I breathe, that you can see the same full moon and the same twinkling stars, and that you feel the same icy keen wind that blows across Lincoln. In some strange way, I feel that you are not a spirit yet, but that you are a man with all a man's needs. I know I can supply those needs and I long to do so with all my heart. You know what a happiness it was to me to mend your clothes, and darn your socks, and comb your hair, and wash your face, oh and cut your toenails. The smallest act of service was a pleasure to me. I have loved and cherished you in every way possible, and now I can do nothing. That is what hurts me most.

6 Wednesday Letter from Aunty Lucy (to say 'it can't be very nice for me' – not Nice!) – masterly understatement. If only I could hear Vic was alive and well! Without this sure knowledge the foundations of my life are tottering.

Write to Vic:

Wednesday, 6th Dec.

I didn't tell you that I had a letter from Mr Eades, not the usual carping letter of sympathy, but a very comforting one. There was one line in it especially so

'Certain it is that Victor cannot drift beyond God's love and care.'

I am glad to be reminded of that, because as I told you last night I feel my own shortcomings so much in not being able to help you. He also assured me of his daily prayers for us both. Oh Vic, surely so many petitions cannot go unheard. It is even more important than ever now that we should keep our 'nine o'clock' dates. You do keep them always, don't you, Vic? It is the only link we have now remember, our only means of communication. I feel it is so very necessary that you should be aware of my being there at that time, that I always arrange it so that I am completely alone at 9 o'clock, and I say as loudly as possible so that my voice may be borne to you on the four winds:

"Vic, my Vic, here I am. It is 9 o'clock, and I want you to know that wherever you are my heart is with you and I love you so very dearly. Let me find you soon, Vic, and always I shall be waiting. Deadbeat, darling, you won't forget. And I'd like to see you in time for your next leave. Here are my lips, Vic, waiting for those scarlet kisses. God bless, darling, till we meet."

I wonder, does my impassioned plea ever reach you? In the absence of any official information as yet, I have been doing my utmost to collect as much 'gen' as possible on my own. Not that I have been very successful so far. It would be much easier if you were on ordinary bombers instead of those special 'hush-hush' expeditions. However, from one source I understand that three aircraft were missing on the fateful night of 27/28 Nov., two over Germany and one over France on a special Signals raid. There is a very good chance, I should think, for the one missing over France. I wonder which of these was yours.

Often and often in the silence of the night, I try to put myself in your 'N for Nina' on that night of nights. I try to imagine some of the difficulties in which you found yourself and to follow the sequence of events up to the time of your touching Mother Earth. Did you have trouble with your oxygen supply? How did you come to be so low? – I thought you flew at 33,000 ft. range out of reach of German AA guns? Did your engines fail? Did you crash-land or did you bale out? Are you safe? – that's the main question.

Won't it be wonderful when I can send you this letter? – or better still give it to you in person? It will be marvellous to see you smile as you read of my silly fears. It will be marvellous to smile at them myself and know that those nameless horrors have been kept at bay.

'Gen' from Map Clerk: '3 Mossys missing a week last Monday, 2 over Germany, 1 over France, on special signals raid."

7 Thursday Letter from Squadron Adjutant at Foulsham: 'Very little news after a/c took off at 02.58 on 27/11 with Bomber attack on Munich, captained by P/O J. Fisher (Canadian). Not landed in occupied territory … should he have survived without being captured

RAF Station Foulsham, Nr Dereham, Norfolk
30th November, 1944

Dear Miss Chessall,

It is with very deep regret that I have to confirm that your fiancé, Flight Lieutenant Henry Victor Alexander Vinnell is missing from operations. There is very little I can tell you about this tragic occurrence at the present moment.

Your fiancé was flying as Navigator in a Mosquito aircraft with his usual captain, Pilot Officer J.G.M. Fisher, a Canadian. They had done many operations together and on this occasion were accompanying a Bomber Command attack on Munich in the early hours of Monday morning the 27th November, 1944. The aircraft took off from here at 2.58am but nothing more was heard of it afterwards. At one time we had hopes that it had landed in Occupied territory on the Continent, but unfortunately this was not so.

Your fiancé had been with us since last May and had always carried out his duties with the greatest of determination and courage. He has shown the highest skill and aptitude for his work; he and his captain made an excellent pair and their loss will be very keenly felt by the Squadron.

I will, of course, send you immediately any further news that I may receive. I must ask you not to pass on any information to the Press as this may prejudice his chances of escape should he have survived without being captured. This is not to say that any information about him is available other than that I have already given, but it is a necessary precaution adopted in the case of all personnel reported missing.

If there is any way in which I can help you or if you have any queries, do please let me know as I will be only too glad to be of assistance. May I send you the deepest sympathy of myself and everybody in the Squadron during this anxious time of waiting for news.

Yours sincerely,

Wing Commander D. W. Donaldson, DSO, DFC

RAF Station Foulsham
3rd December, 1944

Dear Miss Chessall,

I am writing to tell you very sad news, as we have just been informed that articles of clothing belonging to F/Lt. H.V.A. Vinnell and to his pilot, P/O J.G.M. Fisher have been washed up on the seashore, as well as wreckage from a Mosquito. In my earlier letter to you I said that they were missing after a Mosquito sortie to Munich on November 27th 1944.

Although this is not conclusive proof, I am very much afraid that the evidence leaves little doubt that they cannot have survived.

I need not say that we are all distressed to learn this news and that we all join in sending you our deepest sympathy in your very great loss....

Yours sincerely,

Wing Commander D. W. Donaldson, DSO, DFC

1945

COMPLETE SURRENDER

'We succumbed to overwhelming power. The war in Europe is over.'

JANUARY

'Marriage is like finding one's completion, and once having found it, it is like losing half of oneself without it. It is like someone you want to laugh at one moment and run to for comfort the next. It is someone who can make one empty house a home, and a home a haven. It is someone who believes in you when you have lost your belief in yourself. It is someone to whom you can tell your achievements and your failures. And the emotional side of it? – why, it is as natural as the air you breathe and the food you eat, like good health, just as natural and   necessary.' And I married Vic. God help me.

RAF Station Foulsham, Nr Dereham, Norfolk

1st January 1945

Dear Miss Chessall,

Thank you for your letter dated 26th December, 1944.

I quite agree that there is a slight possibility of your fiancé having baled out of the aircraft before it crashed, but if they had done so and had survived, one would have expected them to have been found nearby.

The articles of clothing, (which were found in France a few miles NE of Dieppe), consisted of a cap belonging to the pilot, and an RAF sock to your fiancé. It is quite probable that these were being carried separately as it was contemplated that they would be diverted and would land at another aerodrome on return.

Although from this little evidence it is impossible to reach any definite conclusion, I am afraid that we cannot entertain very great hopes of their survival.

Do let me know if there is any further way in which I can help.

Once again, please accept my deepest sympathy.

Yours sincerely,

Wing Commander D. W. Donaldson, DSO, DFC

---

5 Friday 1 month's Leave granted from Monday. It would be grand if only, if only Vic would come.

8 Monday Leave Ludford. Compassionate Leave.

9 Tuesday Dark days …

11 Thursday I cannot live again until I know that Vic too is alive!! Three months Compassionate Leave granted (one month at a time) on a/c of Mum's illness and her not being able to leave hospital with no-one at home to look after her. Posted to RAF West Kirby with a living out pass, cycling to and from Camp daily.

MAY

2 Wednesday: <u>HITLER DEAD</u> 'Fell at his post in battle of Berlin', says Nazi radio. Hitler is dead. He 'fell for Germany' in the Reich Chancellory in Berlin yesterday afternoon, according to a broadcast from Hamburg at 10.30 last night. Grand-Admiral Doenitz, 54 year old inventor of U-Boat pack tactics, broadcast, claiming that Hitler had appointed him Fuehrer and Commander-in-Chief of the German Forces. Doenitz came to the microphone and declared: 'The military struggle continues with the aim of saving the German people from Bolshevism. We shall continue to defend ourselves against the Anglo-Americans just as long as they impede our aim.' A ghost voice broke in: 'Rise against Doenitz. The struggle is not worthwhile if crime wins.'

The announcement of Hitler's death at fifty-six, after being Fuehrer since January 30, 1933, was preceded by slow Wagnerian music and finally by a roll of drums. During the announcement and Doenitz's speech from Hamburg, the southern German radio network went on broadcasting light music …'

3 Thursday – <u>FULL SURRENDER OF NAZIS IN ITALY</u>

7 Monday – <u>COMPLETE SURRENDER</u>

'We succumbed to overwhelming power. The war in Europe is over. All the German armed forces today surrendered unconditionally to the allies.'

---

9 Wednesday – <u>BRITAIN'S DAY OF REJOICING</u>

Dense crowds in Whitehall, estimated by the police at 50,000 – all cheering like mad – mobbed the Prime Minister when he emerged from Downing Street after his breakfast speech. With the broad grin of victory on his face – and a new cigar clamped between his teeth – Winston Churchill gave his famous V-sign.

Air Ministry, Casualty Branch,
73-77 Oxford Street, W.1
June, 1945

Madam,

I am directed to refer to your letter of 6th June, and to express the Department's regret at the delay in replying thereto owing to the great increase in Casualty enquiries following upon the occupation of enemy territory.

I am to explain that a special unit of the Royal Air Force, the Missing Research and Enquiry Service has been formed to conduct the most exhaustive investigations into the fate of all our aircrews who have not returned. It is felt that you will appreciate that no priority could be given to individual cases, in this sad task, which is of such magnitude that many months must elapse before all areas can be covered and all investigations completed.

I am to assure you that, if it is at all possible to discover any information to throw light on the fate of your fiancee you will be notified at once. In this connection, however, the location of the loss of his aircraft, off the French coast, points to the sad conclusion that both he and his pilot, Pilot Officer Fisher, lost their lives in the sea, in which sad circumstances, the possibility of further news must unhappily be considered to be very small.

I am, Madam,

Your obedient Servant

Air Ministry
73-77 Oxford Street
London W1
4th June, 1945

Madam,

I am directed to inform you, with regret, that in view of the lapse of time and the absence of any further news regarding Flight Lieutenant H.V.A Vinnell, since he was reported missing, action has now been taken to presume, for official purposes, that he lost his life on the 27th November 1944.

In conveying this information, I am to express to you the sympathy of the Air Ministry.

I am, Madam,
Your obedient Servant,

For Director of Personal Services
NATIONAL BABY WELFARE COUNCIL
Official Organ 'Mother and Child'
29 Gordon Square, London, WC1
27 November, 1945

479352 LACW Chessall N
Poplar Villa
396 Pensby Road
Pensby, Wirral
Cheshire

Dear Miss Chessall,

It is with the greatest possible pleasure I write to inform you that you have been awarded five guineas for the very excellent essay you submitted recently for our competition. As you know, we originally offered only one prize, but you and another competitor submitted such splendid entries that the adjudicators decided to award two prizes of five guineas each.

I wonder whether you would be so good as to let me know your age, whether you are still in the WAAF or whether you have been released, and any other details you would care to send. We shall be circulating the results to the press within the next day or two and in consequence are often asked various questions regarding competitors. If you should receive some publicity

I hope you will not mind. The cheque will follow in the course of a day or two when I have secured the necessary signatures.

May I end with a personal note. We of the National Baby Welfare Council are convinced that a realisation of the plans which you and your fiancé made together and which at the time gave you so much happiness will be an inspiration to others. We sincerely hope that, as part creator of this inspiration, you yourself will glean some consolation and comfort in your own personal grief. We would re-echo your own words:

'Let none of them have made this sacrifice in vain.'

Yours sincerely,
Secretary
National Baby Welfare Council

5th December Article published in *Daily Express*: 'This, My Dream Home …by the WAAF whose man went to war'.

I was sitting in the NAAFI with the usual 'cup of char and a wad' when I heard a buzz of excitement from a group of airmen gathered around the pages of an open newspaper and caught a glimpse of a familiar WAAF face – my own. I turned and fled before I could be recognised.

Then an avalanche of letters started to arrive c/o RAF West Kirby and soon it seemed that everyone had heard of 'The WAAF whose man went to war'. It was to be the only memoriam I could give him.

This, my dream home..

By the WAAF whose man went to war

WE have talked about ideal family life a lot, my fiancé and I. We have argued about it, discussed it, and thought of our ideal family so often that to both of us it was almost a reality.

I knew and understood his viewpoint, he knew and understood mine, and together we have worked out what we consider to be a practical scheme for bringing up a family in an ideal way and in those conditions best calculated to promote the health and happiness of its members.

The first essential for an ideal family, we decided, was a happy marriage, based on a firm foundation of mutual love and respect and complete understanding. A child needs all the patience, wisdom and stability that fully satisfied parents can give him, and, above all, he needs to feel safe.

Marriage is no gay, light-hearted affair, to be taken up at the dictates of a fleeting fancy and put down again at its passing. It should be a partnership, a supreme lasting partnership, and nothing must be allowed to jeopardise its inviolability.

'No relations'

A HOUSE is a necessity for the proper growth of a family, and because a family is a highly individual business it must be a separate house.

No community life or living with relations for us, we said, and I think anyone who has been in the Services would agree.

Too much time should not be spent on housekeeping duties, however, and every labour-saving device possible should be employed to reduce these to a minimum. Cooking, washing, cleaning and mending are important and necessary, so important and necessary that I think no wife is worth her keep unless she can do these things well, but her responsibility does not end there.

This is a good beginning, but the main job of a wife is to be a companion and helpmeet to her husband, and the main job of a mother is the training and guidance of her children.

Education in a child's life can be divided into two categories—the conscious education, which can safely be left to the schools, and the subconscious education, which a child imbibes, without any effort on his part, through

NINA CHESSALL

wrote this article

as an entry in the National Baby Welfare Council's essay competition for Waafs — "The Ideal Family Life." She is 27, is working at an R.A.F. station at West Kirby, Wirral, Cheshire. Her essay won—and the Council sent it to the Daily Express because they felt it had a message for all about to marry.

the medium of his environment, companions and home training.

The effects of subconscious education are far more lasting and go far deeper than many parents realise, and it is in this respect that the children of an unhappy marriage are at a disadvantage. The root of so many inhibitions and complexes that develop later in life can be traced to just such a cause. A short course in child psychology for both parents would not be time wasted.

My fiancé thought that a father had just as important a role to play in the education and

upbringing of his children as the mother. It is quite wrong to regard him only in the light of a disciplinarian.

A son looks to his father for a lead in all manly matters and, indeed, in his whole attitude towards the opposite sex. An important point here is that he should be taught the art of self-defence.

We both felt that parents should be really strict about mealtimes, as nothing is worse than bad table manners. Pocket-money should be earned, and boys as well as girls should be given some special task to do. This gives a sense of responsibility, and children should be encouraged to save a proportion of their earnings.

A matter that is regarded lightly and even ignored altogether is the question of spiritual guidance.

It is said by some parents that they do not desire to give a lead in spiritual things, so that their children may be free to make decisions for themselves when they are older.

Such an attitude would be regarded as gross neglect in the study of—say, history, science, mathematics. Why should it apply to religious instruction? A child needs a simple, straightforward explanation of God and the fundamental principles of what constitutes right and wrong.

Two boys, two girls

WE used to say, about the size of our family, that we would have at least one of each sex.

It is a fact that boys brought up in the company of sisters, and vice versa, possess a much more balanced outlook on the opposite sex than those brought up in a family of the same sex.

An ideal number would be two boys and two girls. I think an increased number of married women would be attracted to having a family if they could be assured of a more painless childbirth.

Now I have done what I set out to do. This, my dream family, I pass on to others to make into a reality. My fiancé and I gave it birth in a world at war and, like so many others, he did not return. Let none of them have made this sacrifice in vain.

Nina's prize-winning essay.

This, my dream home...
by the WAAF whose man went to war

Nina Chessall wrote this article as an entry in the National Baby Welfare Council's essay competition for Waafs – "The Ideal Family Life." She is 27, is working at an RAF Station at West Kirby, Wirral, Cheshire. Her essay won – and the Council sent it to the Daily Express because they felt it had a message for all about to marry.

WE HAVE TALKED ABOUT IDEAL FAMILY LIFE a lot, my fiancé and I. We have argued about it, discussed it, and thought of our ideal family so often that to both of us it was almost a reality. I knew and understood his viewpoint, he knew and understood mine, and together we worked out what we consider to be a practical scheme for bringing up a family in an ideal way and in those conditions best calculated to promote the health and happiness of its members.

The first essential for an ideal family, we decided, was a happy marriage, based on a firm foundation of mutual love and respect and complete understanding. A child needs all the patience, wisdom and stability that fully satisfied parents can give him, and, above all, he needs to feel safe.

Marriage is no gay, light-hearted affair, to be taken up at the dictates of a fleeting fancy and put down again at its passing. It should be a partnership, a supreme lasting partnership, and nothing must be allowed to jeopardise its inviolability.

A house is a necessity for the proper growth of a family, and because a family is a highly individual business it must be a separate house. No community life or living with relations for us, we said, and I think anyone who has been in the Services would agree. Too much time should not be spent on housekeeping duties, however, and every labour-saving device possible should be employed to reduce these to a minimum. Cooking, washing, cleaning and mending are important and necessary, so important and necessary that I think no wife is worth her keep unless she can do these things well, but her responsibility does not end there. This is a good beginning, but the main job of a wife is to be a companion and helpmeet to her husband and the main job of a mother is the training and guidance of her children.

Education in a child's life can be divided into two categories: the conscious education, which can safely be left to the schools, and the subconscious education, which a child imbibes, without any effort on his part, through the medium of his environment, companions and home training. The effects of subconscious education are far more lasting and go far deeper than many parents realise, and it is in this respect that the children of an unhappy marriage are at a disadvantage. The root of so many inhibitions and complexes that develop later in life can be traced to just such a cause. A short course in child psychology for both parents would not be time wasted.

My fiancé thought that a father had just as important a role to play in the education and upbringing of his children as the mother. It is quite wrong to regard him only in the light of a disciplinarian. A son looks to his father for a lead in all manly matters and, indeed, in his whole attitude towards the opposite sex. An important point here is that he should be taught the art of self-defence.

We both felt that parents should be really strict about mealtimes, as nothing is worse than bad table manners. Pocket-money should be earned and boys as well as girls should be given some special task to do. This gives a sense of responsibility and children should be encouraged to save a proportion of their earnings.

A matter that is regarded lightly and even ignored altogether is the question of spiritual guidance. It is said by some parents that they do not desire to give a lead in spiritual things, so that their children may be free to make decisions for themselves when they are older. Such an attitude would be regarded as gross neglect in the study of, say, history, science or mathematics. Why should it apply to religious instruction? A child needs a simple, straightforward explanation of God, and the fundamental principles of what constitutes right and wrong.

We used to say, about the size of our family, that we would have at least one of each sex. It is a fact that boys brought up in the company of sisters, and vice-versa, possess a much more balanced outlook on the opposite sex than those brought up in a family of the same sex. An ideal number would be two boys and two girls. I think an increased number of married women would be attracted to having a family if they could be assured of a more painless childbirth.

Now I have done what I set out to do. This, my dream family, I pass on to others to make into a reality. My fiancé and I gave it birth in a world at war and, like so many others, he did not return. Let none of them have made this sacrifice in vain.

From *The Daily Express*, Wednesday 5th December 1945

1945 - 1995

ENDINGS AND BEGINNINGS – 50 YEARS ON

When my mother first showed me the letters shared between her and Vic her fiancé they were still in their original envelopes, stuffed into a suitcase where she had stored them away for over 50 years.

The suitcase was locked and placed in the darkest corner of a wardrobe. Yet, in reading and re-reading them as I came to do, I could feel the power of their love as a vital, living entity which had endured all the years which had passed between. It reached out to me across the years, and captured again the briefest of moments that had been.

I don't know if that same strength of love can be felt in peace-time. I cannot imagine how it must feel to know that every moment you spend together might be your last. Maybe it takes a backdrop of a World War and the daily life and death situations which people face in those times, to make that kind of love real.

However, my mother wanted me to understand through the reading of the letters the way it had been. She believed that same kind of love was out there still, somewhere for me.

The letters came to me at a particularly low point in my life. I had lost the point of living and a reason to go on. Through my own life experiences, I had only known betrayal and mistrust. In sharing her own past, she wanted to pass on a legacy of love.

'*Love is eternal*'. She and Vic had written the words often. They had also been adamant that those words belonged, not just to them, but to all those who came after. My mother also needed to know that their letters would be treasured and kept.

Following Vic's disappearance in November 1944, my grandmother had taken and disposed of everything that belonged to Vic, believing that would help her daughter come to terms with the awful aching uncertainty, and the eventual conclusion that he had gone.

Inside, my mother stopped living. It was as if she held her breath waiting for Vic to reappear. Meanwhile, she continued to exist on automatic pilot.

As a child, I remember the powder-blue wedding dress in protective cover hanging at the very back of the wardrobe, still waiting for the non-event.

Alongside the letters and documents, she showed me the only other two items of which she had kept hold - Vic's silk inner flying gloves, and a rusty nail taken from the gate of Blymhill Church when they exchanged their vows at the altar.

It was a strange feeling, being here, and yet being 'there' at the same time. And over the following months, in reading their words, I came to fall in love with Vic myself who, at the tender age of 21 years, won my mother's heart all those years ago. How I yearned to meet someone like him and to feel their love as my own.

What my mother wanted most of all and which had been denied her by the cruel way in which Vic went, was to have a resting place where she could properly say goodbye, to visit and take flowers, and to know that he was finally at rest. Otherwise, even after fifty years, she clung to a last-ditch hope that he and the pilot had somehow baled out before the destruction of their aircraft, and were alive, suffering from what would be termed today as 'Post-Traumatic Stress', unable to remember who they really were.

For fifty years, she had written and had visits from the pilot's mother. I had even written myself as a child.

Poplar Villa
396 Pensby Road
Pensby, Wirral, Cheshire
15th December 1945

Dear Mrs Fisher

Very many thanks for your kind and helpful letter and I am only too sorry that I have been so long in answering it.

As a matter of fact, I have been very busy carrying out an idea you gave me in your last letter, that of writing a book. So far, I have not had the courage to attempt anything quite so ambitious as a book, and have confined myself to writing short articles. The first of these, entitled: 'This, My Dream Home ...' was published in a National Newspaper last week. If I am able to secure any additional copies, I will send you one. And if not, perhaps you would be interested to read a typed copy, as I dedicated it to my fiancé.

I am enclosing a photograph of myself as you request, but regret that I have no more than five photos of Vic, with which I could never bring myself to part. Please forgive me if I do not send you one …

5 St Michaels Road
Caterham on the Hill
Surrey
1955

Dear Mrs Fisher,

I have been meaning to write to you for a long time, in general, since last Christmas to thank you for our very charming card and in particular, to share with you that I paid a visit to the Royal Air Force memorial at Runnymede during the summer. I think you would be interested in there as I was, as it is really the only spot which is dedicated specifically to all those of our boys who were lost during the war and who have no known graves.

It is a very beautiful and imposing shrine situated on high ground overlooking the upper reaches of the River Thames near to Windsor Great Park, and as I looked out of the long high picture window at one end of the stone gallery packed tight with the engraved names of those we remember only in our hearts, it seemed that all England lay spread out below at their feet, just as it had been on many occasions ten years or more ago when these young men, alive and fearless, were all that lay between us and destruction.

I walked down the long galleries of dead stone, but it seemed to me that the air all around me was vibrant with voices, gay and laughter-loving and full of hope.

Tucked away in a corner, I found engraved the letters of a name that is still able to shatter my heart into a thousand pieces – Vinnell H.V.A. There, I have said it, and what a queer strange thrill it gave me to see it again. I could see my Vic standing there with me, and part of me relived again the joy and the sadness of eleven years ago, and part of me rooted to the spot like the name itself, holding in my arms a little girl with golden hair who so very nearly began life a great deal earlier, and who would undoubtedly have had blue eyes instead of brown.

We left a bunch of flowers at the bottom of the panel of names as a token, and left another bunch in your name for your son, and I will swear they called out to each other in greeting, because there is one impression I got more than any other, and that is that not one of them is lonely any more. They are not now fighting lonely battles with the elements or braving untold hazards alone against the enemy in the sky; they are all together now and part of a great vast brotherhood. OUR time of waiting is over, and they are now waiting for us ....

When Mrs Fisher died, rather than the connection being broken, she had continued in correspondence with Jack's sister, Audrey, as I do today. The question remained for which there was no apparent answer:

'What happened to Mosquito DK292 on that fateful night in 1944?'

Nina and Vic's story is an incredible account of commitment and love. A true romance of the Second World War. In giving it to me, my mother made me promise I would write it as a book to be shared with the rest of the world.

Perhaps in doing so, she felt Vic's name would be honoured, keeping the promise he had made her in terms of writing a book. And in a world split apart by wars and conflict both in and out of families and homes, she felt it had lessons to offer us all still today.

Suddenly, those letters coming to light as they did fifty years on began to have an influence over the relationship my mother and I shared. We grew so close. So much 'Soulmates'. It was as if their love was still active and just as strong.

While my mother began to sort the letters and to jot down reminiscences, I began to scour the libraries for books and information, documents and past newspapers of the day, collecting what can only be described as fragments of an immense jigsaw puzzle to which there was never really going to be an end. It became addictive. The information we found led to more questions, more discoveries, and a variety of truths. And yet, through it all, the book Mum had always talked about writing, the book Vic had first promised he would write; was finally taking shape. And she was excited to be a part of that process.

I contacted an Aviation Historian who specialised in researching and finding lost relatives of the Second World War.

Then, in December 1995, we replied to a letter which appeared in 'Friends of Yours', a supplement of the 'Yours Magazine':

'RAF No 100 Group (Bomber Support) 1943/1945.

A memorial museum association for this group has been formed. Ex-personnel and anyone interested please write for details to ....'

A letter came back swiftly, and in turn sparked off a chain of events which led to my mother and I becoming members of the RAF No 100 Group Association where we came into contact with both Vic's and Jack's RAF colleagues and friends.

My mother, Nina Chessall, died the following year, on 22nd July 1996. Yet, through those few final months before her passing, she felt she had once more been brought close to Vic through the shared memories and photographs of those who wrote to her. I attended the Reunion that year in her memory as I have done each year since. And it is still a moving experience to meet and talk with Vic's best friend as well as others who knew him and to hear in person about that fateful night, to share their own worries and concerns, and experiences which had happened to them.

I exchange letters and cards with them today, together with the family in Canada of Jack Fisher, the pilot. And it is through them that I have gained additional information, documents and stories of that time which has gone at least some way towards gaining a fuller understanding of what happened to Mosquito DK292 in the early hours of 27th November 1944.

I have also found the answer to a question which has haunted me since my mother's death. I found a man who loves me with that same quiet strength and understanding with which Vic loved Mum.   It does exist. I feel Mum, as the 'Guardian Angel' she always promised she would be, played a part in making that happen. She is with me in spirit, sharing my life today.

And now, eight years on from the death of my 'Mother Soulmate', and in the year which marks not only the 60th Anniversary of D-Day, but also in November, the 60th Anniversary of Vic and Jack's final and fatal flight; I feel her urging me to keep my promise, to complete our book and to let their story be told. It is time!

Through their letters, you will have felt something of the depth of feeling that belonged to Nina and Vic.

To continue their story, it is important first to get a feel for the background of how and why No 100 Group was set up, to understand 192 Squadron in terms of a Special Duties Squadron, and to know the key figures and the part they played in bringing The Second World War to a close.

The crest of No 100 Group RAF. The badge depicts Medusa, one of the Gorgon Sisters from Greek Mythology. The sisters had wings, claws, large teeth and snakes for hair. Her image was so frightful that it tuned all who looked upon it to stone.

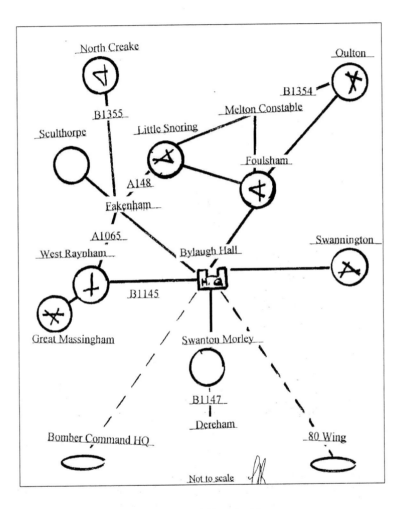

100 Group airfields in Norfolk.

The main reason in forming No. 100 Group was to bring together under one command those units already engaged in various radio countermeasure and bomber support operations.

To considerably enlarge these units and their field of operations, new squadrons would be formed, others would be brought in from other groups, the best in men and materials would be made available, and top priority would be given to fulfil these requirements. The USAAF would be asked to help supply aircraft and to train some personnel.

High security was to be brought in to cover all activities.

During 1943, the Prime Minister and The Chiefs of Air Staff were becoming very concerned about the escalating losses being suffered by our heavy night bomber forces and it was decided that all possible means must be made to reduce this trend. This then gave another good reason for the forming of special bomber support units, notably No. 100 Group.

Duties allocated to the new group were complicated and diverse. Aircraft of the group would first have to use special equipment to find and fix transmissions from enemy wireless, radar, navigational and control systems. These could then be jammed or confused – hence the motto of the group. Jamming and confusion involved the use of other special equipment and the dropping of large amounts of 'WINDOW' (Metallic backed paper strips). The group would also use Mosquito aircraft for bomber stream escort and for locating and destroying enemy night fighters both in the air and on the ground. It would also carry out deception 'SPOOF' raids away from the main target areas.

Systems investigated included VHF R/T air to air and air to ground signals. Attention was also given to the possibility of some form of radio control for the V-1 Flying Bomb and the V-2 Rocket.

For the V-2 a special operation was mounted, known as 'BIG BEN', when a continuous patrol was carried out. American P-38 Lightning aircraft assisted with high altitude patrols in this operation.

U-Boat radio traffic was also investigated. On D-Day, aircraft from the group maintained a continuous radio watch from Cape Gris Nez to Cherbourg for any centimetre signals. All other known radio/radar had been jammed.

As far as No. 100 Group was concerned, it was a continuous cat and mouse game. As fast as enemy systems were found and jammed, new and more complicated systems would appear. Some would operate for only a few seconds per transmission, while others played music as code messages.

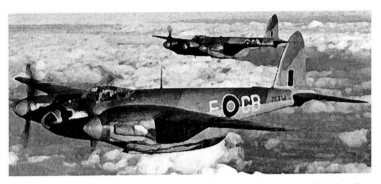

De Havilland Mosquito Mk IV similar to that flown by Jack Fisher and Vic Vinnell

NO 100 GROUP RAF – 192 SQUADRON

'Special Duties Squadron with miscellaneous aircraft for SOE work'

Base: RAF Foulsham – November 1943 to August 1945
(with a detachment to Ford, Sussex)

Disbanded: 22nd August 1945

Aircraft: de Havilland Mosquito Mk. IVs
Vickers Wellington Mk. Xs
Handley Page Halifax Mk. IIIs
Lockheed P. 39L Lightnings

Officer Commanding: Wing Commander D. W. Donaldson, DSO, DFC
(June 1944 – August 1945)

192 Squadron was formed during, and disbanded after the First World War. It was reformed at Gransden Lodge on 4th January 1943 from No. 1474 Flight with Vickers Wellington and de Havilland Mosquito aircraft. On 7th December 1943, 192 Squadron came under the control of 100 Group and moved to Foulsham at which base it remained until the end of the European war

Foulsham is a rural village in the County of Norfolk in England. Situated about 16 miles west of Norwich, and 6 miles east of Fakenham, it is about a mile to the north of the A1067, the junction being landmarked by a large water tower. The market place of Foulsham was rebuilt after a great fire in 1771, and its Georgian houses are dominated by the tower of Holy Innocents' Church, which dates back to the 15th century.

It was during the Second World War that the airfield was opened at Foulsham, and then used by various units of The Royal Air Force and the United States Air Force.

Based at RAF Foulsham, 192 Squadron initially made exploratory flights over enemy territory in order to ascertain and identify the German radar, and to establish the wavelengths used.

For the remainder of 1943 and the early part of 1944, the Squadron's Mosquito establishment, concentrated in C Flight, grew very slowly, only reaching a total of seven by June 1944.

However, the Squadron rapidly expanded after its formation and became the bomber support campaign's 'eyes and ears'.

In 1944, the Squadron began flying in co-operation with the RAF bomber raids over Germany, but their main task was still to keep a check on the enemy radar systems.

During October 1944, the Squadron concentrated on locating signals for enemy missiles, investigating 'Egon' during actual bombing raids and 'Knickebein' and 'Benito' radio guidance systems.

All the squadron's Mosquitos were fitted with at least '*Piperack*' jammers and Main Force support sorties became a regular feature usually being combined with VHF radio traffic monitoring.

The Mosquito's role was predominantly to 'destroy' the Luftwaffe's night fighter arm, a role in which it excelled. 8,000 offensive sorties claimed a total of 267 enemy aircraft destroyed for a loss of 69. Post-war analysis shows that the Luftwaffe developed an almost hysterical fear of the type as an intruder. Every incident rapidly became attributable to the Mosquito and the toll on aircrew nerves and morale far outweighed the actual damage done by the type in air-to-air combat. The Mosquito intruder squadrons such as 192, became the most effective area of the whole bomber support campaign.

Mosquitos flown by the squadron included the Mark IV, one of which was DK292, the aircraft which went missing on 26/27th November 1944 together with Flying Officer Jack Glen Millan Fisher (J/88232), aged 21 years and his navigator Flight Lieutenant Henry Victor Alexander Vinnell (123505), aged 22 years.

ROYAL AIR FORCE OPERATIONS FOR 26/27 NOVEMBER 1944

Main target: Munich, Germany

Aircraft Participation: 270 Lancaster Bombers and 8 Mosquitoes of No
                                         5 Group.

Aircraft Losses: 1 Lancaster crashed in France

Post Raid Report: Claimed by Bomber Command as an accurate
                                         raid with much damage to railway targets.

Minor Targets: 7 Mosquitoes to Erfurt

                                         6 Mosquitoes to Karlsrube (a 'spoof' raid)

                                         20 Electronic Counter Measure operations,

                                         20 Mosquito patrols

                                         31 Aircraft on Resistance Operations

Aircraft Losses: 1 Mosquito lost

                                         1 Lockheed Hudson on a Resistance flight
                                         crashed behind Allied Lines in Belgium.

DE HAVILLAND MOSQUITO MK IV DK292

Aircraft Serial: DK292

Squadron Code: DT-J

Construction Details: de Havilland Mosquito, DK292, was one of a production batch of 50 Mark IV aircraft. This aircraft, made of plywood, was one of the most remarkable warplanes ever produced.

Details of loss: Mosquito Mk IV, DK292, was lost on the night of 26th/27th November 1944, whilst flying on an 'Intruder' mission, in support of Bomber Command operations against Munich.

Location of loss: Reported as 3 kilometres south west of Reichsstrasse, Coesfeld, with the aircraft 99% destroyed.

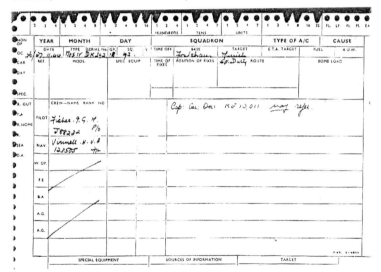

Loss Certificate (front).

Loss Certificate (back).

MARK IV MOSQUITO DK292 – OFFICIAL LOG

1944 November

1st Berlin (sp.) investigate radar FUGE

13th   17.36 back hour later. Electric failure

19th   PATHFINDER

21st   Osnabruch

        Cassel.

26th   0.258 Take Off, Special Flight on own Enemy RT. Instructed to land at Ford (Sussex Coast, England). Failed to land there. Nothing after.

RAF No 100 Group, 192 Squadron, C Flight, Foulsham (15.10.44). Ted Gomersall (centre), Acting OC of the so-called 'Communications Flight' Jack Fisher (on left in flying jacket and capless), Tony Emmett (with moustache),

192 Squadron, C Flight, Aircrew and Ground Staff. Ted Gomersall (second row, far right), Ron Phillips (next to Ted). [Photograph courtesy of Ron Phillips]

WHAT HAPPENED TO MOSQUITO DK292?

It is a strange feeling indeed to stand outside the hangar which is now a grain store, looking out across the former airfield at Foulsham. It is said that in following the footpath alongside you can become surrounded by the hundreds of airmen who still haunt that area.

I have visited it more than once, and I swear that on a clear day, when the air is still, you might hear the engines preparing for take-off, the footfalls of the servicemen, the laughter, the chatter, the noise. You can feel the raw, aching dread of those who lived then and the nervous excitement of the moment. The memory lives on.

I have visited Foulsham Church and stood also at the altar in Blymhill Church, knowing that Nina and Vic stood there sixty years before, filled with hope, and yet at the same time fear that The Dream would not be fulfilled.

They feel so close. The spirit of their love lives on.

This year, 2004, as in previous, I shared another pleasant weekend with members of RAF 100 Group Association in Horsham St Faith at the City of Norwich Aviation Museum, talking and sharing with Vic and Jack's friends and colleagues. It is easy to feel Vic and Jack and others standing close by, as wartime experiences are talked about and shared. It can prove an emotional event for members, including myself. I have grown so close to Vic and Jack in sharing an important part of their lives through their photographs and writings. The Association reunions allow me to talk about Mum and Vic and to reflect on the way it had been for them, as well as to update on additional information found. I know Mum would have loved to talk with those who knew her Sweetheart, to relive the memories, and to dispel the mysteries and myths. There are times when I feel her firmly tapping my shoulder, urging me to ask a question missed, or to spend longer with one who knew Vic most. And as we lay wreaths and make toasts to those who have passed over, I wish with all my heart that I could find that resting place on earth for Vic, for Jack where, for Mum, I might finally have that place to call on and reflect, lingering awhile to place plaque and flowers, before carrying them on in my heart.

The City of Norwich Aviation Museum holds a special section dedicated to the operations of RAF Bomber Command's 100 (Bomber Support) Group which flew on top secret electronic counter measures, deception and night intruder missions from a number of Norfolk airfields, including Foulsham.

In fact, it was the advertisement placed in 'Friends of YOURS' magazine aimed at forming a Memorial Museum Association for RAF 100 Group in the latter half of 1995 by Len Bartram which first put us in touch with others to form the City of Norwich Aviation Museum as it is today, still manned totally by volunteers.

Len Bartram sadly passed away in February 2002, but I remain in contact with his widow, Evelyn, and I know that Len's first letter of many was welcomed so much by my mother:

6th January 1996

'... There was a cover up of most 100 Group operations up to the 1970s, even now all will never be revealed ... In particular 192 Squadron operations were classified, very top secret ... Fl/Lt Vinnell would have been the operator for special equipment carried which could find and identify enemy radio/radar wave-lengths and other equipment which could jam and confuse enemy radio/radar transmissions .. They would operate in support of the RAF main bomber force, they often carried extra fuel tanks and would operate long operations, sometimes flying with the bomber then as a decoy to another target, then to German night fighter assemble areas, then back to and from the bomber stream. Great skill was required by these special operators – who were also the navigators of the aircraft. Most of the 192 aircrew were specially picked to serve in that role... They were also in great danger of being found by night fighters because the equipment they carried sometimes gave off signals the enemy could home in on. But overall, the 100 Group losses were below average, much less than had been expected...'

Ted Gomersall was the first member of RAF 100 Group Association to write to Mum who had actually known and worked alongside Vic and Jack, and I remember her intense excitement as she read his words to her:

'Vic and I were close, and shortly before he and Jack went missing, on the night of 26th/27th November 1944, we had been to London together, when flying was off for some reason. It's a long time ago, but I remember that he introduced me to the Wings Club (in Grosvenor Square) and we gate-crashed some posh parties in Belgravia.

'Bud' George (known universally as George the Automatic Pilot) and Jack Fisher were close friends – I believe they came across to the UK together after initial training in Canada. (George was my pilot.) It is true, as they say, that I too was a special operator/navigator in 192, using equipment to identify enemy radio/radar wavelengths, confusing and jamming transmissions. I would say that Vic was occupied in some such activities on the night of the 26th/27th Nov – hardly an 'intruder' mission, although it could conceivably have been in support of Qud. I see from my log book that I was not flying that night, but was on ops to Neuss on the following night, the 27th.

My wife and I were married in 1937, and during my time in the RAF, we wrote to each other every day – a bit of a struggle at times! However, Hilda has kept all my letters to her and I think I can best help by giving you relevant extracts from them:-

Sunday 26.11.44 … In the evening, Vic and I went to the flicks and saw 'Lifeboat' …

Monday 27.11.44… Jack Fisher and Vic failed to return last night, and we have no news of them yet. There is a slight possibility that they managed to get down in Belgium or France. I do hope so. It's at times like this that one realises the futility of war …but they're probably quite OK at some airfield across the Channel.

Tuesday 28.11.44 …There is still no news of Jack Fisher and Vic, and today they are officially posted as 'missing'. Vic was going to be married on his next leave, and his girl, who is in the WAAF, was trying to get posted to Foulsham. In fact, he was half expecting her coming this week… There is still hope that they put down at some obscure airfield in France. If it had been one of our larger airfields we should have heard by now. And then, of course, they may have baled out over France or Germany. Anyhow, I hope they are both safe …

George, my pilot, is very shaken about Jack Fisher … they were very good friends – rather naturally, I suppose, being the only two Canadians in the Flight at the moment …

Wed 29.11.44 ….. There is still no news of Jack and Vic, and their names have been rubbed off the crew bit …

Thurs 30.11.44 … There is still no news of Jack and Vic, and it begins to look as though they've bought it, reluctantly, as one is to come to that conclusion.

Sunday 3.12.44 Our worst fears about Jack and Vic have been confirmed by the washing up of Jack's cap and a sock with Vic's name on it, on the South Coast yesterday. It seems almost certain that they came down in the drink,but there are certain mysteries about it which will never be cleared up, I suppose …'

He goes on later to say:

'The operation (27/11/44) from which the Mosquito failed to return was a Bomber support Radar/Radio ELINT (Electronic Radio Countermeasure operation in the NEUSS) area of Germany on *the edge of the Rhur (NOT Munich!)*.'

Ted (Acting CO of the so-called 'Communications Flight' at 192 Squadron) became an inspiration to my mother. To think that he had actually been there, talking and sharing with Vic and Jack brought all the feelings back from the past, and left her with a thirst to know more. My mother's reply to Ted Gomersall picks up on the threads and the conflicting accounts which cover the night in question:

23 January 1996

'After all this time, you cannot believe what a wonderful relief it is to actually contact someone who knew Vic as a real person and even shared his life at RAF Foulsham. Up to now, I have only received official statements of 'missing believed killed', plus his silk flying gloves (allegedly washed ashore off the coast of France), the wedding ring, and my letters to him …

For years, I have accepted that Vic's Mosquito came down in the drink, that therefore, there would never be any further evidence of what happened – no wreckage, no body, no grave – and all I have been given are alternative theories, about 'hush-hush' and 'cover-ups' and 'classified information'. I also hear from another quarter that Neuss (in the Reich area) was Vic's destination on the night of 26th/27th Nov which was also your destination the following night. Whereas, at the time, I was told it was Munich.

Thank you for the group photograph. I have never seen a photo of Jack Fisher, although I have been in regular contact with his family in Canada. He was only 21, with 6 sisters, one of whom came to visit us some 10 years later when we lived in Surrey. We also met his mother in Edinburgh for a meal when we lived in Northumberland during a tour of Europe aged 90, a grand old lady. Jack's fiancee also joined us. She has never married, a Scottish lass. She died two years ago.

I tried to contact Vic's father, but he would not answer my letters. Vic's mother died in hospital some short while later. So I feel that I am the only one left to make enquiries on his behalf. And I have no recognisable status for doing so, except perhaps 'unfinished business'.

Please thank your wife for her research into family records. I have kept a day-by-day diary from as far back as 1939, religiously (except for 1945 and 46). It has now become a way of life for me and I am often called upon to settle questions arising from memory gaps.

It is good to reminisce. Thank you for listening. Please, write again soon.

Nina (nee Chessall)

---

3 February 1996

'Dear Nina,

You ask if I have an operational route chart for the operation to Neuss on the 27th November 1944. Yes – herewith! … The words 'Special Duty' and 'Spec. Op' had to be deleted or cut out as a condition of our being allowed to keep these copies. The dotted lines show the route of the bomber stream – our route is the unbroken line with the times of take-off and landing and of turning-points. I would think that our aim was partly divisionary, partly signals investigation, and partly photographing and recording any signals intercepted (if I remember rightly, we recorded on wire!), but not on that occasion, jamming, which was usually reserved for the occasions – including Dresden on the 13th February 1945 – when we orbited the target, at, I must say, a fairly safe height.

I would say that it was fairly unlikely that Jack and Vic's target was Munich. On the only occasion that we went as far as Munich, we had to land and re-fuel outwards at Cradwell Bay, as Munich was very near the limit of our range. In spite of all the pervading security, I think I would have heard of something unusual like that, and in any case, I also believe that in November 1944, the bomber offensive was mainly against the Rhur. ...

The only other thing I would add is that we did not carry out 'intruder' operations as such – other 100 Group Mosquito Squadrons did that – but I suppose our activities <u>could</u> be described as such in a sense....

Ted Gomersall'

Mum and I began writing to other members of RAF 100 Group Association – such as Hank Cooper, another Mosquito Special Operator at RAF Foulsham in 1944. A reply came back by return of post:

29th January 1996

'... Yes, I did know Vic and Jack Fisher. I flew with Jack on a couple of occasions – not on 'ops' but on some trips over the UK.

... I have a visual picture of Vic – an open cheerful face, usually smiling, high forehead, with shortish hair in the front, fairly tall and well-built ... with an absolute dedication to the job in hand and a willingness to do 'the extra mile'.

I can appreciate that Vic had little or nothing to say about his work – our Squadron was 192 SD Squadron – the SD standing for Special Duties. The Squadron started off as a 'Flight' – 1474 Flight and flew from an airfield near Huntington – then it was upgraded to a Squadron (192) and flew from Feltwell and moved to Foulsham in late 1943 and remained there until the end of the war. About this time a new Group was formed in Bomber Command – 100 Group – which had about 6 or 7 stations around Fakenham in Norfolk with about 2 Squadrons on each station. 100 Group's job was to:-
(a) investigate and find out about the German Radio and Radar devices, (b)

to home onto the German aircraft which were using radar and engage them with 100 group night fighters.

Vic's job (along with all 'Special Operators' of 192 Squadron of whom I was one) was concerned with (a) above. Without going into details, it was a fairly exacting task – flying on the main bomber aircraft routes and using (for those times) extensive and accurate radio equipment and measuring gear.

I have looked in my log book and I was not operating on 26/27 November 1944, and I cannot say what the target was – but of course 192 Squadron did not always follow the main Bomber Command route – but struck off somewhere else on some 'other investigation' into Radio/Radar.

However, I can remember the loss (as I was also in the Mosquito Flight – C Flight of 192) and I remember the sadness and gloom in the crew room and the mess.'

Hank Cooper

Martin Staunton, Hon Sec of the RAF 100 Group Association shared his own experience of loss:

15th January 1996

'My brother-in-law was lost on the 22nd March 1945 and my sister, who had only been married for 3 months, spent the ensuing 50 years wondering if her husband had died quickly or had suffered intolerably. The pilot's mother was the Dowager Lady Wynford and even her requests to Bomber Harris and Lord Trenchard failed to give us the answer.

In the course of establishing the Book of Remembrance and Memorial at Oulton for the men of her husband's station we met a man who had served on my brother-in-law's squadron (214) and he produced a flight log which was annotated 'Between turn point E and the target we saw a huge explosion believed to be P-Peter.' As it was the only aircraft missing it meant that her husband's end, although horrifying, was at least quick.

My sister and myself took on a rather daunting task for which we had no qualifications when we set out to commemorate the brave men of RAF Oulton. We have been rewarded by not only knowing what happened but we now have the friendship of a very special group of men. We are honoured to be in their company at reunions, etc. We understand more than most how you must feel...'

Martin Staunton

Bob Collis is an Aviation Historian, with access to air ministry aircraft loss records as well as contacts in Germany, Holland and Belgium in relation to missing World War 2 aircraft.

'... DK292, as a Mk IV Mosquito, had a 'Glass nose' and carried no armament (guns or cannons). It could not, therefore, have been on an 'Intruder' sortie. Such 'Intruder' type operations were usually carried out by fighter or light-bomber aircraft, being directed against enemy airfields and aircraft and almost exclusively at night. Mosquitoes were employed in this role by No 100 Group RAF, but not by 192 Squadron, and never using this aircraft variant.

While Mk IV Mosquitoes in regular squadron service were employed on bombing and reconnaissance work, they served in an entirely different role with 192 Sqn. All bomb aiming and release gear was removed, and instead these aircraft were fitted with specialised receiving, recording and – in a few cases – jamming equipment. Most of the Mosquitoes thus employed had the 'Glass nose' painted over.

The precise nature of the sortie being undertaken by the crew of DK292 when lost remains speculative, but it almost certainly involved ELINT (Electronic Intelligence) work ie. searching for enemy radio and radar transmission and recording the signals on their special equipment. I do not believe that 192 Sqn actually carried out jamming operations with the Mosquito before December 1944, and when they did so, it was in addition to their ELINT duties. The equipment carried was apparently capable of coping with signals up to 3000NHz, but they were more likely to have been carrying a wide range of receiving gear to meet specific operational requirements, plus an array of recording equipment.

Each time an RAF Bomber Command aircraft was lost on operations, a document called a Bomber Command Loss Card (BCLC) had to be made out. Depending on the date and the administrator involved, the BCLCs usually held a few facts about the aircraft, unit, date, target (or operation flown), and identity of the crew. As the war progressed, printed cards were introduced for the task, and more detailed information was often entered, including bomb-load carried, take-off time, last known position and other pertinent facts. As information filtered through via the International Red Cross, intelligence sources, and from the Germans themselves, the cards were updated as to the fate of the crews involved. Occasionally airmen who evaded capture or were repatriated provided information which was added to the BCLCs.

With the surrender of Nazi Germany in May 1945, the RAF wasted no time in sending a team of investigating officers to find and collate details of the many aircraft which had crashed in Germany and the occupied countries. Groups of RAF personnel forming the Missing Research And Enquiry (MRAE) service inspected thousands of captured German documents in an effort to glean information on missing aircraft and crews. Much of this information was added to the BCLSs where a definite identification was made. A great deal of work was done by the MRAE between 1945-48, but their task was not helped by the fact that a number of missing aircraft had come down in territory occupied by the Russians, who would not grant the RAF men access to the areas or the documentation they had captured in them.

I believe that a BCLC is the source of your 'Official Documents' which give a crash location for Mosquito DK292. I have not been able to find a 'Wesfeld' (later found to be a mis-spelling of Coesfeld) on any of my maps of the Munich area, but I suspect it may be a small village or hamlet. It is obvious that the MRAE team found evidence that the Mosquito had crashed at the stated location, either from a German report or wreckage at the crash-site (or both).

As you are probably aware, the names of Flt Lt Vinnell and F/O Fisher RCAF appear on the panels of the Air forces memorial to the Missing at Runnymede, both having no known graves. There are a number of reasons as to why this sad state of affairs may have come about. It may be that Mosquito DK292 exploded, either in the air or on impact with the ground, the resultant destruction being such that the Germans were totally unable to identify the two crewmen. It is also possible that the aircraft crashed into the ground in a power-dive and buried itself. If this occurred in an area of soft ground, ie. Marshland or peat, then there is every possibility the bodies of the crew were not recovered by the Germans. It is also possible that the Germans did in fact recover the bodies of the crew, and either buried them close to the crash-site in an unmarked grave, or interred them in a local cemetery or churchyard as 'Unknown airmen'. I know that this must sound rather brutal and unpleasant, but you have to remember that air crashes of this kind were an everyday event in Germany. In addition, the Allied bombing raids generated an intense hatred of aircrew among the German population, and the formalities of honouring airmen with full military honours at funerals had long been dispensed with by November 1944.

I am in contact with a Bomber Command researcher, who has provided me with a great deal of assistance in my enquiries into these type of losses. He has microfilm copies of the BCLCs for 1939-45, and has confirmed that the stated location for Mosquito DK292 is indeed on the Loss Card. He also has contact with a number of groups and/or individuals in Germany who are involved in aviation archaeology and associated research work. I have enlisted his help ...'

Bob Collis, Aviation Historian, wrote again in March to offer further information regarding Jack and Vic's plane:

7th March 1996

'Further to my last letter, I am pleased to report that I have received further details regarding the loss of 192 Sqn Mosquito DK292 on the night of 26-27 Nov 1944.

192 Squadron's Operations Record Book (ORB) for the night 26-27 Nov 1944 states that four aircraft were detailed to carry out special operations. Two Halifax aircraft, code-letters 'S' and 'X' took off on an operation to the Strasbourg area. Both these aircraft dropped 'WINDOW' radar-jamming foil, and returned safely to RAF Foulsham at 07.15 and 07.12 hours respectively. A third Halifax, 'O' was to have flown the same sortie, but turned off the runway and became bogged down in soft ground, so was withdrawn from the operation that night.

Mosquito DK292, which carried the code-letter 'J', took off from RAF Foulsham at 02.58 hours (27th Nov) for a special duties flight to Munich, to record enemy R/T (Radio Transmitter) activity. The crew were briefed to land at RAF Ford, in Sussex, on completion of their mission. Little else is recorded, other than saying the Mosquito failed to land at Ford, and that nothing had been heard from the aircraft after it took off. The ORB confirms the crew as pilot F/O Fisher and special operator Flt/Lt Vinnell.

The BCLC for Mosquito DK292 confirms that this was the source of your 'official report' regarding the (suspected) crash-site. It gives: 'Place of loss. 3Kms south west Reichsstrasse, Wesfeld. Airframe 99% destroyed.' However, it does state on the card: 'Captured German Document   KE 10.011 may refer.'

So it would appear that there was an element of doubt by the MRAE administrator who made this entry. A German researcher has also been unable to establish the location quoted on the BCLC. He believes the information is incorrect, and is continuing enquiries in Germany on our behalf. Researchers in Holland and Belgium have all confirmed that they have no record of a Mosquito crash in their countries on the night of 26-27 Nov 1944. However, another contact of the 192 Sqn Assocation came up with the most interesting information. He says that Mosquito DK292's task was to monitor the German night-fighter R/T 'chatter' during the Lancaster raid on Munich. He believes that no detailed record of the equipment carried was made, but that on this type of sortie, the aircraft would have probably been fitted with two receivers, a Hallicraft S27U, and anAPR4, as well as a recorder, one of the type code-named 'Blonde' or 'Commando'.

What surprised me was that he says the Mosquito crashed on the shore at Vassonville, France, but there was no sign of the crew, and no bodies were ever recovered. I have no idea of his sources of information, but what he says would certainly seem to tie-up with your information from W/C Donaldson that the aircraft came down 'in the sea off the French coast and was destroyed'.

In 2001, Bob felt he would once more 'give another push' to finding an answer to a final resting place for Vic and Jack:

14th July 2001

'... I have been corresponding for about two years now with a Dutch researcher named Jan (John) Hey. He now concentrates almost exclusively on USAAF aircraft losses in WW2, but has done a tremendous amount of work on other war graves matters in Europe. It was principally his work on compiling nominal registers and details of British, American and

Commonwealth casualties during the MARKET GARDEN operation in 1944 which led to official recognition in the form of an MBE in March of this year.

I sent Jan the known details of the loss of DK292 and crew, and I enclose his reply ...'

Bob Collis N&SAM, BAAC, LAS

18th June 2001

'... It seems that the 192nd Sqdn researcher William Rees has come close to the truth by saying that it crashed on the French coast ... However, in the book 'Roll of Honour Canada' F/O Fisher, the Pilot and a Canadian from Instow, Saskatchewan is recorded and the entry says that he attempted a crash-landing on the beach north of Le Havre but hit a mine. I have a well detailed atlas for France but cannot trace a location with the name of or sounding like Vassonville north of Le Havre. It may (have been) a hamlet that does not exist any more. Anyhow: Le Havre and the entire coastal area of France up to the Belgian border (except for Dunkirk that remained in German hands until the end of the war) was liberated by Canadian ground forces already at the beginning of September 1944 and it is a bit sloppy that the British military authorities did not make a clear record of that accident that occurred in an area well in hand. Just according to the type of mine the aircraft and its occupants will have been blown to bits and no human remains have apparently been recovered ...

I have no knowledge about the contents of the German document KE 10.011. This will be kept in the RAF Air Historical Branch in London ...'

J A Hey

Phil James, MBE, was a close friend of Jack's and I first made contact with him and his wife Vera at the official Opening of the RAF 100 Group Museum. In 1997, he received this reply from the Personnel Management Agency at RAF Innsworth:

21st August 1997

'As promised here is the information I have been able to locate on the loss of Mosquito aircraft DK292 on 28th November 1944.

Mosquito DK292 took off at 02.58 hours on 27th November 1944 accompanying a Bomber Command attack on Munich, Germany. The aircraft was due to return to Royal Air Force Ford at 07.00 hours but nothing was heard of it after take-off. The two crew members were:

Pilot – Pilot Officer Jack Glen Millan Fisher (J88232) – Canadian

Navigator – Flight Lieutenant Henry Victor Alexander Vinnell (123505)

Information was later received that Mosquito DK292 crashed on the French Coast at Vassonville, north of Le Havre, at 6.30am on 27th November 1944. The wreckage was covered by the sea at high tide, but by the direction of the aircraft, it was assumed that it flew into a cliff and exploded on impact. The airframe was completely disintegrated. As the beach was most probably mined, attempts to salvage the wreckage were impracticable. No vehicles could gain access to the beach. The only items recovered were a sock marked N B A Vinnell and an officer's cap marked P/O Fisher 232.

The bodies of the two airmen were never found and from the description of the aircraft having exploded on impact and the disintegration of the fuselage, it was most probable that the remains of the crew were washed away by the tide. Consequently both Pilot Officer Fisher and Flight Lieutenant Vinnell were recorded as Missing Presumed Dead – Lost at Sea and their names recorded on the Runnymede Memorial on panels 246 and 203 respectively. They are also commemorated in the Royal Air Force Books of Remembrance held in St Clement Danes Church, The Strand, London. Pilot Officer Fisher is recorded in Volume 4, Page 63 and Flight Lieutenant Vinnell in Volume 9, Page 16 ...'

PMA (CS)1b(RAF)

For Air Secretary/Chief Executive

Phil has continued to make enquiries on our behalf, and in late 2003 wrote to the Air Historical Branch (RAF), Ministry of Defence and received the following reply which he forwarded to us for our records:

11th August 2003

'... Our records show that this aircraft took off from RAF Foulsham at 0258hrs on November 27, 1944 to investigate Radiotelephony activity in the

Munchen area. It crashed 3km SW of the Reichsstrasse at Coesfeld. The cause
of the crash is not yet known.'

AHB5 (RAF)

These findings are endorsed by John Larder of The Second World War
Experience Centre, home to the Mosquito Aircrew Association archives:

March 2003

'I think you have been given some scrambled information. DK292 force
landed at Freiston Aerodrome, Sussex in March 1944 after being shot down
by an enemy fighter over France. Bill Chorley's Bomber Command Losses –
1944 has DK292 crashing 3 km SW of the Reichsstrasse at Coesfeld which is
North East of Borken.

The usually fairly reliable 'They Shall Not Grow Old' has the aircraft
crashing on a mined French beach and exploding.

The Air Historical Branch confirms Bill Chorley's account of the loss of
the aircraft word for word. Lost investigating railway target activity in the
Munich area. Crashed 2 km SW of the Reichsstresse at Coesfeld in Germany.
Cause of loss not known. I suspect that the crew's grave has been lost and
either their local German burial couldn't be found or else when they were
moved to a larger cemetery their identities were lost …'

The nagging question in Phil's mind was why was the A/C flying over
Coesfeld as it is far from the route from Munich to Ford on the south coast of
England? He wrote again to the Air Historical Branch outlining the confusion
and asking for clarification, to receive this reply:

5th September 2003

'… After having done a thorough search of the casualty file, the following are
the findings. Mosquito DK292 was seen to crash off the French coast, North
of Le Havre at Vassonville, near Dieppe. The plane crashed and exploded on
the shore 250 yards from the foot of the cliff. The salvage was impracticable
as the beach at Vassonville was believed to be mined. Only the heavy parts
such as the engine was left, the rest was washed away by the sea which covers
the wreck except at very low tide.

According to reports, the aircraft exploded on impact and the fuselage was completely disintegrated, it seems highly probable that the remains of the bodies were washed away by the tide.

As the British and Canadian troops were still in the area the local authorities let them do everything, and no records of the crash were kept.

The information I provided you in my last letter was taken from the casualty cards that we hold in this branch. The reason Coesfeld is mentioned may be due to the fact that the aircraft was flying over Coesfeld, and the contact was lost from there onwards ...'

AHB5 (RAF)

We had written earlier to the Personnel Management Agency at RAF Innsworth asking what information they have relating to a crash site for DK292:

30th June 2003

'... Research shows that DK292 took off at 02.58 hours on the 27th November 1944 for a special investigation flight accompanying the Bomber Command attack on Munich. They had been briefed to fly at 25,000 feet whilst over enemy territory. The aircraft was due to return at 07.00 hours at RAF Ford but nothing was heard of it after take off.

Information was later received to the effect that north of Le Havre at 06.30 on 27th November 1944 a Mosquito aircraft crashed and exploded on the shore, 250 yards from the foot of the cliff. Their bodies were never found. They are however commemorated at Runnymede Memorial. ...'

PMA Casualty 2a (RAF)

Through all the reams of research and paper-documented information the crash-site of Vassonville seems increasingly likely to be a final resting place for Vic and Jack.

Richard Forder shares his thoughts:

23rd June 2003

'I can understand your frustration as a number of references merely record that the aircraft was missing with no record of the fate of the aircrew. You mentioned that one document you possessed makes reference to Coesfeld as a possible crash site for the aircraft. As I believe you have already established Coesfeld is a small town just to the west of Munster in Germany. This would have been way off course on their route to and from Munich where they were to record enemy R/T activity during an attack by Main Force Lancasters. You may be aware of the book written by William J and John E Rees 'Espionage in the Ether' that details the wartime story of electronic intelligence and radio countermeasures carried out by 192 Sqn. In this book it records '... On its return journey the aircraft crashed on the shore at Vassonville. No sign of the crew'. This obviously ties in with another version of the crew's fate that you mentioned. I must say that this sounds more plausible than the Coesfeld version. If this is correct one can only speculate that they had been damaged during their sortie and were trying to reach the UK, but ran out of luck as they crossed the French coast and were unable to regain the mainland to put it down. I cannot imagine that they would have set off across the channel without reasonable confidence that they would make UK, particularly as they could have put down at an Allied airfield in France. Another possibility is a sudden catastrophe failure again as they had just crossed the French coast.'

Richard Forder

My mother died on the morning of 22nd July 1996 from cancer. Later the same year, I was asked to send an entry for the 'Silver Message Book' to be read out in response to the Silver Jubilee celebrations on 21st June 1997 of the Norfolk and Suffolk Aviation Museum. In memory of Nina Chessall and Vic Vinnell therefore, the following was made as an entry:

'On behalf of my late mother, Nina Harrington (nee Chessall), who sadly lost her fiancé Vic Vinnell of 192 Squadron when his Mosquito was lost on the night of November 27th 1944, I would wish the Norfolk and Suffolk Aviation Museum every success on its Silver Jubilee celebrations on 21st June 1997. I know my mother would have wished to be with you in person. but I know she will be with you in the spirit of love.

I would also pay tribute to the tremendous and continuing help and support offered by researcher and historian Bob Collis. As a representative of the Norfolk and Suffolk Aviation Museum, through his work, he has added a few more pieces to the puzzle of what became of my mother's fiance when he went missing in November 1944. It was some comfort to her before she died in July last year, to know that there are people who care enough to continue to uncover the mystery that haunted her through life.

Thank you, Bob. And thank you all of you at the Museum who work at keeping alive the spirit of those, like Vic, who died so tragically in the Second World War.'

POSTSCRIPT

It is now ten years since Mum and I first started on our journey to try to trace the final resting place of Vic and Jack. The location of the aircraft DK292 is still not known and a crash site has still not been confirmed.

It would appear that despite reports of the aircraft having crashed onto the beach on the coast of France near Vassonville, the fact that Vassonville is 30 kilometres inland from the coast continues to cast doubt.

And so our search goes on.

However, we have just received a letter from the Personnel Management Agency at RAF Innsworth aimed at clarifying past confusion caused:

20th May 2004

'I apologise if this Department's previous letter dated 30th June 2003 caused you any distress, that was certainly not our intention. It referred to the aircraft crashing off the French Coast North of Le Havre but no mention was made of Vassonville... However, I have now investigated the matter again and can confirm that this aircraft did crash at the hamlet of Vassonville, which is part of the coastal Commune of Saint Martin en Campagne not the town of Vassonville. Hence possibly the confusion. I have highlighted this on the enclosed map ...
    PMA Cas2 (RAF)'

This year, given that it is the 60th Anniversary both of D-Day and the time when Vic and Jack went missing, it seems fitting that Ian and I are planning to visit France, to walk along the French coast where most evidence seems to support the idea that Mosquito DK292 crashed around 6.30am on 27th November 1944.

Audrey Fisher, Jack's sister, informs us that the Canadian Government decided recently that un-named rivers, creeks and mountains would be named after service men that failed to return from World War 2.

To this end, it was decided to name a creek THE FISHER CREEK after Jack Fisher.

But it's still sad that we are unable to have that place to finally stand and pay tribute and remember the love that Vic and Nina shared.

This book therefore, is seen as a fitting memorial to Vic and Nina, and Jack, and to all those who continue to serve in places of conflict and who have stories of their own to tell, but with no resting place to call their own.

If you feel in reading this book that you have information which would be of interest, or would like to share your own experiences, I would welcome hearing from you.

Janine Harrington

Please ask the publishers to put you in touch with us.

ACKNOWLEDGEMENTS

I would wish to make special mention of the following and thank them for continuing friendship and support:

Audrey Fisher and her family; **Len and Evelyn Bartram**, Members of RAF 100 Group Association; **Ted Gomersall**, Friend of Vic, Special Operator/Navigator, 192 RAF 100 Group, Acting CO of the so-called 'Communications Flight'; **Hank and Diane Cooper**, Mosquito Special Operator, 'C' Flight, 192 RAF 100 Group; **Vera and Phil James MBE**, close friend of Jack Fisher; **Richard Forder**; **Trevor Allen DSO DFC**, CO of 'C' Flight, September 1944; **Ron and Marjorie Phillips**, RAF 100 Group, 'C' Flight; **Martin Staunton**, Hon Sec, RAF 100 Group Association; **Martyn R Ford-Jones**, Aviation Historian and Researcher; **Bob Collis**, Aviation Researcher; **Jan Hey MBE**, Dutch Researcher; **James Hillier**, British Air Historian; **Florian Huber**, German Film Crew, NDR Fernsehen; Air Historical Branch (RAF); Ministry of Defence Personnel Management Agency; RAF Innsworth; War Museum Library; **John Larder**; The Second World War Experience Centre (which holds the Mosquito Aircrew Association archives); Norfolk and Suffolk Aviation Museum; The City of Norwich Aviation Museum.

And finally, I would thank **Nick Shepperd** of Woodfield Publishing for making it possible for the story of Nina and Vic to be shared. Through your belief in this book you have enabled the Promise to be kept.

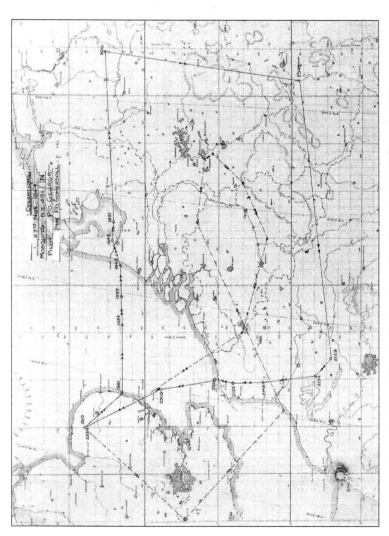

Operational Route Chart for the Operation to Neuss (inner circuit) 27th November 1944.